Changing Ones

Cheyenne *hetaneman*, **1889.** Female berdache in battle wearing a man's breechcloth. National Anthropological Archives, Smithsonian Institution, neg. no. 57204A.

Changing Ones

Third and Fourth Genders in Native North America

Will Roscoe

St. Martin's Griffin
New York

ISBN 0-312-22479-6

Library of Congress Cataloging-in-Publication Data

Roscoe, Will.
    Changing ones : third and fourth genders in Native North America /
by William Roscoe.
        p.   cm.
    Includes bibliographical references and index.
    ISBN 0-312-17539-6 (cloth) 0-312-22479-6 (pbk)
    1. Indian gays--North America. 2. Indians of North America-
-Sexual behavior.   3. Berdaches--North America. 4. Homosexuality-
-North America. 5. Lesbianism--North America.   I. Title.
E98.S48R67   1998
305.3'089'97--dc21   97-41762
                                                            CIP

Design by Acme Art, Inc.
First published in hardcover in the United States of America in 1998
First St. Martin's Griffin edition: May 2000
10 9 8 7 6 5 4 3 2 1

CONTENTS

LIST OF ILLUSTRATIONS AND TABLES

Illustrations

Tables

FOREWORD

Back in 1984, when Will Roscoe came to our literature table at the San Francisco Lesbian/Gay Pride Day Celebration, he shared his ideas regarding research projects that included us as lesbian/gay native persons. At the time we thought he was just a "wannabe," one of those white people who came around yearly to be "blessed" or to romanticize Native Americans. But in the months that followed he would become an adopted brother in our extended family, volunteering his services to the Gay American Indians (GAI) board of directors. With our support, Will was successful in obtaining GAI's first grant in 1985, which helped publish our anthology *Living the Spirit*.

From the get-go Will had Indian patience, sitting through long meetings as we worked through our busy agenda. But through consensus process we published *Living the Spirit*. At times Will has lectured and traveled (often at his own expense) on behalf of our community. I feel a debt to his commitment and courage as a new anthropologist and a true historian for our community. Will has always consulted us on his projects. He has been a true "We'wha," a special cultural ambassador for our times.

Will has always brought to our community a sense of historical and contemporary pride that we should never overlook. Too often the subject of native gender roles has been dismissed or ignored by those who haven't taken the time to appreciate our traditions. It has been individuals like Will, who really know native people, that have embraced this subject. He understands the importance that we third and fourth gender people had and continue to have in our tribes, and the importance of making information about our roles available to the public.

Over the years, Will and I have discussed many issues, such as the problem of professional jealousy and how it holds us back as lesbian/gay people. Many times he has said to me, "Randy, if you don't like what we publish about your community, then you must go out and do your own research and publish your own voices." We did that with *Living the Spirit* and with our forthcoming anthology on AIDS/HIV in the Indian community. More recently, when I mentioned how Indian families are often more important in teaching culture than the tribe or nation, Will quickly got my point. I'm sure that after I left he went to the nearest library to research the subject more.

Will is doubly blessed to be a crossover from our community to his profession. He uses intuitive skills along with historical facts to document his scholarly work. I've visited his university classes and have seen how his students gave him the utmost respect as a lecturer. At numerous community forums in which he has lectured about our community and history, I have seen people walk away feeling proud to be lesbian/gay Americans. I know he is just as well thought of at Zuni as he is here in the Bay Area Indian community. This only proves to me that Will Roscoe is true go-between for us all. When I was asked to write a preface for this book, I eagerly agreed.

In this book, students, scholars, and native people will find the same thorough research, commitment to inclusiveness, and sensitivity to tribal differences and contemporary issues that Will brought to *Living the Spirit* and *The Zuni Man-Woman*. Will really brings to life the traditional role third and fourth gender people played in our tribes. I am inspired by the stories of Hastíin Klah, Osch-Tisch, Running Eagle, and the other third and fourth gender people he documents, and I'm amazed at his detective work with Michael Tsosie in locating the first photograph of a female "berdache," or warrior woman. Here again is an example of how Will effectively collaborates with native scholars and cultural experts to produce results that scholars *and* native people can use. I always look forward to reading Will's books because I know I will find something new, refreshing, and controversial. Will's work should never be placed on a bookshelf to collect dust; it should be read aloud and looked at with great pride as something special.

So with the blessing of our community elders, we honor Will's hard work and dedication in publishing this book. Remember, there are very few of us who have been gifted to share with the world the special role we played as lesbian/gay Native Americans before and after the arrival of the Europeans to our land. We must be thankful to all those who, like Will Roscoe, walk with us in pride.

Randy Burns
Co-founder, Gay American Indians/San Francisco
December 1996

Changing Ones

PART I

"STRANGE COUNTRY THIS": AN INTRODUCTION TO NORTH AMERICAN GENDER DIVERSITY

In 1833, Edwin T. Denig came up the Missouri River to the country of the Crow Indians in Montana to spend the next twenty-three years of his life as a trader for the American Fur Company. He found himself in an unknown land, surrounded by unfamiliar cultures. Of all the differences he encountered none seemed more alien to him than native practices regarding sexuality and gender. Among the Crow Indians, Denig found that some of the most important and respected individuals were men and women who in American and European societies would be condemned, persecuted, jailed, even executed. Their lifestyles would be called immoral and perverse, their sexuality deemed unnatural.

And yet, among the Crows, men who dressed as women and specialized in women's work were accepted and sometimes honored; a woman who led men into battle and had four wives was a respected chief. As Denig wrote, "Most civilized communities recognize but two genders, the masculine and feminine. But strange to say, these people have a neuter," and with a note of exasperation he added, "Strange country this, where males assume the dress and perform the duties of females, while women turn men and mate with their own sex!"[1]

The social universe of native North America was nowhere more at odds with that of Europe and Anglo-America than in its diverse gender roles. Denig's was not a new discovery. Europeans had been encountering "berdaches"—as third and fourth gender people have come to be called in the anthropological literature—since the days of Spanish conquest, and they reacted much as Denig did: with amazement, dismay, disgust, and occasionally, when they weren't dependent on the natives' goodwill, with violence. As Cabeza de Vaca wrote of his sojourn with the Karankawa Indians of Texas in 1540, "In the time that I continued among them, I saw a most brutish and beastly custom, to wit, a man who was married to another, and these be certaine effeminate and impotent men, who goe clothed and attired like women, and performe the office of a woman."[2] Some years earlier, when Vasco Núñez de Balboa encountered forty *pathicos fœmineo amictu* (male homosexuals dressed as women) in Panama, he had them put to the dogs. The scene is illustrated in sadomasochistic detail in Théodor De Bry's famous *Collectiones peregrinationum*.[3] "A fine action of an honourable and Catholic Spaniard," commented one historian a hundred years later.[4]

In 1986, when the U.S. Supreme Court upheld Georgia's sodomy law, the majority opinion cited "millennia of moral teaching" against homosexuality in support of its decision. Ten years later, when legislation called the Defense of Marriage Act was proposed by a twice divorced congressman and signed into law by an admitted adulterer, it was said that no society that allowed people of the same sex to marry has or could survive, that American values were grounded in Judeo-Christian principles that precluded tolerance of same-sex love and gender difference.[5]

In truth, the ground American society occupies once may have been the queerest continent on the planet. The original peoples of North America, whose principles are just as ancient as those of Judeo-Christian culture, saw no threat in homosexuality or gender variance. Indeed, they believed individuals with these traits made unique contributions to their communities. As a Crow tribal elder said in 1982, "We don't waste people the way white society does. Every person has their gift."[6] In this land, the original America, men who wore women's clothes and did women's work became artists, innovators, ambassadors, and religious leaders, and women sometimes became warriors, hunters, and chiefs. Same-sex marriages flourished and no tribe was the worse for it— until the Europeans arrived. In this "strange country," people who were different in terms of gender identity or sexuality were respected, integrated, and sometimes revered. How could this be?

The first goal of this book is to document one of the most distinctive, widespread, and least known aspects of native North America. The result is a strikingly different view of the American frontier. Instead of hypermasculine braves and submissive squaws we find personalities of surprising diversity and complexity. Furthermore, in the ambiguous space of the border zone, native and

European concepts of gender and sexuality coexisted as well as clashed. The legacy for Euro-Americans has been the way in which North American multiple genders influenced the formation of modern concepts of homosexuality and heterosexuality. For native people, the legacy is a darker one, for the greater part of it has entailed their conquest, decimation, dispossession, and colonization. But along the way, the representatives of gender diversity were among those who took strong stands on behalf of their tribes, who sought and found creative strategies by which their people could survive. Their lives challenge the assumption that natives and their cultures have disappeared or been assimilated.

But the significance of native gender diversity is not only in the way it challenges stereotypes. It also undermines many assumptions and theories about the nature of gender and sexuality. The careers of Osh-Tisch, Hastíín Klah, and Woman Chief, for example, convincingly refute (should further refutation be needed) the old medical models of sexual and gender difference as pathological maladjustments, as well as popular associations of gender variation with weakness and incompetence. Berdaches were not failed men or women; they occupied distinct gender roles and behaved according to cultural expectations for those roles.

The evidence of multiple genders in North America offers support for the theory of social constructionism, which maintains that gender roles, sexualities, and identities are not natural, essential, or universal, but constructed by social processes and discourses. At the same time, it challenges certain assumptions of recent work in postmodern cultural studies, feminism, and queer theory. The only societies many of today's influential cultural theorists have considered have been those of the West (and primarily northwest Europe and North America). Few have ever considered cross-cultural evidence; many show a marked disinclination for empirical evidence of any kind. Consequently, certain elements of Western beliefs and epistemology have been essentialized as universal features of human societies. These include assumptions that "sex" and "gender" are relevant categories in all societies and that sexuality and gender are (always) analytically distinguishable; that sexes and genders are binary and dichotomous and that, by extension, only heterosexuality or the attraction between opposites is natural; that ideology and cultural beliefs regarding gender are always essentialist while gender identities and sexualities are always constructed; and that the fluidity of human desire and the ambiguities of human categories make stable identities and cultural continuity impossible. All of these assumptions are called into question by the example of native multiple genders. As we will see, native beliefs about gender and sexuality were avowedly constructionist, acknowledging the malleability of human desire and identity. At the same time, North American multiple genders emerge as roles with great historical depth and continuity, with parallels in societies worldwide.

This journey into the "strange country" of native North America begins with biographical and historical accounts of individuals and their roles. This approach places alternative genders in the context of specific tribes and cultural systems. The reader is invited to identify with third and fourth gender people, to understand the worlds they occupied and the knowledge and experiences they drew on to make their life choices. Eventually, the exoticism of the six-foot-tall male who wore a dress or the female who carried a gun and could use it gives way to an appreciation of the complexity, integrity, and logic of their lives. This first part of the book concludes with an account of contemporary lesbian and gay natives, who have adopted the term "two-spirits" to reflect the non-Western roots of their identities, and their efforts to revive alternative gender traditions. The second half of the book draws on these case studies (and adds to them) to develop theoretical perspectives on multiple genders and their history. The last two chapters review ongoing debates in the study of North American gender diversity and their significance for cultural theory and contemporary social issues.

THE BERDACHE OR ALTERNATIVE GENDER ROLE

The estimated four hundred tribal groups in North America at the time of European contact represented a diverse array of environmental adaptations, subsistence strategies, social organizations, family structures, languages, and religions. They ranged from the egalitarian, loosely organized bands of Inuit hunter-gatherers in the arctic, to the populous farmers and village dwellers of the southeast, who were organized into castes and ruled by chieftains. Many other North American societies combined hunting and gathering with digging stick horticulture. (True agrarian societies, on the other hand, based on intensive food production with draught animals, were not present.)

Rather than technology, native societies emphasized knowledge, especially familiarity with the environment. Consequently, intuitive forms of knowledge were highly developed. Visions, dreams, and trance states were valued as sources of information, direction, ability, and fortune. Ideals of balance, harmony, and integration between humans and nature were widespread. However, those drawn to native religions because of their apparent resonance with Western environmental and New Age tenets would do well to remember the central role of violence in Plains Indian religions and the concern with wealth among Northwest Coast groups.

Most North American societies were only weakly stratified. In the typical tribal social organization leaders were selected (or confirmed) based on competence, and social control was achieved largely through face-to-face interaction. Work roles were organized on the basis of gender. Within these systems, women made important, sometimes the most important, economic contributions to their families' subsistence. Although the life choices and personal autonomy of women varied significantly from matrilineal groups like the Hopis, Zunis, and Iroquois to the warrior-dominated Plains tribes, opportunities for women to acquire prestige and take leadership roles existed in every group.

Alternative gender roles were among the most widely shared features of North American societies. Male berdaches have been documented in over 155 tribes (see Tribal Index). In about a third of these groups, a formal status also existed for females who undertook a man's lifestyle, becoming hunters, warriors, and chiefs. They were sometimes referred to with the same term for male berdaches and sometimes with a distinct term—making them, therefore, a fourth gender. (Thus, "third gender" generally refers to male berdaches and sometimes male and female berdaches, while "fourth gender" always refers to female berdaches. Each tribe, of course, had its own terms for these roles, like boté in Crow, nádleehí in Navajo, winkte in Lakota, and alyha: and hwame: in Mohave.) Because so many North American cultures were disrupted (or had disappeared) before they were studied by anthropologists, it is not possible to state the absolute frequency of these roles. Those alternative gender roles that have been documented, however, occur in every region of the continent, in every kind of society, and among speakers of every major language group. The number of tribes in which the existence of such roles have been denied (by informants or outsider observers) are quite few. Far greater are those instances in which information regarding the presence of gender diversity has simply not been recorded.

"Berdache" has become the accepted anthropological term for these roles despite a rather unlikely etymology. It can be traced back to the Indo-European root *welə "to strike, wound," from which the Old Iranian *varta-, "seized, prisoner," is derived.[7] In Persia, it referred to a young captive or slave (male *or* female). The word entered western European languages perhaps from Muslim Spain or as a result of contact with Muslims during the Crusades. By the Renaissance it was current in Italian as bardascia and bardasso, in Spanish as bardaje (or bardaxe), in French as berdache, and in English as "bardash" with the meaning of "catamite"—the younger partner in an age-differentiated homosexual relationship. Over time its meaning began to shift, losing its reference to age and active/passive roles and becoming a general term for male homosexual.[8] In some places, it lost its sexual connotations altogether.[9] By the mid-nineteenth century, its use in Europe lapsed.

In North America, however, "berdache" continued to be used, but for a quite different purpose.[10] Its first written occurrence in reference to third and fourth gender North American natives is in the 1704 memoir of Deliette.[11] Eventually, its use spread to every part of North America the French entered, becoming a pidgin term used by Euro-Americans and natives alike (see Table 8.1).[12] Its first use in an anthropological publication was by Washington Matthews in 1877. In describing Hidatsa miáti he wrote, "Such are called by the French Canadians 'berdaches.'"[13] The next anthropological use was in J. Owen Dorsey's 1890 study of Siouan cults. Like Matthews, he described "berdache" as a French Canadian frontier term.[14] Following Alfred Kroeber's use of the word in his 1902 ethnography of the Arapaho, it became part of standard anthropological terminology.

Although there are important variations in berdache roles, which will be discussed below, they share a core set of traits that justifies comparing them:

- Specialized work roles—Male and female berdaches are typically described in terms of their preference and achievements in the work of the "opposite" sex and/or unique activities specific to their identities.
- Gender difference—In addition to work preferences, berdaches are distinguished from men and women in terms of temperament, dress, lifestyle, and social roles.
- Spiritual sanction—Berdache identity is widely believed to be the result of supernatural intervention in the form of visions or dreams, and/or it is sanctioned by tribal mythology.
- Same-sex relations—Berdaches most often form sexual and emotional relationships with non-berdache members of their own sex.

The most visible marker of berdache gender status was some form of cross-dressing, although this occurred much less consistently than is usually assumed. In some tribes, male berdaches dressed distinctly from both men and women (see Table 6.1). In other cases, berdaches did not cross-dress at all or only partly. Cross-dressing was even more variable in the case of female berdaches. Often, they wore men's clothing only when hunting or in battle. Similarly, despite the common description of berdaches as "doing the work of the opposite sex," they more often engaged in a combination of men's and women's activities, along with pursuits unique to their status.

Berdaches are also frequently attributed with spiritual powers. This was especially common in tribes, such as those of the Plains, with a vision complex, in which visions or dreams were considered life-defining and believed to convey power. Such beliefs not only justified alternative gender identities, they endowed those identities with special prestige. Even in societies lacking the vision complex, such as the Pueblos of the Southwest, alternative gender roles were sanctioned by tribal myths and portrayed in ceremonies.

The process by which third gender identity was adopted and/or acknowledged varied, but one dominant pattern emerges cross-culturally. Recognition of berdache orientation typically occurred when a boy showed interest and aptitude in women's work or a girl persistently engaged in the activities of boys and men. Significantly, these preferences manifested well before puberty, so that sexual behavior was a less important defining trait. In tribes with a vision complex, supernatural intervention was sometimes credited with determining berdache status, but a close reading of ethnographic and historic reports reveals that in many cases childhood cross-gender interests and skills preceded visions, which merely served to confirm alternative gender identity. Another process has been reported for certain arctic and subarctic groups, in which children were sometimes assigned cross- or mixed-sex identities at birth, which might be modified after puberty (see below). Latitude was still allowed, however, for individual preferences. In those instances when men were required to cross-dress because they were considered cowards or because they were captives, a distinction from true berdache status was recognized (see chapter 9).

Unfortunately, there are few accounts of berdache sexuality. This has led some to claim that berdaches were asexual or that the sexual aspects of alternative genders were not important. Harriet Whitehead has argued that "sexual object choice is part of the gender configuration, but its salience is low; so low that by itself it does not provoke the reclassification of the individual to a special status," and Clemmer has concluded, "The berdache was not only— and sometimes not at all—a sexual role."[15] Ironically, in those cases for which detailed evidence about individual berdaches exists (such as Osh-Tisch and Hastíín Klah), almost nothing has been recorded about their sexuality and personal relationships. However, when the sexual preferences of berdaches *have* been reported a definite pattern emerges. Male and female berdaches were sexually active with members of their own sex and this behavior was part of the cultural expectations for their role.

Indeed, some male berdaches were very active sexually. The Navajo *nádleehí* Kinábahí told Willard Hill that "she" had had sex with over one hundred different men.[16] The Sauk and Fox tribe held an annual dance in which a berdache, or *aya'kwa*, appeared surrounded by all "her" lovers,[17] and Lakota *winkte* bestowed bawdy nicknames as a souvenir of sexual encounters with them. In fact, Lakota warriors sometimes visited *winkte* before going to battle as a means of increasing their own masculinity.[18] In the early eighteenth century, Ojibway men had sex with the berdache Ozaw-wen-dib (Yellowhead), himself an accomplished warrior, "to acquire his fighting ability and courage, by having intimate connection with him."[19] In a similar vein, an Omaha chief once claimed he could change the weather because he had had sex four times with a male berdache.[20]

The active sex life of berdaches led them to be considered fortuitous in all matters relating to sex and romance. Navajo *nádleehí*, Cheyenne *he'eman*, and Omaha *mi"quga* were matchmakers, while the Mohave believed both male *alyha:* and female *hwame:* were lucky in love. If Mohave berdaches became shamans, they specialized in the treatment of sexual diseases (see chapter 7). Pawnee berdaches provided men with love charms for attracting women, while a carved fan from the eastern Sioux depicts male berdaches in a ritual scene associated with the love magic of the elk. (In the Oto origin myth, the figure Elk is described as a berdache.)[21] The autobiography of a Kwakiutl chief provides a rare description of a sexual encounter with a male berdache: "This man, her name was

Frances . . . , she caught hold of me, and when I went there she throwed me right into her bed. My, she was strong—awful strong!"[22]

In forming relationships with non-berdache members of their own sex, third and fourth gender natives were "homosexual" in the Western definition of that term. The native view of such relations was more complex, however. Because berdaches were considered members of a distinct gender, native epistemologies classified relationships with them differently than those between individuals who had the same gender identity.[23] Nor were their non-berdache partners labeled in any way; their gender identities and sexualities remained those of men or women. At the same time, knowledge of berdaches' anatomical sex was never denied, and the sexual acts performed with them were recognized (with distinct terms) as different from heterosexual acts. Some male berdaches had relationships with women, although in most cases they were men who were already warriors and husbands who became berdaches on the basis of a vision or dream.[24] Finally, a few berdaches may not have been sexually active at all, although institutionalized celibacy was a foreign concept in native cultures.[25] The only sexual relationships berdaches are not known to have formed are ones involving other berdaches.

The primary characteristic of third gender sexuality in the native view was not its same-sex nature, but the fact that it was nonprocreative. That is, rather than an opposition of heterosexuality to homosexuality, native beliefs opposed reproductive to nonreproductive sex. (This is especially apparent in the case of native terms for berdaches that literally mean "sterile" or "impotent"—see the Glossary of Native Terms). Reproductive sex was engaged in to obtain children and fulfill one's kinship role. Nonreproductive sex was engaged in for pleasure and emotional rewards. As such, sexual pleasure was valued in its own right—it forged relationships, it was entertaining, it was necessary for good health. In these belief systems, third and fourth genders represented special instances of nonprocreative sexuality and romantic love. Given the relative absence of restrictions on their sexual availability within a kinship-based social organization, individuals in these roles had more opportunities to engage in sexual activity than did men or women. Although long-term relationships between berdaches and non-berdaches were considered marriages, they do not seem to have been the product of alliance politics between families, to have involved bridewealth or brideservice, or to have been governed by restrictions on the social status of the partners. When such relationships dissolved the disputes involved were usually limited to the couple alone, not their families or clans.

Of all the cultural associations of alternative genders, perhaps the least understood is their relationship to warfare. Many observers have attempted to account for male berdaches by suggesting that the role was a social status imposed on men too weak or cowardly to live up to tribal standards of masculinity.[26] This can be disproved on several grounds. Landes's Dakota informants, for example, clearly distinguished between men who were uninterested in or afraid of warfare and berdaches "who had a dream."[27] In fact, male berdaches regularly participated in many aspects of warfare.[28] This ranged from accompanying war parties to provide support, entertainment, and luck, to joining in the fighting, handling enemy scalps, and directing victory ceremonies. Indeed, some berdaches, such as the Crow Osh-Tisch, the Ojibway Yellowhead, and the Southern Piegan, Piegan Woman, were renowned for their war exploits, while the Sioux remember a berdache who tricked the Sans Arc band into putting down their weapons just as their enemies attacked.[29] Third and fourth gender figures appear as warriors in myths and tales, as well.[30] In fact, most native belief systems ultimately viewed berdaches and successful warriors in similar terms—both were the beneficiaries of supernatural power.

The associations of alternative genders with death, whether through roles as undertakers and mourners in California, or as participants in victory or "scalp" dances, is striking. They point to a nexus of beliefs difficult to grasp from a Western perspective, in which nonprocreative sexuality and fertility, creativity and inspiration, and warfare and death are linked, and these links are represented by third and fourth gender persons. The nature of these connections will be explored throughout the rest of this book.

That berdaches were accepted and integrated members of their communities is underscored throughout the ethnographic literature and confirmed by contemporary natives. In some tribes, alternative genders enjoyed special respect and privileges. In a few cases, berdaches were feared because of their supernatural power. If they were scorned, hated, or ridiculed, it was usually for individual reasons and not because of their gender difference, at least until the twentieth century. In some cases, joking relationships have been mistakenly interpreted as evidence of nonacceptance. In fact, individuals in tribal societies were often subject to teasing precisely because they had high status.[31] In other cases, accounts attributing natives with hostility toward berdaches can be shown to reflect the judgments of Euro-Americans or of informants influenced by Christianity. As Drucker observed, "Most of the informants were inclined to be reticent about sexual matters, apparently feeling that they would be putting themselves in a bad light by discussing such things. This attitude accounts for most of the denials of the existence of berdaches aboriginally. I was told repeatedly that such individuals ('jotes') were to be found 'only among Mexicans.'"[32] What is needed at this point is an analysis of a tribe either definitely lacking such a role or hostile to gender difference based on pre-contact values.[33]

There are no reliable data at present concerning the numbers of berdaches in native populations, although careful work in census records and oral histories may make it possible to make estimates for some tribes in the late nineteenth century. In small groups, with populations of a few hundred, there might have been only one or two berdaches in a given generation. In larger communities, their numbers were sufficient for them to be recognized as a social group (as among the Timucua, Hidatsa, Crow, and Cheyenne). Among the Hidatsa of the upper Missouri River, there was said to be fifteen to twenty-five *miáti* in a village, and among the Yuki of California as many as thirty in the tribe.[34] In any case, the importance of a social role for a given society is not a function of the number of individuals who occupy it—the number of chiefs and medicine people was in most cases no greater than that of berdaches, but no one would dispute their importance to tribal society and history.

Some of the points made so far apply to alternative genders for females as well. As Medicine notes, "warrior women," like male berdaches, occupied "socially sanctioned role alternatives." These were "normative statuses which permitted individuals to strive for self-actualization, excellence, and social recognition in areas outside their customary sex role assignments."[35] Blackwood has argued that alternative female roles were socially and ontologically on par with male roles in the sense of being distinct, lifelong identities.[36] Still, it is clear that female alternative genders were not mirror opposites of those for males, nor were alternative gender roles the only avenue by which women engaged in male pursuits, as chapter 4 relates.

Important differences existed between alternative genders in various tribes, as a regional survey reveals:

Southeast. The reports of René Goulaine de Laudonnière and Jacques Le Moyne, who arrived in Florida in 1564 on an expedition to assert French claims to the region, provide a fairly detailed description of male berdaches among the Timucua Indians. Le Moyne painted two pictures of them and engravings based on these paintings were published by Theodore De Bry. One depicts two pairs carrying corpses on stretchers, while two others carry sick or injured persons on their backs. The engraving is captioned "Hermaphrodites as Laborers," and the accompanying text relates that because they are strong, "hermaphrodites" (a term frequently used by Europeans who often assumed without evidence that berdaches were intersexed) accompany warriors to battle to carry provisions and tend to the injured. A second engraving depicts "curly-haired hermaphrodites" bearing baskets of game, fish, and crocodiles to a storehouse.[37]

Alternative gender males among the Karankawa and Coahuiltec Indians of the Texas Gulf Coast also participated in warfare.[38] According to Cabeza de Vaca, "*Hombres amarionadas impotentes*," while dressing and living like women, carried heavy burdens and were larger than other males.[39] In the eighteenth century, Dumont de Montigny observed a role for males called the "chief of women" among the Natchez of the lower Mississippi. They did women's work, including crafts and gardening, assisted on war parties, and had sex with men.[40] Unfortunately, these early reports are the most detailed available for Southeast tribes, although alternative gender statuses appear to have been present among the Creek, Chickasaw, Choctaw, Caddo, and Cherokee (see Tribal Index).

Northeast and woodlands. Although there are no definite reports of alternative gender roles among the Algonkian-speaking and Iroquoian tribes of the Northeast, among the Algonkian Illinois of the Mississippi Valley the status of *ikoueta*, or male berdaches, seems to have been fairly high, judging from the accounts of French explorers and travelers in the late seventeenth century. Males entered the role based on their preference for women's work. They went to war, sang at religious ceremonies, gave advice at councils, and were considered "manitou," or holy. According to Marquette, "Nothing can be decided without their advice."[41] Nearly all the French observers commented on their sexuality—*ikoueta* practiced "sodomy"—typically in the context of a general denunciation of Illinois morality. Similar roles also have been documented among the Winnebago, Sauk and Fox, Miami, and Potawatomi. Among these groups visions or dreams were believed to play a role in determining berdache identity. The Potawatomi considered such individuals "extraordinary."[42] Indeed, the widespread occurrence of this role among Algonkian-speakers of the Plains (the Cheyenne, Arapaho, Blackfoot, and Gros Ventre) and in the subarctic region makes its apparent absence among eastern Algonkians all the more suspect.[43]

Plains. Whereas the traditional cultures of tribes east of the Mississippi were severely disrupted long before the rise of anthropology, the cultures of the Plains have been more systematically studied, and the literature occasionally provides detailed glimpses of alternative gender roles. Table 1.1 summarizes this evidence for four tribes: the Crow; their relatives, the Hidatsa; the Lakota; and the Cheyenne.

The North American vision complex reached its apex among Plains tribes. Men sought visions that would enable them to kill game and enemies, women sought visions as sources of designs and inspiration for their arts, and male berdaches among the Mandan, Lakota, Assiniboine, Arapaho, Omaha, Kansa, Osage, and Oto had dreams and visions of female deities or the moon that confirmed their identity and gave them distinct abilities. The Osage term for berdache, *mixu'ga* (and its cognates in Omaha, Kansa, and Oto), literally means "moon-instructed" (from *mi*, "moon" and *xu'ga*, "to instruct").[44] The most frequently cited skills were those of beading, quillwork, and the manufacture and decoration of myriad products made from animal skins. As Benedict related, "The Dakota had a saying, 'fine possessions like a berdache's,' and it was the epitome of praise for any woman's household possessions."[45] These productive skills were a function of supernatural power—both contact with it and possession of it.

Creativity was only one of the forms this power could take. Lakota *winkte* could also predict the future, and they had auspicious powers in relation to childbirth and childrearing that included bestowing names that were considered lucky.[46] The religious dimension of alternative gender roles was perhaps most fully developed among the Hidatsa and Mandan, horticultural village dwellers,

TABLE 1.1.

Cultural Associations of Plains Male Berdaches[1]

	Lakota	Crow	Hidatsa	Cheyenne	Other tribes
Dreams/ visions	had dreams of Double Woman	had dreams that transformed	had dreams of Woman Above or "mysterious women"		Assiniboine, Oto, Osage, Arapaho, Kansa, Mandan, Ojibwa
Moon	were influenced by moon				Omaha, Pawnee, Sauk/Fox, Osage, Kansa, Oto
Power	were holy, foretold future, brought luck	some were medicine people	had special power	were doctors	Arapaho, Sauk/Fox
Religion	led some ceremonies	selected sun dance pole	had role in sun dance and other rites; were members of Holy Women Society	led scalp dance	
Sexuality	had sex with men and gave them obscene names	had sex with men	lived with men	were matchmakers	Omaha (matchmakers), Pawnee (love magic)
Crafts	were skilled in quill- and beadwork	excelled in crafts	were industrious in crafts	were talented	Ponca
Warfare	joined war parties	joined war parties		joined war parties	

1. See Tribal Index for sources.

and the Cheyenne, who were former village dwellers. Coleman argues that the reason *he´emane'o* directed the all-important victory dance was because they embodied the central principles of Cheyenne religion, which were balance and synthesis.[47]

Arctic and subarctic. Saladin d'Anglure has described the extremely flexible gender system of the central arctic Inuit, in which arbitrary gender assignments along with individual preferences result in complex and varied "gender histories" for many individuals. Boys and girls are raised in accordance with the gender of one or more names selected for them before their birth. Consequently, some children are raised with cross- or mixed-gender identities. Upon reaching puberty or adulthood they may choose to alter such identities or retain them.[48] Saladin d'Anglure considers such individuals (who are often shamans, as well) to be members of a distinct third gender. In addition, the Inuit believe some infants, called *sipiniq,* change their anatomical sex at birth.[49] (Similar beliefs have been reported for the Bella Coola and the Tlingit.)[50] The Athapaskan-speaking Dene Tha (Slavey or Beaver Indians of Canada) have a related belief in the possibility of cross-sex reincarnation.[51] Among the Ingalik, an Athapaskan group of the Alaskan interior, both male and female berdaches have been reported, and male berdaches often had shamanic powers.

Russian explorers, traders, and missionaries were well aware of gender diversity among Alaskan natives. The explorer Lisiansky reported that a Russian priest almost married an Aleut chief to a berdache before being informed that the "bride" was male.[52] Among the Chugach and Koniag, Pacific Eskimo (Yup'ik) groups, such individuals were believed to be "two persons in one."[53] Despite Russian attempts to suppress the role, third gender individuals were esteemed and encouraged by their families, who considered them lucky. Many were shamans. Early observers reported that some feminine boys were raised as girls from childhood by families lacking a daughter.[54]

In the vast subarctic region, alternative genders have been reported for the Athapaskan-speaking Kaska and among the widely dispersed Cree and Ojibway. The linguistic relationship between terms for male berdaches in Algonkian-speaking groups (including the Fox and Illinois) is evident (see Glossary).

Northwest Coast and Columbia Plateau. Among the Northwest Coast Haisla, berdaches were reportedly "fairly common." A supernatural berdache was portrayed in masked dances by the neighboring Bella Coola.[55] Among the Eyak, however, berdaches did not have supernatural power and their status was low.[56] Alternative male genders have been widely reported for the Columbia Plateau region but with few details. Among the Flathead of western Montana and the Klamath of southern Oregon, berdaches were often shamans.[57] The career of one Klamath *tw!ĭnnă´ĕk,* known as Muksamse´lapli, or White Cindy, has been briefly described by Spier and by McCleod.[58]

West and Southwest. Male and female alternative genders have been documented throughout the Great Basin, California, Colorado River, and Southwest culture areas. They are consistently described as doing the work of the other sex, less consistently as cross-dressing. As elsewhere, they formed relationships with non-berdache members of their own sex. Among some groups (Shoshone, Ute, Kitanemuk, Pima-Papago), families held a kind of initiation rite to confirm male berdache identity. The child was placed in a circle of brush with a bow and a basket (men's and women's objects, respectively). The brush was set on fire, and whichever object the boy picked up as he ran away served to identify his gender preference. The choice of the basket signified male berdache status. Among the

Shoshone, who acquired horses and adopted a Plains-oriented lifestyle, male berdaches joined war parties.[59]

In California, third/fourth gender individuals often had ceremonial roles relating to death and burial. Among the Yokuts and Tubatulabal, and possibly the Chumash, male berdaches served as undertakers, handling and burying the deceased and conducting mourning rites.[60] Berdaches also participated in mourning rites among the Monache (Mono), Pomo, Miwok, Achumawi, Atsugewi, and Shasta.[61] Among the Wappo, Mattole, Hupa, Chilula, Tolowa, Maidu, Achumawi, Shasta, and Modoc, male berdaches, and less often female berdaches, were sometimes shamans. One of the last chiefs of the Kawaiisu was a third gender male.[62]

Third and fourth genders among the Yuman-speaking tribes along the Colorado River are the subject of chapter 7, while Navajo *nádleehí* are described in chapter 3. Alternative roles for males (but apparently not females) existed among the Pueblo communities of Isleta, San Felipe, San Juan, Santa Ana, Santo Domingo, Tesuque, Acoma, Laguna, Zuni, and Hopi (see Tribal Index for sources).[63] Among the western Pueblos, man-woman kachinas, or gods, were portrayed in masked dances and ceremonies. The Zuni *lhamana* We'wha was a religious specialist who regularly participated in ceremonies.[64] Other Pueblo berdaches are described primarily in terms of their specialization in pottery and other pursuits of women.

Alternative gender roles also existed among the Papago and Pima of the Southwest and northern Mexico. Like Plains berdaches, Papago *wiik'ovat* taunted the scalps brought home by warriors, and they were visited for sexual liaisons by men to whom they gave obscene nicknames. A fire test was employed to confirm their identity.[65]

A NOTE ON TERMS AND METHODS

Several terms used in this book have specific meanings, the understanding of which is crucial to the arguments I will be making. My subject is North America and its original inhabitants, which encompasses a more diverse group of peoples than do the terms "Native Americans" or "American Indians." To include the Indian people of Canada as well as Alaskan natives (Eskimo/Inuit/Yu'pik, Aleut, and Indian), I use the term "native North Americans."[66] I do not capitalize the term "native" following current typographical conventions (and to spare the reader's eyes since it occurs frequently); nor, for that matter, do I capitalize gay, lesbian, or other ethnic terms except those involving proper nouns like African American and American Indian. Where I do use "Native American" or "American Indian" I mean specifically Indian people in the United States (both terms being widely accepted among those people).

Perhaps the most important distinction in this book is between the terms "sex" and "gender." As used here, "sex" specifically refers to anatomical or biological sex, while "gender" refers to culturally constructed social roles and identities in which sex is one defining element whose importance (and definition) varies. Statistically, the large majority of human bodies across cultures can be classified as either male or female (although perhaps three to five percent cannot for various reasons).[67] Gender roles, on the other hand, diverge considerably across cultures and, as I will argue in this book, are not always limited to two.

Consistent with this distinction, I use the terms "male" and "female" specifically in reference to biological sex, and "men," "women," and "berdaches" in reference to gender roles. Thus, "female alternative gender role" means a role for individuals with a female body but a third or fourth gender identity. I never speak of "male work" or "female lifestyles," since the implication would be that certain work or ways of living were inherent to having a certain kind of body. Rather, I speak of "men's work" and "women's lifestyles," to identify work or life patterns culturally defined as those of men or women. There is little consistency in how native people and anthropologists apply gendered English pronouns to berdaches. Many native languages lack such pronouns, so the problem does not arise. Generally, I use the pronouns appropriate to an individual's anatomical sex—since this was always known to other tribal members. Where berdaches are known to have been referred to by tribal members with specific gendered pronouns I have followed this usage.

In seeking alternatives to terms that imply judgments or tend to pathologize what they describe, I avoid adjectives like "deviance" and "variance" in preference to more neutral terms such as "difference" and "diversity."

The most troublesome term in this book is "berdache" itself. In recent years, calls have been made to replace berdache with "two-spirit." In 1993, a group of anthropologists and natives issued guidelines that formalized these preferences. "Berdache," they argued, is a term "that has its origins in Western thought and languages." Scholars were asked to drop its use altogether and to insert "[sic]" following its appearance in quoted texts. In its place they were encouraged to use tribally specific terms for multiple genders or the term "two-spirit." Two-spirit was also identified as the preferred label of contemporary gay, lesbian, bisexual, and transgender natives.[68]

Unfortunately, these guidelines create as many problems as they solve, beginning with a mischaracterization of the history and meaning of the word "berdache." As a Persian term, its origins are Eastern not Western. Nor is it a derogatory term, except to the extent that all terms for nonmarital sexuality in European societies carried a measure of condemnation. It was rarely used with the force of "faggot," but more often as a euphemism with the sense of "lover" or "boyfriend."[69] Its history, in this regard, is akin to that of "gay," "black," and "Chicano"—terms that also lost negative connotations over time.

The oft-cited 1955 article by anthropologists Angelino and Shedd has done much to perpetuate these misconceptions (and inspire attempts to find alternative terminology). The authors trace the term back to its Persian form but then state, "While the word underwent considerable change the meaning in each instance remained constant, being a 'kept boy,' a 'male prostitute,' and 'catamite.'"[70] This is certainly wrong. As outlined above, the meaning and use of the word underwent significant change when it was imported into Europe (where there were no "slave boys") and even more change when it was carried to North America (where there was no tradition of age- or status-differentiated homosexuality). If the first generation of French visitors to North America used the term in a derogatory sense it soon lost this connotation as it came to be used not only as a pantribal term by natives themselves but as a personal name as well. There is no evidence that the first anthropologists to use the term were aware of its older European and Persian meanings. Washington Matthews, for example, in his Hidatsa ethnography (and in his 1897 Navajo Legends, in which he suggested that such a role was "known perhaps in all wild Indian tribes") appears unaware of any other meaning of the term.[71] Crow Agency physician A. B. Holder's lack of familiarity with the term's European origins led him to report in 1889 that berdache was a word from a native language of the Puget Sound area![72]

More importantly, using "two-spirits" as a transhistorical term raises the same problems as labeling premodern forms of homosexuality "gay," a practice few scholars have employed since historian John Boswell wrote of "gay" people and "gay subcultures" in ancient Rome and was widely criticized for such anachronism.[73] The term "gay," because of its strong associations with modern homosexuality, evokes associations and assumptions that are not valid for other historical periods and cultures whose forms of homosexuality were organized differently. Consequently, scholars have adopted terminology that does not equate past and present, Western and non-Western cultural forms.

In this book I present significant evidence of continuity between identities in past tribal societies and the identities and roles of contemporary lesbian/gay/two-spirit natives. In chapter 8 I argue that models of historical process that pit tradition against change can explain neither the survival of native cultures nor the ways in which they have been transformed. But the evidence I present of continuity is that of symbols and re-established meanings, not of continuously transmitted teachings from one generation to another (with a few exceptions). While I have tried to respect contemporary native sensibilities in my writing, I also think it is important to honor the traditions I write about by remembering that the belief systems and social realities in which they existed endowed them in ways that cannot be easily translated into contemporary experience. For this reason, I have decided not to refer to individuals in historic third and fourth gender roles as "two-spirits," reserving this term instead for those contemporary native people who have begun to identify as such.

This presents a problem, however, for no ready alternative to "berdache" exists. Using tribal terms is one option, and I have done so when possible. But in order to speak of traditional statuses generally, to compare roles of different tribes and those for males to those for females, it is necessary to have an umbrella term to refer to the subject. I can and do write of "alternative genders," "third gender," and "multiple genders." But "female third gender individuals" or "Hastíín Klah, a traditional Navajo alternative-gendered male" seem onerous formulations when there exists a straightforward, historically received term whose only referent for two centuries has been alternative gender roles in North America (the sole definition of the word in the second edition of the *Oxford English Dictionary*). Since "berdache" has no other current usage it does not carry with it expectations based on contemporary lifestyles and identities. Its use emphasizes the distinctiveness of historic roles and the individuals who occupied them, while it maintains continuity in the field of "berdache studies." For these reasons, I continue to use "berdache" when no other term is easily employed.

The goal of this book is to describe and understand native North American gender diversity at its greatest level of articulation—in the same sense that artistic, social, and religious movements are recognized as having high points of development in their history. This has entailed reconstructing these roles as they existed in the period prior to the massive disruption of tribal societies that began with disease and violence and ended with confinement on impoverished reservations. In this task, anthropological field research alone cannot answer every question. Even in tribes in which multiple gender roles have been continuously occupied to the present day, many of their forms, practices, and associated beliefs have not been transmitted. Although anthropological fieldwork can help answer questions about contemporary native sexuality and gender, only ethnohistorical research can truly expand our knowledge of historic berdaches and their roles.

Ethnohistory combines the methods of history and anthropology to study past societies, historical events, and individuals. It differs from anthropology in its focus on historical context and change—how cultures, social organizations, events, and individual actions all shape each other. Ethnohistorians utilize historical records, published literature, archives, visual materials, and artifacts and consult contemporary members of the communities they study.[74] In seeking to understand actions of groups and individuals in the past they draw on anthropological concepts and theories. An understanding of culture often clarifies actions that might otherwise appear mysterious or irrational. Although the discipline of ethnohistory has flourished primarily in North America, its goals are similar to those of the subaltern studies group of India, which has sought to recover the views, understandings, beliefs, and rationales of populations whose voices until now have been ignored or left out of the historical record.

In generalizing about alternative genders, I begin by comparing historically, geographically, and/or linguistically related tribes, then, more broadly, groups within distinct cultural areas (the Plains, Southwest, California, and so forth). Only then do I venture to generalize about these roles as North American phenomena. For this reason, I write of "alternative genders" and "berdache roles" in the plural, rather than "*the* third gender" or "*the* North American berdache."

Another important aspect of my research as been to focus on specific tribes. Biographical and in-depth studies of tribal traditions provide what Gilbert Herdt has termed "the missing key" to the study of third genders, namely, "the understanding of the desires and attractions of the individual and the role in which these influence the establishment of a social status as a third sex." Such desires are linked to the larger social system through what Herdt refers to as cultural ontologies, "local theories of being and the metaphysics of the world; of having a certain kind of body and being in a certain kind of social world, which creates a certain cultural reality; and of being and knowledge combined in the practice of living as a third sex or gender."[75] The case studies in the first half of this book provide good examples of how individual desires are constructed by and expressed through tribal ontologies.

Whereas ethnohistory provides a methodology for reconstructing traditional roles, I have drawn on anthropology, gender studies, and cultural studies to interpret and analyze them. These discourses have taught me to seek the multidimensional aspects of gender constructions—as both social institutions and symbolic systems. Feminist theory, in particular, has attuned me to the power dynamics of gender differences and the relationships between gender roles, modes of production, and social organization. Although I am struck by the regular occurrence of berdaches throughout North America (and their counterparts around the world), the theory of gender diversity developed in this book is based in social and cultural factors. I do not explain why some individuals prefer the work of another gender or have dreams instructing them to become other genders, but I do offer models to explain what happens when individuals manifest such traits—the kind of identity they will have, the expectations others will have of them, the lifestyle they are likely to lead, and the cultural meanings attributed to them.

Cultural studies and poststructuralism provide valuable tools for reading texts, whether those written by Euro-Americans or those from native oral literatures. Deconstructing the imperatives shaping what Europeans could say about non-Western others and how they could say it is indispensable for this research. Only when the rules of discourse have been identified can a given text be utilized confidently as a source of data about another culture. Consequently, at various points in the chapters that follow my focus shifts from native cultures to what was written and said about them by Europeans and what this, in turn, reveals about

European sexuality and gender. I periodically draw on poststructuralist and psychological theories, as well as native theories and models, to interpret the underlying dynamics of Euro-American and native patterns.

Alternative gender roles were one of the most widespread and distinctive features of native societies throughout the continent, yet they are barely mentioned in ethnographies and, until the 1980s, no anthropologist or historian comprehensively studied them. A conspiracy of silence has kept the subject obscured and hidden. In the eight volumes published to date of the Smithsonian Institution's state-of-the-art *Handbook of North American Indians,* berdaches are mentioned in entries for only sixteen tribes—an accuracy rate of barely ten percent based on the number of tribes with alternative gender roles listed in the index here.

A final goal of this book, therefore, is to demonstrate once and for all that any portrayal of native cultures in North America that fails to include gender diversity is flawed, ethnocentric, and, ultimately, wishful. The cases of Osh-Tisch, Hastíín Klah, Running Eagle, Masahai, and the others described in the first half of this book, all figures of historical significance in their tribes, support this conclusion, while the anthropological and historical analyses in the second half reveal the significance of their roles for current theories of sexuality and gender.

Not all parts of this book will speak to all readers. Still, those who seek examples of how third/fourth gender roles were lived should find ample reading, as should those interested in the broader implications of gender diversity. For members of all communities, the example of native North American multiple genders can not only expand our understanding of human diversity, it can open our imagination to personal and social possibilities that have, in our own times, largely been precluded.

"THAT IS MY ROAD": THE LIFE AND TIMES OF A THIRD GENDER WARRIOR

A year after Custer's disastrous defeat at the Little Big Horn, Lieutenant Hugh L. Scott found himself standing on the battleground supervising a hasty burial of the victims' remains. A few months earlier he had been a cadet at West Point. Now he was filling one of the many vacancies in the ill-fated Seventh Cavalry. It was an inauspicious beginning to an otherwise long and distinguished career.

The young lieutenant faced very different challenges from those that had concerned Custer, however. Despite repeated blunders in the 1876 campaigns, the Americans' superior numbers, weapons, and supplies; the aid of Indian allies; and a strategy of systematic attacks on civilians ensured their eventual victory. The army was entering into a new relationship with its former enemies. Once self-sufficient tribes were now wards of the government. It became the army's responsibility to ship and distribute rations for them, enforce order among them, and regulate their social and religious life.

Consequently, young officers in 1877 needed new skills—especially the ability to communicate with natives. Scott applied himself to the task of mastering the Plains Indian sign or gesture language, which made it possible to converse across tribal lines throughout the region; he eventually became a recognized expert on the subject. As Scott recalled, "I began . . . an intensive study of every phase of the Indian and his customs, particularly as to how he might best be approached and influenced, a knowledge that has stood me in good stead many times, has doubtless saved my life again and again, and has also been used to the national benefit by different Presidents of the United States, by secretaries of war and of the interior."[1] Useful indeed—from 1894 to 1897 Scott supervised the captive Chiracahuas Apaches at Fort Sill, Oklahoma, and following the Spanish-American War he carried out assignments in Cuba and the Philippines.[2] Still, he was remarkably open-minded for his time. As his biographer observed, "Scott tended to view and treat men as individuals be they White, Indian, Moro [Philippine], or Negro."[3] In concluding his own memoirs, Scott fondly recalled his "contacts with the peoples of many races and colors by which our lives have been filled with joy and gladness, and which have contributed much to the delightful memories of a soldier's career."[4]

Scott's education in the art of governing the "children of the world" (his own words) began when his troop joined a camp of Crow Indians in the summer of 1877.[5] He was instantly fascinated by the tribe and its "great village of skin lodges," and he thoroughly enjoyed "the color, the jollity, the good-will and kindness encountered everywhere."[6] When he found his canvas army tent poor protection from Montana's dust and flies, he "wandered into the huge buffalo-skin lodge of Iron Bull, head chief of the Crows." He found himself in a strange new world.

> The hide lodge cover was well smoked from the fire and the sun could not penetrate. There was a dim religious light inside that discouraged the flies. Beds of buffalo robes were all around the wall, and the floor was swept clean as the palm of one's hand. The old man, attired only in his breechclout, was lying on his back in bed, crooning his war-songs and shaking his medicine rattle. He was the picture of comfort in that cool, dark lodge, and I said to him, "Brother, I want to come and stay in here with you until we leave"; and he and Mrs. Iron Bull made me very welcome. Theirs was the largest and finest lodge I have ever seen.[7]

The Crows said that "Iron Bull's lodge is like the lodge of the Sun." It was extraordinary not only because of its size but because of the supernatural sanction it represented. According to Edward S. Curtis, "One who had seen a lodge in a vision made his dwelling of twenty hides; but to use more than eighteen would offend the spirits, unless one had received such a vision or bought the right from the man who had seen it."[8]

Over forty years later, Scott returned to Montana a distinguished retired general and a member of the Board of Indian Commissioners. While visiting the Crow Agency he took a side trip to interview the individual who had made Iron Bull's lodge. As Scott learned, the artisan whose mastery of tanning and hideworking created the lodge he so vividly remembered occupied a special status in his tribe. Thanks to Scott's unpublished notes from this meeting the fascinating story of a traditional Crow *boté,* or third gender male, can now be told. Woman Jim, as Scott called him, or Osh-Tisch[9] (Finds Them and Kills Them) as he was known among the Crows, had witnessed the transition from the freedom of camp life to the harsh realities of confinement on a reservation. His life sheds new light on some of the key events of that period.

THE CROW *BOTÉ*

Both male *boté* and warrior women were noted among the Crows by early explorers and traders. According to the German Prince Maximilian, who traveled on the northern plains between 1832 and 1834, "They have many bardaches, or hermaphrodites, among them."[10] In 1856, Edwin Denig also noted the number of berdaches among the Crows. According to Denig, the adoption of *boté* status by boys resulted from the "habits of the child"—in particular, a preference for the work and association of women. "The disposition appears to be natural and cannot be controlled. When arrived at the age of twelve or fourteen, and his habits are formed, the parents clothe him in a girl's dress and his whole life is devoted to the labors assigned to the females." Denig also described Woman Chief, a famous female hunter, warrior, and Crow leader who died in 1854 (see chapter 4).[11]

The Crow explanation for *boté* occurs in a myth in which Old Man Coyote's Wife and Red Woman determine how the Crow people are to live. They establish procedures for tanning skins, starting fires, and taking grease from buffaloes, as well as the length of human life, customs for burial, and the order of the seasons. Then,

> Old-Man-Coyote's Wife said, "I have forgotten something."
>
> Red-Woman said, "You have not forgotten anything." Red-Woman wanted all men and women to be all of the same size and to run all the same way and be the same way.

But Old Man Coyote's Wife said,

> "That way you'll have lots of trouble. We'll give women a dress and leggings to be tied above the knee so they can't run, and they shall not be so strong as men."
>
> That is why men are stronger than women. They made a mistake with some, who became half-men and since then we have had *bāté*.[12]

In this succinct etiology, gender differences are the result of social conventions—the particular dress women wear—not biology. However, in the process of constructing men and women a few "mistakes" can be expected. These fortuitous disjunctions of biology and social convention result in a third gender—the *boté*. As Denig concluded, "Most civilized communities recognize but two genders, the masculine and feminine. But strange to say, these people have a neuter."[13] In other words, Crow *boté* did not cross or exchange genders. While assuming women's clothing and occupations, they still engaged in certain male activities, as we will see.[14]

As Scott noted, *boté* "were honored among their people."[15] They were experts in sewing and beading and considered the most efficient cooks in the tribe. According to one anthropologist, *boté* "excelled women in butchering, tanning, and other domestic tasks"; another reported that their lodges were "the largest and best appointed," and that they were highly regarded for their charitable acts.[16] Indeed, by devoting themselves to women's work, which included everything connected with skins and their use in clothing, robes, moccasins, various accessories, and lodges (or tipis), free of interruption from childbearing and rearing, *boté* were in effect full-time craft specialists.

Crow berdaches fulfilled special religious roles as well. In the sun dance ceremony, for example, a large lodge was constructed around a tall central pole. This pole, a symbolic conduit between the dancers and the Sun Father, had to be secured by individuals who were themselves intermediaries between the community and the supernatural—threshold figures, to use Victor Turner's term. The ceremony that surrounded the felling of the tree used for this purpose required a virtuous woman (that is, faithful to her husband), a captive woman, and one or more *boté*. Each of these individuals occupied an ambivalent, hence spiritually powerful, position in Crow culture. A *boté* actually cut down the tree after announcing, "May all our enemies be like him."[17]

The values of European and American observers, however, led them to single out and denounce Crow customs regarding sexuality and gender. In 1889, when A. B. Holder reported observations of *boté* made during his assignment as a government doctor at the Crow agency, he concluded, "Of all the many varieties of sexual perversion this, it seems to me, is the most debased that could be conceived of."[18] In this century, anthropologist Robert H. Lowie described Crow berdaches as "pathological," "psychiatric cases," "abnormal," "anomalies," "perverts," and "inverts." But as historian Charles Bradley Jr. points out, "Crow morals were simply different, not lacking."[19] In fact, the tribe's matrilineal social organization provided accommodations for premarital, extramarital, and same-sex sexual behavior; divorce, illegitimacy, and adoption; and the economic security of women and children. This was the basis for the sexual freedom attributed to the Crows. Within such a system, if some individuals did not accept or were unsuited for the usual role assigned to their sex, they could still contribute to the community. A man who specialized in women's work, for example, when that work included the production of valuable trade items and articles of apparel that bestowed prestige and beauty, did not forsake a higher social status for a lower one.

INTERVIEW WITH A *BOTÉ*

Scott became aware of third gender males soon after arriving in Crow country: "When I was young, five or six were pointed out to me in the big camp of Mountain and River Crow at the mouth of the Big Horn in 1877. I considered then that it was some sort of a freak, the wearing of women's clothes, and then forgot about it as so many important and interesting things were pressing continually for attention. I have since taken every opportunity to study the matter among the Indians of various tribes."[20] In fact, Scott's research led him to survey not only anthropological texts but the new work of European psychiatrists and sexologists as well, especially Havelock Ellis, and in 1919 he did something almost no anthropologist ever did—he interviewed a berdache.

Scott arrived at Crow Agency in August 1919 to conduct an official inspection on behalf of the Board of Indian Commissioners.[21] Shortly after his arrival he secured the services of a translator and traveled to St. Xavier on the Big Horn River for the express purpose of meeting Osh-Tisch, or "Woman Jim." Scott found the *boté* sitting outdoors under a shade recovering from a case of blood poisoning. "She had a woman's calico dress on and her hair dressed woman fashion."[22] He estimated "her" age to be about sixty-five. Although he was anxious to inquire about *boté* life, Scott noted that "the subject was a very delicate one to broach on such short acquaintance and had to be approached with tact. We got acquainted by talking first about the old Crow chiefs now dead that I knew in 1877—Iron Bull, Blackfoot, Old Crow, Two Belly, etc."

Scott then asked Osh-Tisch why "she" wore women's clothes.[23]

"That is my road," the *boté* replied.

How long had she acted as a woman?

Since birth; she "inclined to be a woman, never a man."

Had anyone, a medicine person, perhaps, told her to become a berdache?

"No."

Did she ever dream about it?

"No."

Did any spirit ever tell her to do it?

"No! Didn't I tell you—that is my road? I have done it ever since I can remember because I wanted to do it. My Father and Mother did not like it. They used to whip me, take away my girl's clothes and put boy's clothes on me but I threw them away—and got girl's clothes and dolls to play with."

When Scott asked if there were any other *boté* in the tribe, Osh-Tisch replied that she was the last. "There were three others recently but they are dead." In her lifetime, she had known of eight, adding, "They have always been far back in history."

Again Scott asked if a spirit or vision directed individuals to become *boté*.

"No, it was just natural, they were born that way."

What sort of work did Osh-Tisch do?

"All woman's work."

Scott added, "She took evident pride in her ability to tan skins and told me she was going to tan a skin and send it to me and then I would see her skill. She handed me a Nez Percé grass bag she had given her by the Nez Percés, saying, 'You have come a long way—I give you this.'"

Osh-Tisch described the lodge she had made for Iron Bull that Scott had so admired. "She said she had made Iron Bull's skin lodge with 25 skins and 22 poles from 36 to 42 feet long, with holes near the points for insertion of buckskin strings to tie them on the pony. It took four or five ponies to carry them. She had made another lodge just as large. The lower ends of [the] poles were five inches in diameter."

Scott continues,

She was most jolly, had a simple air of complete satisfaction with herself, perfectly unconscious of anything abnormal. Obliquely, in answering questions, she said she had never been married, but others she knew had or did everything women did.

When asked if she had any fine buckskin clothes, she said yes, her leg had been very badly swelled three times with blood poisoning from a scratch but now she was recovering. She thought she was going to die and had fine burial clothes ready. Then with great pride, she produced a dark blue woman's dress with abalone shell ornaments, a finely beaded buckskin woman's dress with woman's belt, and leggings. . . .

One could not resist liking her for her frank, simple, jolly manner and evident truthfulness. I gave her some money, which she received in a very dignified way.

"I wish you were going to be at the Crow Fair," Osh-Tisch told Scott as he was leaving. "I am giving things away there and would like to give you something."

Some years later, in 1928, Scott obtained photographs of Osh-Tisch taken by Crow Agent C. H. Asbury. Asbury wrote to Scott,

Some three years ago you suggested you would like to have a picture of Squaw Jim, or Finds Them and Kills Them, of this reservation, dressed in a certain burial garb that he has had for a long time. . . . A few days ago he had the Matron

Figure 1. Osh-Tisch, 1928. Osh-Tisch in front of his cabin wearing clothes he had prepared for his burial. National Anthropological Archives, Smithsonian Institution, photo no. 88-134.

telephone that he was ready to have that picture taken. I went over the day following and made quite a hunt for him and then found him 10 miles from the garb, but I took him to his cabin where the garb was and took three pictures, which I trust you will find of interest.[24]

As a record of an interview with a traditional third gender person, Scott's notes are unique. On their own, however, they do not provide a complete picture of "Woman Jim" or his role in Crow society. The *boté* carefully evaded Scott's questions in two areas, sexuality and religion—and for good reason. As we will see, these aspects of Crow life had been subjected to ongoing interference by representatives of the U.S. government since the 1880s.

OSH-TISCH: ARTIST, MEDICINE PERSON, WARRIOR

At the time of Osh-Tisch's birth in 1854, the tribe still roamed the northern plains freely in search of game and other resources, and a *boté* like Osh-Tisch, as Scott discovered, could still earn respect by mastering traditional tribal arts. In those years, the tribe's berdaches pitched their lodges together and were looked upon as a social group. They called each other "sister." As Osh-Tisch's reputation grew they came to consider him their leader.[25]

What Scott failed to learn was that Osh-Tisch was also a powerful medicine person as a result of a vision he had had as a youth. In this vision, Osh-Tisch was taken underwater by water spirits where he received the power to be a mediator of spiritual forces, an in-between person. A record of this vision still exists in the form of a lodge constructed by Osh-Tisch that survives to the present day. The lodge is covered with green striped canvas awning—canvas being the alternative to buffalo hides after the 1880s—and the interior lining is made of three green and black striped Hudson Bay blankets sewn end-to-end. The joining of the blankets creates double black lines, and between these are sewn green and blue ribbon ties (used to fasten the liner to the inside of the lodge). All these elements relate to Osh-Tisch's vision—blue ribbons to symbolize water, green for grass. Inside the lodge the diffuse light that filters through the well-smoked canvas is much like sunlight viewed underwater. In 1906, Osh-Tisch sold the lodge, but he took the medicine bundle that hung inside with him and therefore retained the right to recreate it. It still can be seen occasionally at Crow Fair, where the granddaughter of its purchaser and her family sometimes set it up.[26]

The physician Holder wrote what may be the earliest description of Osh-Tisch. "One of the bote of my acquaintance is a splendidly formed fellow," he wrote in 1889, "of prepossessing face, in perfect health, active in movement, and happy in disposition. . . . He is five feet eight inches high, weighs one hundred and fifty-eight pounds, and has a frank, intelligent face—being an Indian, of course, beardless. He is thirty-three years of age and has worn woman's dress for twenty-eight years." Holder offered the *boté* money to undergo a medical examination, and true to nineteenth century faith in biological determinism, he inspected his genitals to determine whether they were "in position and shape altogether normal"—they were. According to Holder, this *boté* had lived for two years with a well-known male Indian. "It is not, however, the usual habit of the bote to form a 'partnership' with a single man. He is, like the female members of this tribe, ready to accommodate any male desiring his services." The preferred sexual practice of *boté*, Holder reported, was to perform fellatio on men.[27] (Little had changed sixty years later, when Ford and Beach reported that four *boté* in the tribe were regularly visited by young men for oral sex.[28])

The prestige Osh-Tisch enjoyed among the Crows was due in no small part to an incident that occurred while he was in his early twenties, when he earned the name by which he is remembered today. In 1876, Osh-Tisch joined the forces of General George Crook and fought in the Battle of the Rosebud. Although this engagement is less well known than Custer's famous last stand, one historian has argued that it "involved more troops, had fewer casualties, lasted for most of a day, and was of far greater historical significance."[29] The Sioux and Cheyenne that fought Crook to a stand-off at Rosebud Creek went on to annihilate Custer's command at Little Big Horn eight days later. Indeed, Crook barely missed Custer's fate.[30]

The Crows had their own reasons for joining the army's campaigns against the Lakota and their allies. The infiltration of these traditional enemies into the Crow homeland threatened their hunting grounds and villages. When Crook's representatives called for volunteers, 175 Crow warriors "offered themselves." Among them were Plenty Coups, who was to become the last traditional chief of the Crows, and Osh-Tisch, the last traditional *boté*.[31]

We do not know why Osh-Tisch joined this expedition. It may have been from a desire to revenge the death of a loved one or the result of a vision or both. In any case, when the Crows arrived at Crook's camp a reporter noted three women among them. He assumed they were "wives of the chiefs," but one was, no doubt, the *boté* Osh-Tisch.[32] Fortified by the Crows and Shoshones, Crook's column of 47 officers, 1,000 men, and 1,900 horses and mules proceeded to the headwaters of the Rosebud Creek. [33]

On the morning of June 17, after several hours of forced marching, the general called a bivouac and sat down to a game of cards with his officers. At that moment, the Sioux and Cheyenne attacked. The Indian allies held off the assault while Crook's men organized. According to one participant, "If it had not been for the Crows, the Sioux would have killed half of our command before the soldiers were in a position to meet the attack." The Crows and Shoshones prevented disaster at least two more times that day; once saving Crook's own position and later rescuing an isolated detachment. They also performed daring individual rescues.[34] On one of these occasions, Osh-Tisch played a prominent role.

A young woman named Pretty Shield had watched the Crow warriors leave her village to join Crook. Fifty years later, she recalled their adventures for the journalist Frank Linderman:

> "Did the men ever tell you anything about a woman who fought with Three-stars on the Rosebud?"
>
> "No," I replied, wondering.
>
> "Ahh, they do not like to tell of it," she chuckled. "But I will tell you about it. We Crows all know about it. I shall not be stealing anything from the men by telling the truth.
>
> "Yes, a Crow woman fought with Three-stars on the Rosebud, *two* of them did, for that matter; but one of them was neither a man nor a woman. She looked like a man, and yet she wore woman's clothing; and she had the heart of a woman. Besides, she did a woman's work. Her name was Finds-them-and-kills-them. She was not a man, and yet not a woman," Pretty-shield repeated. "She was not as strong as a man, and yet she was wiser than a woman," she said, musingly, her voice scarcely audible.
>
> "The other woman," she went on, "was a *wild* one who had no man of her own. She was both bad and brave, this one. Her name was The-other-magpie; and she was pretty."

Pretty Shield described how these two, the "wild one" and the "half-woman," brought glory to the Crows by their brave deeds that day. When a warrior named

Bull Snake was wounded by a Lakota and fell from his horse, Finds Them and Kills Them "dashed up to him, got down from her horse, and stood over him, shooting at the Lacota [sic] as rapidly as she could load her gun and fire." The Other Magpie rode around them, inveighing the Lakota with her war song and waving her coup stick (an object used to strike enemies in demonstrations of bravery). According to Pretty Shield:

> "Both these women expected death that day. Finds-them-and-kills-them, afraid to have the Lacota find her dead with woman-clothing on her, changed them to a man's before the fighting commenced, so that if killed the Lacota would not laugh at her, lying there with a woman's clothes on her. She did not want the Lacota to believe that she was a Crow man hiding in a woman's dress, you see."

Just as The Other Magpie struck the Lakota with her coup stick, Finds Them and Kills Them shot and killed him. "The-other-magpie took his scalp," Pretty Shield recalled. "She was waving it when I saw her coming into the village with the others. Yes, and I saw her cut this scalp into many pieces, so that the men might have more scalps to dance with."

"The men did not tell you this," Pretty Shield confided to Linderman, "but I have. . . . and I hope that you will put it in a book, Sign-talker, because it is the truth."[35]

Another dramatic rescue occurred when Colonel Guy V. Henry was seriously wounded by a bullet that struck him in the face. Stunned, he sat on his horse for several minutes in front of the enemy before tumbling to the ground. According to a witness, "As that portion of our line, discouraged by the fall of so brave a chief, gave ground a little, the Sioux charged over his prostrate body."[36] The Crows rallied and counter-charged. Plenty Coups recalled, "We rode *through* them, over the body of one of Three-star's chiefs who was shot through the face under his eyes, so that the flesh was pushed away from his broken bones. Our charge saved him from being finished and scalped."

Henry's ordeal was not over. According to Plenty Coups, "They tied two poles between two mules and put the wounded chief on a blanket they had lashed to the poles. When the mules came to a steep hill the ropes broke and the mules ran away, pitching the suffering chief head-first down the hill. . . . No Indian would have done such a thing with a badly wounded man."[37]

Osh-Tisch told Scott that he "had fought with General Crook (Three Stars) in the Rosebud 17 June 1876 and next day an officer shot through the face was thrown out of an ambulance or travois face down in the mud and she [Osh-Tisch] had pulled him out, and he had laughed."[38] Another witness reported that "after the dirt had been wiped off, and some water had cleared [Henry's] throat, he was asked the somewhat absurd question of how he felt. 'Bully,' was his somewhat unexpected reply. 'Never felt better in my life. Everybody is so kind.'"[39]

Figure 2. "Squaw Jim and his Squaw. Jim with the Mirror," ca. 1877-1878. This earliest known photograph of a berdache shows Osh-Tisch (on the left) not long after his exploits in the Battle of the Rosebud. Photograph by John H. Fouch; Fort Keogh, Montana Territory. Courtesy of Dr. James Brust.

The next day, the Crows and Shoshones abandoned Crook's expedition. According to Pretty Shield,

> "The return of the Crow wolves [warriors] and these two women to our village was one of the finest sights that I have ever seen. . . . I felt proud of the two women, *even of the wild one* [italics mine], because she was brave. And I saw that they were the ones who were taking care of Bull-snake, the wounded man, when they rode in.
> "Ahh, there was great rejoicing."[40]

This statement underscores the difference between Crow and European attitudes toward sexual and gender difference. Pretty Shield considered the "real" female in her story more deviant than the *boté*. In American society, the reverse could be expected. But since Osh-Tisch was still half-male, his participation in the men's activity of warfare drew less notice from other Crows than that of The Other

Magpie. Pretty Shield's story also casts doubt on the theory that berdaches were simply males seeking to escape the "hypermasculine" warrior role of Plains Indian men.

The young *boté* had earned his name, Finds Them and Kills Them. A year or so later, he posed for John H. Fouch in the earliest known photograph of a North American berdache.[41] Osh-Tisch sits with a female companion in front of a blanket strung between two trees. He wears a dress made of manufactured cloth with an elaborate decorative print, earrings, a beaded necklace with what appears to be a piece of abalone shell pendant and also a silver dollar hung on a string, several metal bracelets on both wrists, and undecorated moccasins. He holds a framed mirror and a brush on his lap. His companion is dressed more simply, with a manufactured blanket draped around her shoulders and a plain dress. An awl case is pinned on her dress.

The caption on the photograph reads "Squaw Jim and his Squaw. Jim with the Mirror." Whether Osh-Tisch had a relationship with a woman at this time is not confirmed. It is possible that the second figure is The Other Magpie. Fouch was the first post photographer at Fort Keogh, which was established in 1877. The story of the Crow man who dressed as a woman, fought in the Battle of the Rosebud, and aided a wounded officer, and the Crow woman who fought with him, was no doubt still current. Fouch may have taken advantage of an opportunity to photograph its two principal characters. That he misunderstood the subtleties of Crow relationships and gender roles in the caption he wrote is not surprising. What is certain from the photograph, based on Osh-Tisch's dress and accoutrements, is that the *boté* warrior had already acquired wealth and prestige.

AGENTS OF ASSIMILATION

With only one man killed, the Crows returned from the Rosebud remarkably unscathed. Their culture and social organization would not fare so well in the next decade. The time when a young warrior could earn glory in warfare—and a *boté* could gain fame making lodges—was nearly past. As Plenty Coups said, "When the buffalo went away the hearts of my people fell to the ground, and they could not lift them up again. After this nothing happened." Bitterly, Pretty Shield recalled, "There is nothing to tell, because we did nothing."[42]

In the 1870s, Crow life came under the direct supervision of the United States government. This was an especially difficult transition for the tribe, which had never fought the Americans and had not been defeated by them. But the ideology of the period did not countenance cultural pluralism. All Indians had to be assimilated into white society, whether they had been friendly or not. In practice, this meant rigorous regulation of religious and social life by Indian agents, school teachers, missionaries, and the military. These "agents of assimilation" did not always act in concert, but they shared common goals.

Government policies during this period regarding allotment of tribal land to individuals, reduction of reservations, and compulsory education have been well documented, but the clash of cultures was equally dramatic in the area of sexuality and gender roles. Government officials and agents regularly complained about irregularities in Crow morality. "I know of no tribe of Indians where vice is as prevalent," wrote agent Henry E. Williamson in 1887, and in 1889, Holder attributed acceptance of the *boté* "not to any respect in which he is held, but to the debased standard of the people among whom he lives."[43] Agents took direct action "to crush the formerly open viciousness" by "meting out severe punishment." Even after the turn of the century, Crows who engaged in premarital and extramarital sex, common law marriage, native divorce, or polygamy were routinely jailed by agents. Legal marriage was enforced by sending couples under guard to the nearest Christian minister.[44]

Osh-Tisch did not escape this campaign of morals. As Lowie reported, "Former agents have repeatedly tried to make him don male clothes, but the other Indians themselves protested against this, saying that it was against his nature."[45] In 1982, tribal historian Joe Medicine Crow related these events to anthropologist Walter Williams:

One agent in the late 1890s was named Briskow [Briscoe], or maybe it was Williamson. He did more crazy things here. He tried to interfere with Osh-Tisch, who was the most respected *badé*. The agent incarcerated the *badés*, cut off their hair, made them wear men's clothing. He forced them to do manual labor, planting these trees that you see here on the BIA [Bureau of Indian Affairs] grounds. The people were so upset with this that Chief Pretty Eagle came into Crow Agency, and told Briskow to leave the reservation. It was a tragedy, trying to change them. Briskow was crazy.[46]

What is extraordinary about this account is the intervention of the chief. In other tribes, missionary and educational influences made native leaders reluctant to defend berdaches. In 1879, the only Hidatsa berdache fled to the Crows when his agent stripped him, cut off his braids, and forced him to wear men's clothing.[47] But the Crows continued to view *boté* as integral, even necessary members of their society. It was a chief's duty to protect them.

Efforts to reshape Crow customs regarding sex and gender took other forms. Children were required to attend government-run boarding schools in which any expression or use of native language and customs was severely punished, boys and girls were segregated, and girls were not allowed to leave the school until husbands had been found for them. In such an environment, children with *boté* tendencies were quickly identified. According to Holder, when a Crow boy was found secretly dressing in female clothes in the late 1880s, "He was punished, but finally escaped from school and became a boté, which vocation he has since followed."[48]

The Crows preferred the day schools operated by religious denominations, which allowed children to return home each day. In fact, the desire of Crow families in the Lodge Grass area for a day school led them to invite another agent of assimilation to the reservation. In 1902, a delegation under the leadership of Medicine Crow traveled to Sheridan, Wyoming, to seek the help of a young Baptist minister, William A. Petzoldt.

As one Baptist historian noted, "The Crows did not ask for the gospel; they wanted schools, but the coming of the Petzoldts meant the coming of the gospel."[49] Like many missionaries, the Reverend and Mrs. Petzoldt rendered valuable services to their neighbors and formed lasting friendships. But they also sought radical changes in Crow culture. From his pulpit, Petzoldt regularly denounced Crow dances and marriage practices along with the boté role. According to Thomas Yellowtail, "When the Baptist missionary Peltotz [sic] arrived in 1903, he condemned our traditions, including the badé. He told congregation members to stay away from Osh-Tisch and the other badés."[50]

However, the Baptist day school opened in 1909 was popular. Parents camped nearby, and children rode their horses to school.[51] The Crows adopted an ecumenical attitude toward Christianity, merging its tenets easily with their traditional beliefs.[52] In the end, Petzoldt's denunciations did not alter the lifestyle of Osh-Tisch, but they did have an impact on the younger generation. According to Thomas Yellowtail, Petzoldt "continued to condemn Osh-Tisch until his death. . . . That may be the reason why no others took up the badé role after Osh-Tisch died."[53]

AN ENVIABLE POSITION

In the 1880s, Osh-Tisch had received an allotment of land near St. Xavier. Early census records show him as the head of his own lodge, living with a niece, nephew, brother, and other adults and children. By 1891, however, he was living alone with a three-year-old child named Brings Horses Well Known, listed as his adopted son. Interestingly, in the next census, from 1895, the child is identified as *female* and an adopted *daughter*. Perhaps Osh-Tisch was raising a boté child. In any case, Brings Horses Well Known continued to live with Finds Them and Kills Them at least until his sixteenth birthday, in 1904.[54]

When Lowie began his research among the Crow in 1907, Osh-Tisch still enjoyed a "reputation of being very accomplished in feminine crafts." Lowie described the middle-aged boté as five feet, seven inches tall and "of large build."[55] In 1919, Scott noted that Osh-Tisch held an "enviable position" in the tribe.

Osh-Tisch maintained a far-ranging network of friends, visiting the Nez Percé in Idaho and the Hidatsa and Mandan at Fort Berthold, North Dakota. He earned a reputation as the best poker player in the region.[56] Eventually, he established cordial relations with Crow agents. At the turn of the century, he regularly called on Agent Reynolds's wife and sold her grass bags. Daughter Carolyn remembered "Maracota Jim" (that is, *mi:akà:te,* "girl") as "pleasant" and "good-natured."[57]

Of these sacks, my mother had a collection, because she was a customer of "Maracota Jim," who visited the Nez Perce occasionally and brought home these sacks, which were a unique craft of that Idaho tribe. . . . Maracota Jim was an unfortunate soul who was probably glad to get away from his native tribe and go visiting. At home, he was forced to dress like a woman, in a short dress, heavy leather belt, blanket, head-scarf. Perhaps, as a boy, he had not measured up to the Crow idea of manliness. He was not an old man when we knew him. He was a pleasant person, and good-natured about this insult. But one can understand why he spent so much time among his friends the Nez Perce. Perhaps he could dress as he pleased among them. However, he came home now and then with the beautifully made sacks, of all sizes. He always called on my mother, his customer and a kind person. She stuffed the large sacks with straw and used them for extra pillows on the davenport.[58]

Although her understanding of the Crow third gender role is faulty, this frontierswoman had found a rationalization that enabled her to accommodate interaction with Osh-Tisch. In fact, a "keepsake" inserted into the book by the publisher adds the following clarification: "And her meticulous research continues even past publication of this work. She concludes Crow mothers would not force cross-dressing on their children; this would be contrary to the 'free and easy life,' but rather, 'Maracota Jim was garbed like a woman; and Crow friends tell me, he dressed like a woman because he wanted to.'"

Although Crow life had changed drastically, Osh-Tisch found ways to continue to use his traditional skills and knowledge. In 1926, the *boté* who had gained fame for his work with buffalo hides won a ribbon at the Yellowstone County fair for his handsewn quilts (now a "traditional" art among the Crows and others). He also received first and second place awards for collections of wild roots, berries, and meats, prepared and dried according to traditional techniques.[59]

Osh-Tisch died on January 2, 1929, at the age of 75.[60] Having outlasted and outwitted efforts over the course of three decades to change his "road," his story can be counted as one of the personal triumphs of American Indian history.

When Thomas Yellowtail stated that no other Crows became *boté* after Osh-Tisch, he may have had a specific aspect of the role in mind—the ceremonial function of *boté* in the sun dance. When the sun dance was revived in 1941, after a lapse of sixty-five years, the role was not included. But individuals identified as *boté* have been a part of Crow life in the generations since Osh-Tisch. Today they are likely to identify as "gay" or "two-spirit." Many are active in powwows and other aspects of contemporary Crow culture. As we will see in chapter 5, they are not alone in recovering aspects of historical roles. In the end, the efforts of the agents of assimilation failed. The struggle of Osh-Tisch, or Finds Them and Kills Them—third gender warrior, artist, and medicine person—was not in vain.

THREE

THE ONE WHO IS CHANGING: HASTÍÍN KLAH AND THE NAVAJO *NÁDLEEHÍ* TRADITION

In 1913, a young man from Iowa named Arthur Newcomb decided to make his living in an unusual way. He would move to the barren tracts of western New Mexico and become a trader to the Navajo Indians. That year he purchased the trading post at Pesh-do-clish (Blue Mesa), a nondescript stop along the rutted, often washed out dirt road from Gallup to the junction of New Mexico, Arizona, Utah, and Colorado called the Four Corners.[1] He was joined by his wife, Franc Johnson (1887-1970), a teacher from the government boarding school at Fort Defiance, the following year.[2] The Newcombs had picked a remote and austere setting to raise a family. As their friend Mary Wheelwright wrote, "Mrs. Newcomb tried year after year to make a little grass grow in front of the house, and there was one precious tree. The great charm of the place was that by climbing out on the mesa you had a bird's-eye view of the two valleys where you could watch the Navaho life coming and going."[3]

The couple had made their home in the ancestral lands of the *dziłtł' ahnii* clan.[4] The local matriarch, Ahson ('Asdzaan) Tsosie, or Slim Woman, granddaughter of the chief Narbona Tso who had been killed by American soldiers in 1849, resided with her daughter and four granddaughters just three miles east of the post. Her son, Hastíín Klah,[5] lived nearby. They were one of the wealthiest families in the region. Together they owned over two thousand sheep, as well as cattle and horses, and held valuable farm lands.[6]

Hastíín Klah reached out to the couple soon after their arrival. They discovered that the dignified, middle-aged bachelor was an individual of remarkable talents with a special status in his community. Klah, for his part, was eager to learn from the Newcombs about the white world, and he was willing to teach Arthur the Navajo language.[7] Their friendship lasted nearly twenty-five years. At his death, Arthur Newcomb declared, "He was one of the finest men I ever knew, and the best friend I ever had."[8] Years later Franc Newcomb warmly recalled "pleasant memories of long winter evenings before the huge open fireplace, sometimes with a baby in my lap or perhaps with my hands busy sewing some small garment while I listened to the deep voice of Hosteen Klah recounting traditions of his people or tribal events that took place long before he was born."[9] She dedicated one of her books to Klah's memory and wrote his biography.[10]

While Klah was eager to learn about Anglo-American culture from the Newcombs, he was nonetheless an ardent traditionalist, an accomplished medicine man (*hataałii*), and a skilled weaver. He was also a *nádleehí*, or berdache. Thanks to the writings and recollections of Newcomb and other Americans he befriended, it is possible to gain a glimpse of a worldview otherwise lost to us—the thoughts and imagination of a highly intelligent, deeply spiritual, traditionally trained third gender person.

Hastíín Klah is certainly the most famous *nádleehí* in Navajo history. He enjoyed significant prestige within the tribe and made lasting contributions to Navajo art, religion, and politics. At the time of his death, he counted among his friends wealthy patrons of the arts, famous artists and writers, respected anthropologists, and countless Navajos whom he had aided and cured. Anthropologist Gladys Reichard described him as "one of the most remarkable persons I ever knew."[11] Today, Klah is remembered as the first master weaver of sandpainting tapestries and the cofounder of the Wheelwright Museum of the American Indian in Santa Fe. Yet Klah's identity as a *nádleehí* is often overlooked. A review of his life reveals that his achievements were only possible because of the special status he held.

THE PEOPLE

Members of the Athapaskan language family, the ancestors of the Navajo originally lived in Canada and Alaska. At some time in prehistory, groups of these

Athapaskans began migrating southward. Eventually some reached the South-west, perhaps between 1000 and 1400 C.E., and subdivided into the Navajo and Apache tribes. Originally nomadic hunter-gatherers, the Navajos began to engage in agriculture under the influence of the village-dwellers they called the Anasazi, the forebears of the Pueblo Indians. When the Spaniards began to colonize New Mexico, they found the *diné,* or "the people," as they call themselves, living in dispersed family groups that shifted residence seasonally. Acquiring sheep and horses, the *diné* expanded their subsistence base to include herding and periodic raids on their neighbors for crops and goods. In this period Navajo culture and ceremonialism flourished.

Matrilineal and matrilocal customs ensured the high status and prestige of Navajo women. Homes and lands passed from mothers to daughters; husbands lived with their wives' families; divorce could be initiated by either party. The eldest woman in the household, along with her sisters, controlled the use of family lands and sheep. Since children belonged to their mother's clan, there was no illegitimacy. In this social organization, the third gender role enjoyed high status and prestige.

The term *nádleehí* was used to refer to both female and male berdaches. Female *nádleehí* gained prestige in men's pursuits such as hunting and warfare, while male *nádleehí* specialized in the equally prestigious women's activities of farming, herding sheep, gathering food resources, weaving, knitting, basketry, pottery, and leatherwork. Many *nádleehí* combined activities of men and women, along with some traits unique to their status. By engaging in both farming and sheepherding, along with the manufacture of trade goods, they were often among the wealthier members of the tribe. The only activities that male *nádleehí* did not perform were warfare and hunting, which were strictly male, and carding and spinning wool, which were reserved for women.[12]

In an episode in the Navajo origin myth (*aɬnaashii adeesdeelgi,* where the people moved opposite each other), a *nádleehí* confidently lists all the skills he has mastered: "'I myself plant, I myself make millstones, that's settled,' he said. 'I myself make baking stones. I make pots myself and earthen bowls; gourds I plant myself. I make water jugs,' he said, 'and stirring sticks and brooms,' he said."[13] In this account, the men and women decide to live on opposites sides of a river, and the *nádleehí* serves as an adviser and a mediator. Actual *nádleehí* performed a similar function by serving as go-betweens in arranging marriages and affairs.[14]

There was significant variability in how *nádleehí* dressed. Reichard reports that they wore either men's or women's clothing.[15] Some, such as the male *nádleehí* Charlie the Weaver, photographed by James Mooney in 1893 and by A. C. Vroman in 1895, appear to have alternated between a unique style of dress, neither that of men or women, and women's dress. Other male *nádleehí,* such as Kinábahí, photographed by anthropologist Willard Hill in the 1930s, routinely dressed as women.[16] Still others—such as Hastíín Klah—did not cross-dress at all

Figure 3. Charlie the Weaver, ca. 1895. The Navajo *nádleehí* known as "Charlie the weaver" (on the right) dressed in a style distinct from both men and women. The caption by photographer A. C. Vroman reads "Charlie and Friend." Seaver Center for Western History Research, Los Angeles County Museum of Natural History, neg. no. V-714.

(or did so only on ceremonial occasions). According to Father Berard Haile, "the *nádleeh* who retains male dress and the one who prefers female dress are not differentiated in name."[17] Matthews, however, writing in the 1890s, stated flatly that *nádleehí* "dress as women,"[18] and even in the 1930s Hill noted that many Navajo continued to associate cross-dressing with *nádleehí* status. (He once overheard an older Navajo remark, "There must be a great many more [*nádleehí*] among the whites than among the Navaho because so many white women wear trousers."[19]) Men who did not marry were also assumed to be *nádleehí*. Haile reported that "even the priests of St. Michael's Mission were thought of as *nádleeh*, and natives asked if we were deprived of testicles."[20] By the 1930s and 1940s, however, white ridicule and changing Navajo attitudes had created significant pressures on *nádleehí* not to cross-dress.[21] In the absence of this traditional marker of their status, one finds them described simply as "bachelors" or men "not interested" in women.[22] A recently published dictionary defines *nádleehí* as "transvestite, homosexual."[23]

Of the many anthropologists and observers of the Navajo, only the self-trained Haile has been forthcoming regarding the sexuality of the *nádleehí*—"a name," he once wrote, "which implies that the man is proficient not only in feminine accomplishments, but also practices pederasty."[24] Elsewhere he reported that "of the white [sic!] and native *nádleeh* who came under my observation, or of whom I made inquiries, the evidence showed them to be active pederasts and sodomites."[25] Most *nádleehí* formed relationships with members of their own sex, although some male *nádleehí* married women. One Navajo told Hill, "If they marry men, it is just like two men working together."[26] That *nádleehí* were expected to be sexually active with men is indicated by the episode of the Navajo origin myth in which the men and women separate. The *nádleehí* joins the men, and among the services he provides them is sex.[27]

Unfortunately, little is known about female *nádleehí*, although Hill stated that they were equal in number to male berdaches in traditional times.[28] According to one report, they hunted and went to war, and a case is known of a Navajo woman who led a war party against the Hopi to avenge her son's death.[29] Haile described a woman considered by some Navajos to be a *nádleehí*. She was "industrious, swings an axe as well as any man, and is generally respected." She married a man, but soon after the marriage he took her sister to be his wife and bear his children. The female *nádleehí* then adopted and raised the children.[30] Although the published versions of Navajo origin myths account for only the male *nádleehí*, Navajo scholar Wesley Thomas has identified a telling that describes the origin of both male and female berdaches, and has a female *nádleehí* present in the separation episode.[31]

In the 1930s, Hill recorded comments from a variety of elders that underscore the respect accorded to third gender individuals:

> If there were no *nadle*, the country would change. They are responsible for all the wealth in the country. If there were no more left, the horses, sheep, and Navaho would all go. They are leaders just like President Roosevelt.

> A *nadle* around the hogan will bring good luck and riches.

> You must respect a *nadle*. They are, somehow, sacred and holy.[32]

For all these reasons, families welcomed a *nádleehí* in their midst. Children with berdache tendencies were given special care and encouragement. According to Hill, "As they grew older and assumed the character of *nadle*, this solicitude and respect increased, not only on the part of their families but from the community as a whole." *Nádleehí* were often given responsibility for managing family property and acting as the head of the household. They supervised agricultural as well as domestic work.[33] Their affinity for wealth led some to earn reputations as successful gamblers.[34] Because of their unique psychological and social attributes, many *nádleehí* also became religious specialists. In pre-reservation times individuals with *nádleehí* traits consistently received religious training.[35] In fact, *nádleehí* identity was as much a sacred occupational status as a secular social role.

Religion and religious beliefs were a pervasive aspect of Navajo life. Central to Navajo belief is the idea that everything in the world is connected by a kind of spiritual electricity. The condition of balance and harmony within this network of energy is called *hózhǫ́*. As Witherspoon explains, "*Hózhǫ́* refers to the positive or ideal environment. It is beauty, harmony, good, happiness, and everything that is positive, and it refers to an environment which is all-inclusive. . . . Positive health for the Navajo involves a proper relationship to everything in one's environment, not just the correct functioning of one's physiology."[36] When *hózhǫ́* is disrupted by contact with things considered dangerous or by witchcraft, the result is physical and mental illness (Navajo belief does not distinguish the two).

Medicine men restore *hózhǫ́* with complex ceremonies—sometimes called chants or sings—that produce harmony and balance by re-enacting the creation of the world with the patient at the center. As Witherspoon argues, the ritual language and images used in these ceremonies are ways of extending thought into the world and actively shaping its form, much as mythological figures "think" the world and its occupants into existence.[37] Mastering the details of these ceremonies, including countless songs, prayers, dances, medicines, and other procedures, and acquiring the necessary materials, requires years of apprenticeship and training.

A key feature of Navajo ceremonies is the sandpainting made on the floor of the ceremonial hogan from sand, ground stones, and shells in a variety of colors. The word for sandpainting, *'iikááh*, literally means "they come, as into an enclosure." "They" are the gods, who are drawn to the rites by the beauty of the sandpaintings and serve as mediators between humans and the sources of spiritual energy.[38] At the climax of the proceedings the patient is seated in the center of the sandpainting and sand from it is rubbed on the patient—effecting a literal identification of the individual with the gods and with holiness. In the Blessingway ceremony, the patient sings:

> Earth's body has become my body
> by means of this I shall live on.
>
> Earth's mind has become my mind
> by means of this I shall live on.
>
> Earth's voice has become my voice
> by means of this I shall live on.[39]

Navajo conceptualizations of nádleehí have confused many outsiders. As Haile noted, "Outsiders may wonder why [nádleehí] should designate the real, congenital hermaphrodite, as well as our transvestite, pederast, and sodomite."[40] The reason is that Navajos saw all these kinds of people, which Anglo culture distinguishes, as sharing the characteristic of bridging or combining genders. This trait was more important in defining a person as nádleehí than their sexuality. In fact, many Navajo expected nádleehí to combine sexes physically as well as psychologically. Hill's informants reported that "real" nádleehí were hermaphrodites and others were "pretend" nádleehí, while Haile attempted to distinguish the "real or congenital" nádleehí from the "pseudo-nádleeh"—although he admitted that the two were "popularly not distinguished."[41] However, there is no evidence of a higher than average human incidence of intersexuality among the Navajo. Perhaps tribal members assumed such an occurrence among humans because hermaphrodism was common among their sheep as a result of inbreeding.[42]

In fact, the assumption that nádleehí were hermaphrodites reflects central beliefs in Navajo philosophy. In myths male and female principles are consistently offset, sometimes by the pairing of supernaturals, sometimes within a single supernatural being.[43] Nádleehí are an example of the latter. However, this was seen not as a crossing or switching of genders, but as a state of continuous fluctuation between them. Rather than juxtaposing male and female (as in the true hermaphrodite) or androgynously blending the two, nádleehí were simultaneously male, female, and hermaphroditic.[44] This is the literal meaning of the term nádleehí, "the one who is (constantly) changing."[45]

As Witherspoon has shown, an emphasis on motion and change is characteristic of Navajo language, philosophy, and art. This, in turn, is related to the belief that natural phenomena and human beings alike have both inner and outer forms. The inner form (nilch'i biisizíinii, "in-standing wind soul" in the case of humans) is the animating intelligence believed to activate outer forms and endow them with their specific properties.[46] In such a belief system, anatomical sex is merely the outer form of an inner, psychological form. Since the inner form of nádleehí was hermaphroditic, many Navajo assumed that their outer, physical form would reflect this condition. At the same time, the practice of always representing male and female simultaneously, as a symmetrical pair, means that both principles are always present, whether as outer or inner forms, and consequently all beings have both male and female qualities. Nádleehí, in this regard, merely represent that special case in which these principles are offset within a single individual rather than by the pairing of two.

Consequently, even though Navajo work and social roles were allocated according to gender, gender did not delimit an individual's social experience. As one of Hill's informants explained, "A boy may act like a girl until he is eighteen or twenty-five; then he may turn into a man or he may not. Girls do the same thing."[47] Certain religious observances provide all Navajos with a chance to assume a different gender position. During the Yeibichai ceremony, for example, the mask of the female Yé'ii god is held before the face of each initiate, who looks through the triangular eyes of the mask. Together these two triangles form a diamond—the symbol of Changing Woman, the Navajo Earth Mother. What the initiates learn to see is a female view of the world.[48]

THE MAKING OF A MEDICINE MAN

Klah was born in the midst of some of the most traumatic events in Navajo history. In the 1860s, some twenty years after entering the Southwest, the U.S. government had yet to achieve control of the region. The lifestyle of the Navajos in particular was seen as an obstacle to white settlement and economic development. And so, in 1863, Kit Carson launched a slash-and-burn campaign that resulted in the surrender of thousands of Navajos. The prisoners—including Klah's parents—were marched three hundred miles across New Mexico to a desolate reservation at Fort Sumner called Bosque Redondo. The Navajos refer to the ordeal as the Long Walk. By 1867 they were nearly starving, and the government began to allow them to return to their traditional lands. Hastíín Klah was born that December, soon after his mother and father settled in western New Mexico on the eastern slopes of the Chuska Mountains. His childhood was divided between summers spent in the mountains behind Toadlena and winters near Sheep Springs in the Tunicha Valley.

At an early age, Klah showed an interest in religion. By the time he was ten he had learned his first ceremony from his mother's uncle, while his aunt shared with him her extensive knowledge of native plants.[49] Given his interests and skills, Klah's family began to make arrangements to further his training.

While in his early teens, Klah went to live with relatives on the western side of the Lukachukai Mountains. It was in these mountains that he made a discovery that foreshadowed his future career. High up on a canyon ledge, he found a cave in which a medicine man had left his ceremonial bundle. The walls of the cave were painted with images of Navajo gods. Klah decided that the medicine man was trying to preserve his ceremonial knowledge. The experience made a deep impression on him, and a small arrowhead from the cave became his first piece of ceremonial equipment.[50]

Not long after this, Klah's status as a nádleehí was formally confirmed. There are conflicting accounts of how this occurred. According to Newcomb, Klah was in a serious horse-riding accident, and in the course of his recovery he was discovered to be a "hermaphrodite." Gladys Reichard, on the other hand, reported that Klah had been emasculated as an infant by Ute Indians when his family was returning from Bosque Redondo.[51] However, Klah was not born until *after* this journey.[52] In any case, both stories are improbable. Klah showed no physical sign of infant emasculation and such a late discovery of hermaphrodism by his family is unlikely.[53] Some of the confusion concerning his status is probably due to the fact that he did not cross-dress. According to Reichard, "He dressed in men's clothes at least in recent years and there was nothing feminine about him unless an indescribable gentleness be so called. The reasons the Navajo called him 'one-who-has-been-changed' [i.e., *nádleehí*] were chiefly that he wove blankets and was not interested in women."[54]

The fact that Klah recovered from a serious accident was evidence of his religious powers, as were his berdache inclinations. As Newcomb wrote, he had entered a "very special category": "The Navahos believed him to be honored by the gods and to possess unusual mental capacity combining both male and female attributes. He was expected to master all the knowledge, skill, and leadership of a man and also all of the skills, ability, and intuition of a woman. Klah during his lifetime lived up to these expectations in every way."[55]

WEAVING AND A WORLD'S FAIR

Once his *nádleehí* identity had been confirmed, Klah was "expected to assist" his mother and sister in their weaving—an important source of income for the family. During the 1880s, Klah mastered skills that would later make him famous, learning to weave smooth, finely patterned rugs.[56]

Navajo women had been weaving blankets from wool since the eighteenth century. By the early 1800s, Navajo blankets were regularly traded to Spanish settlers and other Indian tribes as far away as the Great Plains. Weaving was an art practiced by the majority of women, a part of their life cycle. Through weaving, women expressed such values as self-control and self-esteem, creativity and beauty, and balance between the world of animals and plants—symbolized by the fibers and dyes used in weaving—and the world of humans.[57]

Klah began weaving at a time of great change in Navajo crafts production. After an artistic and technical peak in the mid-nineteenth century, weaving had begun to decline. The arrival of the railroad in the region in the early 1880s brought cheap manufactured clothing and blankets that quickly displaced handmade items. At the same time, it also brought an influx of traders.[58] They established posts throughout the reservation and encouraged weavers in a variety of ways, providing dyes, yarns, and even pictures of the designs they considered desirable. By the 1890s, two-thirds of the items woven by Navajo women were for nontribal use, and white buyers were beginning to use blankets as rugs. As art historians Berlant and Kahlenberg note, "If the transition from blanket to rug marked the end of an art form, it also established a basis for continued economic and social stability."[59] Eventually regional styles of weaving emerged. The style popular in Klah's area, which became known as Two Grey Hills, developed around 1915.[60]

By the time he was in his mid-twenties, Klah already had earned a reputation as a weaver. In 1893, this brought him to the attention of the organizers of New Mexico's exhibit at the World's Columbian Exposition in Chicago. They wanted to send Navajo artists to the fair, but they felt it would be more convenient to send only men—and so they were referred to Klah, apparently unaware that, by definition, a male weaver among the Navajo was a *nádleehí*. Klah spent the summer working before crowds of American sight-seers. According to Newcomb, the blanket that he completed in Chicago was the first he wove entirely on his own.[61]

The presentation of native people and cultures at the Columbian Exposition set a pattern for the display of ethnicity followed by many subsequent world's fairs.[62] Fairgoers could contemplate "prehistoric architectural monuments and habitations, natural and artificial cave dwellings, lacustrine dwellings, sweat houses, cliff dwellings and skin lodges, implements of war and the chase, furniture and clothing of aboriginal, uncivilized and partly civilized races."[63] Best of all, they could observe "living Indians" occupying mock villages and purportedly engaging in their normal daily pursuits. Here the gaze of the anthropologist and the colonialist was made accessible to all comers, as perhaps the peculiar combination of democratic and imperialist impulses in fin de siècle America required. Finally conquered, the so-called savages now could be viewed sympathetically, as colorful primitives.

There is another side to the display of native culture, however, and that is the way in which beautiful objects can have an appeal across cultural boundaries. Appreciation of native arts was one of the first areas in which Euro-Americans were able to perceive native people as their intellectual and creative equals. It is no coincidence that so many activists in the campaign against the U.S. government's program of forced assimilation also promoted the preservation, improvement, and marketing of native arts and crafts. If beautiful pots, baskets, and weavings were what it meant to embrace cultural pluralism, then most Americans in the early twentieth century were willing to accommodate the continuing presence of tribal communities.

TRADERS AND FRIENDS

When Franc Newcomb arrived at the trading post at Blue Mesa on her wedding day in 1914, "The first Navaho who came to our living room to greet the new bride was Hosteen Klah." Klah presented her with an untanned fox pelt, "all gold and white, with only a spot of black on the tip of the tail and a black nose." Newcomb had it made into a stole that she "was proud to wear for many years."[64]

Franc Newcomb's association with Klah lead to some extraordinary cultural experiments and not a few adventures. "There were star-filled nights," she later wrote, "when we drove the car to their sacred ceremonies and listened to the rhythmic chorus of the singers as they joined in the chants. Often we took our places in the dark circles of branches, in some high mountain place and watched masked and painted dancers salute the central fire."[65] That such a friendship could develop between a white woman and an Indian man at that time was no doubt due to the fact that, as Reichard put it, Klah was not "interested" in women—and the parties concerned could take this for granted.[66]

When the Newcombs opened their trading post, Klah was already an accomplished medicine man and weaver. Still, his religious training was not complete. Whereas most medicine men learned one or two ceremonies in a lifetime, Klah eventually mastered eight.[67] According to Newcomb, the rites he studied were all cultural or peace chants—distinct from the ceremonies of war.[68] Only in 1917, when he was forty-nine years old, did he decided to hold his first independent Yeibichai, or Nightway, ceremony.

> He told Arthur that he had conferred with and compared ceremonies with every Yeibichai chanter in the Navaho tribe—there were none he had not contacted. He had learned something from each one, and now there was nothing more for him to learn. He said, "This fall I will hold the greatest Yeibichai that has ever been held on the Reservation since before the Navahos were taken to the Bosque Redondo, and I will ask everyone to come and criticize. If there is any mistake or omission, I will start studying all over again."[69]

"I am sure," wrote Newcomb, "that this ceremony was the equal of those held in the days of Narbona's chieftaincy when the Navaho people were called "The Lords of the Soil.""[70] Newcomb estimated that nearly 2,000 Indians from several tribes attended. The climax of the event was a great "give-away" in which Klah distributed goods and sheep representing one-third of his worldly wealth and announced his intention to devote the rest of his life to spiritual concerns.

He was now at his full powers and prestige as a medicine man. Newcomb wrote that during the flu epidemic of 1919 and 1920, which claimed hundreds of lives, "He was the most successful doctor of any I heard about, losing only one member of his family."[71] According to Reichard, his generosity and skill as a medicine man made him beloved among Navajos.[72] In her biography of Klah, Newcomb tells a dramatic story that confirmed to her his powers. The Newcomb family was returning with the medicine man from a trip to Santa Fe in October 1935.

> We had gone about forty miles when heavy, wind-blown clouds darkened the sky and hard gusts made driving difficult. Suddenly I looked across the mesa to my right and exclaimed, "What's that?" Everyone looked that way and Arthur said, "It's a cyclone!" He stopped the car and we watched the black hourglass column as it spun and swayed on a path that would take it across the road about a half-mile in front of us. We were already beginning to feel the side

winds sucking in toward the center, when, to our horror, it turned directly toward us. . . . I told the girls to hurry and rushed to climb into the car. But not Klah. He started walking slowly toward the whirling mass, which was approaching with the sound of a thousand swarms of bees. Stooping now and then to pick up a pinch of earth or part of a desert plant, he put the accumulation into his mouth even while he was chanting. We could not very well turn around and go away, leaving him to face the tornado alone, and anyway, it was now much too late to make our escape, so we simply sat there— four of the most frightened humans anyone ever knew. Klah continued to walk slowly into the eddying wind, then suddenly held up both hands and spewed the mixture in his mouth directly at the approaching column and raised his voice to a loud chant. The column stood still for a moment and then divided in the center of the hourglass, the upper part rising to be obscured by the low hanging clouds and the lower half spinning away at right angles to its former course like a great upside-down top. Klah turned around and came back to the car.[73]

If Klah's 1917 Yeibichai ceremony was the largest gathering of Navajos since the time of Narbona, it was also of a different order. Narbona was a war chief who commanded all the Navajo warriors east of the Chuska Mountain. But in Klah's day the Navajos were at peace and facing a hard accommodation to reservation life. Klah aided this accommodation in three ways—by seeking to preserve his religious knowledge, by expanding the artistic and market potentials of Navajo art, and by developing a synthesis of Navajo ideology.

When Newcomb attended Klah's Yeibichai ceremony, she became fascinated by the sandpaintings he made and later attempted to reproduce them on paper. Klah encouraged her efforts and eventually Newcomb developed a remarkable skill for drawing the complex designs entirely from memory (sketching during the ceremonies was prohibited). This was the beginning of a project that resulted in the preservation of some five hundred sandpainting images.

The friendship between Newcomb and Klah also resulted in a lasting contribution to the art of Navajo weaving. This began in 1919. According to Newcomb,

> One day as Klah was helping me with my sand-painting collection, I asked why he did not weave a rug with a ceremonial design. He said that the sacred symbols should not be put into a rug that would be placed on the floor and walked on day after day. I assured him that a blanket of this type would never be used on the floor but would be hung on the wall of some museum. He said he would think about it .[74]

After consulting with his family, Klah decided to weave the "Whirling Logs" sandpainting from the Nightway ceremony—a design he would return to several times.

It is not known exactly when and where the first sandpainting weaving was made. Two of the earliest experiments are reported to have come from the Chaco Canyon area east of Klah's home in the 1890s. They were sold to the trader Richard Wetherill, who had arrived in 1896 with the Hyde Exploring Expedition.[75] According to author Erna Fergusson, Klah was friends with Wetherill.[76] They may have met when the Expedition investigated Klah's area in 1897 and commissioned him to weave a copy of a blanket fragment it had found.[77]

So, although Newcomb takes credit for proposing the idea, Klah was probably aware of earlier attempts to weave sandpainting designs. In 1916, he had taken a step in this direction by weaving a blanket depicting Yeibichai dancers (a ceremonial scene but not a sandpainting image), which he sold to Ed Davies at Two Grey Hills.[78] A key point, however, is that Klah's development of sandpainting weaving was only possible because of his *nádleehí* status. He combined his knowledge of religion, the domain of men, with his knowledge of weaving, the art of women. Most sandpainting tapestries made since Klah's time have been collaborations between a medicine man and a female relative.

Klah's artistic experiments involved a great deal of risk. By tradition, sandpaintings were always swept away at the end of the ceremony. They were never made in permanent form, for to do so was considered spiritually dangerous. As Reichard explains, "If one can realize even fractionally how deeply religious belief, of which the sandpainting is only a small part, influences the behavior of the Navajo, he can begin to comprehend what it means to them to depict these things in a permanent medium like paper or tapestry. One can exert his mind even further and attempt to realize what it meant to the first person who broke the taboo of evanescence."[79] Despite these taboos, by the turn of the century some Navajo medicine men were cooperating with anthropologists to record their chants and sandpaintings. Two of Klah's teachers had been informants for Washington Matthews.[80]

Still, Klah's Yeibichai blanket created a stir. According to Newcomb, "When other medicine men and Navahos found out about this rug, there was quite a furor, and they demanded that Klah hold an 'evil-expelling' rite and that the rug be destroyed."[81] The excitement did not subside until the rug was removed from the reservation. In 1919, Arthur Newcomb hired a guard to watch over Klah's "Whirling Logs" tapestry until it was completed. Klah seemed to have felt, however, that his powers as a medicine man could protect him; he performed religious rites continuously when weaving.

Klah's sandpainting tapestries were an instant success. His first attempt was purchased by a wealthy collector while still on the loom. Soon he was receiving more orders than he could fill. He held ceremonies to protect his two grandnieces, who were also weavers, and gave them each large looms to work on, while he built himself an even larger one.[82] Together they produced some sixty-five tapestries; Klah wove at least twenty-two of these himself. In

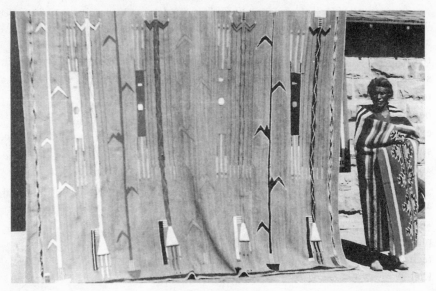

Figure 4. Hastíín Klah, ca. 1921. Hastíín Klah next to his sandpainting tapestry from the Hail Chant. Wheelwright Museum of the American Indian, Santa Fe.

the midst of the Depression, they sold for as much as five thousand dollars.[83] Most are now in museums.[84]

According to Rodee, "His personal style was distinctive from the beginning. He used only backgrounds of tan undyed wool from the bellies of brown sheep. His dyes were carefully prepared from local plants and indigo and cochineal, although later he would come to use commercial dyes. He wove exceptionally large rugs, about twelve feet by twelve or thirteen, on specially constructed looms."[85] The care Klah took because of his special subject matter resulted in new standards of excellence for Navajo weaving. The return to native dyes, in particular, became an important element of the art's subsequent revival.

Sandpainting tapestries, however, remained controversial. The interest of white buyers in religious content created a lucrative market for such items, but traditional sentiment barred its exploitation. As Parezo argues, religious images had to be "secularized" before they could be "commercialized." From the Navajo point of view, artists had to demonstrate that these images could be depicted in permanent media and sold without bringing harm to themselves and the community. Parezo credits two groups with overcoming these problems: Navajo singers and white scholars interested in preserving Navajo culture; and Navajo artisans and white traders interested in exploiting the market for native crafts.[86] Klah and Newcomb represent both groups. According to Newcomb, "After a few years had passed and neither Klah nor the girls had suffered ill effects, many weavers decided to make 'figure blankets,' which were beautiful and brought high prices, but no one else dared make an exact copy of a ceremonial sand painting."[87]

In fact, as Rodee reports, "Many weavers specializing in ceremonial patterns now do so in spite of great personal discomfort. They think they are performing a sacrilegious act, incurring the dislike and resentment of their neighbors."[88] In the end, the lasting precedent established by Klah's tapestries was not their subject matter, but the status they earned as objects of art. The transition from rug to tapestry—and from the floor to the museum wall—marked the difference between a craft and a fine art. Eventually, the interest of collectors in Klah's work extended to all styles of weaving. Navajo artists not only found commercial success, they began to influence non-Indian artists, including key figures of the abstract expressionist movement, such as Jackson Pollack.[89]

While only a few weavers followed Klah's example in weaving sandpaintings, artists in another medium now commonly employ religious designs. In the 1930s and 1940s, Navajos began to make permanent sandpaintings with pulverized materials glued on wood. According to Parezo, Fred Stevens, the pioneer of this technique, "used Hosteen Klah, his father's clan brother, as his model, employing Klah's arguments and techniques to prevent supernatural displeasure."[90] A tourist market for these items emerged in the 1960s and 1970s, and today the production of these souvenirs is an important source of income for many Navajos.

COLLEAGUES AND COLLABORATIONS

Klah's friendship with the Newcombs led to other important contacts. Most significant among these was the wealthy Bostonian, Mary Cabot Wheelwright (1878-1958). Remembered by her friends for "her independent spirit, her peppery humor, and her dedication to the study of comparative religion," Wheelwright had lived a sheltered existence for the first thirty-nine years of her life.[91] Never married, largely self-educated, she appeared destined for the quiet life typical of the well-to-do Victorian daughter. Her passion, sailing off the rugged coast of Maine, was her only bond to an otherwise remote father.[92] But after the death of her parents, as one acquaintance recalled, she "flung side her lap robes, and decided that it was time to begin to live."[93] In 1918, at the age of forty, she made her first trip to the Southwest.[94] There, as she later wrote, "I seemed to get near to something I had always wanted, a more simple type of civilization, more adventuresome and more exciting than the safety of Boston."[95]

In 1921, Wheelwright bought one of Klah's tapestries in Gallup.[96] Soon after this, she and some traveling companions arrived at the Newcomb trading post on horseback. The Newcombs provided the party with accommodations and offered to introduce them to Klah, who was leading a Nightway ceremony at a remote site some seventy miles away. When they arrived, as Wheelwright recalled, "The dancers were to be seen through the whirling snow, while the fires blew out sideways. Out of this turmoil appeared Klah, calm and benign." When Wheelwright asked Klah to explain the meaning of the dances, he replied, "Why do you want this information?" Because, she explained, she was interested in religion. Klah replied, "How deep is the sea?"[97]

Wheelwright's experience of Navajo spirituality had a profound effect on her. She once described her reactions in a letter to a friend: "The morning ceremony of a path of life outside the hogan is so beautiful that it broke me the first day and I had a good cry and felt like a new person. The contrast was too much for my wires to carry without giving out. It was a great relief and one of the big experiences."[98] By the late 1920s, she was devoting much of her time and resources to the study of Navajo culture. She sponsored research by several scholars, and she worked with traders to encourage the revival of traditional weaving techniques.

Wheelwright's friendship with Klah was based on deep mutual regard. She wrote,

> I grew to respect and love him for his real goodness, generosity—and holiness, for there is no other word for it. He never had married, having spent twenty-five years studying not only the ceremonies he gave, but all the medicine lore of the tribe. He helped at least eight of his nieces and nephews with money and goods. . . . When I knew him he never kept anything for himself. It was hard to see him almost in rags at his ceremonies, but what was given him he seldom kept, passing it on to someone who needed it. . . .
>
> Our civilization and miracles he took simply without much wonder, as his mind was occupied with his religion and helping his people. It was wonderful to travel with him, as he knew the ceremonial names and legends of all the mountains, rivers and places, and the uses and associations of plants and stones. Everything was the outward form of the spirit world that was very real to him.[99]

According to Wheelwright, Klah himself proposed that she record his ceremonial knowledge: "Klah said that he had begun to realize that while it was all right for Navajo boys to go to school, that, after they had been there, they could not memorize the long myths; consequently he was beginning to feel that he would like to have this old knowledge recorded, and he asked me to record his songs."[100] When Klah warned her of the supernatural dangers involved in such a project she replied, "I am not afraid."[101] Their collaboration began in 1927. Over the next ten years, Wheelwright transcribed hundreds of Klah's songs and myths, often in cooperation with Newcomb, who drew the corresponding sandpaintings. With Klah's help, she contacted other medicine men as well.[102] Klah also worked with Gladys Reichard, who recorded his telling of the Hail Chant myth, and Harry Hoijer, who made wax recordings of his chants of the Navajo origin myth.[103]

As the friendship between Wheelwright and Klah developed, Newcomb noted that "many of Mary's friends and relatives had wondered why she spent so much of her time and money on the Navaho Reservation. They did not see how she could be so much interested in a medicine man and his primitive religion. Since she could not bring them all to the Navaho country to meet Klah, she decided to take Klah to her summer home in Maine to meet them."[104] In the summer of 1928, Klah and the Newcombs traveled across the United States by car to Northeast Harbor, Maine.

The white world must have puzzled Klah, for all along the way his party was denied food and accommodations because of the color of his skin. Yet, when he finally arrived in Maine, he was the guest of honor at a reception attended by some of the wealthiest and most influential people of the day. Through it all Klah remained perfectly at ease. He took long walks in the nearby woods and told Wheelwright that "he was sure that Bego chidii [a berdache deity] . . . was in Maine because it smelled so sweet."[105] At one point, Wheelwright arranged for Klah to attend a formal Japanese tea ceremony. The proceedings made a deep impression on him, and he later asked Newcomb, "What sickness is that tea ceremony used for?" Newcomb tried to explain that the ceremony was not for curing any illness, but for Klah the drinking of an herb infusion had to be part of a healing rite, and he always referred to the session as "the tea medicine ceremony."[106]

In 1930, Klah again traveled to visit Wheelwright, this time to her ranch outside Santa Barbara, California. For Klah this trip was especially meaningful because the Navajos believed that Changing Woman (the Navajo Earth Mother) lived in an island off the coast of the Pacific.[107] On these and other trips—including ones to Phoenix and to Wheelwright's ranch at Alcalde on the Rio Grande—Klah recited myths, songs, and religious lore for transcription. No doubt he felt more comfortable doing this off the reservation, where it was less likely to attract the attention of other Navajos.

Klah had spent a lifetime mastering the cultural traditions of his people. His career had been carefully nurtured by his family, who early on recognized his talent. He was certainly one of the most knowledgeable medicine men on the reservation. He was the last qualified to perform several important ceremonies. Consequently, he had begun to train a successor before 1917—his nephew, Beaal Begay. But in the summer of 1931, quite unexpectedly, Begay died. It was a bitter disappointment. Klah was in his sixties, and there was no time to train another student.[108]

Wheelwright had also been thinking about her legacy and had decided to use her inheritance to found a museum devoted to Navajo religion. That autumn, when she asked Klah if he would be willing to place his ceremonial equipment and documentation in a place where they would be preserved and could be studied, Klah agreed. He was already beginning to have dreams of his own death.[109]

Wheelwright had two goals in mind for her museum: "Although I believed strongly that the museum should be a depository for the lore of the Navaho for their benefit in the future, I felt it should also be an open door for the American people into the wonderful world of their fellow-citizens, the Navaho."[110] To finance the project in the middle of the Depression, Wheelwright sold two of her family homes.[111] Klah participated in all aspects of the museum's planning, working closely with architect William Henderson. The result was a unique design that recreated the experience of emerging from the underworld—as the Navajo origin myth describes—and attending a Navajo ceremonial. In its original configuration, visitors entered the museum by ringing a bell at the doorway. A curator led them down a set of stairs, then back up again into the exhibition hall, where, Wheelwright hoped, they would experience a "sense of surprise and wonder" as they viewed displays of sandpaintings and artifacts and found themselves "face to face with the strange world of Navajo religion."[112]

As a result of Klah's collaborations with Wheelwright, Newcomb, and others, the record of his cultural contributions is extensive. Other aspects of his life have been almost entirely unrecorded, however. In particular, there is little evidence concerning his sexuality and personal relationships. To what extent Newcomb or Wheelwright inquired into this side of his life is unknown. However, Navajo tradition does not remember Klah as being celibate. One contemporary medicine man reports that Klah had sexual relations with men throughout his life, while descendants of his relatives believe that he may have been married to a woman when he was a young man.[113]

FINAL JOURNEY

In 1934, Klah was asked to return to Chicago to demonstrate sandpainting and display his tapestries in the New Mexico state exhibit at the Century of Progress Exhibition. He was sixty-seven years old. According to Newcomb, he made a colorful outfit for the occasion:

> Klah bought velveteen for his sister to make three shirts of different colors. . . .
> He bought several pieces of checked and striped calico and made trousers in the
> native fashion. He did not take all of his coral and turquoise beads, but he did
> wear a large silver concho belt, three strings of white shell beads, and two heavy
> turquoise bracelets. Tom Shorty was paid to make him a new pair of red deer-
> hide shoes with a large silver button on each, and I gave him three silk
> headkerchiefs in bright colors.[114]

In Chicago, Klah made a different sandpainting every day without repeating a design once, but he found the endless press of the crowds overwhelming. White people were "like leaves in front of a west wind," he later told Newcomb.[115] When Franc and Arthur arrived they found him enervated by the heat and depressed by the crowds. They arranged to drive him immediately back to New Mexico. At least one historic moment occurred that summer, however, when Klah became the second berdache in American history to meet a president.[116] He returned to New Mexico with his guestbook signed by Franklin Roosevelt. According to Newcomb, the book was one of Klah's "prized possessions."[117]

Klah's last sojourn in the white world appears to have left him disillusioned. Despite his willingness to form friendships with Anglos and to adapt traditional ways to changing times, he found the white world alien. As he told a reporter in Gallup,

> The Americans hurry too much. All the time you hurry and worry how you are going to hurry and worry more. You go thru life so fast you can't see beauty. I live the way I did when I came here first in 1893. I am happy. That is why I come. I want to show the white people that I am happier than they are because I don't have all those things to worry about.[118]

Klah's sister, Ahdesbah, died in 1936. After this, according to Newcomb, Klah was "a very lonely person," and he began to spend most of his time at the trading post.[119] In February 1937, at the age of 70, he contracted pneumonia. The Newcombs took him to a hospital in Gallup. With Arthur holding his hand, Klah gave his family instructions for disposing of the sacred objects and medicine bundles he had spent a lifetime accumulating.[120] He died only a few months before the dedication of the Museum of Navaho Ceremonial Art (renamed the Wheelwright Museum of the American Indian in 1976) in Santa Fe.

THE DREAMER'S VOYAGE

Hastíín Klah has left an identifiable body of work that rivals the output of many Western artists. If we can assume that the designs Klah chose to weave in his sandpainting tapestries reflect myths and themes that had personal importance for him, it becomes possible to explore the imagination and psychic life of a third gender person. One of the designs Klah wove most often was the Whirling Logs image from the Nightway (or Yeibechai) chant—a ceremony he had spent twenty-six years studying. Differing versions of the myth associated with the ceremony have been recorded, but Klah is likely to have been most familiar with the one recorded by Matthews as told by one of Klah's teachers.[121]

The story begins by introducing the hero, who is called simply the Visionary or Dreamer. The Dreamer lives alone with his grandmother (and is, therefore, unmarried). Although he has already acquired ceremonial knowledge, he wants to travel to a place called "Waters That Flow Around" to see the sacred cross of whirling logs said to be there. He decides to travel down the San Juan River in a hollowed-out log. He spends twelve days preparing in secret, but when he starts the log sinks into the mud. The Dreamer's brothers seek help from the gods, who take the hero to meet with them. When the hero explains his goal, the gods tell him,

> "That is a trifling cause for which to risk your life. You have been to the great places of the holy ones and have seen much. The things you now wish to see are insignificant compared to those you have already seen."
>
> "You have taught me much," he responds; "you have shown me much; I have seen all the sacred places except this and I shall never rest till I behold it. I am determined to go; for not until I have gone there shall I know all."[122]

The gods decide to help him—but he must start his journey over. Floating down the river, he encounters various obstacles and animal gods who require that he make offerings to them. Finally, the log floats into a lake surrounded by high cliffs and touches shore. At this magical place, the hero is greeted by the Fringe Mouth gods who show him a sandpainting. As he glances at it, the hero collapses in a fit. He is revived by the chief Fringe Mouth god, who presses the horn of a mountain sheep to his body. The hero memorizes these procedures to take back home with him.

Back in his log, the hero finally floats into the lake of swirling waters where two logs form a cross. On the arms of the cross are seated the Holy Ones, who use their staves to guide the logs and sing as the Dreamer approaches. The gods teach the hero two versions of the Whirling Logs sandpainting—the image Klah often wove. After he learns a third sandpainting, the gods tell him, "Now you have learned many mysteries. With these you may treat your people when they are ill. In this work you may help one another. You will work for the sick; they and their people will work for you." The hero acquires additional skills in farming, cooking, and building hogans and then returns to his relatives.

It is easy to see how Klah was able to identify with the central figure of this myth. As a youth, his thirst for sacred knowledge led him to discover a cave filled with ceremonial remains. At the same time, his curiosity exposed him to danger. Like the hero of the myth, he was seriously wounded, and, like him, he learned the ceremony that was held to cure him. Surviving his injuries, he demonstrated to others his supernatural power and emerged from the ordeal as a culture bearer with a new identity, that of *nádleehí*.[123]

Yet another source of insight into Klah's outlook as a *nádleehí* lies in his treatment of the deity, Begochídíín. Luckert has argued that Begochídíín is among the oldest gods of the Navajo.[124] Originally, he was a trickster figure with power over game animals and hunters.[125] As such, he was pansexual, and many of the stories about him are quite bawdy. He sneaks up on individuals at embarrassing moments and grabs their genitals or gets between couples when they are making love. One translation of his name is "the *bego* who touches"—*bego* being the exclamation he makes.[126] Luckert believes that a change in his character occurred when the Navajos shifted from hunting and gathering to a combination of horticulture and herding. Begochídíín came to be credited not only with the creation of game animals but domestic animals as well, and with providing the first seeds. He was identified as the inventor of pottery and the first *nádleehí*.

Begochídíín plays a key role in the Mothway myth, which accounts for the origin of exogamous marriage and the Mothway ceremony, which cures the madness caused by incest. In the myth, Begochídíín takes care of the young male and female Butterfly People by "encircling them all time and never letting them out of his sight."[127] They address him as their aunt, uncle, and granduncle. His love for them is so excessive that rather than allow them to marry outsiders, he masturbates them, touching their genitals and saying "Bego." The parents too are possessive, and when they are asked to give up a daughter in marriage they say, "No, you must know that she was nursed by me. I raised her, therefore I love her much and do not care at all to give her to another person."[128] When Begochídíín leaves for another country, the Butterfly children commit incest to avoid marrying outsiders. This makes them go wild, and, like moths, they rush into burning flames and many die. Even when the flames are extinguished, they stagger about as if drunk.

Typical of matrilineal societies in which brothers and sisters maintain close and cooperative relations throughout their lives—often closer and more permanent than marriages—the myth is concerned only with brother-sister incest.[129] However, it presents the problem of incest as one of possessive love on the part of parents—this is what leads brothers and sisters to turn to each other. Begochídíín is instrumental both in sustaining this state of affairs and in triggering its resolution. He represents a form of sexuality that does not require an other— masturbation. Combining (or alternating between) male and female, he epitomizes the potential of complete self-autonomy and lack of differentiation. When he leaves, however, a crisis occurs. Failure to go outside the group for sex leads to "burning"—more desire, not its release. Ultimately, the survival of the group requires relinquishing certain of its members to other groups.

The incest taboo solves the problem of parental possessiveness through the requirement that brothers and sisters marry outside the immediate family. In the myth, a rock ledge is constructed to separate the brothers and sisters. When they can no longer see each other, they quiet down. "Therefore," the narrator explains, "there is absolutely a mutual fear of their lower parts between brothers and sisters. The mere thought of such a thing is to be feared. This became known at that place."[130] The myth also provides the rationale for matrilocal marriage, a practice by which daughters do not have to be given up to outsiders (because husbands live in their wives' homes).

By Klah's time, Begochídíín was a complex figure. According to one account, he was born from a flower impregnated by a ray of sunlight.[131] Because Begochídíín was his youngest son, the Sun Father spoiled him and gave him dominion over many things. (Of course, overprotected sons are common figures in mythology, but here it is the father, not the mother who indulges the son—and a distinctly nonpatriarchal father at that, apparently unperturbed at the prospect of a third gender son.) Thus, Begochídíín is the source of a medicine made from flowers, and his home is always sweet-smelling. He has power over wind and insects—the procedure that Klah used to protect the Newcombs from the whirlwind is taught by Begochídíín in the Hail Chant. Having been born from sunlight, he is usually invisible, but he can appear at any time and take many forms. He travels by cloaking himself in haze, which can be of different colors. Hence, some Navajos recognize as many as four distinct Bego figures, including White, Yellow, and Black.[132]

In Klah's telling of the Navajo origin myth, Changing Woman travels to her home in the Pacific Ocean where she is greeted by Begochídíín, walking across the water. According to Klah, "His hair was shining and little rays of light shone and sparkled from him."[133] Elsewhere, Klah describes him as fair-skinned, with red or yellow hair and blue eyes, and dressed as a woman.[134] Others have described him as an old man, or as a boy who turns into a man, or as alternating between old and young—much as the term *nádleehí,* or "the one who is changing," suggests. In other words, Begochídíín fluctuates in both age and gender, the key social distinctions in most tribal societies.

Begochídíín appears prominently in two myths told by Klah—the story associated with the Hail Chant (recorded by Reichard and Wheelwright), and the Navajo origin myth (recorded by Wheelwright). Klah's account of Begochídíín in the Hail Chant myth corresponds with the older, trickster version of the god: A body of people is traveling when they spy a boy in the distance behind them throwing dust and dirt into the air. Eventually, their curiosity is aroused, and they send a party to investigate. When they arrive where the boy had been, they find only a small yellow worm. As they crowd around it, the worm leaps into the air. It leaps four times and turns into a man out of whose mouth pours forth masses of bees. (In Reichard's version, Klah describes the man as having gray eyes and red hair and being dressed as a woman.) The insects light upon the people, "getting into their hair, eyes, and ears, and stinging and frightening them badly."

They begged the man to stop sending these bees to torment them, but he did nothing but laugh and laugh, and sent forth more bees in swarms until the people were in great agony. At last they gave the man a Yellow Kehtahn [prayerstick] and he drew in his breath and sucked all the bees back into his mouth. . . . Then they saw that the man was Begochiddy, and were greatly amazed. . . . Begochiddy told the people that he would go with them and watch over them, and the people were glad and went on their way, when suddenly

Figure 5. Hastíín Klah, ca. 1925, working on one of his sandpainting tapestries. Photograph by Dane Coolidge. Bancroft Library, University of California, Berkeley.

Begochiddy disappeared from their midst and they did not see him go, so they knew that he had gone up into the sky.[135]

As accords a trickster figure, Begochídíín confounds the people and spreads pestilence. (According to Reichard, Klah declined to describe the sexual dimension of Begochídíín's behavior because "it was too dirty to tell to women.")[136] Only when the people offer the apparently malign being a prayerstick does its other aspect emerge—that of a benevolent deity whose benefits are (paradoxically) a function of the capacity to bridge good and evil. The trickster becomes a transcendental figure, a savior who lives in the sky and answers the prayers of the people. In Klah's telling of the origin myth, this transcendent aspect is fully realized. Born of pure light (a sunbeam and a sunray), Begochídíín is present throughout the narrative, responsible for creating (and recreating) mountains, plants, animals, and humans. (In other versions, these functions are fulfilled by different figures.) He is even responsible for the birth of Changing Woman, whom he raises. After Changing Woman causes a flood to purify the world, Begochídíín appears standing on a great rainbow, his hands spread out in gladness.

Donald Sandner, a Jungian analyst who has worked with Navajo medicine men, considers Begochídíín "a reconciling symbol which brings together good and bad, high and low, pure and impure, male and female, and as such he is one of the most daring intuitive concepts of American Indian religion—an ingenious attempt to express the basically paradoxical nature of man in the image of a god."[137] As C. G. Jung observes, such tricksters typically combine traits of animals, humans, and gods. For that reason, they often serve as symbols of the self, the total psyche in both its conscious and unconscious dimensions.[138]

Androgyny—whether thought of as a combination of male or female, or as that which is *neither* male or female—is another common symbol of this unity. In the Christian tradition, for example, the figure of Christ combines human and divine traits, and is often portrayed in an androgynous manner. However, as Jung points out, Christ is not an adequate symbol of the self, because Christian belief requires any negative aspects of God to be split off and projected onto the anti-Christ.[139] Begochídíín's malignant side, on the other hand, is not ignored or repressed. For this reason, he is a more apt symbol of the self—he is divine, human, *and* animal, good *and* evil. Further, as a figure who spanned Navajo history, he was an excellent vehicle for representing continuity within change at the beginning of the reservation period. Klah's version of Begochídíín bridges not only male and female, but *all* forms of social difference—including age and race (Klah described him as fair-skinned).

Reichard and others have argued that Klah exaggerated the role of Begochídíín, promoting him into a kind of supreme being.[140] Klah himself always insisted that his telling of the Navajo origin myth was "the Great, Old story."[141] In fact, a comparison of the traits attributed to Begochídíín by Klah with those found in other sources, as Table 3.1 summarizes, reveals that the only traits unique to Klah's telling are the role of law giver, the raising of Changing Woman, and the ability to cause sores. What is distinct about Klah's Begochídíín, however, is that he synthesizes traits mentioned separately in other sources. In other words, Klah's contribution was less one of innovation than that of combining and reconciling variant tellings.

Klah's career provides a rare glimpse into the relationship between archetypal figures of androgyny and the life of an individual who identified with them. Although scholars have long studied symbolic and ritual forms of androgyny, the social roles based on these representations are too often overlooked or dismissed. (Mircea Eliade, for example, described the social enactment of androgyny as symptomatic of a "confusion of levels").[142] As Klah's life shows, far from being psychologically undeveloped or marginal, third gender individuals could project images of wholeness that served as ideals for an entire society. Indeed, some forty years after Klah's death Sandner found medicine men who attributed the same transcendental status to the *nádleehí* god Begochídíín.[143]

BERDACHE ARTIST AND PRIEST

While Klah's innovations in weaving had a concrete economic impact, his contributions in a second area were no less significant. Klah became a synthesizer of Navajo

TABLE 3.1.

Themes in Accounts of Begochidíín

	Other versions[1]	Klah's version[2]
Sun's son; sun's uncle; child of daylight & ray of sun	•	•
Moon bearer; associated with moon	•	
Born from flower, flower medicine	•	•
Reverses age	•	•
Berdache, cross-dressed	•	•
Bisexuality	•	
Obscene behavior	•	•
Incest theme	•	
Fertility/increase	•	•
Cause of sores		•
Control of winds	•	•
Creator of Holy People	•	•
Creator of Changing Woman		•
Creator of mountains	•	•
Creator of wild and domestic animals	•	•
Creator of seeds, plants	•	•
Inventor of pottery	•	
Patron of hunters	•	
Creator/master of insects	•	•
Law giver		•
Gives aid	•	•
Answers prayers	•	•

1. Matthews 1897: 86-87, 226; 1902: 31; 1907: 58-59; Fishler 1953: 11, 14-17, 27, 105; Buxton 1923: 303; Hill 1938b: 99, 126; Haile 1949: 100; 1978: 82-90, 161-68, 171-72; Luckert 1978: *passim*; Sandner 1979: 38, 78, 114-17.

2. Faris 1990: 183, 195, 214, 227; Klah 1938: 11; Reichard 1944a: 21-22; 1944b: 7, 11, 13, 47, 49, 105; Klah 1942: passim; 1946: 5-8, 33, 40, 120; 1951: 1; Newcomb 1949: 3.

traditions and beliefs. As Reichard put it, "He rationalized many phases of religion and was much more aware of consistency in our sense than any other Navaho I ever met."[144] In creating his synthesis, Klah seems to have applied a principle of Navajo weaving. Witherspoon describes this as "creative synthesis, . . . bringing together elements of diverse characteristics into a single, balanced, and harmonious whole."[145]

By integrating the diffuse beliefs and practices of Navajo religion, Klah helped develop it into a vehicle for tribal identity and unity. Prior to the reservation period, the Navajos were a dispersed, semi-nomadic people. Extended families were the largest political units. But in the twentieth century, the tribe needed to be able to present a united front in its dealings with the U.S. government, which was actively seeking to reduce the size of reservations and to suppress traditional culture.[146] As Kluckhohn and Leighton observe, "In the absence of a codified law and of an authoritarian chief, it is only through the myth-ritual system that the Navahos can present a unified front." Klah appears to have reached the same conclusion. His familiarity with so many ceremonies led him to seek the continuity of his tribe's decentralized system of knowledge. In explaining the relationship between these ceremonies to Wheelwright, for example, he compared them to a group of trees, rather than a single tree with branches.[147] Eventually, as Reichard wrote, "After hours of thought and discussion scattered through a lifetime he had come to the conclusion that the ultimate in Navajo attainment was 'universal harmony,' a state of being with no tangibility. This is a notion of oneness and in it all elements in the universe are submerged."[148]

Klah also made a lasting cultural contribution by seeking the preservation of his religious knowledge. Years before Native American studies, tribal museums, and institutions like the Navajo Community College, Klah sought ways to preserve Navajo traditions. Although his ceremonies were not transmitted to the next generation, some of his ceremonial equipment, which had been placed at the Wheelwright Museum, has been returned to the community and is used today by practicing medicine men.[149]

While fulfilling Navajo expectations for a traditional *nádleehí,* Klah was also very much a figure of the twentieth century, willing to explore multiple cultural perspectives. He was, truly, an avant-garde berdache.[150] Like Nampeyo, who revived Hopi pottery by studying shards from an archaeological dig, and Maria Martinez of San Ildefonso, the first Pueblo potter to sign her work, Klah innovated to preserve traditional cultural forms and values.

Reichard provides an insightful assessment of his character:

> He was a person of many facets. One became instantly acquainted with him, one constantly found in him depths not easily plumbed, uncanny intuition, capacity for quiet and bubbling humor, a sure stability and, at the same time, a wide, even experimental tolerance. His voice was gentle and low, though interesting, his actions never impulsive, but energetic and swift, his principles and convictions unshakable. . . . His was an intuitive, speculative, imaginative mind, far from conservative, though he remained orthodox. He was always ready to examine new ideas, he harbored certain notions probably held by no other Navaho, unless taught by him.[151]

Today, the *nádleehí* tradition continues in parts of the Navajo reservation. Anthropologist Carolyn Epple has worked with several self-identified *nádleehí* traditionalists and teachers. While these contemporary *nádleehí* have diverse ways of identifying and defining themselves in relation to Western categories such as "gay," "homosexual," "bisexual," and "queen," they all emphasize traditional concepts of interconnection, transformation, change, and cyclical process.[152] In many respects, the circumstances of the Navajos today, the largest tribe in the United States, epitomize the dynamism and ambiguities of the postcolonial milieu. The tribal community encompasses fully assimilated Navajos living in towns and cities, along with families whose lifestyles and practices are among the most traditional of any tribe in North America. The effort to reconcile the divergent values and beliefs of Navajos and Anglo-Americans is bound to produce confusion, contests over meaning, and competing claims to tradition. As one Navajo told Epple, "If you were to ask what is a *nádleehí,* no one could really say."[153]

The contemporary context of Navajo life also produces creative mediations. Erna Pahe, a Navajo community activist in San Francisco, draws on both traditional philosophy and feminism when she describes the modern lesbian and gay community:

> We're the one group of people that can really understand both cultures—as mothers, as females, as young girls versus fathers and men. You go out there into the straight world and it's really amazing the stereotypes. Men can do this and women can't do that. Or women can do this and men can't do that. In our culture, in our little gay world, anybody can do anything. I mean, you find some very good mothers that are men. And you find very good fathers that are women. We can sympathize, we can really feel how the other sex feels. . . .
>
> I think that society is ready for that kind of atmosphere where we don't have to compete against each other over sexual orientation, or we don't have to feel like the men play a bigger role in society than women do. I think it's time for that neutralness, where people can understand just how to be people.[154]

In traditional Navajo society, individuals who occupied other genders had a place in the cosmic order—and, therefore, responsibilities to the common good. As Klah's life shows, in return for the acceptance of individual differences tribal society gained outstanding service and invention. In the twentieth century, Indian tolerance and white intransigence toward diversity in sex and gender have often clashed. But thanks in part to the efforts of Klah, some of the artistic and spiritual insights afforded by the social experience of the *nádleehí* have been saved—for contemporary Navajos who are tracing the continuity of their traditions as well as non-natives whose own society does not include such identities and who might not otherwise know of the social vistas they offer.

WARRIOR WOMEN AND WOMEN CHIEFS: ALTERNATIVE IDENTITIES AND GENDERS FOR NATIVE WOMEN

INTRODUCTION

In the maps and books made by Europeans following their discovery of the Americas, the so-called New World was frequently illustrated by the figure of an Amazon queen. She reclines in a pose typical of European depictions of the nude—except for the inclusion of a bow and arrows, war club, or sometimes a bloody, severed head.[1] To translate the erotic appeal of such an image for Renaissance male viewers into contemporary terms we need only imagine her feathered headdress and club replaced with a whip and a pair of stiletto heels. The New World was from the beginning an erotic horizon for male Europeans, a land where pleasures and evils banished by Christianity had taken root and flourished.

Derogatory accounts of Native American "squaws" appeared early in the contact literature and became one of its staples.[2] Native women were often denounced for their lasciviousness on the one hand, and their brutishness on the

Figure 6. **America as an Amazon**, 1581. In this engraving by Philippe Galle America is figured as a headhunting warrior woman.

other; they both attracted and repelled. Or their "drudgery" and "slavery" was piously bemoaned and unfavorably contrasted to the elevated position of Woman in European societies. The other side of invective, especially for the Spaniards, were erotic fantasies of a Rabelaisian cast—monsters, cannibals, warrior women. When Hernán Cortés reported stories of an island north of Mexico rich in pearls and gold and inhabited by Amazons it was named California, after the Amazon queen Califia in a popular novel of the time.[3] In 1529, Nuño de Guzmán led an expedition hoping to find the Amazons of California—and their gold.

The New World was an a-topia, a Marquis de Sade Eden, which either titillated or horrified European men depending on the particular dynamics of their sexual repression. If Spanish conquistadors were beguiled by native women (and for various reasons willing to intermarry with them), the English viewed the sexual landscape of America with fear and loathing. The Puritans considered themselves akin to Abraham entering the land of the Sodomites; they arrived prepared to do battle with the instruments of Satan, the native inhabitants.[4] Over time, Anglo-American iconography transformed the buxom Amazon into a desexualized Indian Princess. As such, she was adopted as the original figure of the new American nation.[5]

Somewhere beyond the poles of sexual repression and the return of the unconscious in the form of perverse impulses that circumscribe the field of European discourse, lies the reality of native women's lives. In fact, the women that Europeans encountered in the Americas were neither the shock troops of Califia nor the minions of Venus. They were, however, often more powerful, more sexual, and far more autonomous than women at any level of the European social order.

In the Southeast, Hernando de Soto's ill-fated expedition was hosted for a fortnight by a Creek female leader whom the Spaniards called the "queen of Cofitachequi."[6] The English also encountered women they termed "queens" among the natives of Virginia and New England.[7] Some of these women deserve recognition as heroes of Native American resistance. Weetamoo, a chief of the Pocasset Indians, was "as potent a prince as any round about her, and hath as much corn, land, and men at her command."[8] A "severe and proud dame," as Mary Rowlandson described her, she assumed her office from her husband following his death.[9] At the outbreak of King Philip's war, she led over three hundred warriors, but these were eventually reduced to less than thirty. In 1676, while trying to escape the region, she drowned in the Taunton River. The English fished her body out and gleefully displayed her head on a pole.[10] Here we see what the fantasy of Amazons and severed heads is really about—European castration anxieties irrupting as paranoid and murderous impulses alternately projected on and directed at the feminine Other of the New World.

Our view of native women has been distorted by what author Rayna Green calls the "Pocahontas perplex," in which "Indian women have to be exotic, wild, collaborationist, crazy, or 'white' to qualify for white attention." In reality, as Green points out, most native women leaders and cultural brokers sought to manage and minimize the negative consequences of change on their people.[11] In any case, Pocahontas and her sisters resist complete sentimentalization, as literary historian Leslie Fiedler has argued.[12] The fatal linkage between Indians and sexuality in the minds of white Americans makes it impossible for an Indian woman to symbolize purity. The lesson that the story of Pocahontas teaches— reconciliation of the races through sex and marriage—remains unassimilable.[13] In popular portrayals the "Indian princess" who accepts white culture and Christianization, betraying her people in the process, invariably dies before the end of the story (or, as in the Disney production *Pocahontas* [1995], historical facts are grossly altered to avoid interracial consummation).[14]

Today anthropologists and scholars in Native American studies continue to offer divergent views of native women. Many of these differences reflect larger debates within feminism and gender studies concerning the relative emphasis that should be placed on the systems of dominance that relegate women to secondary status compared to the ways in which women resist these systems. Feminist anthropologists concerned with male domination have offered various theories, attributing it to women's role in childbearing (which results in their exclusion from more prestigious public roles) and ideological oppositions between reproduction and production, and nature and culture, in which women are identified with the former (to their detriment) and men with the latter. This has led several theorists to argue that male domination of women is a universal feature of human societies, that "social systems are, by definition, systems of inequality."[15] A key goal of this research has been to show that women's status is never a simple consequence of their biology, but a product of social processes.

However, many students of Native American cultures as well as native women themselves have objected to the broad characterizations of tribal societies frequently found in research focusing on male dominance. As native anthropologist Beatrice Medicine argues, sweeping descriptions of Plains tribes as male-dominated warrior societies and Plains women as passive and dependent obscure the "rich complexity of female gender roles and the variety of relations between women and men."[16] DeMallie adds, "The stereotypical portrayal of Lakota society as dominated by males is only correct to the extent that it characterizes a culture in which the activities of men were considered to have greater symbolic value than the activities of women. To describe it as a male-oriented society characterized by psychological warfare between the sexes is to impose on the Lakotas our Western categories and meanings, and our conceptions of the appropriate relationship between the sexes."[17]

Many studies of native North American women challenge one of the central assumptions of feminist theories—that women constitute a class by their common treatment and common interests, which are distinct from those of men. Such a view, as DeMallie suggests, is at odds with tribal values and goals, which emphasize complementarity and interdependence between men and women. Consequently, many scholars of native North America have shifted their focus from the analysis of male dominance alone to the ways in which women gain autonomy in tribal societies and how they resist domination when it occurs. Anthropologists such as Alice Schlegel and Eleanor Leacock have argued that native North America provides examples of egalitarian societies in which women and men have "different but equal" roles and sources of prestige.[18] Some Native American feminists, such as Paula Gunn Allen, have shown how many tribal philosophies incorporate woman-centered values, concepts, and practices.[19]

Of course, the differences between these approaches—one that analyzes power relations and one that focuses on women's resistance—are not absolute, and scholars of both schools probably would agree that some differences in status and prestige between genders do exist in tribal societies *and* that women are not merely victims of social forces. On the other hand, both approaches share a common shortcoming, which is a tendency to view women in tribal societies as an internally undifferentiated class. Too many students of native cultures unquestioningly accept tribal ideologies (but not social reality) that define women in terms of their reproductive and social role as mothers, even though women lead very different lives before marriage and after menopause, periods that can accumulatively account for a larger portion of their life spans.[20] Accepting motherhood as the common denominator of women's gender roles leads scholars to overlook the frequency and significance of women's participation in activities defined as male—or to treat this participation as random and incidental when, in fact, it was often the expected behavior of women of a certain status and age.[21]

Many of the discrepancies in how native women have been portrayed are based on the differing experiences of women from high-status families and those from low-status families or those lacking kin; of elder women and young, newly-married women; of women with talent, ambition, or recognized powers and those who were not so gifted. These distinctions of family, age, and ability existed even in hunting-gathering groups conventionally described as egalitarian. Native women's lives were also differentiated in terms of the identities and social roles open to them, whether through inheritance, supernatural intervention, or their own achievements. This diversity has been overlooked as well, and one result has been confusion regarding female berdache roles and lesbianism.

Harriet Whitehead, for example, in an important theoretical essay has argued that female berdaches were rare because, "For someone whose anatomic starting point was female, the infusion of an official opposite sex component into her identity was by no means so easily effected." Consequently, "female deviations into aspects of the male role . . . were not culturally organized into a named, stable category comparable to that of the 'berdache.'"[22] Evelyn Blackwood and others have criticized the biological essentialism of Whitehead's assumptions about women's abilities.[23] Even so, Whitehead's discussion is better than the complete dismissal of the subject by many others.[24]

The question of lesbianism, or relationships between non-berdache women, has been equally obscured. Marla Powers, in criticizing Hassrick's discussion of lesbianism among the Sioux for his reliance on ethnocentric categories, asserts, "There is no 'hint' that there were any kind of sanctions for 'female inversion.'"[25] But, having rejected Hassrick's terminology she offers nothing in its place, leaving the question of whether Sioux women ever loved each other or engaged in men's occupations unanswered. The implication is that these patterns were absent. In fact, evidence of lesbianism among the Sioux and other tribes does exist, from reports of incidental homosexual behavior between women, to ongoing relationships, to tales and myths in which lesbian sexuality has a role.[26] Specific terms for lesbian sexual practices have been recorded for the Flathead, Sanpoil, Cheyenne, Mohave, and other languages (see Glossary).

The difference in the lives of male and female berdaches means that these roles are not merely complements of each other. For this reason, Walter Williams introduced a distinct term for such women, calling them "amazons," but this label has been criticized by several writers. As Jason Cromwell points out, accounts of so-called amazons since the times of the classical Greeks emphasized their

Figure 7. Sioux women, 1890. This photograph by John Anderson shows "two women, both ninety years old, who never married and who lived together until they died" (Dyck 1971: 106). Nebraska State Historical Society, A547: 2-149.

femaleness and consistently identify them as women.[27] Female berdaches, on the other hand, occupied a distinct gender role. They were not thought of as women (or even female in some cases), and their behavior, temperament, and appearance consistently differed from that of women. In addition, Blackwood argues that use of the term "amazon" has the effect of excluding alternative genders for females from the general study of berdaches. Although the Old World meaning of "berdache" is no more appropriate for Native American females than males, both alternative genders share some traits and were conceptualized in similar ways by native people. As Blackwood argues, if the term "berdache" should continue to be used in discussing roles for males, then it can and should be used in discussing female roles as well.[28]

The Mohaves provide a good example of the complexity of female identities in traditional native societies. The myth relating the birth of the first male berdache or *alyha:* opens by describing four women in the house of the god Mastamho. Mastamho assigns each woman a particular role. One is the mother about to give birth to the *alyha:*, another is to be her midwife. To the third, Mastamho says, "You are the one who will be a doctor, I think," and to the fourth, "You are the one who will not listen to what your kin say to you; you will be loose." Each of these identities represents a distinct social type and temperament.[29] The qualities of mothers constituted the ideal for Mohave women. Those of shamans were equally distinct, if viewed more ambivalently.[30] The "loose" woman also was a recognized type, referred to as *kamalo:y.* Traditionally, *kamalo:y* were believed to be under the influence of urges beyond their conscious control. Like female berdaches, or *hwame:*, they "throw away their house-keeping implements and run wild."[31] Unlike *hwame:*, however, their promiscuity was heterosexual. In sum, the theme of the myth is not merely the origin of *alyha:* but more generally the elaboration of gender, which includes a subdivision of "women" into four distinct identities.

Interestingly, *hwame:* are not included here (although female shamans were often *hwame:*).[32] Since they occupied a distinct gender, *hwame:* were not thought of as women. Instead, their origin is related in a separate episode:

> Mastamho was singing. He called a girl Hatšinye-masam-merīke [Little-girl-white-bean]. He said to her: "Listen!" She said: "Yes, I hear." Mastamho said: "If you hear all that I sing, do you know it?" She said: "Yes." Then he said: "Let me hear you sing it." Then she sang: she sang to him: "Vanālye, stand back!" She sang what he had sung. Then he said: Yes, now you have it. It is good. You have not lost a word." She was the first Hwami.[33]

The Mohave situation is not unique. Other tribes recognized not only distinct genders like the *hwame:*, but also specialized identities within the category of "women." To this should be added the evidence of women routinely engaging in "men's" work. Advancing our understanding of native women's role alternatives at this point requires adopting a broader frame of reference that does not define the subject so narrowly that relevant data are left out. When the inquiry is expanded from the question of whether female berdaches were present or not, to questions about the nature of female leadership and role alternatives more generally, the relevant data become much greater. It is clear that third and fourth gender roles were patterns of female autonomy and leadership but, as evidenced by the Mohave example, other alternatives existed as well.

Within this continuum of female roles, female berdaches can be defined as anatomical females occupying a named social status involving cross- or mixed-gender economic and social behavior, sometimes partial and/or occasional cross-dressing, and sometimes relationships with (non-berdache) women. Marriage avoidance is a consistent theme in the lives of many female berdaches. In addition to the economic and social dimensions of the role, there is often a spiritual element—females who became berdaches were inspired by dreams or visions, had shamanic powers, or were sanctioned by tribal myths. Many of these traits are similar to those of male berdaches, but their exact configuration tends to be more variable. At the same time, in nearly every tribe with a documented female berdache role, male berdaches were also present. As I will argue in chapter 6, both male and female berdaches belonged to distinct alternative gender roles. In tribes in which the same term was used for both, they belong to a third gender role. Where distinct terms were used, male berdaches represent a third and female berdaches a fourth gender role. Although male berdache roles have been documented in every region of North America, female roles appear to be concentrated among groups west of the Rocky Mountains.

In addition to third/fourth gender roles, at least two other patterns of female autonomy and alternative identities can be found in North American societies. In the Plains, although almost no instances of named alternative roles for females have been documented, a good deal of evidence exists of women's participation in warfare and hunting. In the area east of the Mississippi, a third pattern is represented by women chiefs like Weetamoo. Despite the extremely broad nature of these distinctions, there are relevant socioeconomic and cultural differences between the tribes of these regions that help account for these differing female roles.

INDIAN QUEENS

The "squaw queen" Weetamoo was not unique. Native American "queens" are known to have existed in Algonkian- and Muskogean-speaking tribes from Massachusetts to Georgia. Among the Coastal Algonkian they were called *sunksquaw;* in Virginia, *wiroansqua.*[34] Roger Williams defined the Narragansett word *saunks* as "the Queen, or Sachims Wife" (plural *saunksquuaog* or *sunksquaw*), but *sunksquaw* were much more than chiefs' wives.[35] Coastal Algonkians were semi-sedentary village dwellers who engaged in a productive mix of gardening combined with hunting and gathering. Leadership roles were hereditary within high status families.[36] Kinship practices (which in some cases may have been matrilineal) allowed women to inherit these offices, or to succeed their brothers or husbands. Once a woman became a *sunksquaw,* she ruled in her own right, and if she married (or remarried), her husband held no special office.[37] (Indeed, Weetamoo's second husband was described as an "insignificant fellow."[38])

Women's inheritance of chiefly rank has been documented for the Massachusett, Natick, Saconnet, Wampanoag, Narragansett, Western Niantic, Scaticook, Piscataway, and Powahatan groups, and for the Delawaran Esopus in the Hudson Valley.[39] The Plymouth Pilgrims encountered a woman chief when they attacked the Massachusetts in 1621. The leader of the Massachusetts confederacy at that time was a woman they called Squaw Sachem, or the "Massachusetts Queen."[40] Other *sunksquaw* in the seventeenth century include Quaiapan (or Magnus or Matantuck), noted as one of six Narragansett chiefs in 1675, who led her warriors against the English until her death the following year; and Awashonks, a Saconnet woman who also fought against the English and was "somewhat celebrated for her masculine qualities."[41]

Although *sunksquaw* have some similarities with female berdaches, especially involvement in warfare, there is one important way in which they differ. Being a *sunksquaw* was not incompatible with heterosexual marriage; in fact, marriage was the primary way by which Algonkian women became chiefs. Nor is there any evidence of *sunksquaw* cross-dressing or engaging in men's subsistence activities. Another crucial factor was family background. It appears that only women from high status families became *sunksquaw*. In sum, Algonkian women chiefs represent a mode of female autonomy linked to social stratification and inherited leadership. These social practices can be related, in turn, to the productivity and cultural specialization afforded by the mixed subsistence pattern of these tribes. In such societies, women's access to power was enhanced by if not contingent upon heterosexual marriage. Although individual ability and temperament were no doubt important factors in the cases of women who became *sunksquaw*, low status women with these traits had little chance of becoming chiefs.

The only evidence of a cross- or mixed-gender role for women among groups east of the Mississippi comes from the Algonkian-speaking Illinois, among whom, according to the French traveler Lahontan, "some young Women will not hear of a Husband, through a principle of Debauchery. That sort of Women are call'd Ickoue ne Kioussa, i.e. Hunting Women: for they commonly accompany the Huntsmen in their Diversions."[42] If the model outlined here is valid, the reference to marriage refusal and participation in men's subsistence activities suggests that *ickoue ne kioussa* were true female berdaches.

WOMEN WARRIORS

The one Plains tribe with positive evidence of a female berdache role, the Cheyenne, were also Algonkian-speakers. The term *hetaneman* was defined in a dictionary published in 1915 by Rudolphe Petter, a Mennonite missionary to the Southern Cheyenne, as "hermaphrodite (having more of the female element)," in contrast to the *he'eman*, or male berdache, which was "hermaphrodite (having more of the male element)."[43] According to a Cheyenne consultant of Winfield Coleman, the *hetaneman* "were often great warriors who accompanied the warrior societies in times of war. Some of these . . . even sat with the Chief Council and had an effective voice."[44] Further evidence of *hetaneman* comes from two ledger book drawings by a Cheyenne artist.[45] Both depict a bare-breasted woman firing a rifle (see frontispiece). She is dressed like the male members of the Hohnuka, or Contrary society, who fought wearing only their breechcloths.[46] Petter's personal copy of his dictionary also includes some interesting handwritten additions, including the terms *heemanèvo ehazistoz*, "[illegible] . . . acts of sapphism, autophysical love among women" and *heeo zetaomeaeuowathaazess*, "sapphism, Lesbian love, tribadism: women 'owning themselves,' consorting only with women in sexual gratification."[47]

Aside from the Cheyenne *hetaneman* there are no other confirmed instances of female berdache roles among Plains tribes. Yet the evidence of women's participation in both hunting and warfare is extensive. Plains women accompanied war parties and raids, joined battles, counted coup, received honors, and sometimes led expeditions.[48] In several tribes, there were associations of women who had been to war or women's auxiliaries to warrior societies.[49] In almost all tribes, women participated in victory dances and war rituals. Further, the most famous cases of women as warriors and leaders in North America come from this region. Their behavior, as we will see in the cases of Kuilix, Woman Chief, and Running Eagle, incorporated mixed gender and third gender traits. They distinguished themselves from women who occasionally joined a raid or battle by participating in warfare on a routine basis, being successful in battle, and becoming leaders. Being warriors was clearly part of their identities, not an occasional activity. At the same time, they do not appear to have occupied a named social status, and in this regard they cannot be considered female berdaches.

One might argue that the careers of these Plains women reflect the tumultuous conditions of the nineteenth century, when their tribes were locked in a desperate armed struggle with the United States. As one male leader after another fell before the advancing wave of violence, women occasionally stepped in to fill the breach. Such an explanation may have validity, but it must also be recognized that every aspect of Plains Indian life was changing in this period. It would be hard to say what was "normal" for any institution or social role. Indeed, if female berdache roles did not exist in Plains tribes, the careers of the women described here might be taken as evidence that such roles were emerging (or were covert categories), a process brought to a sudden halt by the tribes' military defeat.

The following cases also serve to illustrate how Plains women warriors and chiefs have been caught up in the "Pocahontas perplex." In all three cases, the available evidence comes from non-ethnographic sources—the observations and reminiscences of white frontiersmen. Their accounts reflect both their biases as men and their reliance on popular literary formulas.

Kuiliy: "Renown for Intrepidity on the Field of Battle"

The Salish-speaking Pend d'Oreille (or Kalispel) and Flathead (or Salish) tribes of western Montana illustrate all the patterns of women's participation in war found in the Plains region—from ceremonial roles to participation in battles to ongoing roles as warriors and leaders.

The Jesuit fathers Pierre Jean De Smet, Nicholas Point, and Gregory Mengarini arrived in Montana in 1841 intending to "reduce" the Flatheads and Pend d'Oreilles to missions (much as their brethren had done among the natives of Paraguay). Instead, they found themselves accompanying their would-be converts on treks to the plains to hunt buffalo and fight their enemies. The tribes, for their part, welcomed the missionaries, hoping they would provide them with supernatural aid. But when the Jesuits began to scold them with "fatherly rebukes" and "exhortations" because they continued to give "themselves up to their old war-dances, to savage obscenity and to shameless excesses of the flesh," attitudes quickly changed.[50] As relations worsened, the Flatheads refused to sell the priests provisions. In 1850, St. Mary's mission in the Bitterroot Valley was abandoned.[51]

The Jesuits were especially baffled by the active role of Flathead and Pend d'Oreille women in warfare. Women joined dances dressed as warriors, and they frequently entered battle. As De Smet observed in 1846,

> Even the women of the Flathead mingled in the fray. One, the mother of seven children, conducted her own sons into the battle-field. Having perceived that the horse of her eldest son was breaking down in a single combat with a Crow, she threw herself between the combatants, and with a knife put the Crow to flight. Another, a young woman, perceiving that the quivers of her party were nearly exhausted, cooly collected, amidst a shower of arrows, those that lay scattered around her, and brought them to replenish the nearly exhausted store.[52]

At least one Pend d'Oreille woman distinguished herself in war and appears to have been a recognized leader. Her native name was Kuilix, "The Red One" (or "Red Shirt"), referring to a bright red coat she wore—probably part of a British military uniform.[53] She was known to whites as Mary Quille or Marie Quilax. Father Point drew and painted her and described her in his journals and letters. He relates an occasion in 1842 when a small group of Pend d'Oreilles came upon a large party of Blackfoot and attacked them. When the sounds of gunfire reached the Pend d'Oreilles camp, the other warriors rode out to join the fray. According to Point:

> The first Pend d'Oreille to dash out at the enemy was a woman named Kuilix, "The Red One," . . . Her bravery surprised the warriors who were humiliated and indignant because it was a woman who had led the charge, and so they threw themselves into the breach where nature's shelter had protected the enemy. The Blackfeet immediately shot four shots almost at point-blank range; yet not a single Pend d'Oreille went down. Four of the enemy—some claim it was only two—managed to escape death by hiding in the thickets, but the rest were massacred on the spot.[54]

Kuilix was also present at a battle with the Crows in 1846. According to Point, "The famous Kuilix . . . accompanied by a few braves and armed with an axe, gave chase to a whole squadron of Crows. When they got back to camp, she said to her companions, 'I thought that those big talkers were men, but I was wrong. Truly, they are not worth pursuing.'"[55] Point's illustration of the episode

Figure 8. Kuilix, 1846. This drawing by Father Nicholas Point shows the Pend d'Oreille woman warrior Kuilix in battle against the Crows. The Pierre Jean De Smet Papers at Washington State University Libraries.

bears the caption, "A woman warrior's swift about-face left the enemy stupefied."[56] According to Point, Kuilix was "renowned for intrepidity on the field of battle."[57] De Smet referred to her as the "celebrated Mary Quille" and an engraving of her based on Point's drawing appears on the title page of his 1844 *Voyages aux montagnes rocheuses.*[58]

Of the three Plains warrior women discussed here, the evidence is strongest for considering Kuilix a female berdache. Her success as a warrior, the fact that she led men in war, and her partial cross-dressing are all traits of female berdaches. Such a status is known to have existed among the neighboring Kutenai, while Flathead terms suggesting such a role have been recorded (see Glossary).

Woman Chief: "Fearless in Everything"

The career of Woman Chief of the Crow Indians includes not only participation in hunting, warfare, and leadership, but a sexual dimension as well—she married four women. An account of her life was recorded by Edwin Denig, who knew her over the course of twelve years.[59]

Born into the Gros Ventre tribe in the first decade of the nineteenth century, she had been captured by the Crows when she was about ten. According to Denig, "As in the case of the Berdêche [berdache] who, being male inclined to female pursuits, so this child, reversing the position, desired to acquire manly accomplishments." She was "taller and stronger than most women," and "long before she had ventured on the warpath she could rival any of the young men in all their amusements and occupations, was a capital shot with the rifle, and would spend most of her time in killing deer and bighorn, which she butchered and carried home on her back when hunting on foot." She did not, however, cross-dress. When the Crow man who had adopted her was killed, she took over responsibility for his lodge and family, "performing the double duty of father and mother."[60]

Woman Chief became a warrior on the occasion of a Blackfoot attack on her village. Taking up her gun, she killed several of the enemy while escaping injury herself. Within a year, she was leading her own war parties, counting coups, and taking scalps. "In every battle . . . some gallant act distinguished her. Old men began to believe she bore a charmed life which, with her daring feats, elevated her to a point of honor and respect not often reached by male warriors. . . . The Indians seemed to be proud of her [and] sung forth her praise in songs composed by them after each of her brave deeds."[61] According to Denig, she led large war parties and "is fearless in everything, has often attacked and killed full-grown grizzly bears alone, and on one occasion rode after a war party of Blackfeet, killed and scalped one alone (within sight of our fort on the Yellowstone), and returned unharmed amid a shower of bullets and arrows."[62]

Eventually, Woman Chief acquired four wives, which only increased her stature in the tribe. According to Denig, she was recognized as the third highest leader in a band of 160 lodges, and at a council of the Crow and Cree she sat in fifth place among the Crow chiefs.[63] She could advance no higher, however, since, as an adopted member of the tribe she lacked the necessary family network for such a career. Nonetheless, for twenty years she "conducted herself well in all things appertaining to war and a hunter's life."[64] The Swiss artist Rudolph Kurz, who met her in 1851, described her as "neither savage nor warlike." The "Absaroka amazon" "sat with her hands in her lap, folded, as when one prays. She is about 45 years old; appears modest in manner and good natured rather than quick to quarrel." Denig described her as "tolerably good-looking."[65]

Woman Chief continued to go to war into her forties. In 1854, she decided to visit the Crow's long-time enemies, the Gros Ventres. Initially welcomed into their camp, when the Gros Ventres discovered who she was they killed her and her four companions.[66]

Beyond these sketchy facts Woman Chief's life fades into the mists of frontier mythology. It was probably the basis for the character called Pine Leaf in James Beckwourth's 1854 memoir. Beckwourth was an emancipated mulatto who had traveled to the Rocky Mountains in the 1820s. Joining the Crows, he distinguished himself as a warrior and for a time served as a war leader. According to Beckwourth, Pine Leaf (Bar-chee-am-pe) was "one of the bravest women that ever lived. . . . She possessed great intellectual powers. She was endowed with extraordinary muscular strength, with the activity of the cat and the speed of the antelope." When her twin brother was killed during a raid on their village, Pine Leaf "solemnly vowed that she would never marry until she had killed a hundred

Figure 9. Pine Leaf. James Beckwourth's character, Pine Leaf, as illustrated in his 1856 memoir.

of the enemy with her own hand." "Whenever a war-party started, Pine Leaf was the first to volunteer to accompany them. . . . She seemed incapable of fear; and when she arrived at womanhood, could fire a gun without flinching, and use the Indian weapons with as great dexterity as the most accomplished warrior."[67]

After serving with her on several war parties, Beckwourth asked Pine Leaf to marry him. She responded, "Do you suppose I would break my vow to the Great Spirit? He sees and knows all things; he would be angry with me, and would not suffer me to live to avenge my brother's death." When Beckwourth persisted, she replied, "Well, I will marry you."

"When we return?"

"No; but when the pine-leaves turn yellow."[68]

Several days passed before Beckwourth realized that pine leaves do not turn yellow.

Beckwourth's treatment of Pine Leaf underscores the very different fate of native women warriors in the texts of Euro-Americans when compared to the treatment of male berdaches. Whereas men dressed as women evoked dismay and disgust, female berdaches were viewed in terms of the stereotype of the Indian Princess. To democratic American frontiersmen the desire of a woman for access to the privileges and rewards of the male world merely affirmed in their eyes the superiority of their role. The effort of some native women to escape their (allegedly) slavelike status struck American men as noble and stirring, garnering their fascination and paternalistic sympathy. As the early explorer and geographer David Thompson noted in describing the interest of frontiersmen in the life of the Kutenai female berdache Qánqon, "The story of the Woman that carried a Bow and Arrows and had a wife, was to them a romance."[69]

Warrior women and women chiefs came to occupy a small but significant place in American literature, according to the rules of the Pocahontas perplex— they were mysterious, enticing, but ultimately tragic figures. Other romanticized accounts of women warriors include Emerson Bennett's *The Prairie Flower; or, Adventures in the Far West* (1850) and *Leni Leoti; or, Adventures in the Far West* (1851), A. B. Meacham's *Wi-ne-ma: The Woman Chief* (1876), and, more recently, Rose Sobol's *Woman Chief* (1976) and Frederick Manfred's lurid *The Manly-Hearted Woman* ([1975] 1985).

Running Eagle: "I Shall Never Marry"

Perhaps the most mythologized native woman warrior is Pi´tamakan, or Running Eagle, of the Blackfoot (Siksikas) Indians of Montana and Canada. James Willard Schultz, a popular writer who had been adopted by the Blackfoot in the late 1870s, published two versions of her story, a short summary in 1916 and a book-length, novelized account in 1919 titled *Running Eagle: The Warrior Girl*.[70] Schultz's informant was Tail Feathers Coming Over the Hill, who had grown up with Running Eagle and placed her death in the 1840s.

In the 1916 version Running Eagle is described as the oldest child of two brothers and two sisters. When she was fifteen both her parents died. Rather than abandoning their lodge to live with relatives, however, Running Eagle insisted on keeping her brothers and sisters together and becoming the head of the lodge. At the same time, she refused to marry. According to Tail Feathers Coming Over the Hill, "Many young men and many old and rich men wanted to marry her, and to all she said 'No!' so loudly, and so quickly, that after a time all knew that she would not marry." Meanwhile, she developed an extraordinary interest in warfare and the activities of warriors. "All she talked of, all she thought about, was war."[71]

At the age of twenty, Running Eagle joined a raiding party and successfully stole six horses. Invited to count her coups at a medicine lodge ceremony, she was given the name of an honored chief, Pi´tamakan.[72] After additional raids against the Crow, Sioux, and Flathead, she became a leader, and "warriors begged to be allowed to join her parties." She wore men's clothes when on a raid and women's clothes in camp, but she also hosted feasts and dances "like any man."[73] Running Eagle counted coup three times by actually seizing the gun of an enemy. On her ninth raid, her camp was taken by surprise. She and five men were killed.[74] Tail Feathers Coming Over the Hill concludes with the words, "And so passed Pi´tamakan, virgin, and brave woman chief of our people."[75]

Schultz elaborated this account in several ways to produce *Running Eagle*. To her original motives for becoming a warrior—marriage refusal and interest in war—he adds an account of her childhood that portrays her as a tomboy. When her mother insists that she take up lodge work, Running Eagle replies, "I wish that I was a boy . . . but if I cannot be one, I can at least do a boy's work. I shall not tan hides, I shall not do lodge work, I shall continue to help my father!" She earns the nickname *sakwo´mapi akikwan,* or "boy-girl."[76] Schultz introduces yet another motive (or at least hints at one) when Running Eagle decides to start hunting again after taking over domestic responsibilities following her parents' deaths. To do the lodge work, she takes in a "tall, slender, fine-looking woman" named Suya´ki, who had been mistreated by a recently deceased husband and "wanted nothing more to do with men."[77] That Schultz was aware of the lesbian overtones of the relationship becomes apparent in his subsequent handling of it.

The primary means by which Schultz interjects drama into Running Eagle's story is by attributing heterosexual motives to her. As in the earlier version, she initially rejects all proposals and declares, "I care not what people say of me so long as I do right. As for marrying . . . I shall never marry! I shall never be any man's slave!"[78] However, in the novel Schultz turns this resolution into a religious vow and devotes the second half of the book to this theme. The other motives for Running Eagle's career—her tomboy childhood, her attraction to warfare, her disinclination to marry—drop out of the picture. Instead, Schultz emphasizes her beauty and feminine appearance (and has her cry in more than one episode). She is irresistibly attractive to men. "Never, never had they seen a woman so beautiful, so graceful as she was in her gorgeous man's war costume."[79] Whereas Running Eagle's initial refusal to marry settles the matter in the 1916 version, in the novel her resolve is repeatedly tested by men who declare their love for her. This leads her to undertake no less than two vision quests, both of which reaffirm the vow, which increasingly seems like a penance.

The agenda behind Schultz's transformation of Running Eagle becomes clear when the novel is read as an allegory of Euro-American, not Indian, gender roles. Schultz projects the anxieties of his own time concerning women's roles onto the liminal space of the American frontier, a frontier of gender as well as geography. Much as the contradictions of Walt Disney's animated film *Pocahontas* represent late-twentieth-century anxieties over female autonomy and femininity, one can hear in the voice of Schultz's Running Eagle echoes of early twentieth-century feminists. He has her declare that "it was time for us girls and unmarried women to show the men that we can do much more than just day-after-day lodge work. That the less we depend upon them for what we need, the more they will respect us."[80] At the same time, by giving her a tomboy background and a female "lodge-mate" who is also a marriage protester, Schultz evokes the vulgar stereotype of feminists as man-hating lesbians. He spends the rest of the novel putting this bogey-woman to rest. Suya´ki marries a Yanktonai chief, and the ambiguities of Running Eagle's sexuality are resolved by the long denouement of her vow.

Thus the marriage-resisting tomboy becomes a frustrated, unrequited hetero-sexual, a sad victim of primitive religious belief. Yet, Schultz's treatment of Running Eagle and his attitude toward feminism can be seen as essentially sympathetic, albeit through the revanchist move of reclaiming her as a role model by heterosexualizing her story. Potentially an "Indian queen," Schultz casts her instead as an "Indian princess"—less sexual, less threatening to Anglo-Americans, and less transgressive than the full-fledged Amazon who once graced the maps and imaginations of European men.

John C. Ewers also published an account of Running Eagle, collected nearly thirty years after Schultz's book appeared. His source was Weasel Tail, who placed the warrior woman's death in 1860.[81] Weasel Tail had learned about Running Eagle from White Grass, who had joined war parties under her leadership.

> Running Eagle was a large, strong woman. When she was still young, her husband was killed in a fight with the Crows. Seeking some way to avenge his death, Running Eagle prayed to the sun, and thought she heard the sun answer, "I will give you great power in war. But if you give yourself to any other man you will be killed."
>
> In a short time Running Eagle became a successful leader of sizable war parties. When on the warpath, she wore men's leggings, a peculiar loin cloth doubled over like a diaper, and a woman's dress. Although men who went to war under her leadership respected her highly, she was never proud. She insisted upon cooking for the men of her party, and she also mended their worn moccasins. When one young brave complained that it was not proper for a Blackfoot war leader to have to mend moccasins, she replied, "I am a woman. You men don't know how to sew."
>
> One winter White Grass joined an expedition of about thirty men under Running Eagle's leadership, bound southward to the Crow country beyond the Yellowstone. They had not gone far before one of the younger men began to grumble because the leader was a woman. Running Eagle heard him and said, "You are right. I am only a woman." Then she sang her sacred war song, "All of you bachelors, try your best." The dissenter was so impressed by her manner that he decided to stay with the party to observe how this woman behaved.

Running Eagle then located and killed three buffalo on her own and successfully lead the party in battle against the Nez Perces.

The following spring White Grass joined another expedition led by Running Eagle:

On the Sun River they sighted a camp of Flatheads who had crossed the Rockies to hunt buffalo on the plains. Running Eagle confided to her followers, "Last night I dreamed that some horses were given to me. Tonight we shall find them in the Flathead camp."

Shortly before daybreak the Piegans silently approached the tepees of the sleeping Flatheads. Running Eagle swiftly gave her orders: "Brothers, catch the horses you can rope outside the camp. I am no good with a rope. I'll go into the camp and see what's there." She sang her war song and prayed to the sun. "Sun, I am not a man. But you gave me this power to do what I desired." Then she walked quietly into the enemy camp, quickly cut loose five prize horses picketed near their owners' tepees, and led them away. Meanwhile, the men of her party roped a goodly number of the loose horses. When Running Eagle returned, the party was ready to make a fast getaway. She then told her comrades, "I'll take the lead. I am only a woman. I'm not as strong as you men. Keep any of those who may fall asleep on their horses from falling behind." For two days and two nights they rode without stopping to sleep. After the party reached their home camp, Running Eagle gave a bay and a roan to her eldest brother and a horse to each of her other relatives.

Eventually Running Eagle's luck ran out. When the Flathead realized that a woman was stealing their horses, they set a trap. The next time Running Eagle entered their camp she was challenged by a guard. Unable to respond in the Flathead language, she was shot and killed on sight. According to Weasel Tail, "Some of the old Blackfoot Indians claimed that Running Eagle lost her life because she had broken her promise to the sun. She had fallen in love with a handsome young member of her war party, and she had not resisted his advances."[82]

The differences between the Schultz and Ewers versions include such basic details as the date of Running Eagle's death (1840s in Schultz, 1860 in Ewers) and the motives for her going to war (revenge for the death of her parents and tomboy interests in Schultz, revenge for the death of her husband in Ewers). The most significant difference in Ewers is the absence of the marriage protest theme, which is prominent in both accounts by Schultz. Instead of a "virgin" warrior girl, she is a widow. On the other hand, a vow not to marry plays a role in both accounts. In Ewers it is clearly presented as the condition for her participation in war, so that, by implication, she chooses war over remarriage. Ewers also foregrounds Running Eagle's visionary and medicine powers, along with her self-deprecating manner, which bespeaks confidence in her supernatural powers while it conforms to the expected demeanor for Blackfoot women. The more recent reminiscences of Beverly Hungry Wolf, a contemporary Blackfoot woman, further clarify the supernatural basis of Running Eagle's gender difference—she engaged in men's activities because she had had a man's vision. This had given her "the power that men consider necessary for leading a successful warrior's life."[83]

In the ethnographic literature the women of Blackfoot tribes (the Blackfoot or Siksikas, Piegans, and Bloods or Kainah) are described as thoroughly subjugated by men, who consider them mentally inferior and suited only for domestic work and childcare.[84] As Oscar Lewis explains, "The behavior considered ideal in Piegan women is submissiveness, reserve, faithfulness, and kindness."[85] He goes on to summarize the features of Blackfoot society that keep women subordinated, including bride price, patrilocal residence, a sexual double standard, wife beating, male-only associations, the exclusive participation of men in tribal government, and the control of key sources of prestige by men.[86]

At the same time, a set of alternative identities for women has been documented among the Blackfoot, similar to those outlined in Mohave mythology. These include the *nâtoyi´*, the sun dance or sacred woman; the *ninauake* (Northern Piegan; *ninaki,* Northern Blackfoot), the favorite or "sits-beside" wife; the *matsaps,* or "crazy woman"; and the *ninauposkitzipxpe* (Northern Piegan; *ninawaki,* Northern Blackfoot), the manly-hearted woman.[87] Recognizing the systematic nature of this identity set, Seward published a diagram illustrating how each of these identities represents a variation of conventional women's behavior. The sun dance woman varies in the degree of her virtue, the manly-hearted woman in the degree of her assertiveness, the *matsaps* in her extramarital sexuality, and the favorite wife in marital affection.

Of particular interest is the role of the manly-hearted woman. In contrast to the normally reserved and deferential behavior of conventional women, manly-hearted women were known for their aggressiveness, independence, ambition, boldness, and sexual freedom. While the character of many manly-hearts did not emerge until they were adults, others were recognized in childhood because they played boys' games and gave themselves the names of great warriors. Manly-hearts excelled in both men's and women's work. They were known for speaking out in public and for using vulgar language like men. In 1939, Lewis found that all the medicine women on the Brocket Reserve (and 13 percent of all married women) were manly-hearts. Some had learned men's songs and performed them during ceremonies.[88]

Nonetheless, manly-hearted women differ from female berdaches in several respects, the most important being the means by which they become manly-hearts. Lewis found that only married women were manly-hearts; unmarried women with similar behaviors were not called such. It is also significant that Blackfoot societies were stratified in terms of wealth (although various practices mitigated the transference of wealth across generations). Only wealthy women from prominent families became manly-hearts. Often they had been *manipuka,* or favored children, singled out for special treatment. Such women acquired wealth through their own work, through gifts from their family, and through inheritance. Many were widows who had inherited their husbands' property. The majority of manly-hearts were over the age of fifty.[89]

In other words, manly-hearted status was defined not only in terms of gender difference, but in terms of economic status and age, as well. In this regard, it shares certain characteristics with the status of women chiefs among eastern Algonkians. It was the product of a society in which women were subjugated by an ideology that treated them as an undifferentiated class. At the same time, there were two ranks of women. High status women, being near wealth and prestige through kinship and marital ties, had opportunities to acquire them that poor women did not. However, these opportunities were limited to women who married. A woman who refused to marry not only gave up the chance to acquire wealth from her husband, but it was unlikely that her family would support her decision and continue to provide the gifts or inheritance needed to become a manly-heart.

Running Eagle does not conform to any of the alternative female identities for Blackfoot women. Although she is credited with certain traits similar to those of manly-hearted women (assertiveness, success in both men's and women's work, wealth, sponsoring feasts, participating in men's ceremonies—and, in Ewers' account, she is a widow), and she was reportedly a holy woman who sponsored sun dances, one of her traits has no place in the Blackfoot female gender paradigm—her refusal to marry.[90] This makes her more like a female berdache than a manly-heart.

If Blackfoot social structure does not provide a context for Running Eagle's career, Blackfoot history does. At the time of her birth in the early nineteenth century, the Blackfoot had just completed a radical social transformation that began with the acquisition of horses around 1730.[91] The mobility horses afforded geometrically increased the tribe's capacity for hunting and raiding. Equally significant were the changes this brought about in gender roles. Horses and guns were men's possessions, and men controlled the food and wealth they produced. This resulted in a significant decrease in the social and sexual autonomy of women—although their economic contributions, including traditional gathering activities and the processing of the myriad products derived from buffalo, and their roles in religion remained important.[92]

It does not seem so surprising after all that in Running Eagle's generation—grandchildren of the first Blackfoot to mount horses—there should appear the stirrings of complaint against the excessive constraints being imposed on women and girls. In fact, De Smet noted Blackfoot women's criticisms of their status in the 1840s.[93] There is also evidence that Running Eagle's story became the basis for protests in subsequent generations. Schultz has described two women (Otter Woman and Lance Woman) who cited Running Eagle to justify their own attempts to participate in war parties.[94] Elsewhere he relates that a lake in Glacier National Park was named after "a long-ago woman of the Pikuni, who was noted for her love of the war trail."[95] In the 1930s, Lewis found that although women considered the unconventional behavior of manly-hearts "immodest and dread the thought of their own daughters becoming manly-hearted," they also "speak with envy and admiration of the courage and skill of manly-hearted women and look upon their deviations as a form of female protest in a man's culture."[96]

This observation may be generalizable. Plains women, in the period immediately before the reduction of their tribes to reservations, may have been in the process of creating a role for female autonomy and leadership.[97] If so, it would have been distinct from the inherited *sunksquaw* status of the eastern United States and from female berdache roles of the far West, although sharing some traits with both.

Retellings of Running Eagle's story have not ceased. In 1984, the Bilingual Education Program of the Heart Butte School District in the Blackfeet Indian Reservation reprinted Schultz's 1916 account in an illustrated pamphlet titled "The Story of Running Eagle: Pi'tamaka as told by Tail-Feathers-Coming-over-the-Hill." While the text is unchanged, the framing of it gives the story new significance. Now, the audience for Running Eagle are young members of the Blackfoot tribe being educated in schools on the reservation. The story has been selected for their reading not as an artifact of a distant, exotic culture, but because Running Eagle is seen as an appropriate role model, one that upholds tribal values and provides a positive image for young women. To whatever extent Running Eagle may have articulated a protest against the male-dominated aspects of Blackfoot society, her voice has now reached a generation who can act on it.

ALTERNATIVE GENDERS

Even when allowance is made for the more systematic study of native groups west of the Rocky Mountains, the number of references to female berdaches in this region is striking.[98] Nearly absent in the Plains and eastern United States, in the West they have been documented from Alaska and Canada to California and the Southwest—although, in most cases, the sources do little more than indicate their presence. A summary of this evidence appears in Table 4.1. (See the Tribal Index for sources and the Glossary of Native Terms.)

Some regional variations in these roles can be discerned despite the sketchiness of the data. As described in chapter 1, among Inuit-Eskimo and Athabaskan-speaking groups of the arctic and subarctic females were sometimes raised in accordance with names of male ancestors chosen for them before their birth, or they were given a male or mixed gender assignment because their family lacked or desired a son. Among the Kaska, parents sometimes raised a daughter to be

TABLE 4.1.

Tribes with Female Berdache Roles[1]

	Hunt/ men's work	Go to war	Cross-dress	Relations with women	Shamans	Notes
Arctic, Subarctic						
Aleut[2]						term for "woman transformed into a man"
Eskimo/Inuit (Alaska, Canada)	•			•	•	mixed gender status based on ancestral names; infants whose sex changes at birth
Pacific Eskimo/ Yupik	•					Koniag girls raised as boys; "man-woman" daughter of Chugach chief
Ingalik	•		•			
Kaska	•	•	•	•		raised in place of boy
Plains, Woodlands						
Cheyenne		•				
Illinois	•					"hunting women" who refused to marry
Northwest Coast						
Haisla	•		•			
Carrier, Haida	•		•			female who hunted, married to a man
Nootka		•				women who became warriors and chiefs after supernatural experiences
Tlingit		•				women war leaders
Quileute, Quinalt	•			•		
Columbia Plateau						
Thompson, Lillooet	•		•			
Okanagon	•					"women who were not interested in getting married and liked to hunt"
Sanpoil						"transvestism" denied but term for female homosexuality recorded
Kutenai	•	•	•	•	•	case of Qánqon
Flathead						terms for "lesbianism" and "homosexualism between women"
Klamath	•			•	•	same term for male role

"like a man." Such a woman hunted, wore masculine attire, rejected the sexual advances of boys, and "apparently . . . entered homosexual relationships."[99] In the nineteenth century, Dall related another pattern of female gender difference—marriage resistance. He described a Bering Strait Inuit woman who "despised marriage," preferred men's work, and formed a relationship with another woman.[100] A third mode of entrance into alternative gender status by females has been reported for the Ingalik, among whom female "transvestites," called "man

	Hunt/ men's work	Go to war	Cross- dress	Relations with women	Shamans	Notes
Great Basin						
Northern Paiute	•		•	•	•	same term for male role
Southern Paiute			•	•		
Shoshone	•		•			same term for male role; sometimes a result of visions
Ute	•		•			female berdache did women's work, never married
Washo						present
California						
Achumawi	•		•	•	•	result of dreams in one case
Atsugewi			•			
Yuki	•	•				
Wiyot	•		•			
Tolowa						present
Wappo					•	
Wintu				•		female homosexuality; some lived with men
Yana						present
Shasta					•	
Pomo	•					same term for male role
Nisenan						same term for male role, initiated as men, never married (to men?)
Mohave, Mari- copa, Quechan, Cocopa, Tipai, Yavapai	•	•	•	•	•	see chapter 7
Southwest						
Navajo	•	•				same term for male role
Apache		•		•	•	female homosexuality reported; case of Lozen
Papago	•	•				female berdache cowboy, never married (men?)
Pima						present but no special term
Zuni	•					same term for male role; initiated in kachina society

1. See Tribal Index for sources.
2. The absence of bullet entries here and in other cases below indicates that sources report an alternative female gender status, but no other data about the role.

pretenders," were identified in childhood when they insisted on dressing as boys and participating in men's activities.

Among the Northwest Coast Nootka, Drucker found that questions about "female transvestites," "almost invariably call forth tales of women who became

Figure 10. Lozen and Dahtetse, 1886. The Apache warrior woman and shaman Lozen and her companion Dahteste (top row, sixth and fifth figures from the right) among the Chiricahua prisoners enroute to Florida. Courtesy of the Arizona Historical Society/Tucson. AHS. #19,796.

famous war chiefs in ancient times, through a supernatural experience in which they receive medicines and rituals for strength and bravery."[101] Traditions of women war leaders also have been reported for the Tlingit.[102] In the Columbia Plateau, California, and Great Basin regions, third/fourth gender females were sometimes shamans. This association appears to have been strongest among the Mohave; *hwame:* were often powerful doctors specializing in sexually transmitted diseases (see below). Among the Navajo, female berdaches were reported to have been equal in number to males.[103]

An interesting case is that of the Chiricahua Apache "Woman Warrior" named Lozen, or Little Sister. The sister (or cousin) of Victorio, the famous Warm Springs chief, she received the power to heal wounds and locate the enemy as a result of a vision quest undertaken when she was a young woman. This made her invaluable on raiding and war parties. Her skills in riding, fighting, roping, and stealing horses and her bravery were legendary. Victorio reportedly said, "Lozen is as my right hand. Strong as a man, braver than most, and cunning in strategy, Lozen is a shield to her people."[104]

When Victorio died in battle in 1880, Lozen joined Geronimo's band and fought with him until his surrender in 1886. On more than one occasion she played a role as a mediator in negotiations with the army, together with a woman named Dahteste (Tah-des-te). Although Dahteste was married, she and Lozen appear to have been partners at this time and during the band's captivity in

Florida and then in Alabama (when Dahteste's husband left her). In a photograph of the Chiricahuas shortly after their capture, Lozen and Dahteste appear huddled together holding hands. Anthropologist Morris Opler was told, "They say that there were two women at Fort Sill who lived together and had sexual relations together." These were undoubtedly Lozen and Dahteste, although Lozen died in Alabama in June 1889, before the group was moved to Fort Sill. Dahteste later remarried but mourned Lozen's death the rest of her life.[105]

Lozen has received the same romanticized and heterosexualized treatment as Running Eagle and Woman Chief. Improbable tales are told of unrequited love and a vow never to marry.[106] The verifiable facts of her life support the conclusion that Lozen was a female berdache.

One reason for the frequency of female berdache roles in the West has been suggested by Blackwood, who points to the egalitarian nature of the tribes in which these roles appear. Many groups throughout the Great Basin, Southwest, and California subsisted on hunting-gathering and/or desert farming, and they lacked status distinctions based on wealth and hereditary leadership. This distinguishes them from the horse-based hunting-raiding tribes of the Plains and the semi-sedentary horticulturalists east of the Mississippi. Band-level, unstratified social organization appears to favor the presence of female berdache roles, perhaps because, as anthropologists often find, women have more autonomy in hunting-gathering societies. In such societies, marriage often represents a loss of freedom for women.[107] Resisting (or delaying) marriage therefore becomes a viable strategy for increasing autonomy in a way that it is not in stratified societies in which women are economically dependent on husbands and/or elders. Pursuing a female berdache lifestyle is a logical extension of this strategy.

Not every occurrence of female berdaches can be explained by this model, however. Northwest Coast natives were village-dwellers known for their three-tiered caste system and hereditary chieftainship. Yet female berdaches were present in some of these groups. Perhaps further investigation will reveal an association between women war leaders and membership in high status families in these tribes—the pattern of female leadership typical of eastern Algonkians. The mountain tribes of the Kutenai, Flathead, Kalispel, and Shoshone, who adopted a Plains-oriented lifestyle, are also exceptions to this model. It is likely that the presence of female berdache roles in these tribes predates the acquisition of the horse and was part of an earlier hunting-gathering pattern.

Female berdaches were often conceptualized as complementary to male berdaches. This is evidenced by informants who describe both roles as a set and especially by those native languages in which the same term is employed for both (for example, the Klamath, Northern Paiute, Pomo, Nisenan, Shoshone, Navaho, and Zuni). Females in third/fourth gender roles are often explained, like male berdaches, in terms of childhood preferences for dress and work roles.

The tribes with known female berdache roles share two other general characteristics. None of them were full-time horticultural communities.[108] (Only the Pueblos west of the Mississippi relied on agriculture to the extent that they established permanent villages.) Another commonality is the presence of a vision complex. Supernatural intervention was often credited with influencing women to become warriors and hunters. De Smet related a case of a Shoshone woman "who once dreamed that she was a man and killed animals in the chase. Upon waking, she assumed her husband's garments, took his gun and went out to test the virtue of her dream; she killed a deer. Since that time she has not left off man's costume; she goes on the hunts and on the war-path; by some fearless actions she has obtained the title of 'brave' and the privilege of admittance to the council of the chiefs."[109]

The early nineteenth-century Kutenai Qánqon-kámek-klaúla (Sitting in the Water Grizzly, shortened somewhat derisively to Qánqon) also illustrates the role of supernatural experience in the career of a female berdache. Initially, Qánqon claimed that her white husband had used supernatural power to transform her into a man—although her tribespeople refused to accept this fiction.[110] Her own claims of supernatural powers were taken more seriously, however, and she was remembered as a successful healer. She cross-dressed, carried a gun and a bow and arrows, and courted women. Eventually, Qánqon became a mediator between white traders and natives in the Pacific Northwest and appears to have originated prophecies that contributed to a pantribal revival movement.

As in the case of alternative roles for males, sexual object choice was not the primary defining characteristic for female berdache status. Nonetheless, female berdaches were sexually active, most often forming relationships with non-berdache women. What is known of female berdaches like Qánqon and the Mohave *hwame:* described below, however, suggests that many had heterosexual experiences, as well, and that their sexuality was more variable than that of male berdaches. In many cases, female berdaches are described simply as women who "never marry"—whether they were celibate or formed relationships with women instead is unstated. In these cases, it is difficult or impossible to separate the motivation of marriage resistance from desire for sex with women. On the other hand, the existence of specific terminology for female-female sexuality in some languages (see Glossary) indicates that the sexuality of female berdaches and women was not as inhibited nor as invisible as has been assumed.

Masahai Amatkwisai: "What Can Be the Matter with All These Women?"

All of the elements of female berdache roles just described—social, economic, spiritual, and sexual—are illustrated by the life of Masahai Amatkwisai, a female berdache or *hwame:* of the Mohave tribe in the late nineteenth century. Thanks to the 1937 account of the psychoanalytic anthropologist George Devereux, her case is frequently cited in the literature of anthropology and gender studies—and frequently misunderstood.[111]

Prior to the arrival of the Americans, the Mohave were a semi-sedentary, semi-horticultural people who lived along both banks of the Colorado River near the borders of California, Nevada, and Arizona. Today they reside primarily in two locations, the Fort Mohave Indian Reservation, near Needles, and the Colorado River Indian Reservation, at Parker. This is a consequence of a division that occurred in 1859, when most Mohaves relocated from Fort Mohave to Parker. A conservative faction remained at Needles but found itself cut-off from government services and plunged into poverty. In this period, the Mohave population decreased from an estimated 4,000 in 1872 to barely 1,000 in 1910.[112]

Masahai was born sometime in the 1850s (or 1860s) into the Huttoh branch of the tribe, which traditionally occupied the central Mohave Valley. Her family was among those who remained in the vicinity of Fort Mohave and Needles. Following Mohave patrilineal practices, she belonged to her father's clan, Nyoltc. With five brothers and two half-sisters, hers was a large and prominent family considered among the *pipa tahan*[a] or "best of people." Her aunt had been married to the famous chief Irataba. Masahai's full name was Masahai Matkwisa Manye:, which means "Alluring Young Girl Who is Pleasing."[113] It was actually a man's name, the kind a Mohave man might choose as a way of gaining luck in attracting the kind of women it describes. In fact, Masahi was quite lucky when it came to finding female lovers.

Of her early years, Devereux reports nothing. Upon arriving at adulthood, she is said to have never menstruated, although she looked feminine and had well-developed breasts.[114] She did not cross-dress, or at least not routinely. Devereux was told that she wore short skirts "like a man," which could either mean that she wore a variation of the men's breechcloth or, conversely, a variation of the traditional knee-length woman's bark skirt, but not the full-length "Mother Hubbard" dress that many Mohave women had adopted. The Mohave referred to her as "he" (in English) and considered her a *hwame:* (although today when referring to her they say "she").[115]

It is not clear if she underwent formal initiation as most *alyha:* did. Her dreams gave her the power to cure sexual diseases. This power also made her lucky in love, as well. Through her income from doctoring, her hard work as a farmer and hunter, and, later, through prostitution, she had enough money to be considered prosperous in Mohave terms: she could afford shoes.[116]

Masahai's first wife was considered very pretty—so pretty that men kept teasing her and trying to seduce her. They would say, "Why do you want a transvestite for your husband who has no penis and pokes you with the finger?"[117] Unimpressed, Masahai's wife replied, "That is all right for me, if I wish to remain with her." Yet another suitor tried to persuade her by saying, "She has no penis, she is just like you are. If you remain with her, no 'other' man will want you afterwards."[118] Although Masahai's wife asserted that her partner was an excellent provider, she decided to leave Masahai for this man. But finding this husband less satisfying, she eventually returned to Masahai.

In the meantime, Masahai had begun attending dances. She sat with the men and brazenly described her wife's genitals, while flirting with girls—all typical male behavior. This earned her an obscene nickname, Hithpan Kudhape (Split Vulva, which refers to one of the sexual positions used by *hwame:.*) It was "such a bad insult that no one dared called her that to her face."[119] Eventually, the relentless teasing of Masahai's wife led to their breakup.

Masahai's next wife was also teased, and a rivalry developed between her and her predecessor. Masahai was unperturbed. "Never mind what she tells you. She wants to come back to me, that is all." Eventually the two women met at a dance and a fight erupted between them (urged on by men). Masahai and her former wife's husband watched serenely, as befit their masculine pride, until a bystander pushed the combatants onto Masahai and all three rolled around in the dirt. Some time later, this wife also left Masahai.

Disappointed and resentful, Masahai painted her face like a warrior and took out her bow and arrows. However, instead of going to the house of her second wife's seducer to seek revenge, she went to a nearby camp and began courting yet another woman.

> The married woman she wished to visit leered at her and insultingly spoke to her the way one woman speaks to another woman: "She thinks maybe that the bow and arrows suit her. She thinks she is a man." These remarks did not appear to ruffle Sahaykwisa: [Masahai]. She calmly replied: "Yes, I can shoot game for you," and then left. We think she must have felt encouraged, because we say that if a girl or woman insults her suitor, he can be pretty certain of winning her in the end.[120] A few days later Sahaykwisa: visited this woman once more and asked her to grind corn for her, which is precisely what a bride is supposed to do the moment she reaches her new husband's camp. Surprisingly enough, the woman complied and ground corn for the hwame:. The news of this spread like wildfire all over the reservation, and people said: "I bet she will get herself another wife. What can be the matter with these women to fall for a hwame:?"[121]

Indeed, when Masahai called upon the woman a third time, she left her husband and eloped with the *hwame:*. The husband, a 35-year-old man named Haq'au, did nothing at that time. "He could not very well fight with a transvestite," Devereux was told.[122] Masahai lived with her third wife on the southern outskirts of Needles. (One of these wives is identified in a 1911 census as "Owch kwita-hiyoova, female wife of Masahai Kwisa.")[123]

Masahai's ability to obtain wives was believed to be related to her shamanism and power to cure venereal diseases. According to Devereux's informants, "She was a good provider, worked hard and took great pleasure in bedecking her wives with beads and pretty clothes."[124] While female shamans were believed to be powerful, *hwame:* were especially sought after because their ability to treat venereal disease was considered one of the most powerful skills of all.[125]

Even so, Masahai's third wife also left her and returned to her husband. Masahai again painted herself like a warrior and stood on the outskirts of her former wife's camp on the northern edge of Needles. This behavior was considered synonymous with that of a witch. Haq'au, her former wife's husband, ambushed her in the bushes and raped her, proclaiming that he would "show her what a real penis can do."[126] After this, Masahai did not take a wife again. The Mohave believed she had intercourse with the ghosts of her former wives, whom she had bewitched, in her dreams.

Following her rape, Masahai began to drink and to "crave" men. According to Devereux, she became a *kamalo:y,* or lewd woman, and engaged in prostitution. This began when she was around the age of twenty-five. Prostitution was not the defining characteristic of *kamalo:y,* however. Rather, such women were understood as being subject to sexual desires beyond their conscious control. For this reason, no moral judgment was implied by the term *kamalo:y.* Nonetheless, the more extreme behavior of some *kamalo:y* was cited as the reason for sexual assaults on them.

In his 1937 article, Devereux treats Masahai's rape as the event triggering her involvement in heterosexuality and prostitution, and much of his subsequent analysis of her "deviancy" is predicated on her assumed psychological reaction to it. However, in a later article he reported that Masahai "occasionally supported her 'wife' by prostituting herself to white men," which would mean that the prostitution *preceded* the rape.[127] Nor does "occasionally" sound like the compulsive behavior of a *kamalo:y.* More likely, Masahai's life changed as the result of several factors, of which the trauma of rape was one. Mohaves typically do not view rape as categorically different from any number of ways in which an individual might be forced to do something against his or her will. Since being the victim of rape was not stigmatizing in and of itself, the source of trauma for Masahai would have been the negation of her identity as an *hwame:* and the disrespect shown her by her assailant.[128]

Eventually Masahai fell in love with Tcuhum, a man of her own clan twenty years her senior. But Tcuhum refused to have sex with her, saying, "You are a man."[129] Masahai used her powers as a shaman to bewitch him. He died without ever naming her as his bewitcher, which Mohave interpret as meaning that he secretly did love her. Masahai then became lovers with his son, Suhura:ye, who was about 40 or 45 years old, and his friend, Ilykutcemidho: of the O:otc clan, who was about 50.

Masahai had now crossed the line between doctoring and witchcraft. Consequently, deviant behavior was expected of her. According to Devereux, "Like most Mohave bewitchers she began to look for a chance of being killed, for only a murdered shaman will join the ghosts of his victims in the other world."[130] Accusations of witchcraft were widespread within the Yuman tribes in this period.[131] Kelly has documented fourteen cases of individuals being killed for witchcraft among the Cocopa between 1880 and 1945.[132] Contemporary Mohave recall several infamous cases of witchcraft from the turn of the century and believe that the witches of that period were particularly powerful. Hivsu: Tupom[a], Devereux's primary informant for Masahai's life, was a confessed witch who had also committed incest.[133]

Masahai and her two male lovers traveled together some 30 miles north of Needles, where they planned to work for a living. On the trip, Masahai got drunk and openly boasted of killing Tcuhum with her witchcraft. Angered, her two lovers picked her up and threw her into the Colorado River, where she drowned. Her body was found two weeks later near Needles, and Hivsu: Tupo:m[a] helped give her a traditional cremation. The best estimate is that this occurred in the 1890s. Masahai was approximately 45 years old.[134]

It is important to note what is missing from Devereux's case history—details of Masahai's ordinary life, her upbringing, her shamanic practice, her relations with her family. Another reading might recognize her as an individual with an identity crisis in an historical period in which her tribe was under extreme duress. She seems to have experimented with all of the alternative identities for Mohave women—*hwame:*, shaman, *kamalo:y,* wife. The only female role that Masahai did not fulfill was that of mother.

Devereux's analysis of Masahai's life history has all those elements of orthodox psychoanalysis that make it odious. He portrays her as a maladjusted, self-destructive, violence-prone lesbian. Citing no evidence, he speculates that she defensively rejected her family before they could reject her.[135] He compares her demise with that of Greek heroes: "The harder these tragic personages struggle against their character, which is also destiny, the deeper they sink into the quicksand of their fate."[136] Her lesbianism was a reaction against her "real" femininity. Her self-destructive urges led her to provoke violence against her. She is to be blamed for her own victimization.

In fact, three of Masahai's brothers, numerous nieces and nephews, and one of her former wives were alive at the time of Devereux's research in the early 1930s. Some of these relatives were neighbors of Devereux's interpreter and key informant, Agnes Sevilla, but Devereux made no attempt to interview them, and he was dissuaded by Sevilla from talking to the former wife: "She is still quite touchy about that episode and does not like to be reminded of it."[137]

Quite a different picture of Masahai Matkiwsa: emerges from the memories of contemporary Mohave, including descendants of her relatives. She is recalled primarily as a powerful shaman who specialized in love magic, and less for her status as a *hwame:*. Her demise is considered the result of a shamanic practice that was, if anything, too successful. Mohave shamans seek to capture the souls of others to accompany them when they transition to the afterlife. According to contemporary Mohave, Masahai "got tired of this life." Since she had captured so many souls through her shamanism she was ready to die and therefore sought her death. As Devereux explains, the shaman

> segregates these dead souls 'in his place,' their souls visiting him at night and, if of the suitable sex, having intercourse with him (or her). Eventually he will come to fear that another witch may kidnap his retinue of souls, and/or he will long for their constant presence. As a result, he will taunt the relatives of his victims, by confessing to witchcraft, whereupon the witch is killed. It must be stated that a witch only kills those whom he loves.[138]

In this regard, witchcraft represents both the excess and the limit of Mohave sexuality. As we will see in chapter 7, there were few other safeguards against antisocial forms of sexual desire—lust, compulsiveness, sexual jealousy. The witch served as the negative example of unrestrained desire—an individual whose sexuality was out of control—and was subject to avoidance and other sanctions by the community.

In the end, Devereux's own evidence makes it clear why Masahai's behavior cannot be interpreted as abnormal and viewed as a symptom of her sexual-gender identity—her behavior conformed in every way to Mohave expectations for a *hwame:*, a shaman, and, finally, a witch. While these were, indeed, ambivalent roles in Mohave culture, they were not marginal. If anything such individuals enjoyed a surplus, not a deficit, of the power all Mohave aspired to obtain—the skills and luck bestowed by dreams.

CONCLUSION

In this chapter, three patterns of alternative female identities and roles were examined. Among tribes on the eastern seaboard, the role of *sunksquaw,* or woman chief, provided an opportunity for certain women to enter positions of leadership and participate in war. In the Plains region, several cases of women warriors and chiefs have been documented, along with the institution of manly-hearted women among the Blackfoot/Piegan, which was shown to be similar to the role of the Algonkian *sunksquaw.* Female berdache roles, on the other hand, were concentrated primarily among tribes west of the Rocky Mountains. Their occurrence was shown to be related to the egalitarian social structure of the tribes in this region and the importance of women's subsistence activities. In these predominantly gathering and hunting societies women were less dependent on opposite-sex marriage and could, by becoming berdaches, forgo it altogether. In sum, throughout North America role variation, alternative identities, and individual differences were, in varying forms, a part of women's lives in every native society.

FIVE

TWO-SPIRIT PEOPLE: GAY AMERICAN INDIANS TODAY

THE WHITE MAN'S DISEASE

When the Twin Rainbow Drum and Dancers stepped out at the 1992 San Francisco Lesbian/Gay Pride Parade it looked as if a tornado had scooped up a powwow in Oklahoma and plopped it down on the other side of a postcolonial rainbow. The Gay American Indians organization (GAI) had been marching under the banner "First Gay Americans" since the 1970s, but their appearance that year was their most visible—and extravagant—yet. Over twenty members, plus friends and family, had been rehearsing for several weeks, creating costumes, props, instruments, dance steps, and songs. The symbol of the San Francisco parade is the rainbow flag, and the GAI group embraced it as their own. The dancers were bedecked in rainbow everything—flags, headdresses, shawls, and crowns all decorated with Day-Glo feathers in rainbow arrays.

As the group made its way up Market Street, Twin Eagle dancers were encircled by Swan dancers, while Rainbow Maidens danced around them all, waving rainbow staffs. Finally, a set of Pony dancers pranced outside the circle. The Rainbow Drummers brought up the rear. GAI co-founder Randy Burns, wearing a chief's headdress in rainbow feathers reaching down to his knees,

Figure 11. GAI in front of banner, 1990. Gay American Indians organization marching in Lesbian/ Gay Pride Parade in San Francisco. Photograph by Will Roscoe.

alternately strutted for the onlookers and helped a GAI member in a wheelchair navigate the trolley tracks that carve up San Francisco's thoroughfare. The group was cheered wildly all the way to the Civic Center, where a fifteen-foot-high tipi had been set up to receive them.

The Twin Rainbow Drum and Dancers were emblematic of the evolution of consciousness that occurred among lesbian, gay, bisexual, and transgender natives in the 1980s and 1990s. For some, this took the form of a gesture to the past and the revival of alternative gender traditions. The San Francisco Twin Rainbow Drum and Dancers were staking a claim to another vital dimension of Native American life—the postmodern, pantribal powwow. Since the early twentieth century, powwows often have been the source for creative, sometimes idiosyncratic expressions of "Indianness" and Indian identity, and with them Indian unity and political consciousness.

The appearance of the Rainbow Dancers also marked a turning point in the politics of the San Francisco Indian community. Two days earlier, the group had premiered their costumes and dances at a community meeting during which articles of incorporation for a new community center were presented and a name selected. It would be called the Indian Center of All Nations (ICAN). The name held special significance because of its emphasis on inclusiveness. In 1990, San Francisco's American Indian Center had been forced to close its doors after years of alleged mismanagement. Some of its staff had been hostile to GAI and openly homophobic; on occasion lesbian and gay natives had been refused services. Consequently, following the center's demise, local lesbian and gay natives were prominent in efforts to create a new center that would be more responsive to the community, a center open to Indians of *all* nations and, as its by-laws spelled out, all genders—that of "two-spirits" as well as women and men.

The founding of ICAN represented the culmination of a local struggle by gay natives for acceptance and visibility that began in 1975 when Barbara Cameron (Hunkpapa) and Randy Burns (Northern Paiute) founded Gay American Indians.[1] Before that time native people who dared to come out of the closet encountered homophobia of surprising vehemence. "Before Alcatraz," recalls Maurice Kenny (Mohawk), referring to the occupation of that island by Indian activists in 1969, "it was just about impossible to stand up and say who you were. If you had a job you'd get fired. Your family might disown you. You certainly would be ridiculed."[2] Or worse. As one of the primary contacts for lesbian and gay natives throughout the country, Randy Burns has collected some horrifying stories: "We've even had incidents where gay Indian people have been murdered, sadistically, on our reservations. When you read it in the local news it doesn't say 'gay Indian person,' but other contacts we have say, 'That brother was gay.'" In the early 1990s, attacks on gay men at the Pine Ridge Reservation in South Dakota resulted in at least one death.[3]

When not confronted with open hostility, gay native people have encountered silence and invisibility. As Erna Pahe (Navajo) explains, "Even when I go back home now, we never talk about it. It's the activities or ceremonies that our family is going to. The spiritual way is always put as a priority. Your personal side of life is a little different." Mindful of this, writer Paula Gunn Allen (Laguna Pueblo/Sioux) debated for a year before publishing her groundbreaking essay on Native American lesbianism, "Beloved Women," in 1981. "I decided I could take the risk—I don't live there [on the reservation]. But there are young gay Indians who do and they have to hear this."

Burns and others credit "the Christian influence with our people" above all with undermining traditional acceptance of gender difference and homosexuality. In fact, the "disappearing" of the berdache was the end result of actions by countless government officials, school teachers, missionaries, and local whites. Indian agents did not hesitate to regulate the most intimate aspects of native lives. On some reservations as related in chapter 2, berdaches were rounded up, their was hair cut, and their role was suppressed. In government- and church-run boarding schools children with third or fourth gender tendencies were quickly spotted and severely sanctioned. Indeed, many of the punishments used at these schools had the effect of completely inverting traditional values—runaway boys, for example, were forced to wear girls' dresses.[4] The sign of a role once authorized by tribal mythology and fully integrated into tribal society became a mark of humiliation.

Even without the inculcation of anti-gay attitudes by the various agents of assimilation, native people could not avoid being influenced by white values. Once prejudices were acquired, the isolation of Indian communities provided few occasions for them to be challenged. For many natives today, homosexuality is completely "other," a phenomenon imagined to belong to the urban white man and categorized with the other catastrophes attributed to him—disease, alcoholism, emotional dysfunction. "We do not want to receive your publications," wrote the editor of the Indian magazine Akwesasne Notes to the gay journal RFD in 1977, "because they encourage a kind of behavior which our elders consider not normal and a detriment to our way of life."[5] Such attitudes are held by leaders and traditionalists who, in other contexts, acknowledge the traditional acceptance of gender difference. However, given the associations of homosexuality as constructed by Western medical and psychiatric discourse—as weakness, depravity, and compulsion—it is not surprising that some natives fail to perceive any connection between it and traditional third and fourth genders.

Despite these obstacles, GAI grew from a social club in the 1970s into an organization of several hundred members in the 1980s, offering social and support services. Its efforts in lobbying Indian, gay, and non-gay agencies to improve their outreach to gay natives eventually paid off. "It's taken more generations for us to get to where we're at now," said Pahe, chair of the GAI board of directors in 1985, "but we've found a new tool now and that tool is speaking out." Even so, when the group celebrated its tenth anniversary, it was still the only formal organization of lesbian and gay natives in North America.

That would change in a dramatic way within a few short years. Before the decade was over, GAI was joined by gay native groups in major cities throughout the United States and Canada. An international network of lesbian and gay native activists, professionals, writers, and artists emerged, and a movement to revive multiple gender traditions took form. GAI and writers like Allen and Kenny had laid the groundwork for this growth. But the event that triggered it had its origin far outside native communities: the HIV/AIDS epidemic.

In San Francisco, this occurred in 1987 when Jodi Harry (Miwok), one of GAI's founding members, received a diagnosis of AIDS. Until then, no one in the GAI community was known to have had AIDS. As Bart Amarillas (Pima), a GAI board member who himself died of AIDS, told me, "I thought AIDS was a white boy's disease." Randy Burns recalls, "We came here to openly express our self-love and self-acceptance as homosexuals. . . . Like our [non-Indian] gay and lesbian counterparts, we were all young and oversexed and that made our community vulnerable to the AIDS virus." That spring day when Jodi was diagnosed he went home to his small apartment on Haight Street and committed suicide. His body was found by members of the organization several days later.

Jodi was not the first Native American in San Francisco with AIDS. Due to serious underreporting and nonreporting it is almost certain that other Native Americans had already died. But Jodi was the first victim of the epidemic widely known in the Bay Area Indian community. That was the first shock. The second was that he took his own life instead of turning to the community for support.

GAI members founded the Indian AIDS Project soon after Jodi Harry's death and dedicated their work to his memory and that of another member who died in 1987, Herbie Jeans (Navajo/Otoe). Given the circumstances, no one noted at the time that a landmark had been passed. After ten years, suddenly there was a second project involving gay Native Americans in San Francisco. Soon there would be new organizations, as well, drawing in new volunteers and producing new community leaders. Eventually, volunteer programs would be superseded by funded programs with professional staffs. In 1988, the American Indian AIDS Institute was founded by members of GAI and the community to provide educational, advocacy, and support services. In 1994 it was joined by the Native American AIDS Project, which, by 1997, was serving some 120 clients in San Francisco.[6]

In Minneapolis, similar developments occurred. American Indian Gays and Lesbians (AIGL) was founded in 1987 with the goal of creating a social structure for gay natives, based in traditional cultural values. At its peak, AIGL had members representing some thirty different tribes. The organizers soon realized, however, the need to commit themselves to AIDS-related programs. As members became active in the Minnesota American Indian AIDS Task Force, the National Indian AIDS Media Consortium, and other projects, AIGL took a "sabbatical" in the early 1990s. In 1997, the group reformed to sponsor the Tenth Annual International Two-Spirit Gathering (discussed later in this chapter).[7]

HIV/AIDS issues also were a priority from the beginning for Gays and Lesbians of the First Nations, founded in Toronto in 1989. Among its stated goals, the group sought to improve the quality of life of "aboriginal persons infected and affected by HIV/AIDS." By 1992, the organization had three hundred members from sixteen Indian and Inuit nations. With funding from both local and national sources, it maintains an office, holds talking circles and healing circles, organizes image awards and drag shows, publishes a newsletter (with significant space devoted to HIV information), and sponsors a Two Spirits Softball Team, as well as offering HIV/AIDS services. Also in 1989, activists formed WeWah and BarChee-Ampe in New York City.[8] Like the Toronto group, WeWah and BarCheeAmpe moved quickly to address AIDS-related issues in the native community, helping to establish the HIV/AIDS Project in 1990 at the American Indian Community House.[9] In 1991, it hosted "Two Spirits and HIV: A Conference for the Health of

Gay and Lesbian Native Americans," and the following year it participated in demonstrations against celebrations of the quincentennial of Columbus's arrival in the Americas.

Other organizations founded in this period include Nichiwakan, in Winnipeg, Canada; Tahoma Two-Spirits, based in Seattle; Vancouver Two-Spirits, in British Columbia; and Nations of the Four Directions, in San Diego. By the mid-1990s, organizations of gay/lesbian/two-spirit natives also were active in Washington, D.C. and Nashville, Tennessee.

Native activists and organizations who have sought to prevent the spread of HIV in their communities have encountered a number of obstacles. In San Francisco, Randy Burns and the Indian AIDS Project discovered that neither local nor national health authorities, and none of the nonprofit agencies serving individuals with AIDS, were collecting statistics concerning Native Americans. Natives were routinely being counted as "white," "Latino/Hispanic," "black," or "other." No one knew how many native people in San Francisco and the Bay Area had acquired the disease, or what, if any, services they were using. New York organizers encountered similar problems.[10]

The Centers for Disease Control (CDC) did not list American Indians (or Asian Americans) as separate racial groups for HIV and AIDS reporting until 1988. Federally funded studies in Seattle and Los Angeles have since confirmed the serious underreporting of native AIDS deaths. Ron Rowell, executive director of the National Native American AIDS Prevention Center, estimates that total native AIDS cases may be three to ten times greater than CDC statistics.[11] Despite the lack of adequate statistics, factors such as injection drug use, alcohol use, transmission of other STDs, and a high rate of bisexuality indicate that native populations are significantly at risk.[12] A 1990 study in San Francisco found that 15 percent of Indian men who had sex with men reported daily alcohol use and 73 percent used condoms only sometimes. Some 68 percent of respondents were unemployed.[13]

By mid-1997, a total of 1,677 cases of AIDS had been officially documented among Native Americans. In San Francisco, Randy Burns estimates that over sixty members of the GAI community have died from AIDS. Routes of transmission are predominantly male to male (50 percent) but injection drug use is a factor in 34 percent of all native cases (compared to 17 percent of white cases), and 14 percent of native men with AIDS report both sex with men and injection drug use. Infection rates among native women, at 16 percent of all native cases, are similar to those of other women of color but over two times those of white women. In 1997, the clients of the Native American AIDS Project in San Francisco were 25 to 30 percent heterosexual, with an increasing number of injection drug users and/or commercial sex workers.[14]

The efforts of activists and professionals throughout the country have slowly convinced health authorities and agencies to monitor, study, and serve native populations. The National Native American AIDS Prevention Center (NNAAPC) in Oakland, founded in 1987, has played a key role in this process. Funded by the Centers for Disease Control, NNAAPC provides education, training, and support services to natives and native organizations throughout the United States. The Center operates a telephone hotline and funds satellite programs including media and information services and case management programs.[15]

Native people with HIV face a variety of special problems. On many reservations, irrational fears of AIDS combined with homophobia create an environment of extraordinary hostility. Many reservation Indians depend on the Indian Health Service (IHS), which has long been criticized for its quality of care. Until recently, the staffs of these small hospitals and clinics received little or no training in HIV treatment and its emotional and social impacts. In 1991, the AIDS coordinator for IHS admitted that due to severe underfunding "decisions are being made at facilities such as 'Do we do this elective surgery or that gallbladder surgery?' and 'Do we get pentamidine for an AIDS patient or give chemotherapy to someone with cancer?'"[16] Five years later comprehensive AIDS care was still not available through IHS.[17] Confidentiality at these facilities has been a problem as well. In small tribal communities, personal information can quickly become common knowledge. In 1990, a (non-gay) Lakota man sued the Indian Health Service after medical information was released to his employer, the Rosebud Sioux Tribe of South Dakota, which fired him.[18]

Urban Indians with HIV face other difficulties. Urban Indian health clinics typically require proof of tribal enrollment, which many mixed blood, dislocated natives, and adopted natives lack. Those who do access these clinics often encounter unveiled hostility. A 1990 survey of clients and counselors in Indian chemical dependency treatment centers found extremely negative attitudes toward gays and bisexuals.[19] Those natives unable to access Indian services typically depend on Medicare or Medicaid, but they tend to avoid Western medical care except for emergencies. When they do seek services from mainstream institutions they often encounter racism and cultural insensitivity. Native people with AIDS all too often show up in emergency rooms desperately ill with advanced opportunistic infections. Native women with AIDS face additional difficulties. Many programs are designed for male populations, while women with HIV have special needs for child care, family services, transportation services, and respite.[20]

In contrast, when comprehensive case management services are delivered by native providers, client retention rates are as high as 90 percent.[21] The Ahalaya Project in Oklahoma City has developed a service delivery model that integrates traditional healing, referral services, emergency food and shelter services, health-oriented case management, secondary prevention services (alcohol and drug treatment), and social and psychological support.[22] This model is now the basis for comprehensive case management services funded through NNAAPC at ten urban and rural sites throughout the United States.[23]

Other obstacles are culture-specific. Among Navajos, the mention of death or even the name of a dead person are carefully avoided; to talk about death is considered tantamount to wishing it on someone. Nonetheless, HIV/AIDS had become a distinct reality on the reservation, with 56 diagnosed cases by 1994.[24] Created to address the need for education and services, the Navajo AIDS Network began as a volunteer organization in Chinle, Arizona in 1990. In 1992, it helped organize the Navajo Nation AIDS Network Conference in Gallup. The following year it received funding to provide case management services as well as prevention programs and sex education. The organization has successfully encouraged medicine men to treat tribal members with HIV.[25]

Other tribal and reservation organizations that have undertaken culture-specific AIDS/HIV initiatives include Chugachmiut in Alaska (where natives account for 17 percent of all reported AIDS cases), the Tuscarora tribe of North Carolina, and the Swampy Cree Tribal Council and the Cree National Tribal Health Centre in Canada, which have produced brochures in English, Ojibway, Cree, Dene, and Dakota. In upstate New York, education and support services are now provided to each of the six nations of the Iroquois confederacy by a satellite project of the American Indian Community House. The California Rural Indian Health Board has sponsored gatherings of medicine people to discuss the use of traditional healing methods to prevent and treat HIV infection, and in 1994, the San Diego County American Indian AIDS Task Force organized a retreat to provide traditional spiritual services for natives living with HIV/AIDS and other conditions—some 367 individuals attended. Many agencies, such as the San Francisco Native American AIDS Project, now have traditional healers on staff or available by referral.

Native safe sex educators often face challenges that require creativity and humor. Earl Polk, an AIDS prevention specialist with the Yukon-Kuskokwim Health Corporation in Bethel, Alaska, explains the difficulties he faces in talking about condoms to audiences that speak little or no English:

> We had a hard time figuring out what to call a rubber in Yupik, because we didn't have a word. And I was just looking around, I was calling them *aliiman,* or glove; or *kaapuaq',* the little hair net that old ladies wear. And I'd call them *malagg'aayaq,* which is a beaver hat. I'd call them everything. Then I began to ask people to come up with a Yupik word that would effectively describe what a rubber is. And we finally came up with "*uc'uum caqua,*" which means the man's pouch, male-part-pouch. And it does the job.[26]

Doctors and translators seeking to provide HIV education to Inuktitut (Inuit) speakers devised the acronym ASAPI by using the first syllable of three words that mean "from the blood, the things which protect, are taken away."[27]

Other problems associated with the epidemic are not unique to gay native people. As HIV/AIDS programs and organizations become increasingly professionalized to obtain funding, there is a tendency to "de-gay" the disease. Gay/ two-spirit native men have had to continually advocate to ensure that they are represented and served by these organizations. In 1994, the only program in Los Angeles addressing HIV prevention was administered by the American Indian Clinic, yet it did not offer gay-specific prevention programs and had no gay staff members. In Oklahoma City (which has the Indian Health Service's largest number of HIV/AIDS cases) only three percent of all prevention funding in the county was targeted for gay men of color, and a single project struggled to provide services for gay/two-spirit natives.[28] To address this and other concerns, a group of activists from around the country formed Positively Native in 1993, a national organization "for, by and about Native American Indians, Alaskan Natives, and Native Hawaiians infected with HIV/AIDS."[29] Lobbying on a national level on behalf of gay native men with HIV was also undertaken by the Campaign for Fairness, a coalition of gay men of color co-chaired by Anguksuar (Richard LaFortune [Yup'ik]) in the early 1990s.

Of course, the disease itself is a constant source of setbacks. At least half of the individuals who were members of the GAI board of directors when I began working with the organization in 1984 are now dead, and not only from HIV but other causes all too typical of the conditions of native people in North America. Problems of morale and continuity of leadership, as well as the need to continually renew consensus, plague efforts to address HIV and AIDS in native communities. Nonetheless, by the mid-1990s the efforts of native activists and professionals to improve services to their communities was having measurable results. Over one hundred prevention education efforts had been established and 12 case management programs were serving natives throughout the United States and Canada.[30] According to CDC reports, AIDS deaths decreased by 32 percent among American Indians and Alaskan Natives in the first half of 1996, a greater decline than among any other ethnicity.[31]

In the late 1990s, priorities for native HIV/AIDS activists, educators, and service providers include improving government and agency awareness of native populations and their cultures; guaranteeing confidentiality; ensuring the inclusion of tribal governments, organizations, and urban Indian agencies in legislation to fund HIV/AIDS programs; gaining access for natives to quality care and state-of-the-art treatments; offering testing in rural areas; and obtaining insurance coverage for traditional healing. With the scheduled dismantling of the Indian Health Service and its replacement by tribally operated facilities and managed health care programs funded by block grants, the attainment of these goals is far from certain.

The epidemic has had some indirect consequences of a more positive nature. The fight against HIVAIDS is of necessity a fight against homophobia. This has prompted a coming out process in both urban and reservation communities.[32] Gay native people, many of them professionals who had hesitated to come out before the epidemic, are now respected leaders in gay and AIDS-related organizations. As Ron Rowell notes, "If we're not visible, we can never get people to talk about what's important."[33] On a personal level, many gay Indian men stricken by the disease have been welcomed back into their extended families. This coming out process has included lesbians as well as gay men. Erna Pahe in San Francisco; Carole LaFavor, Yako Myers, and Sharon Day in Minneapolis; and Leota Lone Dog in New York City have been tireless HIV/AIDS educators and advocates.[34]

The community leaders and professionals addressing the AIDS epidemic today do so with a special appreciation of the impact disease can have on a community. As Rowell observes, "Our struggle is—as it has been for so long—a struggle for survival as a people. An epidemic that primarily affects those individuals in their most fecund years can destroy a tribe's future. It has happened in our history, and it can happen again. However, we are tough, and we are determined. We will survive the AIDS challenge. We have 30,000 years of experience in America to help us do so. We know an enemy when we see one."[35]

FROM GAY TO TWO-SPIRIT

While the need to address the HIV/AIDS epidemic led gay native organizations throughout North America to adopt similar goals and programs in the 1990s, consensus also emerged around issues of identity and self-definition. Much of it derived from lesbian and gay natives' growing awareness of alternative gender traditions in their historical cultures. Some of this awareness was based on memory—that is, orally transmitted knowledge of family and tribal traditions. Much of it, however, was based on history—knowledge recovered through ethnohistorical research. Two books had a significant impact in fostering this awareness: Walter Williams's *The Spirit and the Flesh* (1986) and GAI's *Living the Spirit* (1988). Both have been widely read, and their impact on lesbian and gay native organizers in the late 1980s is evident. The WeWah and BarCheeAmpe group in New York, for example, was named after two figures described in *Living the Spirit*.

For Lee Staples (Ojibway), helping lesbian and gay native people recover their spiritual traditions was a primary motivation in founding American Indian Gays and Lesbians. "When I was drinking I thought all there was to our lives as gays was the bar scene and sex," he said in a 1990 interview, "but to explain our lives as Indian gays and lesbians is to look at our personal journeys. It has much more depth on a spiritual level."[36] Among the goals of AIGL was to celebrate and remember "our roles as gay and lesbian people in our traditional indigenous cultures" and to reclaim "the spirituality of our cultures." Gays and Lesbians of the First Nations in Toronto also included the reclaiming of "the sacred role of 2-Spirited people" among its goals.

In 1988, AIGL hosted "The Basket and the Bow: A Gathering of Lesbian and Gay Native Americans" at the Minneapolis American Indian Center. (The name referred to the traditional test for gender identity given in some tribes, described by Clyde Hall at a planning meeting for the gathering held during the 1987 lesbian/gay March on Washington.) The gathering was attended by over 60 participants from Canada and the United States. Workshops addressed topics ranging from chemical dependency to AIDS, coming out, and relationships. A women's pipe ceremony and a give-away were also held. The gatherings became annual events, now called the International Two-Spirit Gathering. Location and responsibility for coordination has shifted among groups throughout North America. By the fourth gathering, held in Eugene, Oregon in 1991, the event included a powwow, talking circles, sweats, a give-away, a fry bread contest, and a salmon feast as well as various workshops. Subsequent gatherings have been held in Arizona (1993), Kansas (1994), New Brunswick (1995), and British Columbia (1996). Spiritual practices have been an important feature of all these events, along with a commitment to a drug- and alcohol-free environment.[37]

Another important series of events was inaugurated by Beverly Little Thunder (Lakota). In 1985, Little Thunder and her lover had come out at a Lakota sun dance and were asked to leave. The dance leaders told them they should "go have their own ceremony for their own kind." Little Thunder took their advice to heart and organized a wimmins sundance, which has been repeated in subsequent years.[38]

By the end of the 1980s, these developments had coalesced into a cultural revival movement centered on recovery of berdache traditions and practices.[39] At the third annual gathering held in Winnipeg, Canada, in 1990, participants embraced the term "two-spirit" (sometimes rendered as "two-spirited") as an alternative to both berdache and gay. The term is the English translation of the Anishinabe/Ojibway term *niizh manitoag*.[40] Its use quickly spread. In 1991, a group of students from the University of California at Berkeley (Lori Levy, Michael Beauchemin, and Gretchen Vogel) produced a short documentary entitled *Two-Spirit People,* featuring native scholars, writers, and community leaders using the term. In 1992, Gays and Lesbians of the First Nations in Toronto changed its named to 2-Spirited People of the 1st Nations. Sue Beaver (Mohawk) explains the philosophy underlying the change: "We believe there exists the spirits of both man and woman within. We look at ourselves as being very gifted. The Creator created very special beings when he created two-spirited people. He gave certain individuals two spirits. We're a special people, and that's been denied since contact with the Europeans. . . . What heterosexuals achieve in marriage, we achieve within ourselves."[41]

In 1993, at a conference entitled "Revisiting the North American Berdache, Empirically and Theoretically" participants expressed a strong preference for use of "two-spirit." This was followed by an article by anthropologist Sue-Ellen Jacobs and native scholar Wesley Thomas that argued that use of the term "berdache" perpetuated "colonial discourse." "Two-spirit" was recommended as a replacement not only for the "archaic term" berdache, but also as the preferred term for contemporary natives "who are lesbian, gay, transgendered and transsexual."[42]

The rapid adoption of the term is striking. When I interviewed lesbian- and gay-identified natives in 1985, they all expressed discomfort with the European meanings of the term "berdache" and most used "gay" to refer to historic alternative gender roles and persons (although Paula Gunn Allen made an argument for using "dyke" and "queer"). Members of alternative gender roles, as Randy Burns explained, were "our traditional gay Indian people." In an article in *Out/Look* magazine in 1988, I cited this statement and other examples of how native lesbians and gay men spoke of these historic roles. At that time, "gay" seemed the best alternative to "berdache"—it suggested a lifestyle and an identity as well as a sexuality. By making the qualification "*traditional* gay role," the native scholars and writers I spoke to acknowledged the differences between past and present identities.[43] No one at that time claimed to be a "berdache." They cited many traits they felt they shared with "berdaches" but pointed to the spiritual responsibilities of the role as a key difference between it and contemporary identities.

After the Winnipeg gathering this attitude changed, and the emphasis shifted from differences to continuity. In a 1992 article, psychologist and educator Terry Tafoya (Taos/Warm Springs) alternated seamlessly between past and present tense when using the new term:

> The status of the Two-Spirited person was valued in many Native communities, since an ordinary male sees the world through male eyes, and an ordinary female sees the world through female eyes. However, a Two-Spirited person (who possesses both a male and female spirit, regardless of the flesh that is worn) will always see further. For this reason, many Two-Spirit people have become Medicine people, leaders and intermediaries between men and women, and between tribal communities and non-Native people. Their greater flexibility provides greater possibilities to discover alternative ways of seeing oneself and the world.[44]

Given the way American social movements often turn upon strategic claims and redefinitions of words, symbols, and histories, it is not surprising that lesbian and gay native people would propose a label of their own to express and consolidate their self-awareness. Insisting that anthropologists and other representatives of elite discourse use this term is a symbolic gesture but one that alters the dynamics of an historical relationship that has all too often involved one-way transfers of knowledge. The creation of self-chosen terminology has been part of the history of African American, Latino/Chicano, lesbian/gay, and other movements. Indeed, native pantribalism in the twentieth century provides many examples of newly forged symbols of Indian identity. What is distinctive about the use of "two-spirit" is that it has been deployed as a panhistorical as well as a pantribal term.

Curtis Harris (San Carlos Apache) explains the motivations underlying the shift to "two-spirit." "We adopted it because it does encompass more traditions than any of the other terms that we've come across, and it also is a fairly accurate reflection in terms of how most of our communities see us." He adds, "We started to use this term because we didn't feel comfortable in many cases in simply defining ourselves by the colonizers' culture which said that you were now going to be either gay or lesbian or bisexual."[45] In other words, native people are rejecting not only the antiquarian term "berdache," but the entire taxonomy of Western discourse on sexuality. In contrast, Harris attributes traditional tribal culture with an almost postmodern appreciation of the fluidity of identities. "In our communities, many of our communities, the tradition of sexuality is that you're at one point on a Circle, and that all the points are connected, and you can be at any point on the Circle at one period in your life, and you don't necessarily have to be at one end of the line."[46] Tafoya makes a similar observation: "Most Native communities tend not to classify the world into concrete binary categories, . . . but rather into categories that range from appropriateness to inappropriateness depending on the context of a situation."[47]

The popularity of "two-spirit" is a function of its double appeal as a statement of both sexual and racial identity.[48] Yet another advantage to the term, as Leota Lone Dog (Lakota/Mohawk/Delaware) points out, is that it is inclusive of men and women—whereas use of "lesbian" and "gay" "already sets up a division."[49] With the use of "two-spirit" contemporary natives align themselves with traditional culture and can make a claim for acceptance that no other gay minority group in the United States can—not on the basis of some abstract principle of rights or inclusion, but because they are representatives of original tribal cultures and, as such, stand at the forefront of native resistance to white hegemony. Such a discursive move, while anachronistic, gains two-spirit natives access to a rich heritage of images, practices, and role models. As Anguksuar wrote in 1990,

Some of the qualities that have traditionally been associated with the Gay and Lesbian American Indian people are: generosity, skill in arts and healing, leadership skills, certain abilities in the use of magic, and the preservation of old knowledge, and the last but not least, we are regarded as good luck.

These are some of the traditions we live up to in our everyday lives, and for which we consciously and unconsciously strive. As we look at the future, these are some of the things we see, which, as it turns out, are old and were never completely forgotten.[50]

BACK ON THE REZ

Many of the developments described earlier in this chapter occurred or originated in urban centers where lesbian/gay/two-spirit natives have been migrating since the 1950s in search of sexual freedom and economic opportunities (or because they were subject to government relocation). Back on the "rez," as many call the reservations they grew up on, these developments unfolded differently, and sometimes not at all. In some cases, when memory of multiple gender traditions has survived, a fascinating process of cultural accommodation and elaboration is underway. "Gay," "lesbian," and "bisexual" individuals within reservation communities are becoming more visible, and tribal members are seeking to understand and reconcile memories of alternative gender traditions with modern sexual patterns and identities.

At Zuni, I do not think the term "two-spirit" would be recognized by anyone (except individuals I have spoken with), nor would "berdache." "Gay" and "homosexual" are well known and used, with the assumption that these behavior patterns include a component of gender difference as well as same-sex orientation. In other words, understandings of Anglo-American sexual categories are "contaminated" with traditional Zuni categories. In a similar way, the act of "coming out," that is, making a public statement about one's identity, can be accomplished entirely within the terms of traditional culture. A man, for example, might start baking his own bread (women's work). Since ovens at Zuni are located outside the house, such an act becomes a public declaration of one's gender identity and, many Zunis will assume, sexual orientation.

Zunis are increasingly aware of gay tribal members and speculate on whether there are more of them today or whether they are simply more visible—and why. One conversation I had in the early 1990s with a tribal elder began with his question, "Was We'wha a homosexual?" Most of these conversations, however, occur in the Zuni language. In 1987, I was told that the traditional term *lha'ma* or *lhamana* was still applied to historical figures like We'wha, but that a new word had been coined, *lhalha,* which meant "homosexual."[51] Six years later, however, I was told that yet another term, *'e'tsawak'i* ("girl-boy"), had been coined to refer to men considered similar to traditional *lhamana,* while the word *lhamana* (often pronounced *lha'ma*) was being used to mean "gay." Clearly, Western categories like "gay" and "homosexual" are having an impact on Zuni discourse. Yet despite semantic drift, the traditional category of gender difference is continually reproduced, whether as *lha'ma* or *'e'tsawak'i.*

The Zunis have been remarkably resilient when it comes to traditional attitudes regarding sexuality and gender. In many other tribes, including other Pueblo communities, this is not the case. In 1993, I participated in a conversation with individuals from Zuni and Taos pueblos. The Taoseño described the relentless teasing he had experienced growing up as a gay man in the village. I took the opportunity to press my friend from Zuni on the issue: Doesn't this ever happen at Zuni? Doesn't a kid get singled out at high school and teased for being gay? No, he replied flatly, "because we still have Ko'lha'ma [the berdache kachina], and so it's still respected." In contrast, Jacobs has described how the traditional third gender role of a northern Tewa-speaking pueblo has lapsed and how the respect once accorded the sexual and gender difference of *kwidó* has not carried over to tribal members who today are gay or homosexual. She was told that homosexuals are "mixed-up people who can be cured."[52] In the early 1980s, when a young member of the tribe was discovered having sex with another boy, he became the subject of repeated assaults by his father and other male members of the community. Eventually tribal elders intervened, asserting to the father that his son "was special and would have to be protected within the reservation for the sake of the Pueblo." Sadly, this did not end the attacks.[53]

Similar processes have been observed in other tribal communities. In the early 1980s, Walter Williams was told that among the Crow "there are some today, transvestites, homosexuals, or gays you call them, but they don't have any ceremonial role." When he asked what the difference between *badé* (*boté*) and "gay" was, his informant replied "they were the same." Other Crows also translated *badé* as "gay." Among contemporary Lakota, Williams found various outlooks toward traditional and contemporary roles. "'Gay' and *winkte* are different," one self-identified Lakota *winkte* told him. "*Winkte* is a gay with ceremonial powers." Other Lakotas lamented that younger gays "don't fulfill their spiritual role as *winktes*." One consultant, Michael One Feather, identified himself as gay before he was aware of the *winkte* tradition. Later he found older relatives who explained and instructed him in aspects of the traditional role. Now he identifies "both as a *winkte* and as gay."[54]

Carolyn Epple has found that among contemporary Navajo who identify as *nádleehí* there is widespread awareness of and interest in Anglo-American gay culture. One *nádleehí*'s favorite film was the popular 1990 documentary on New York's black drag scene, *Paris Is Burning*.[55] In fact, interstate highways, international air travel, satellite dishes, VCRs, and the internet are all contributing to a breakdown of the rural/urban divide in native America. Lesbian and gay natives who never leave their reservation communities (and there are many) know relatives and friends who have, and they are exposed to Anglo-American sexual attitudes and practices through schools, interactions in nearby towns and cities, and, of course, media.

POSTSCRIPT: NATIVE LESBIAN AND GAY LITERATURE

Gay/two-spirit natives have been active not only in politics and community work. They have been making notable contributions in literature and the arts as well. The recognized elder of gay native writers is Maurice Kenny (Mohawk), whose 1976 essay "Tinselled Bucks: An Historical Study of Indian Homosexuality" (published in *Gay Sunshine* and reprinted in *Living the Spirit*) served as a call to arms for activists like Randy Burns and Barbara Cameron in San Francisco. Kenny had been inspired by 1960s native revivalism, and in his essay he cited a wide range of ethnographic and literary references to two-spirit roles and male homosexuality, concluding with an optimistic prediction of their restoration. "We were special!" he boldly declared in his poem "*Winkte*"; "We had power with the people!" Kenny's publications were followed in 1981 by Paula Gunn Allen's (Laguna Pueblo/Sioux) essay "Beloved Women: Lesbians in American Indian Cultures" (reprinted in *Sacred Hoop*). Allen wrote: "Under the reign of the patriarchy, the medicine-dyke has become anathema, her presence has been hidden under the power-destroying blanket of complete silence. We must not allow this silence to prevent us from discovering and reclaiming who we have been and who we are."[56]

The decision to come out in their writing was a significant one for both Kenny and Allen. Born in 1929 and 1939 respectively, tribal homophobia, fostered by government- and church-directed campaigns of assimilation, reached a peak in their lifetimes. Until the 1970s, lesbian and gay Indians found it necessary to migrate to urban areas to act upon their desires, maintaining uneasy relationships with their families and reservation communities. As Kenny writes in his poem "Apache," "in the night of smoke / safe from reservation / eyes and rules / gentle fingers / turned back the sheets." Nonetheless, both Allen and Kenny (along with Daniel David Moses) were included in the canonical *Harper's Anthology of 20th Century Native Poetry* (1988).

Two native lesbians—Barbara Cameron (Hunkpapa), co-founder of Gay American Indians, and Chrystos (Menominee)—appeared in Cherríe Moraga's and Gloria Anzaldúa's anthology, *This Bridge Called My Back*, published in 1981. Two years later eleven lesbians appeared in Beth Brant's (Bay of Quinte Mohawk) *A Gathering of Spirit: Writing and Art by North American Indian Women* (1983; 1984), which was the first anthology of native writing edited entirely by a native person. The collection included poems and short prose from Cameron, Chrystos, Allen, Janice Gould (Koyangk'auwi Maidu), Terri Meyette (Yaqui), Mary Moran (Métis), Kateri Sardella (Micmac), Vickie Sears (Cherokee), Anita Valerio (Blood/Chicana), and Midnight Sun (Anishnawbe).

The first specifically gay and lesbian collection of native writing was *Living the Spirit: A Gay American Indian Anthology*, published by Gay American Indians.

With over twenty native contributors, contents included traditional myths and tales, poetry, short stories, essays, interviews, and a variety of visual and graphic images.

Chrystos has published three books of poems and contributed to numerous literary magazines. Her writing spans the spectrum from angry denunciations of white expropriation of native cultures to love poems of exquisite tenderness and eroticism. Beth Brant, in addition to promoting the work of other native writers, has published collections of her own stories and poems. Other native lesbians who have published book-length works include Vickie Sears and Janice Gould. Active gay male authors include Clyde Hall ("M. Owlfeather") (Lemhi Shoshone), Terry Tafoya (Taos/Warm Springs), and Canadian Daniel David Moses (Delaware). Moses has had several plays produced and has published both plays and poetry. William Merasty (Cree) has also produced plays in Canada.

Native lesbian and gay writers share with other native authors a sense of integration with the natural world and a close-knit community, survival against enormous odds, and a proud (sometimes idealized) past. Irony and self-mocking humor are common. Also typical is a path of development that includes both alienation from and a return to tribal communities. At the same time, lesbian and gay native writing is distinct from that of other native and gay authors in its celebration of eroticism. One finds this especially in the work of Paula Gunn Allen, Chrystos (who has published a volume of erotic poetry, *In Her I Am* [1993]), and Judith Mountain-Leaf Volborth (Blackfoot/Comanche). At the same time, one is also likely to find a heightened sense of the internal problems of native communities—whether alcoholism, violence, sexism, or homophobia. But the bicultural experience of gay/two-spirit native authors can also be a source of powerful connections. In "A Long Story" in her collection *Mohawk Trail,* Beth Brant juxtaposes an account of Indian mothers at the end of the nineteenth century whose children were forcibly taken to boarding schools with that of a contemporary lesbian mother who loses her children in a custody battle.

Unlike their non-Indian counterparts, two-spirit/gay native people are not haunted by the lack of a past or a sense of social contribution. By connecting to the heritage of multiple genders, lesbian and gay natives in North America are forging a unique vision of what it means to be gay. Rather than a literature of alienation, their work constitutes a literature of survival and affirmation based on the hope of visions and communal traditions. In the words of Beth Brant,

> There is a generosity in the works of Janice Gould and Vickie Sears and other Native lesbian writers. . . . I find this kind of generosity so Indian in its simplicity and affirmation. Beginning a new tradition while following the edicts of older traditions. For what we do, we do for generations to come. We write not only for ourselves but also for our communities, for our People, for the young ones who

are looking for the gay and lesbian path, for our Elders who were shamed or mythologized, for the wingeds and four-leggeds and the animals who swim, for the warriors and resisters who kept the faith.[57]

PART II

GENDER WITHOUT SEX:
TOWARD A THEORY OF GENDER DIVERSITY

THE PROBLEM OF DESCRIPTION

In 1669, the Spanish traveler Francisco Coreal observed practices among the natives of Florida that both intrigued and baffled him. He wrote,

> The men are strongly inclined to sodomy; but the boys that abandon themselves thus are excluded from the society of men and sent out to that of women as being effeminates. They are confused with the Hermaphrodites which they say are found in quantity in the country of the Floridians. I believe that these Hermaphrodites are none other than the effeminate boys, that in a sense truly are Hermaphrodites. Be that as it may, they employ them in all the diverse handiworks of women, in servile functions, and to carry the munitions and provisions of war. They are also distinguished from the men and the women by the color of the feathers that they put on their heads and for the scorn that they bring on to themselves.[1]

What is interesting about Coreal's report is not so much the glimpse it offers of berdaches in a tribe that has long since disappeared. By his time, the presence of alternative genders in Florida had been known for at least a century. Rather, his report illustrates a phenomenon that began with the earliest published accounts of the New World and continues to this day. What Coreal wrote reflects as much his readings of earlier reports ("they say")—and his efforts to resolve their contradictions (garçons efféminés or Hermaphrodites?)—as it does his actual observations.[2]

As James Clifford observes, "Literary processes—metaphor, figuration, narrative—affect the ways cultural phenomena are registered, from the first jotted 'observations,' to the completed book, to the ways these configurations 'make sense' in determined acts of reading."[3] Indeed, what has been written about North American gender diversity in the past five centuries has been powerfully shaped by hegemonic Western discourses on gender, sexuality and the Other. As a result, the texts that describe berdaches often create as much confusion as understanding.

Whereas native languages had distinct terms for berdaches, Europeans, having no comparable roles, had no appropriate terms to describe their particular combination of gender, sexual, economic, and religious traits. Unable to name the gestalt, they labeled those parts of multiple gender roles that could be correlated to European experience. Consequently, the literature that documents these roles employs a bewildering array of terms that seem to shift in every generation. The French travelers who observed the Illinois of the Mississippi Valley between 1680 and 1720 wrote variously of men who "assume the female dress, and keep it all their life" (Marquette); "hermaphrodites" (Membre, Hennepin, Lahontan, "Tonti"); "a Bardache" (Deliette); "sodomy" (Hennepin, Deliette, Lahontan); and "effeminacy . . . carried to the greatest excess" (Charlevoix).

Although "berdache" has been routinely used by anthropologists since the end of the nineteenth century, it rarely appeared in texts before then. Rather, the semantic continuum that emerged early in the contact literature was delimited by "hermaphrodite," a term from classical mythology referring to a condition of anomalous or mixed physiological sex, at one pole, and "sodomite," a term from religious discourse referring to sexual acts (primarily anal intercourse between men), at the other.[4] Most observers have sought to align their descriptions with one or the other of these poles. "I inferred they must be hermaphrodites," wrote Pedro Font in 1775 regarding male berdaches among Yuman tribes, "but from what I learned later I understood that they were sodomites."[5]

The gender and the sexual dimensions of berdache roles became so detached in European discourse that often it is hard to tell if writers are discussing the same phenomenon. In 1703 Lahontan observed, "Among the Illinese there are several Hermaphrodites, who go in a Woman's Habit, but frequent the Company of both Sexes." The next sentence reads, "These Illinese are strangely given to Sodomy."[6] A relationship between "Hermaphrodites" and "Sodomy" is implied, but only by the juxtaposition of the sentences. Similarly, the text attributed to Tonti reports the practice of "infamous vice" with "prostitute boys." This renders the boys effeminate, and, as additional punishment, the tribe makes them dress and live as women. A sentence about polygamy and jealousy in male-female relations intervenes, and then the text reads, "*Hermaphrodites* are very common amongst them, but whether it be an effect of the climate or not, I do not pretend to determine."[7] Here the rupture between terms ("prostitute boys" and "hermaphrodites") is even more pronounced—although the two subjects are still contained within the same printed page.

Many readers of early chronicles have interpreted the divergent terms used in them as referring to discreet subjects, and, like Coreal, they tried to resolve these discrepancies. Dumont de Montigny addressed a confusion he perceived in "almost all the authors" regarding "hermaphrodites" in the Louisiana territory. Although he had never seen a "real" (*véritables*) hermaphrodite, he described the role of dress-wearing Natchez men called the "Chief of Women."[8] Others were indifferent to these distinctions. The frontier diarists Kurz and Denig used "berdache" and "hermaphrodite" interchangeably. According to Denig, "Berdêches or hermaphrodites" resulted from the "habits of the child," not natural causes.[9] Such usages should warn readers away from literal interpretations of terms. Dorsey, for example, reported that a Ponca boy who played with girls was called a "hermaphrodite."[10] Gatschet translated a Klamath word as "hermaphrodite" but quoted a native who defined the term as "a man wearing woman's clothes."[11]

Attempts to resolve the confusion created by the use of so many different terms typically have singled out one trait and subordinated others to it. Usually, the choice is made between gender difference and sexuality. The chronicler of an early nineteenth-century American expedition, for example, invoked both terms of this binary but subsumed the gendered aspects of the role under the sign of "sodomy": "Sodomy is a crime not uncommonly committed; many of the subjects of it are publicly known, and do not appear to be despised, or to excite disgust; one of them was pointed out to us; he had submitted himself to it, in consequence of a vow he had made to his mystic medicine, which obliged him to change his dress for that of a squaw, to do their work, and to permit his hair to grow."[12] In the twentieth century, Kroeber, Benedict, Devereux, and others have defined berdache roles in sexual terms, as a form of "institutionalized homosexuality."[13]

Most writers, however, have chosen gender over sexuality. Angelino and Shed, while warning against relying on "the mere outward sign of attire," defined berdache as a "transvestite," a "person of one anatomic sex assuming part or most of the attire, occupation, and social—including marital—status, of the opposite sex."[14] Theirs has become the canonical definition of berdache in the anthropological literature. Kroeber was the first to use the term "transvestite" in reference to berdaches in his *Handbook of California Indians* (published in 1925 but completed in 1917).[15] The term "transsexual," introduced in 1948, has also been used to describe berdaches.

Although the distinction between transvestism as cross-dressing and transsexualism as cross-sex identification is recognized in the field of psychology it is rarely observed in studies of native North Americans, in which the terms "transvestite," "transsexual," and "homosexual" appear interchangeably. The results are sometimes oxymoronic. Reichard once referred to a Navajo *nádleehí* as a "transvestite" even though he did not cross-dress, and a dictionary of Mississippi Valley French defines "berdache" as "a hermaphrodite; a homosexual."[16] In sum, even though the old mythologically derived terminology for homosexuality (hermaphrodite from Hermaphroditus; catamite from Ganymede; sodomy from Sodom) was eventually replaced by the purportedly scientific language of medicine and psychiatry, the new terms (transvestite/transsexual and homosexual) still reproduced the dichotomy of gender/sexuality.

The atomization and reconfiguration of North American gender diversity into a Western object of knowledge often has rendered the subject unrecognizable to native informants.[17] When investigators use terms such as "inversion," "homosexuality," and "transvestitism" in interviews, natives frequently deny their presence. Hopis who reported a First Mesa berdache nonetheless refused to acknowledge the presence of anything "which could be called homosexuality."[18] Similarly, Olson reported of the Haisla that berdaches of both sexes were common but "homosexuality is unknown."[19] Gayton's Yokuts informants also affirmed the presence of berdaches but denied "homosexuality or transmuted habits."[20] Apache informants found the categories used by Marvin Opler so alien that they responded with "counterquestioning on American urban culture."[21] These examples leave one wishing that ethnographers reported the exact questions and terms used in their interviews. Clearly, Western categories like "gay" and "homosexual," which lack native equivalents, create confusion and tend to encourage informants to comment on Western practices rather than their own.

Elsewhere, I have argued that the alternative to single-dimensional definitions and reliance on terms identified with a specific historical period is a multidimensional model, in which gender and sexual differences are defined in terms of *sets* of traits.[22] Such an approach is essential for comparative research. Although each society has its own linguistic categories and associated meanings that can be compared and contrasted, social science research is also concerned with how people conduct themselves in daily life. Use of a multidimensional model makes it possible to inventory all the characteristics observed in a given cultural context associated with a status such as "berdache" or "homosexual," whether or not they are formally labeled. These traits might include named social roles and identities, gender difference, economic specialization, religious roles, and homosexuality. Such inventories can then be used to make complex and systematic comparisons of roles in different societies.

One way of defining berdache roles in multidimensional terms is to describe them as distinct genders. Martin and Voorhies first suggested that berdache roles were genders in their 1975 book, *Female of the Species*. In a chapter titled "Supernumerary Sexes," they noted that "physical sex differences need not necessarily be perceived as bipolar. It seems possible that human reproductive bisexuality establishes a minimal number of socially recognized physical sexes, but these need not be limited to two."[23] In 1978, Kessler and McKenna specifically termed berdache roles "a third gender category, separate from male and female."[24] In 1983, Jacobs also defined berdache status as a third gender and argued that such a characterization was more accurate than that of gender-crossing.[25] Subsequently, Blackwood proposed the "rigorous identification and labeling of the berdache role as a separate gender." "The berdache gender...," she argued, "is not a deviant role, nor a mixture of two genders, nor less a jumping from one gender to its opposite. Nor is it an alternative role behavior for nontraditional individuals who are still considered men or women. Rather, it comprises a separate gender within a multiple gender system."[26]

As promising as it seems, a multiple gender paradigm raises several questions. Clearly, not every instance of sexual or gender variance represents the presence of a socially acknowledged third or fourth gender role, nor is every named social role the equivalent of a gender. As Murray argues, the criteria for labeling a given social role as a gender need to be spelled out.[27] But before that question can be addressed an even more fundamental issue must be resolved. What, after all, *is* gender if there can be more than two? And how and in what kind of societies do multiple gender roles occur?

The rest of this chapter will discuss the theoretical basis for a multiple gender paradigm, beginning with the deconstruction of the sex/gender binary that has been the basis of most recent work in gender studies. This will be followed by an exploration of the relationship between multiple genders and prestige systems. A methodology will then be described for addressing some of the outstanding questions in the study of North American gender diversity.

GENDER WITHOUT SEX

If genders can be multiple and autonomous from sex it becomes crucial to clarify exactly what "gender" refers to. In fact, definitions of gender are rare in the literature of gender studies. Derived from the Latin *genus* (kind, sort, class) "gender" is widely used today to distinguish socially constructed roles and cultural representations from biological sex. This particular use of gender, however, is fairly recent. Haraway has traced it to the "gender identity" research of the psychoanalyst Robert Stoller in the late 1950s.[28] Actually, popular belief and official discourse alike have long acknowledged the role of social learning in sex-specific behavior. Anthropologists and other social scientists were studying "sex roles" for at least two decades before the adoption of the term "gender." In Euro-

American societies, however, biological sex long has been considered both the origin point and the limit of sex-role differences. What we call gender, in this view, *should* conform to sex, a belief that is rationalized alternately on moral and natural grounds. The study of non-Western cultures, however, reveals not only variability in the sociocultural features of sex roles, but wide variation in beliefs concerning the body and what constitutes biological sex.

Previous theoretical work on berdache roles has taken the correspondence between sex and gender for granted, and this has skewed the interpretation of berdaches in both subtle and fundamental ways. This problem is perhaps best illustrated by Whitehead's 1981 essay, "The Bow and the Burden Strap." She writes, "A social gender dichotomy is present in all known societies in the sense that everywhere anatomic sexual differences observable at birth are used to start tracking the newborn into one or the other of two social role complexes. This minimal pegging of social roles and relationships to observable anatomic sex differences is what creates what we call a 'gender' dichotomy in the first place."[29] Callender and Kochems echo this idea when they state that gender "is less directly tied to this anatomical basis, although ultimately limited by it."[30] All these authors employ Angelino and Shedd's definition of berdaches as "gender-crossers."[31]

Unpacking these statements reveals two propositions: that social gender is based on the "natural facts" of sex; and, since there are only two sexes, that there are only two genders. It follows that if an individual is not one, then he or she must be the other. The only variation possible in a dichotomous system is an exchange of one gender for its "opposite" or some form of gender-mixing, but there is no possibility that cannot be defined by reference to male or female. Thus Schlegel writes, "I see no evidence that societies socialize children for anything but two genders, depending on their sexual identification. Intermediate or anomalous persons such as berdaches or transvestites appear to be trying, to the degree that they are able, to take on the characteristics of the opposite sex, not some intermediate gender."[32] It follows that in such a system there can be only one sexual orientation, the attraction of these opposite sexes, or heterosexuality.[33]

The unquestioned assumptions of a binary gender paradigm have important implications for the way in which alternative gender roles are interpreted. Whitehead, for example, begins by linking their presence to the widespread North American belief in the power of dreams and visions. This "vision complex" had an implicit economic dimension, in that random contact with the supernatural was believed to bestow skills and luck in activities that resulted in wealth and prestige. Such beliefs served to rationalize differences in individual success within otherwise egalitarian communities. At the same time, Whitehead observes, the activities that generated prestige were also coded for gender, so that gender, like skills and good fortune, was viewed as somewhat random. Thus, gender became an achieved status, a kind of rank or standing.

The fact that Native American women had relatively equal access to wealth and prestige through food and crafts production, child-bearing, and household administration meant that some men might decide to pursue these activities, as well. In fact, Whitehead attributes overtly opportunistic motives to male berdaches. To gain the "material prosperity and cultural respect that accrued to the assiduous practitioner of female crafts," they quit "the battlefront . . . of male prestige . . . to take up a respectable sort of lateral position—that of ultra-successful female."[34] In other words, their reputation for excellence in these crafts is merely another form of masculine supremacy: of course he's better, he's a man. According to Whitehead, "The culturally dominant American Indian male was confronted with a substantial female elite," which he found profoundly "disturbing." "It was into this unsettling breach that the berdache institution was hurled. In their social aspect, women were complimented by the berdache's imitation. In their anatomic aspect, they were subtly insulted by his vaunted superiority. Through him, ordinary men might reckon that they still held the advantage that was anatomically given and inalterable."[35] Whitehead cites no specific evidence in support of this generalization, however, and Callender and Kochems have convincingly argued for the opposite conclusion: that women often *encouraged* males who were berdaches. It indeed seems unlikely that such a role could have flourished without women's approval.[36]

Whitehead's conclusions reflect her reliance on the analytical distinction between sex and gender. In this binary, sex, defined as biological and anatomical, is opposed to gender, defined as a learned, sociocultural role. Sex is universal, and even though gender constructions vary among societies, they are ultimately motivated by the universal fact of sexual dimorphism. Deconstructing this binary, however, reveals that the relationship between the terms is in fact hierarchical. Anatomy has primacy over gender, and gender is not an ontologically distinct category but merely a reiteration of sex. In Whitehead's text this becomes apparent when she argues that female berdache roles were less frequent than male roles because female anatomy imposed limits on the possibility of gender-crossing.[37] But this argument raises the question, If gender differences are anchored to an "anatomic-physiological component," on what grounds can we argue that gender roles are not in fact natural (that is, mirroring and/or determined by biology)? If we accept the contention that having a female body makes it more difficult to become a berdache, have we not conceded that gender is indeed biologically determined?

The assumption that gender dualism is a universal fact of human social life can be criticized on both empirical and theoretical grounds. It may be arguable that all societies have *at least* two genders, and that these two genders are linked to perceptions of physiological differences, but what constitutes anatomical sex, which organs (or fluids or physiological processes) are considered the signs of maleness and femaleness, have been shown by scholars in several fields to be as much social constructions as what has been termed "gender." Historian Thomas Laqueur, for example, has traced the shifting conceptions of bodies over the course of Western history and shown how a Greco-Roman model of female sexual organs as internal versions of male organs gave way to the modern notion of two distinct, fixed, and incommensurable sexes.[38]

The analytical distinction of sex and gender has been an important tool in anthropological and feminist research since the work of Margaret Mead. To this fundamental distinction, Gayle Rubin has added the insight that gender identity is not a "natural" developmental process following sex assignment (with occasional deviations), but the product of comprehensive interventions by social institutions and processes—the sex/gender system.[39] The case of gender diversity in native North America and elsewhere, however, reveals the limits of these concepts. As several theorists have recently argued, studies of gender need to shift their focus from how sexed bodies acquire gender roles and identities, to how bodies acquire sex. As feminist theorist Judith Butler notes, "The question is no longer, How is gender constituted as and through a certain interpretation of sex? (a question that leaves the 'matter' of sex untheorized), but rather, Through what regulatory norms is sex itself materialized? And how is it that treating the materiality of sex as a given presupposes and consolidates the normative conditions of its own emergence?"[40]

The intention of drawing a line between sex and gender is not enough, however. The means to do so must exist, and this is what a multiple gender paradigm provides. A multiple gender paradigm takes the original insight underlying the sex/gender distinction, that biology is not destiny, along with Rubin's understanding of how social systems produce gender, to the next logical level—the analysis of sex itself as a social construction. While allowing that morphological differences in infants motivate a labeling process, a multiple gender paradigm recognizes that the markers of sex are no less arbitrary than the sociocultural elaborations of them in gender identities and roles. As feminist theorist Elizabeth Grosz argues, "It is not simply that the body is represented in a variety of ways according to historical, social, and cultural exigencies while it remains basically the same; these factors actively produce the body as a body of a determinate type."[41]

North American data make it clear that not all cultures recognize the same anatomical markers and not all recognize anatomical markers as "natural." In Zuni belief, for example, a series of interventions were considered necessary to ensure that a child had a "sex" at all.[42] This began before birth, when the parents made offerings at various shrines to influence the sex of the developing fetus. In fact, the infant's sex was not believed to be fixed until birth. If a woman took a nap during labor, the sex of her child might change. (The Inuit and others, as related in chapter 1, also believe that the sex of a fetus can change at the time of birth.) Following birth, interventions to influence physical sex continued. The midwife massaged and manipulated the infant's face, nose, eyes, and genitals. If male, she poured cold water over its penis to prevent overdevelopment. If female, the midwife split a new gourd in half and rubbed it over the vulva to enlarge it. In such a cultural context, knowing the kind of genitals an individual possesses is less important than knowing which cultural interventions are employed in relation to anatomy and which bodily features and/or physiological processes are believed to endow bodies with sex.

If sex is a social construction, it cannot provide the "transcendental signified" for defining gender. The challenge, therefore, is to define sex without presupposing the naturalness of its forms and to define gender without reducing it to a reiteration of sex. This can be accomplished by recognizing sex as a category of bodies, and gender as a category of persons. The first entails the criteria for being recognized as human (that is, as having genitals that can be categorized in the terms used by a given social group). The second involves distinctions between kinds of persons within the group. This shifts the emphasis from assumptions about biological differences to the social processes of categorization by which a body is acknowledged as being human.

Gender in this view is a multidimensional cultural category that presumes sexed personhood but is not limited to sex or sex-specific traits; indeed, in North America, individual, acquired, and ascribed traits outweighed sex-assignment in determining gender identity. So while gender categories often include perceptions of anatomical and physiological differences, these perceptions are mediated by language and symbols. Nor can we assume the relative importance of perceptions of physical difference in the overall definition of gender in a given society. Further, those physical differences that are a part of a culture's gender categories may not be constructed as dichotomous or fixed, or viewed as determinants of social behavior. By extension, the presence of multiple genders does not require belief in the existence of three or more physical sexes, but, minimally, a view of physical differences as unfixed, or insufficient on their own to establish gender, or simply less important than individual and social factors, such as occupational preference, behavior and temperament, religious experiences, and so forth.

In this view, gender categories are both "models of" difference (to borrow Clifford Geertz's terminology) and "models for" difference. They are used not only to explain the world, but they also serve as templates and instructions for gender-specific behavior and temperament, sexuality, kinship and interpersonal roles, occupation, and religious roles. For individuals, gender identities function as the prerequisite for acquisition of other identities and roles. They are "total social phenomena," in Marcel Mauss's terms. A wide range of institutions and beliefs find simultaneous expression through them, a characteristic that distinguishes gender roles from other social statuses.[43]

Various evidence supports the conclusion that berdaches occupied culturally recognized alternative genders. On the one hand, a dual gender model clearly fails

TABLE 6.1.

Mixed Gender Traits of Male Berdaches

Assiniboin	Male berdache who does work of both sexes (Lowie 1909: 42)
Cheyenne	*He´emane´o* dress as old men (Grinnell 1923, 2:39)
Chugach Eskimo	*Aranu:tiq* do work of both sexes (Birket-Smith 1953: 94)
Crow	Osh-Tisch dresses as man to fight in war (chapter 2)
Flathead	Berdaches "occasionally" dress in men's clothes (Teit 1930: 384)
Ingalik	Berdache who dresses as a man (Osgood 1940: 460; Snow 1981: 611)
Isleta, San Felipe	Variability in dress (Parsons 1932: 246)
Klamath	Berdache who does not wear a dress (Spier 1930: 52)
Kutenai	Male berdache wears pants under a dress (Schaeffer 1965: 218)
Lakota	*Winkte* accompany war parties and hunt (Medicine 1983: 268); some alternate between work and dress of men and women (DeMallie 1983: 244)
Miwok	Only one of five reported berdaches cross-dress (Gifford n.d.)
Monache	Some alternate between work and dress of men and women (Gayton 1948: 274)
Navajo	Variability in dress of *nádleehí* (Hill 1935: 275; Reichard [1928] 1969: 150)
Pima	Neither male or female "inverts" assume the dress of the opposite sex (Hill 1938: 339)
Southern Paiute	"Though not dressing like a woman . . ." (Lowie 1924b: 282)
Timucua	Berdaches distinguish themselves from men and women (Coreal 1722: 33-34)
Shoshone	"Transvestism . . . was unstandardized, varying with the individual" (Steward 1941: 252-53)
Zuni	Male *lhamana* receives male initiation; buried in male part of cemetery (Roscoe 1991: 126-27)

to account for many of the behaviors and attributes reported for them—for example, berdaches who did not cross-dress or attempt to mimic the behavior of the "opposite" sex or berdaches who engaged in a combination of female, male, and berdache-specific pursuits. Reports of mixed gender traits for male berdaches are summarized in Table 6.1; Table 4.1 documents even greater variability for female roles.

At the same time, the use of distinct terms to refer to berdaches, a practice that prevented their conceptual assimilation to an "opposite" sex, is positive evidence that berdache status was viewed as a separate category. These native terms have a variety of translations, from the obvious "man-woman" (for example, Shoshone *tainna'-wa'ippe*) to "old woman-old man" (Tewa *kwidó*) to terms that bear no relation to the words for "man" or "woman," or simply cannot be etymologized (Zuni *lhamana*). In many tribes, the distinction of berdaches from men and women was reinforced by sartorial practices and the use of symbols, such as the distinct color of feathers worn by Floridian berdaches. In other cases, as I show in *The Zuni Man-Woman,* the religious functions of berdaches and the life cycle rites they underwent were specific to their status. Similarly, among such tribes as the Zuni, Navajo, Mohave, and others, mythical accounts of the origin of berdache status place that event in the same context in which male and female genders were established (as if to say, "when the gods made men and women, they also made berdaches").[44]

If berdaches simply exchanged one of two genders for the other, then they can be interpreted as upholding a heterosexist gender system, but if they are understood as entering a distinct gender status, neither male nor female, something more complex is going on. A multiple gender paradigm makes it possible to see berdache status not as a compromise between nature and culture or a niche to accommodate "natural" variation, but as an integral and predictable element of certain sociocultural systems.

MULTIPLE GENDERS AND THE DIVISION OF LABOR

Whitehead argues that the origins of berdache roles lie in the widespread North American "vision complex." In this belief system, dreams and especially visions are credited with the power to convey skills and knowledge to individuals. Since such dreams could come to anyone, the allocation of ability and success in these societies occurred somewhat randomly. It sometimes happened that men acquired women's skills and, therefore, women's sources of prestige. Because North American societies lacked what Whitehead terms "full prestige differentiation," growth in social specialization was accommodated by an elaboration of gender categories. The (male) berdache role, in her view, was a "cultural compromise formation founded on an incipient, though never fully realized, collapse of the gender-stratification system."[45] Although Whitehead's insight regarding berdache roles as instances of social and economic specialization is valuable, her adherence to dual gender assumptions leads her to view such roles as derivative, a "compromise" of the two essential genders (that is, sexes) of male and female. In a multiple gender paradigm, on the other hand, the only thing that berdache roles "compromise" is the Western assumption that genders are limited to two.[46]

The distinction between sex as a construction of the body and gender as a primary category of personhood has significant implications when analyzing the division of labor in nonclass societies. Strictly defined, the description "*sexual* division of labor" should be applied only to social systems in which productive tasks are allocated on the basis of beliefs about male and female bodies. The corresponding ideology of such a system would be that these two kinds of bodies have different capabilities. A *gendered* division of labor, however, is more complex. If we understand gender as a special category of personhood, then a gendered division of labor is a means of accomplishing production by assigning tasks not to bodies but to *types of persons* whose skills are intrinsic to and inseparable from their total being. This being, in its most fundamental form, is male, female, or possibly another gender. Thus, depending on individual skills and inclinations, gender assignments can be flexible and can diverge from sex. At the same time, most tribal cultures, especially those in which visions are credited with bestowing skills and inclinations, do not view gender identities as being chosen.

Gender categories can include some traits and behaviors that might be linked to biology but many more that are not. In a gendered division of labor, women are said to specialize in pottery not because it is a task that requires little upper-body strength, but because creation is conceptualized as female. In other words, rather than opposing (female) reproduction to (male) production, many North American belief systems view women's reproductive role as a model for their work roles and a metaphor for production in general. At the same time, because productive skills and activities are viewed as intrinsic to specific types of persons, each skill set and productive process comes to imply an identity. Gender is a property of activities and objects as much as a trait of individuals, so that doing women's work imparts the traits and identity of a woman and doing men's work imparts the traits and identity of a man.

Because gendered divisions of labor are concerned with whole persons rather than their labor power alone, new roles are not conceptualized as skill sets that any number of individuals might learn. Rather, specialization within a gendered division of labor takes the form of a proliferation of types of persons, a process that may have been accelerated in North America with the spread of sedentary horticulture. This means that specialized gender roles are not accidental by-products of the random way in which skills are allocated in societies with a vision complex. Rather, the multiplication of gender categories is a logical and predictable way in which certain social systems change over time. Gender diversity is an inherent potential of gendered divisions of labor.

THE UNIFIED ANALYSIS OF GENDER DIVERSITY

Describing and understanding multiple gender roles requires not only new conceptualizations of sex and gender, but new methodologies as well. One approach has been proposed by anthropologists Jane Collier and Sylvia Yanagisako, who argue that studying the complex and interrelated phenomena of gender and kinship requires a unified analysis. Because their three-part program avoids reliance on such dichotomies as sex/gender, nature/culture, and domestic/public it is especially relevant for the analysis of gender diversity.

The first element of their program is the *cultural analysis of meaning*. Here the objective is to explicate the cultural meanings people realize through their practice of social relationships. At this stage of analysis the investigator needs to ask, "What are the socially meaningful categories people employ in specific contexts, and what symbols and meanings underlie them?" In terms of gender diversity, we would want to know what kinds of beliefs are associated with and necessary for the formulation of multiple gender categories. Are sex, gender, and sexuality viewed as natural, constructed, inborn, or acquired traits? Were berdaches anomalies, monsters, or prodigies? How was gender diversity conceptualized in terms of the categories and meanings associated with kinship, economics, politics, religion, and other social institutions?

The second phase of a unified analysis involves the construction of *systemic models of inequality*. This is accomplished by analyzing the structures that people create through their actions and tracing the "complex relationships between aspects of what—using conventional analytical categories—we might call gender, kinship, economy, polity, and religion."[47] Such "ideal typic models" of how power and social difference are organized in various societies are particularly valuable for comparative purposes. In the case of berdaches such models would identify their relationship to the division of labor and their position as producers and consumers in the circulation of prestige and social power.

Being synchronic in nature, systemic models have a built-in bias toward the persistence and continuity of social orders. For this reason, Collier and Yanagisako include *historical analysis* as the third element of their program, pointing out that the ideas and practices that seem to reinforce and reproduce each other from a systemic perspective can be seen to undermine and destabilize each other from an historical perspective. Historical analysis also leads to the consideration of individual factors in social developments—the motivations, desires, and self-generated meanings of the individuals who participate in "events" and occupy social roles—and the examination of the construction of subject positions.

A unified analysis can help address several questions about North American gender diversity. The example of berdache roles among the Plains and Pueblo tribes, for example, raises questions about the relative importance of cultural beliefs compared to socioeconomic factors in constructing multiple genders. Whereas Plains tribes are well known for the value they placed on visions and intuitive knowledge, the Pueblos—as Ruth Benedict pointed out in her classic study, *Patterns of Culture*—lack a vision complex. The cooperative ethos of Pueblo communities, fostered by the collective nature of agricultural production and village living, de-emphasized all forms of individualism. Direct contact with the supernatural was not sought and not welcomed. As Benedict noted, "If a Zuñi

Indian has by chance a visual or auditory hallucination it is regarded as a sign of death. It is an experience to avoid, not one to seek by fasting."[48] The very notion of individual contact with and use of supernatural power was suspect—this was the activity of witches. Instead, all dealings with the supernatural were invested in priesthoods and religious societies. Although some Pueblo berdaches were religious specialists, and their supernatural counterparts were portrayed in ceremonies, if they were considered "holy," it was not because of their berdache status as such, but because of their religious training, which required the mastery of complex oral literature and ceremonial procedures.

Despite the absence of a vision complex, berdaches have been documented in a majority of Pueblo communities. The economic basis of their status was the same as that of Plains berdaches. Pueblo women produced and distributed food and durable goods, and these products were coded as female. Specialization in these activities by males entailed no loss in social standing. Pueblo and Plains beliefs were distinct, however, in how they legitimated multiple genders. Among the Zunis, berdaches were sanctioned not by individual contact with the supernatural but through tribal myths that related the creation of a third gender as an autonomous category. Unfortunately, not enough data have been collected on Pueblo beliefs concerning the individual sources of berdache inclination. According to Jacobs, for example, the Northern Tewa believe that the exposure of an infant's genitals to the light of the moon will cause it to be a *kwidó*.[49] Among Plains tribes the moon was widely associated with berdache status, but, typical of Pueblo patterns, Tewa belief involves not a dream or vision of the moon but merely accidental exposure.

The examples of Plains and Pueblo societies provide evidence that multiple genders occur in societies with diverse subsistence patterns and belief systems. At the same time, social organization in both regions was based on a gendered division of labor with gendered social specialization. Plains and Pueblo berdaches were first and foremost craft specialists. To this economic dimension, Plains cultures added beliefs that the skills of berdaches were bestowed by supernatural intervention. As is typical of such beliefs, once established they become self-perpetuating. Consequently, as Callender and Kochems note, beliefs attributing holiness and supernatural power to berdaches are far more elaborate that necessary to account for occasional variation in occupational preferences.[50]

By combining Whitehead's insight into the relationship between berdache roles and social specialization with an understanding of how divisions of labor produce multiple genders, some interesting hypotheses arise. We might predict, for example, that as a given society with a gender-based prestige system and division of labor increased its capacity to produce surpluses and support economic specialization (by adopting or intensifying horticultural production, for example) both women and berdaches would take advantage of the new opportunities for acquiring prestige, and their status would increase accordingly.

If populations grew as well, the number of individuals with multiple gender identities in a given community would increase, too. Eventually, they might begin to function collectively, along the lines of a priesthood.

Evidence from North America does suggest that berdaches enjoyed high social and economic standing in sedentary, horticultural communities; in some groups, it appears that a berdache priesthood indeed had developed.[51] In Florida, for example, berdaches functioned collectively in tending to the sick and injured and in burying the dead. Among the Hidatsa of the northern Plains, there were as many as fifteen to twenty-five berdaches in a village. According to Bowers, they were an "organized group," a "special class of religious leaders" who collectively fulfilled various ceremonial functions. Among the Hidatsa's relatives, the Crows, boté pitched their tipis together and were recognized as a social group, while Cheyenne he´emane'o collectively led the scalp dance. Both of these tribes were formerly horticultural.[52]

The third phase of Collier and Yanagisako's unified analysis—the study of historical factors and social change—is also crucial in explaining the presence and status of multiple genders. Whitehead, for example, links the presence of berdaches to social systems that lack "full prestige differentiation," with the implication that societies with more complex socioeconomic systems would not have such roles. In fact, examples of societies with diversified prestige systems can be found in the Pacific Northwest Coast area. Tribes from southern Alaska to northern California were stratified into ranks of nobles, commoners, and slaves; lineages and whole tribes were ranked; titles, names, property, and leadership roles were inherited; wealth was ostentatiously displayed; and distinctions were drawn between prestigious and lowly occupations. At the same time, at least half of these groups had male, and some had female, berdache roles.[53]

The most complete picture comes from reports on the Bella Coola. In this tribe, as in many others, entry into berdache status was based on preference for the work of the other gender, which was credited to the influence of Sxints, the supernatural patron of berdaches. In mythology, Sxints is the first berry-picker—an important seasonal food item—and he guards a bevy of heavenly young maidens. He is also identified as one of the ancestors of a Bella Coola village. Portrayed in masked dances, according to McIlwraith, "His face is that of a woman, his voice that of a woman, but he has masculine characteristics as well."[54] Third gender status was well-integrated into the Bella Coola system of social ranking. According to McIlwraith, the position of first berry-picker, held by a woman who had the right to decide when berry harvesting could begin, depended on the ownership of an appropriate ancestral name. Occasionally, a male berdache was given one of these names.[55]

In short, berdache roles indeed can be present in societies with "full prestige differentiation." In Northwest Coast groups, this was because production and prestige were still based in gender categories—that is, types of persons defined by

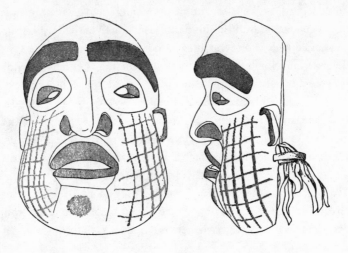

Figure 12. Skhints. Mask of the Bella Coola male berdache god Skhints. From Boas 1898a.

intrinsic productive skills—even though a system of ranking had developed.[56] As historical research often reveals, rather than lapsing, cultural forms change and continue as the social systems they are a part of evolve.

Yet another case in which historical factors are crucial in understanding multiple genders is the Navajo *nádleehí*. We saw in chapter 3 the high status that *nádleehí* could attain. Yet in the anthropological literature the Navajo are described as nomadic foragers and hunters whose culture was only somewhat modified by the adoption of farming from the Pueblos and sheepherding from the Spaniards. How could such a social system support the full-time specialization of a *nádleehí* such as Hastíín Klah? A synchronic, or social-structural, model does not account for this. A diachronic analysis, however, which examines Navajo historical development offers some answers.

The tribe's ancestors arrived in the Southwest in small nomadic bands of hunter-gatherers.[57] It is quite likely that these groups already had alternative gender roles—such roles were present among the historic Great Basin tribes, who pursued a similar subsistence pattern. The Navajo's encounter with the ancestors of the Pueblo Indians, however, gave them a new food source (corn) along with new crafts and religious practices. Women seem to have been both the vehicles and beneficiaries of these developments. Although farming and weaving were men's activities among the Pueblos, the former became a joint activity of Navajo men and women, and the latter became a women's art.

With the acquisition of the horse and sheep in the late seventeenth century a new phase of Navajo history began. Sheep became the property of the matrilocal household and in many cases the outright property of women. Consequently, women's status increased even more. Their labor alone could provide the family's basic subsistence. At the same time, they produced textiles, pottery, basketry, and other valuable exchange goods. With the horse, men were able to conduct regular raids on Pueblo and Hispanic villages. These new sources of food and wealth enabled some families to support talented members in various specializations—in particular, religion. *Nádleehí* were uniquely positioned to benefit from all these developments, both those involving men's roles (by specializing in medicine) and women's (by weaving).

By the beginning of the reservation period, the association of *nádleehí* and wealth was legendary. Further, as we saw in the case of Hastíín Klah, the disruption of traditional patterns in this period, which brought an end to men's roles as warriors and raiders, did not adversely affect the economic basis of the third gender. Klah flourished because changes in Navajo subsistence patterns provided unique opportunities for individuals skilled in both men's and women's activities. Being ambitious and talented, he took advantage of these opportunities and was undoubtedly not the only *nádleehí* to have done so. His career reveals how historical factors help account for the presence and status of alternative gender roles.

CONCLUSION

A multidimensional model recognizes not one but several defining characteristics of berdache roles, including gender, sexuality, social role, productive specialization, and religious functions. Such a model also leads to a new understanding of gender in relation to sex. Acknowledging that cultural interventions construct not only gender identities but serve to "materialize" the body as well (in Judith Butler's sense) requires a definition of gender that does not assume that anatomical differences are perceived the same in every culture. If gender is defined as a category of personhood that entails multiple expectations for behavior and temperament, sexuality, kinship and interpersonal roles, occupations, and religious experience, then male and female berdaches clearly occupied roles distinct from the gender roles of either men or women. Conversely, characterizations of berdaches as crossing or mixing genders, as men or women who "assume the role of the 'opposite' sex," are reductionist and inaccurate.

A consideration of the relationship of multiple gender roles to modes of production, relations of exchange, and the division of labor reveals that these roles were not niches for occasional (and presumably "natural") variations in sexuality and gender, nor were they accidental by-products of unresolved social contradictions. As instances of socioeconomic specialization, they were predictable and logical developments within tribal economies based on a gendered division of labor. A society's mode of subsistence alone, however, does not predict the presence of multiple genders. Whereas sedentary horticultural communities may have provided more opportunities for specialization, it was among the semi-sedentary, dispersed Navajo, for historical reasons, that a third gender appears to have enjoyed the highest status of any such role in North America.

In sum, the minimal conditions for the presence of multiple genders are as follows:

- A mode of production and division of labor organized in terms of gender categories, with possibilities for women's specialization in production and distribution of food and exchange goods;
- A belief system in which gender is not viewed as determined by anatomical sex or anatomical sex is believed to be unstable, fluid, or non-dichotomous, and, therefore, autonomous third/fourth categories are conceptually viable;
- Specific historical developments that create opportunities for individuals to construct and practice such roles and identities.

SEVEN

DREAMS OF POWER: THIRD AND FOURTH GENDERS IN YUMAN CULTURE AND HISTORY[1]

"HE WILL BE A LEADER"

In 1902, the Mohave shaman Nyavarup related the myth accounting for the origin of the Mohave male berdache or *alyha* for Alfred Kroeber. Nyavarup was one of the last Mohave doctors who knew the myth and the accompanying rite—an initiation ceremony that marked the entry of boys into the alternative gender status of the *alyha:*. Published seventy years later (nearly a decade after Kroeber's death), this text offers a rare glimpse into a traditional view of gender diversity.[2]

The narrative opens in the house of the god Mastamho at the sacred mountain Avikwame. Four women are seated in assigned directions around him—the shaman/leader, the *kamalo:y*, the mother about to give birth, and the midwife (see chapter 4). With instructions from Mastamho, the infant is delivered:

Now the baby lay there, looking around. "Sit back from him there," Mastamho said, "That boy knows much—more than you all: he will be a leader." The baby was looking this way and that, its eyes winking. Then it said: "I want a name. What will you call me?" Mastamho said: "He is a boy, but I think we will give him not a boy's name, nor a man's but a girl's. I call him Hatšinye-hai-kwatš'iše [little-girl-doctor]."[3]

Mastamho picked up the baby, held it in his hands, "I will tell you all about him. I want you to learn what I will teach about this child." Then he sang, swaying his hands from side to side with the child on them, and the four women danced to his motions.

When he laid the child down, the boy thought: "I am a boy; but shall I wear a breech-clout or not? Shall I wear girl's clothes or boy's?"[4]

When the boy becomes old enough to play, Mastamho subjects him to a series of tests. He gives him a bow, but the boy throws it away. He makes a prettier bow and arrow, and the boy throws them away as well and begins playing with girls. So Mastamho gives him a new name and makes him a set of stave-dice. The boy proceeds to play dice and laugh like a woman. Therefore, Mastamho instructs all the women and girls that the boy has the game of dice, and that "he will be the head one [of gambling]." Mastamho sings while the boy listens, and then he dances to the four directions. The god magically produces a bark skirt and gives it to the boy. He then instructs the *alyha:* in leading the women in dance. He is to walk backward before them as they follow—the standard pattern for Mohave dances. "He sang loudly, and they all sang with him, and as he sang he blew saliva on them" (a shamanic technique).[5] Following the singing and dancing, Mastamho leads the people south to Miakwa'orve, where he has created a *mat'ara,* or "party zone," and the women dance again.[6]

The myth associates *alyha:* with key domains of Mohave social life, including gambling, shamanism, and dancing. The first two are closely linked to Mohave concepts of the supernatural, the source of both luck and the power to heal or doctor, while dancing, as we will see, was related to tribal patterns of sexuality. When the evidence concerning *hwame:* related in chapter 4 is considered, it becomes clear that third and fourth gender roles were a prominent feature of Mohave culture. By combining this evidence with reports from the Mohaves' Yuman-speaking relatives a comprehensive picture of multiple genders in this region emerges.

The Yuman tribes of southern California, Arizona, and Nevada originally shared a common language and subsistence pattern, that of desert hunter-gatherers. The Upland Yumans (Havasupai, Walapai, Yavapai) and California Yumans (Ipai/Diegueño, Tipai/Kamia, and groups in Baja California) continued to pursue this pattern well into the nineteenth century. The Colorado River Yumans, however, ancestors of the Mohave, Quechan, Maricopa, and Cocopa, had switched to agriculture some time before they were first observed by Europeans in the early sixteenth century. A comparison of multiple genders among these groups, therefore, provides a unique opportunity not only to examine how different social organizations shape such roles, but also how these roles change when the social organizations they are a part of change.

The Mohave were not only the largest of the Yuman tribes, they appear to have been recognized as cultural leaders by other Yumans.[7] Most of the information on Mohave alternative genders is found in the writings of George Devereux, who worked with informants in the southern or Parker branch of the tribe beginning in 1932.[8] Devereux's interest in human sexuality (albeit from an orthodox psychoanalytic perspective) led him to inquire into the subjects of gender difference and homosexuality to a much greater extent than most ethnographers before or since.

Devereux learned that males who became *alyha:* and females who became *hwame:* were identified while they were young children based on observations of their interests and skills. As one informant explained, "When there is a desire in a child's heart to become a transvestite [sic] that child will act different. It will let people become aware of that desire. They may insist on giving the child the toys and garments of its true sex, but the child will throw them away."[9] Because *alyha:* were considered "somewhat crazy," parents were ambivalent about children with such tendencies.[10] However, *alyha:* were not normally teased or bothered. "It is their nature to behave that way," Devereux's informants told him. "They cannot help it."[11]

In addition to fixed personality traits expressed through childhood interests, Mohaves credited predestination, social influences, and, above all, dreams with shaping *alyha:* or *hwame:* identity. As Alfred Kroeber observed, "Not only all shamanistic power but most myths and songs, bravery and fortune in war, success with women or in gaming, every special ability, are dreamed."[12] Gender was among the "abilities" acquired through dreaming. In fact, Mohaves believed that such life-shaping dreams originally occurred when individuals were still fetuses in their mothers' wombs and then recurred around the time of puberty, revealing their adult identities.[13] If a child showed a pronounced interest in the activities of the "opposite sex," it was considered evidence that their prenatal dreams were those of an *alyha:* or *hwame:*. The parents would say, "If our child wishes to go that way, the only thing we can do is make it adopt the status of a transvestite [sic]."[14]

Devereux's clumsy rendering, "make it adopt the status of a transvestite," is a reference to the formal initiation rite held to confirm *alyha:* (and perhaps also *hwame:*) identity. Although ritual "tests" were employed in neighboring tribes to determine or confirm alternative gender status, the Mohave rite is unique in North American records for its complexity. While functioning partly as a test, it was also a fully developed rite of passage. It was conducted by four non-berdache men who had had the appropriate dreams. All preparations were done in secret so that (ideally) the youth was surprised when the proceedings began. His willingness to undergo the rite at this moment was considered the ultimate confirmation of berdache identity.[15] The participants spent the night before in a house preparing a traditional woman's skirt made of shredded bark. (Mohave men regularly made these skirts.[16]) The initiate lay between two women who sat beside him, and the men sang a series of songs describing how they had been with the god Mastamho (in their dreams) when he instituted the rite. The next morning, the two women carried the youth outdoors. One singer put on the willow-bark skirt and danced to the river. The initiate followed and imitated his movements. They bathed in the river, and then the two women gave the new *alyha:* a front apron and back skirt and painted his face white. After four days he was painted again. Following this rite of passage, the *alyha:* adopted a woman's name.

The proceedings follow the three-part pattern of rites of passage described by Arnold van Gennep and Victor Turner. The boy spends a night lying in a prone position under the watch of two women (the phase of separation); the next day he is led in a dance to the river where he publicly strips and enters the water (the period of liminality); after four days his face is painted and he is reintroduced into the community with his new identity as an *alyha:* (incorporation).[17] The existence of this rite is additional evidence of the significance of *alyha:* status. Such proceedings entailed the commitment of both human resources (four male specialists and two women were required) and goods (items used in the rites, food for feasting, payment for specialists).

Statements of Mohave informants parallel those that have been recorded throughout North America crediting male berdaches with special talents in domestic work and women's crafts. The Mohave believed *alyha:* were innately drawn to and skilled in these activities. *Alyha:* and *hwame:* sometimes became shamans (*kwathidhe:*), too.[18] Devereux consistently passes over these references, however, to focus on the particulars of their sexual lives. He reports that *alyha:* insisted on being referred to by female names and with female gender-references. They practiced receptive oral and anal intercourse, and while they achieved orgasm, they discouraged their partners from touching or even referring to their male genitals. They used the word for clitoris to refer to their penises, the term for labia majora for their testes, and the word for vagina for their anuses.[19] They formed both casual and long-term relationships with men who were not berdaches. When married to men, *alyha:* were referred to as wives. They had a reputation for industriousness and, except when teased, for being peaceful persons.[20]

Devereux speculates that *alyha:* were considered desirable wives because young girls "cannot be counted upon to settle down," and he attributes the willingness of men to marry *alyha:* to their "incessant search for new thrills in travel, war, love and humour."[21] He also reports that only prominent persons were able to obtain *alyha:* wives.[22] Still, men who took *alyha:* wives and women with *hwame:* husbands were subjected to teasing, which Devereux suggests was the source of the brittleness of such unions.[23] However, serial monogamy was the standard marriage pattern among the Mohave and other River Yuman tribes.

What has earned *alyha:* a permanent place in the ethnographic literature is Devereux's account of their elaborate mock pregnancies. These were carried out in excruciating detail, including the simulation of pregnancy through self-induced constipation followed by the "birth" of a stillborn fecal fetus. The whole production culminated with the burial of the "fetus" and the observance of the appropriate mourning rites, which the *alyha:* required "her" husband to join. Devereux also reports that *alyha:* simulated menstruation by scratching themselves until they bled and then required their husbands to observe the appropriate taboos. They did not, however, attempt to nurse infants.[24]

The behavior of *hwame:* appears to have been more variable. In childhood, they associated with boys and joined their activities. "They throw away their dolls and metates [used to grind corn], and refuse to shred bark or perform other feminine tasks. They turn away from the skirt and long for the breech-clout."[25] However, *hwame:* did not insist on male physiological terminology to refer to their genitals[26], and one informant told Devereux that *hwame:* did not always take male names. Also, some women became *hwame:* after having children. For this reason, *hwame:* were sometimes compared to *kamalo:y* or "loose" women (see chapter 4). *Hwame:* ignored their own menses but followed the taboos required of husbands when their wives menstruated or were pregnant. They did not necessarily cross-dress, although Devereux states that in "ancient times" they wore male garments. *Hwame:* were often shamans, and as such they were considered exceptionally powerful.[27]

Like men, *hwame:* found wives by attending dances or by visiting girls or married women by day—circumventing direct contact with girls' parents, who were not likely to approve of the courtship.[28] Nonetheless, *hwame:* were known to be devoted mates and excellent providers who took special pride in seeing their wives finely dressed.[29] (Devereux suggests that they were like Mohave men in this regard, whom he believed were more faithful than the women.[30]) They adopted the attitude and postures of the typical Mohave male, taking special delight in sitting among the men at gatherings and bragging salaciously about their wives' sexual attributes.[31] They had sex with their wives in a variety of positions, without assuming distinct active/passive roles.

As the *alyha:* myth indicates, male berdaches were believed to have a special relationship to gambling. Devereux was told that *alyha:* "will watch a woman's gambling game which we call the Utah-game [or Utoh]—as though they were under a spell. This game will fascinate them. They will try to participate in this game whenever they see it."[32] The game, significantly, is played with much explicit sexual humor; there are four pieces, one male (black), one female (red), and two mixed (black and red).[33] The luck of *alyha:* extended to their husbands as well—Devereux was told that some men married *alyha:* precisely for this reason.[34] In his telling of the *alyha:* myth Nyavarup provided an aside explaining that berdaches have special powers for curing venereal disease.[35] This was also said to make them lucky in love. Conversely, non-berdache shamans who specialized in the cure of venereal disease, such as Kuwal (Nopie), were said to be lucky in acquiring *alyha:* as wives.[36] According to Nyavarup, men gave *alyha:* beads when they had sex with them.[37] The nexus of all these associations is supernatural power manifested as luck in love and gambling, and as shamanism. Power attracts others—it is (and the Mohave are not alone in this attitude) "sexy."

The origin myth designates the *alyha:* as a dance leader. At least one dance in which *alyha:* played a role was the victory ceremony or "scalp dance."[38] The dance has been described by Kroeber, Stewart, and Fathauer, based on informants' memories and second-hand accounts.[39] The *kʷaxot* (party leader) placed the scalp on a pole, which was given to two older women (two being the usual number) called *yakatha:alya.*[40] The pole was set up in a *mat'ara.* Adorned and painted like warriors, the *yakatha:alya* danced around the scalp, attacking it, shooting arrows at it, and insulting it. Eight times the scalp was raised high into the air, and the people shouted and threw dust on it. Young men and women painted their hair white and danced for four days and nights.[41]

Both Devereux and Kroeber report that *alyha:* participated in this ceremony.[42] According to Devereux, old women who had lost relatives to the enemy taunted those who did not join the war party by fashioning a wooden penis or twisting their bark skirts to form a protuberance and poking them with it, saying "You are not a man but an *alyha·.*"[43] (According to Devereux, "The true alyha themselves were not considered cowards for not going to war."[44]) Stewart also reports that old women were prominent in the dance, wearing eagle feathers and painted like warriors.[45] The *alyha:* themselves joined in the phallic teasing.[46] It is not clear whether the women in Stewart's account and the *alyha:* in Devereux's were fulfilling the office of the *yakatha:alya;* however, the actions they perform correspond to those that Fathauer attributes to *yakatha:alya.* The element "*alyha*" in the term *yakatha:alya* is suggestive.

That the participation of *alyha:* in the scalp dance was a formal role is suggested in a myth recorded by Kroeber accounting for the origin of the ceremony.[47] In this narrative, the central figure is Nyohaiva, an insect who represents a woman born at the beginning of the world (when the differentiation of animals and humans, and male and female, was not yet complete). Nyohaiva "comes to life" at Miakwa'orve (the tribal "party zone"), and she immediately announces that she has "dreamed well" and wants to tell her dreams to the people. She travels a short distance and establishes another dance place, announcing "All will come to this place. They will come here to play and sing and have a good time. That is how I want you to become married." On subsequent travels she teaches songs to one group of people and shows a Walapai how to hunt. When she encounters four old men, all brothers, who plot to kill her, she declares war on them. She changes her dress and hairstyle (making them more masculine) and paints her face with four horizontal stripes. Putting the enemy to sleep by means of a magic ball created from her spittle, she cuts off the head (that is, the scalp) of one of the brothers with her thumbnail. With the head hidden under her dress, she takes the people to a place where there are four *alyha:* called Alyha:-tuyāme (walk in a circle), Alyha:-tokwīme (stand in one place), Alyha:-tšaôre (step on the heel of one in front), Alyha:-mīṭ-kusāma (far see?).[48] Nyohaiva then leads a scalp dance, throwing the head up four times and singing songs about it. Then she ties it to a willow pole and announces, "When there is war and a scalp is taken, people will do as I have done. They will dance and enjoy themselves. All will be happy and will play and sing."[49] She throws the head south, where it turns into a rock, and then turns herself into a stone called Avi-soqwīlye, or Hawk Mountain.

Kroeber notes that Nyohaiva is for all purposes a *hwame:* (at one point in her travels she causes confusion because her hairstyle is that of a woman although she is assumed to be a man). He concludes that the behavior attributed to her and the presence of the *alyha:* in the myth reveal "a definite functional relation between inversion and war in Mohave culture."[50] The myth also suggests that the roles of the four *alyha:* were formal ones. If they were in fact serving as the *yakatha:alya,* then it may be possible to clarify one of the earliest reports of Yuman berdaches.

In 1540, the Spaniard Hernando de Alarcón traveled up the Colorado River and observed that "the women go about naked. They wear a large bunch of feathers, painted and glued, tied in front and behind. They wear their hair like the men. There were among these Indians three or four men dressed like women."[51] Such males would have been obvious since Yuman women normally did not cover their breasts. Further upstream, in what is believed to be the territory of the Quechan,[52] Alarcón obtained additional information:

> At this place the old man showed as something amazing, a son of his dressed as a woman and used as such. I asked him how many such men there were among them. He replied that there were four, and when one died, a search was made for all the pregnant women in the land, and the first boy born was chosen to exercise the function of women. The women dressed them in their clothes, saying that if they were to act as such they should wear their clothes. These men could not have carnal relations with women at all, but they themselves could be used by all marriageable youths of the land. They received no compensation for this work from the people in the region, although they were free to take from any house what they needed for their living.[53]

The "old man," probably a local leader, clearly had no reticence about pointing out his son to the Spaniards and describing his special status. (In fact, one of Devereux's informants claimed that only members of prominent families, the *pipa tahan*[a] [best people] became *alyha:*.[54]) There are no subsequent reports of the number of *alyha:* being fixed at four—unless the chief was referring to a formal office in a dance such as that described in the Nyohaiva myth. In that case, if one of the four *alyha:* officiants died, there would have to be a procedure for replacing him. Alarcón's report may be a distorted account of this process. Similarly, the report that "the women dressed him" may be a reference to the role of women in the *alyha:* initiation rite as described above. That berdaches were forbidden "carnal relations" with women seems unlikely given the permissive attitudes of Yuman groups regarding sexuality and the absence of social control mechanisms other than gossip. More likely, *alyha:* did not have relations with women because they did not desire them. The statement that they "could be used by all marriageable youths" again reflects the sexual freedom of River Yumans as seen through the antierotic lens of counter-reformation Catholicism. They received no compensation for "this work" because it was not "work" in any native sense but merely one of many allowable pleasures.[55]

Ethnographic reports on other Yuman-speaking tribes confirm and clarify Devereux's Mohave data. Among the Quechan, both male *elxa'* and female *kwe'rhame* have been reported, although *elxa'* are said to have been more numerous.[56] Both were believed to be transformed at puberty by their dreams, especially ones involving messages from plants like the arrowweed, which was believed to change sex itself.[57] One of Forde's informants related a dream told him by an *elxa'*. He had traveled to a mountain near the site of an ancient Quechan settlement.[58] When he awoke he laughed with a woman's voice "and his mind was changed from male into female" (note the emphasis on "mind" rather than physiology).[59] *Elxa'* were believed to have more power than ordinary males and to have a peaceful influence on the tribe. As among the Mohave, a rite was held to publicly recognize their status.[60] In the 1850s an army officer described a Quechan *elxa'* : "She is gigantic in size, muscular, and well-proportioned. Her breasts are not developed like those of a woman, but she dresses like one of the gentler sex, and it is said she cohabits with a man. She is in disposition mild, and often hangs her head with a mental blush at the jokes of her companions."[61]

Kwe'rhame were also believed to be transformed by dreams, especially of men's weapons. However, parents tended to discourage girls from becoming *kwe'rhame* more than they did boys who wanted to be *elxa'*.[62] Forde's informants believed that *kwe'rhame* did not menstruate or that their secondary sex characteristics were

Figure 13. Quechan *kwe'rhame*, ca. 1890s. This only known photograph of a female berdache shows a Quechan woman wearing a man's breechcloth and men's bow guards on her wrists. Courtesy of the Southwest Museum, Los Angeles, Photo #N5506.

undeveloped. They were as active in warfare as men.[63] A photograph dating from the 1890s shows a Quechan woman with all the attributes of a *kwe'rhame* (see fig. 13). Wearing only a man's breechcloth, the woman stands with one hand on her hip in a characteristically male pose. She wears massive amounts of beaded necklaces, indicative of status and wealth, and bow guards on her wrists, a male accoutrement. Although this woman remains unidentified, there was at least one Quechan *kwe'rhame,* who married a woman, reported at this time.[64]

The Maricopa believed that dreaming of any one thing too much could change the gender of boys and girls.[65] "They had, in fact, too much of this dreaming; that is why they changed their mode of life. The change was caused by some spirit," as one informant explained. This usually occurred at puberty, although berdache tendencies were often apparent at an earlier age. If a Maricopa boy threw away his bow and took a basket or used a metate, elders commented, "He is going to turn out to be a berdache." According to Spier, an îlyaxaiˊ did not become a shaman. Although he was given the power to cure and sing, he was given too much power. Consequently, "other spirits" took the boy, "changing him into a woman."[66] Sometimes a berdache was called yĕsaʹaˊn, "barren person," which was considered more polite. Reportedly, men approved of îlyaxaiˊ and "treated them like girls," sometimes marrying them, while women were "uneasy" about them. As in the case of male berdaches, girls who dreamt too much became kwîRaxamĕˊ. Such women dressed like men and married women. In a tribe of about 300 in the early twentieth century, Spier's informant remembered one îlyaxaiˊ in his generation and one in the previous, and one kwîRaxamĕˊ.[67]

The Maricopa associated îlyaxaiˊ with certain sacred mountains. Sierra Estrella, the most revered of these, was believed to have a berdache living inside it. Hence it was called ᵃvialxyaˊʹ, Berdache Mountain.[68] Any man who dreamt of it became an îlyaxaiˊ.[69] Another mountain at Yuma was called by the same name. In dreams, these mountains appeared as young girls. Sierra Estrella invited the Yuma mountain to gamble, and each time one lost, a male from his side became a berdache.[70] Berdaches were associated with sacred mountains in Mohave tradition as well. As we have seen, the first alyha: was born at Avikwame mountain, and in an unpublished tale recorded by John Harrington an alyha: character who has been at a dance changes into a rock at the end of the story.[71]

Among the Cocopa, male berdaches, or elha, were also recognized early in childhood. They talked like girls, sought the company of girls and women, and learned women's work.[72] There may have been a ritual to acknowledge them.[73] Girls who became waRhameh played with boys, made bows and arrows, and hunted. They dressed their hair like men, had pierced noses, and were described as muscular. Reportedly, they did not menstruate and their breasts were small, although their genitalia were still female. They fought in war like men, married women, and established households.[74]

Among the Upland Yumans, however, evidence of multiple genders is less clear. Yavapai have denied the presence of berdaches, although Devereux mentions a Yavapai "lesbian transvestite" who committed suicide.[75] A Walapai informant described a Havasupai man "who dressed like a woman, did woman's work, and lived with a man," but he knew of "none such" among his own tribe.[76] However, another Walapai affirmed the presence of male berdaches and seemed to have had a recent example in mind.[77]

Among California Yumans reports of berdaches are also sketchy, with the exception of the Tipai (Kamia) tribe, whose origin myth prominently features a female berdache.[78] In this myth, as in River Yuman origin myths, Mastamho creates humans at Wikami. He assigns them to four tribes and instructs them to disperse. The Tipai migrate south with the Quechan, then go on alone to the

Salton Sea. Some groups continue west to become the Ipai, who have no seeds and live by hunting and gathering alone. At this point, Mastamho sends a figure called Warharmi, described as "half-man, half-woman," and the twins, collectively named Madkwahomai, to bring seeds and agriculture to the Tipai. Traveling along the Colorado River, they collect feathers for headdresses and then paint their faces for war. When they arrive in the Imperial Valley, the Tipai initially flee except for one woman who marries one of the twins. The twins then give the Tipai clans weapons and instruction in their use.

In this myth, Warharmi is a culture-bearer who brings the arts of agriculture and war. Although she lacks a direct parallel in myths from other Yuman groups, several Yuman goddesses share traits with her. Like Warharmi, some provide seeds (a Havasupai goddess), teach and participate in war (the Mohave Nyohaiva), and are associated with twins (the Mohave Qua-kuiña-haba/Kwa'akuya-inyohava; the Ipai Sinyaxau).[79] The closest parallel is Nyohaiva, a woman warrior who, like Warharmi, instructs the people in the use of war feathers and paint.[80]

Why does a female warrior have the role of introducing agriculture and the war cult in this myth? One possibility is that the process of transmission described in the myth models an historical event. The Tipai of the Imperial Valley have been described as desultory farmers who planted whenever advantageous flooding occurred but readily abandoned their crops if more plentiful wild plants or game appeared elsewhere.[81] According to Drucker, they relied on their upland relatives to bring them seed grain, a scenario that resonates with that described in the myth.[82] A purely speculative hypothesis might be that an actual female berdache, perhaps a leader of a group of colonists, brought seed grain and planting skills at a critical point in Tipai history.

An answer to this question in mythological terms, on the other hand, would begin by noting that Warharmi is a mediating figure. She bridges geographic distance (from the heartland of Yuman culture to its desert margins), but also the domains of agriculture and warfare. She brings seeds but arrives dressed and painted for war and frightens the Tipai. In fact, the motif of conveying agricultural knowledge through an intermediary occurs elsewhere. Earlier in the same myth, for example, Mouse comes to life when the original creator's blood flows into the ground, and he then takes his place in teaching the people when to plant and harvest crops.[83] In a similar way, Warharmi substitutes for Mastamho in transmitting agricultural knowledge. In the Maricopa origin myth, the creator god selects Coyote to take over the role of instructor.[84] In the Cocopa telling, the creator god himself returns to fulfill this function, but in the form of a spirit whose arrival triggers an earthquake.[85] In each case, a mediating figure substitutes for the creator god to teach the people agriculture. Mouse and Coyote, for example, are common characters in native North American folklore. Both are liminal figures with disproportionately great powers. In this context, Warharmi, too, appears as

TABLE 7.1.

Cultural Associations of Yuman Third and Fourth Genders

	Mohave	Quechan	Maricopa	Cocopa	Tipai	Ipai	Upland Yumans
Berdaches present	M/F	M/F	M/F	M/F	F*	M	M?/F
Berdache dreams	M/F	M/F	M/F				
Initiation rite	M/F?	M		M?			
Shamans	M/F	M?					
Gambling	M		M*				
Dancing	M						
Luck (in love)	M/F						
Scalp dance	M/F*						
Warfare	F	F		F	F*		
Berdache mountains	M		M				
Origin myth/tales	M/F		?		F		
Agriculture					F*		

*Documented in myths or tales.

a mediating figure whose ability to bridge male and female suits her for the function of both bridging and transmitting agriculture and war.

In sum, the cultural associations of multiple genders, as shown in Table 7.1, cut across a broad range of Yuman social life:

Power. Berdaches, along with shamans, warriors, and tribal leaders, were leading examples of the power of dreams to shape individual personality and destiny. Berdache dreams not only conveyed supernatural power, they transformed the individual, giving him or her a distinct social status. The associations of *alyha:* with gambling, in particular, link them to core beliefs concerning luck, skill, and destiny.

Pleasure. While the dreams of berdaches associate them with the domain of religion, the skills attributed to them also place them within the domain of *arro'oi,* or play.[86] For the Mohave, dancing, gambling, contests, and love-making were linked, having been established together by Mastamho at Miakwa'orve, the tribal "party zone." The first *alyha:* is lead to Miakwa'orve for his training. The myth describes him as leading dances, gambling excessively, and enjoying sex with men.

War. Third and fourth genders are also linked to the war complex. Female berdaches were warriors, and in Mohave and Tipai myths they lead war activities.

Male berdaches participated in the Mohave scalp dance, while the berdache mountains of the Maricopa gambled to determine the outcome of battles.

Agriculture. The Tipai berdache Warharmi is credited with introducing agriculture. In Mohave mythology, agriculture and multiple gender roles are established together at Avikwame.

THE FECAL FETUS

According to Devereux, Mohave berdaches consistently, indeed rigorously, behaved according to the precepts of a cross-gender model—as individuals of one anatomical sex who wished to become the "opposite sex": "The transvestite [Devereux uses this term interchangeably with homosexual] must attempt to duplicate the behavior-pattern of his adopted sex and make 'normal' individuals of his anatomic sex feel toward him as though he truly belonged to his adopted sex."[87] If so, then the Mohave case throws doubt on the characterization of berdaches as occupying third or fourth genders. If male berdaches not only wore women's clothing but imitated women's reproductive processes, and female berdaches did the reverse, then the Mohave gender system would appear to be dichotomous, and gender-crossing the only alternative possible. But is this the Mohave view? Or does the emphasis on cross-gender behavior in Devereux's report reflect his commitment to an orthodox Freudian theory of homosexuality as a sexual pattern "caused" by cross-gender identification?[88]

In fact, there are several reasons for reviewing Devereux's reporting. To begin with, the evidence of cross-gender behavior that he presents all relates to *alyha:*. His data concerning *hwame:* do not show them engaging in mimetic cross-gender behavior. Although he treats the two roles as complements they clearly do not parallel each other in every respect. Further, Devereux himself made no direct observations of either male or female berdaches, relying instead on the memories of informants recalling individuals and events of the late nineteenth century and often relying themselves on second-hand reports. He cites only three specific sources for his data on berdaches—Nyahwera, reputedly the last Mohave who knew the *alyha:* initiation songs (but not a berdache himself); Tcatc (Chach Cox), who had heard about (but not seen) the *alyha:* ceremony in her youth and was related to the *hwame:* Masahai Amatkwisai; and Hivsu: Tupom[a] (Dan Lamont), a male shaman who had known Kuwal, a Mohave from Parker who in the late nineteenth century married a series of *alyha:*.[89] Devereux's generalizations appear to be based strictly on these cases, even though he notes that only one of Kuwal's berdache wives was Mohave, the others belonging to the neighboring Quechan tribe.[90] (Forde, who conducted his research at the same time as Devereux, does not report gynemimetic behavior on the part of Quechan berdaches).

Needless to say, Kuwal's stories were not about the cultural meaning of the *alyha:* role but, in typical Mohave fashion, the humorous escapades he had had with them. "When alyha· get an erection," he confided to the young Hivsu: Tupom[a], "it embarrasses them, because the penis sticks out between the loose fibers of the bark-skirt. They used to have erections when we had intercourse. Then I would put my arm about them and play with the erect penis, even though they hated it. I was careful not to laugh aloud, but I chuckled inwardly. At the pitch of intercourse the *alyha·* ejaculate."[91] Devereux himself notes that creating a comical situation was "a thing paramount in the Mohave pursuit of sexual pleasure."[92] In short, much of what he repeats as evidence substantiating psychoanalytic theories was told precisely because it was outlandish and humorous.

Based on Devereux's account, it would be tempting to define Mohave berdaches as transsexuals, individuals who wished to change their anatomical sex. A closer look at his data, however, reveals significant differences between Western transsexualism and Mohave *alyha:* and *hwame:*. The goal of modern transsexuals has been to appear so convincing as members of their chosen sex that others never suspect they had been anything but that sex.[93] In the case of *alyha:*, however, the practice of holding public ceremonies to confirm their status made any such fiction impossible. Further, since Mohave women did not cover their breasts (because they were not viewed as sexual organs), *alyha:* were always identifiable, and the identities of both *alyha:* and *hwame:* were widely known within the tribe.[94] Nor is there evidence of *alyha:* attempting to alter their genitalia or enlarge their breasts.

In fact, the extreme gynemimetic behavior Devereux attributes to the *alyha:* is unique. There are no comparable reports from any other tribe, not even among the Mohave's linguistically related neighbors. The challenge, therefore, is to account for the faked pregnancies and other cross-sex attributes reported by Devereux. Here a unified analysis of cultural meanings, socioeconomic structure, and historical factors, as outlined in the previous chapter, provides an effective approach.

The first test of whether Mohave berdaches actually crossed sexes would be to determine if the Mohaves believed sex to be dichotomous and fixed, thereby precluding a third option. In fact, a close examination of the evidence reveals that the social labels and categories of the Mohave are more compatible with a multiple gender paradigm than a binary system. While acknowledging the anatomical sex of children, Mohave belief considers them "unfinished" without the dreams that serve to confirm gender identity. The narrative of the first *alyha:* underscores the malleability of gender assignment.[95] Doubtful of the infant's nature, Mastamho resorts to a series of tests. When the child expresses a preference for girls' toys and activities, Mastamho gives him appropriate training, clothing, and a female name. Neither this myth nor the tellings reported by Devereux provide precedence for a fiction of anatomical change.

In fact, a variety of comments indicate that, in the minds of many Mohave, *alyha:* and *hwame:* retained qualities of their original gender. "You can tease an hwame:," one Mohave told Devereux, "because she is just a woman, but if you tease an alyha·, who has the strength of a man, he will run after you and beat you up."[96] Although *alyha:* adopted female personal names, they did not assume the clan name borne by all the women within a lineage. In fact, the face-painting design applied to *alyha:* at the conclusion of their initiation—"a vertical stripe down from each eye and another down the nose to the mouth"[97]—has been identified as a men's style.[98] The goal of this rite, as Devereux's informants "emphatically stated," was not to transform the sex of the initiate but to effect the transition from boyhood to adult *alyha:*. All this is consistent with the interpretation of *alyha:* and *hwame:* roles as autonomous categories of personhood distinct from those of men and women.[99]

Not all social statuses, of course, are gender roles. What distinguishes gender roles, as argued in the previous chapter, is that they are multidimensional, and that they constitute individuals' primary identity, a point of reference for their sexuality, productive activities, personal relations, and social responsibilities. At a cultural level, they are a total social phenomena, templates for the construction and organization of other domains of social life. In fact, many of the social roles established in Mohave myths, such as shaman and warrior for males and the roles of mother, midwife, doctor, and *kamalo:y* for females, are "gendered" in that each is attributed with a distinct temperament as well as a set of skills or behaviors according to the model provided by male and female gender roles. But entering into the role of *kamalo:y* or shaman did not entail a change in primary gender identity. Devereux's informants, on the other hand, consistently explained *alyha:* and *hwame:* behavior as being typical not of men or women but of *alyha:* and *hwame:*. In fact, Devereux provides an example of Mohaves explicitly using a four-pole gender paradigm. When he asked them to classify degrees of shamanic power, they ranked male shamans first, followed by women, *alyha:,* and *hwame:*.[100]

Of course, the Mohave were no more consistent in their everyday application of terms and labels than Americans are today when they call individuals heterosexual or gay. These were all "fuzzy" categories in practice, their meaning subject to negotiation.[101] (Mohaves, for example, considered a "businesslike, intellectual" white woman a *hwame:*.)[102] To say that, overall, the Mohave thought of *alyha:* and *hwame:* as distinct gender roles does not mean that they applied this distinction rigorously or carried it out to its logical conclusion in every instance.

Shifting from analysis of cultural categories to a consideration of social-structural factors, we find little unique about Mohave social organization to account for the cross-gender behavior attributed to *alyha:*. If the Mohave did not have a division of labor based on gender, the behaviors that marked berdaches might shift from productive activities to other traits, such as anatomy, but there is no evidence that this was the case. Instead, the economic and religious underpinnings of Mohave multiple genders were the same as those in other tribes. *Alyha:* and *hwame:* were individuals who engaged in specialized activities as a result of supernatural sanction.

Assuming that Devereux was not in error (and that his informant was not playing a joke on him), there are two alternative explanations for his report. One is that the behavior Devereux described was atypical. The second is that (some) *alyha:* did manifest cross-sex identification, but because this was enacted at the level of discourse and ritual (and not surgically) it was understood by Mohaves as figurative, not literal.

In fact, Devereux's only source of information on *alyha:* pregnancies appears to have been Hivsu: Tupom[a], who was repeating the stories of his friend Kuwal. A possibility that Devereux does not seem to have considered is that the behavior of Kuwal's wives may have been specific to the dynamics of their relationships with him—and that in a small society such as Mohave, with a population in the late nineteenth century of less than 1,000, the behavior of two or three *alyha:* could easily represent "tradition" for a given generation. A comment reported by Devereux provides a clue: "Some men who had enough of it [marriage to an *alyha:*] tried to get rid of them politely, alleging barrenness of the alyha:. But no alyha: would admit such a thing. They would begin to fake pregnancy."[103] In other words, imitating pregnancy may have been the desperate stratagem of an individual threatened with the loss of a lover, not unlike hysterical pregnancies in women. Getting the husband to participate in mourning rites for the stillborn fecal fetus amounted to his capitulation to the fantasy and, therefore, a victory for the *alyha:*.

A second explanation is suggested by a variety of Mohave linguistic and symbolic practices. The primary means by which *alyha:* enacted their cross-gender identification was by linguistically reclassifying their sexual organs. In this they followed Mohave discursive practices, which frequently used "penis" and "vagina" as synecdoches. A man in retort to his wife who asks him to fetch water might say, "I have a penis and you have a vulva—it befits you to bring water—or bring me your skirt, and put on my breechcloth."[104] The speaker is not claiming that his penis makes him incapable of fetching water, rather "penis" and "vulva" are symbols for male and female gender roles.

Other cultural themes underlying the faked pregnancies of *alyha:* have less to do with gender than with patterns associated with shamanism and with a general anal preoccupation as evidenced in Mohave mythology, naming practices, individual fantasies, and sexual behavior.[105] In one version of the origin myth, the daughter of the cultural hero Matavilye is impregnated after swallowing her father's feces, a magical act that causes his death.[106] Conversely, another legend relates how, when some starving parents let their child fall into the river, a coyote appears who defecates watermelon seeds, which instantly grow into mature plants, making infanticide unnecessary.[107] Here the theme of death (feces) producing life (plant food) is clear.[108] Mohave nicknames frequently make allusion to the anus or feces, and Devereux found that both Mohave men and women had a distinct preference for anal intercourse.[109]

To a striking degree, the anus and vagina were interchangeable in Mohave representation and sexuality. If this was an expression of a cross-sex fantasy, however, it was a collective fantasy of which the anal pregnancy of the *alyha:* was merely a special case. In Mohave terms, such mimetic pregnancies (if they occurred) were not hysterical delusions on the part of *alyha:* but ritual and symbolic manipulations of "dirt" in Mary Douglas's sense of a form of pollution that mediates life and death.[110] The *alyha:*'s fecal fetus was the product of an entirely different order of thought and behavior than that which underlies contemporary transsexualism. There was no possibility of "passing" as a woman in traditional Mohave society, but through magic the *alyha:* could approach the female mystery of the creation of life.

In imposing the categories of orthodox psychoanalysis on his data, Devereux obliterates the Mohave point of view. For him, *alyha:* and *hwame:* roles were simply ways that the Mohave acknowledged the "inevitable": that there are always some individuals who have "abnormal tendencies." These roles "provided certain persons swaying on the outskirts of homosexuality to obtain the desired experience and find their way back to the average tribal pattern without the humiliation of a moral Canossa."[111] That this migration from the "outskirts" to the "average" was, to the Mohave, an exemplary confirmation of the power of dreams and the malleability of gender and sexuality, that it was motivated not by the need for sexual release but by the desire for an appropriate identity capable of fulfilling deep-seated motivations, and that such individuals, therefore, were not marginal but central to Mohave social life and representation—all this is lost when Western moral qua scientific categories of the "normal" and the "abnormal" are deployed. As this analysis suggests, Mohave beliefs and practices were far more complex than those of a dichotomous sex/gender system.

GENDER DIVERSIFICATION IN YUMAN CULTURAL EVOLUTION

The associations of multiple genders with such key domains of Yuman social life as dreaming, supernatural power, entertainment and sexuality, and warfare counter their portrayal as marginal deviants. The rest of this chapter will attempt to explain the prominence of multiple genders among River Yumans in terms of changes in social specialization and marriage practices that occurred when their ancestors switched from a food gathering to a food producing economy.

The dawn of agriculture among the prehistoric Yumans, who have been termed the Hakataya, is difficult to date due to the lack of surviving artifacts and the paucity of excavations.[112] Pottery first appeared in the Hakataya region sometime after 500 C.E., having dispersed from the Hohokom people on the middle Gila River.[113] It reached the lower Colorado River around 800. After 1100, a branch of the Hakataya termed the Amacava adopted a sedentary lifestyle near the confluence of the Gila and Colorado Rivers. It is likely that they were beginning to farm. They are believed to have migrated from the California desert and to have had a social organization similar to that of the historic Tipai and Ipai.[114] Some of these Yumans continued to migrate up the Colorado River into the highlands of northern Arizona.[115] In the 1100s, they established villages and farmed. When rainfall patterns changed and farm outputs decreased in the 1300s and 1400s, however, these eastern Hakataya pueblos were abandoned and the people reverted to hunting and gathering.[116] Their descendants are the Upland Yumans, whose historic culture resembles that of Great Basin Paiutes more than that of their River Yuman relatives.[117]

Consequently, Yuman cultural evolution was not a straight-line development from hunting-gathering to horticulture. Some groups retained older patterns; others combined the two; still others alternated between them.[118] Nonetheless, the adoption of even part-time farming and semi-sedentary residence by the River Yumans was a significant change from hunting and gathering.[119] The archaeologist Gordon Childe termed a similar socioeconomic transformation in the ancient Near East a "revolution." Instead of moving from resource to resource in groups of related families, River Yumans were able to establish semi-permanent residences of individual patrilocal families that on their own could produce all the food they needed.[120] Gathering and hunting supplemented the diet, and, if crops failed, families were ready to disperse to higher elevations and revert to full-time gathering and hunting.[121] Extensive regional trade networks also provided access to alternative food supplies as well as goods, and this fostered further economic specialization.

At the same time, because hunting and gathering remained an important back-up technology, the gendered division of labor associated with it remained in place, and the tasks of cultivation were not integrated into it. Rather, the work of preparing land, planting seeds, and harvesting crops was organized in a purely ad hoc manner and was neither assigned nor coded according to gender. Husbands and wives worked together in the fields at tasks largely of their own choosing. Only the heavier work of clearing brush was performed primarily by men.[122]

As Frederic Hicks has argued, one of the most significant social changes resulting from this economic transformation affected the nature of the lineage system. Among hunting-and-gathering California Yumans, patrilineal clans were localized economic and political units with semi-hereditary leaders. Among River Yumans, clans were a system of nonlocalized descent groups with few, if any, formal functions except to regulate marriage, and there were no clan leaders. Hicks attributes this to the need of River Yumans to relocate whenever the constantly shifting river adversely affected their farmlands. Over time, as families left to find new lands, localized lineages lost their territorial identities. Since there were no social groups larger than extended families with claims to land, families could relocate anywhere in the territory of the tribe not already occupied. The practice of abandoning the home and lands of the deceased facilitated this process. The lapse of formal decision-making and political functions by clans also led to the development of non-hereditary chieftainship based on individual competency and the powers conferred by dreams.[123]

Thus, a growth in social specialization was one outcome of the adoption of agriculture. Multiple genders, which were present among all the historic Yuman groups and, therefore, probably part of the proto-Yuman cultural complex, also appear to have been elaborated in this transition. Significantly, this occurred within the context of a gendered division of labor. That is, social specialization did not take the form of institutions or corporate bodies—River Yuman clans were not functioning bodies, there were no religious societies, and religious specialists were individual practitioners. Rather, specialization took the form of a proliferation of types of persons. In this process, gender roles served as templates for the construction of new roles. In fact, berdache roles may have been the first instances of gender "spin-offs" and the model for others. In Great Basin hunting-gathering bands, berdaches were the only full-time specialists whose productive activities were distinct from those of the standard male or female role. Other specialized identities, such as leader or shaman, remained part-time—most of these individuals continued to engage in the productive activities of men. The frequent references to the skills of male berdaches, on the other hand, under-scores that they were not merely fulfilling the productive expectations for women, but *specializing* in certain aspects of women's work.

At the same time, the supernatural elements of alternative gender status so pronounced among River Yumans are insignificant in most reports from Great Basin tribes, including Upland Yumans. Berdaches in these groups were not usually shamans, nor were special dreams mentioned as triggering the adoption of alternative gender identities or other social roles. Among the Yavapai, for example, shamans obtained their power through trance states rather than dreams.[124]

River Yuman beliefs and practices concerning dreams were, in contrast, much more complex. Because dreams were believed to convey individual skills, social identities, luck, and destiny, the domains of religion and production were, in effect, coterminous. Individuals' economic roles were functions of skills intrinsic to the category of personhood they occupied and this, in turn, was a function of personal contact with the supernatural. Further, the emphasis on dreams rather than visions or trances meant that access to supernatural power was universal. According to Fathauer, nearly all Mohave report skill- or luck-bestowing dreams of some kind.[125] Although the individuality of dreams could potentially authorize an unlimited variety of idiosyncratic and even antisocial behaviors, River Yuman religion ingeniously synchronized dreams with an extensive body of tribal mythology. As Joe Homer, who narrated the Quechan origin myth to Harrington, explained,

> It takes four days to tell all about Kwikumat and Kumastamxo. I am the only man who can tell it right. I was present from the very beginning, and saw and heard all. I dreamed a little of it at a time. I would then tell it to my friends. The old men would say, "That is right! I was there and heard it myself." Or they would say, "You have dreamed poorly. That is not right." And they would tell me right. So at last I learned the whole of it right.[126]

Whereas dreams served to authorize individual behavior, tribal myths authorized customs, institutions, and social roles. As Fathauer relates, "The typical response of Mohave informants attempting to convey an understanding of almost any aspect of their culture was to narrate the parts of the origin myth pertaining to the subject of inquiry."[127] This synthesis of dreaming and myth telling had the effect of both encouraging new behaviors and simultaneously constructing those behaviors into social roles and customs. Through this process, River Yumans were able to produce and conceptualize the growth in social specialization associated with the transition to agriculture.

Those individuals whose dreams made them *alyha:* or *hwame:* enjoyed a double sanction—the supernatural power of their dreams was confirmed by myths that decreed that "From the very beginning of the world it was meant that there should be homosexuals [*sic*]."[128] Fathauer underscores the significance of this sanction:

> The Gods are tribal Gods, and the specialists are tribal representatives. If they do not dream, the duties which *mastamxo* prescribed cannot be carried out and the tribe is unable to function adequately. The people are dependent upon the individuals who have the power to fill the essential statuses. . . . Religion and mythology, therefore, clearly reinforce the strong sense of tribal unity character- istic of the Mohave by channeling supernatural contacts through a series of indispensable tribal officials who automatically receive the power necessary for the existence of the people.[129]

A second significant change triggered by their economic transformation occurred in the marriage practices of River Yumans. Upland and California Yumans practiced arranged marriages, bridewealth and brideservice, and patrilocal resi- dence; restrictions on female sexuality were severe.[130] Walapai and Yavapai women who committed adultery could be beaten and abused.[131] Unmarried pregnant girls were unheard of among the Yavapai, and boys were routinely advised against early intercourse.[132] Among the Mohaves, on the other hand, men and women established marriages with no formalities simply by sleeping together, and there were no formal rules regarding residence after marriage. As

Devereux observed, "Unlike Western society, where children break away from the paternal family—not always successfully—only when they are ready to settle down in earnest with a spouse, the Mohave transition from life with the family to life with one's successive spouses is almost imperceptible."[133] Divorce was easy and frequent. Adulterers were rarely punished; unmarried mothers were common.[134] The Mohave system of patrilineal clans served only to enforce incest prohibitions and to provide names by which all the women members of a clan were known (along with nicknames or other identifiers). These clan names were especially expedient as a means of identifying a woman's sexual availability in relation to incest rules—a practical concern given the absence of other restraints.

All this is in accordance with instructions provided in the Mohave origin myth. Mastamho assigns Thrasher and Mockingbird to teach the people about marriage and sexual relations. A beautiful woman "with long hair reaching to the middle of her thighs and white paint on it" is identified, and the two leaders tell the men: "Some of you go to her. If she does not like you, she will not have you; but if she likes you, she will marry you. Go and try to take this good-looking woman's hand. If she takes yours it will be because she likes you; but if she does not like you, she will refuse to let you take her hand."[135] In short, marriage is to be voluntary and based on mutual attraction; women's right of refusal is absolute. These practices were paralleled among the Quechan, Maricopa, and Cocopa. There were no gift exchanges, brideservice, wedding rites, strict residence rules, or harsh punishments for adultery in any of these groups.[136]

The lapse of brideservice and bridewealth among River Yumans was likely another consequence of the changes in their subsistence pattern. As extended families became self-sufficient productive units, the need to create larger distribution networks (through bridewealth and/or ongoing gift exchanges) and to appropriate the labor of the young (directly through brideservice for the wife's family or indirectly through the requirement that young men work to accumulate goods for bridewealth) decreased. Equally significant were practices that circumvented the accumulation of wealth, such as burning the home and belongings of the deceased, periodic give-aways by chiefs and leaders at ceremonies, and the non-hereditary transmission of offices.[137]

The minimization of marriage among River Yumans had a variety of consequences. Since there were few constraints on the sexual availability of women in general and men could return to their fathers' homes to eat and sleep, marriage was not crucial to establishing adult male status. Consequently, men did not engage in warfare to acquire the prestige or goods necessary to obtain wives but because their dreams foretold warrior careers. According to Stewart, warriors lived spartan lives and "were uninterested in women and sex, few of them marrying until they had grown too old for combat."[138] At best, success in war made men more sexually attractive to women, and with economic considerations minimized, sexual attraction was what one looked for in a partner.[139] Nor were women under any particular pressure to marry, since they, too, could return to (or remain with) their natal household throughout their lives.

This made it possible for sexuality to emerge as a distinct domain of meaning and practice. As Devereux observed, "Sex, to the Mohave, is something very natural, pleasant, not very important emotionally, easily obtainable and just a bit insipid. After the earliest years of puberty all sorts of extraneous 'frills' have to be added to provide the required element of 'thrill.' This 'thrill' may consist in minor atypical modes of heterosexual behavior, or else coarse humor is injected into the sex act. The Mohave will actually devote some time to thinking up sexual 'stunts,' to make the act more exciting."[140] Even so, Devereux's informants considered their present-day exploits pale compared to the feats of the ancients. "Our ancestors could copulate until they died," he was told.[141]

Upland and California Yuman marriage practices, on the other hand, resemble the patterns described by Jane Collier as "brideservice" and "equal bridewealth" societies.[142] In these societies, men must acquire wives by either working for their wives' families (brideservice) or by providing gifts based on their own labor or that of their kin (bridewealth). Collier argues that how men go about meeting these requirements, the role of their elders in providing or not providing the resources necessary to marry, and how disputes concerning women are resolved all serve to define the nature of politics in nonclass societies and, ultimately, the sources of inequality between men and women.[143]

In both brideservice and bridewealth societies, daughters have a distinct value to their families, whether in goods or services, while their marriages help them forge cooperative bonds and exchange networks with other families. On the other hand, women do not need or want husbands as long as they have their fathers' households or other kin to live with. For them, marriage represents a decrease in freedom. They want lovers, not husbands. Controlling the sexuality of daughters and wives therefore becomes an ongoing concern. Some of these attributes can be found among River Yumans. As Collier's model predicts, the creator gods in Yuman myths are male, not female, and girls' puberty rites celebrate themes of health and sexuality, rather than fertility as such. Women's sexuality is seen as stimulating male pursuits such as warfare. (Indeed, attacks on women by enemies, and the capture of women in reprisal, seem to have been frequent sources of conflict in the region.) At the same time, women are frequently portrayed by men as bad housekeepers and unfaithful wives. Older women were more valued as wives, because they had "settled down."[144]

But on closer examination, River Yuman societies do not fit any of Collier's types. A key reason is that hunting and meat distribution, which Collier sees as the source of men's prestige, their alliances with each other, and their power over women, plays very little role in River Yuman economies.[145] A second reason, described earlier in this chapter, is that marriage practices were effectively depoliticized. This was a function of the changes in the lineage system and the fact that agricultural production was not organized according to the gendered division of labor used for hunting and gathering. Those activities of men that earned them prestige were not directly linked to their economic roles. Rather, the generosity of men who became leaders was based on their *distribution* of food and goods, which required the cooperation of the women of their families, who controlled the storage and preparation of all foods.

In the societies Collier describes, antagonistic heterosexual relations are contrasted to the domain of men's relations, which are represented as equal and harmonious. In River Yuman culture, sexual relations are represented as a domain of play and humor in which one can win or lose but can always reenter the game later on equal footing. In this domain of pleasure, both fertility and marriage are equated with sexual intercourse. As the female warrior Nyohaiva declares, "They will come here to play and sing and have a good time. That is how I want you to become married." Rather than being contrasted to a domain of harmonious relations between men, (hetero)sexuality among River Yumans was contrasted to shamanism. When Thrasher and Mockingbird instruct the people in courtship, and a shaman attempts to approach a woman, they tell him, "This is not the place to acquire power and learn to be a doctor: we are teaching other things: we are showing how to sing and dance. This is no place for a doctor to come to."[146] The Mohave shaman, as suggested in chapter 4, serves to mark the boundary between acceptable and antisocial sexuality. Fear of shamans who become witches as a result of sexual compulsion takes the place in River Yuman societies of exaggerated fears and representations of female sexuality and menstrual blood, which serve in other native societies to check sexual conduct.

In short, what asymmetry existed between men and women in River Yuman societies was not a function of marriage politics. Ultimately, it was men's dreams that enabled them to acquire greater prestige and a modicum of social power, because these dreams could lead to roles that extended their sphere of alliances and influence beyond their immediate family. The premiere source of prestige for Mohave men was warfare—but without the correct dreams foretelling success there was no point in pursuing a career as a warrior. Further, warriors were not good candidates for husbands, since they did little work and expected to die. Still, they enjoyed high status, and their potential for violence no doubt led others to fear them. This gave them social power, but it was not power that could be used to arrange marriages for themselves or others.

Before concluding that River Yuman societies illustrate a public/domestic dichotomy of men's and women's roles, evidence that Yuman women had access to public roles and participated in warfare needs to be considered. The role of *hwame:* is the leading example of how some women's dreams resulted in their participation in men's pursuits. Both *hwame:* and women could also become shamans, and both were involved in warfare, from joining war parties and engaging in combat to participating in victory dances and scalp rituals.[147] Still, the primary way women acquired prestige remained childbearing. According to Devereux, the Mohave viewed women's role in childbearing as a direct counterpart to men's role as warriors—both promoted tribal welfare, dominance, and continuity.[148] It is important to stress, however, that having children gained them this respect regardless of their marital status.

There were indeed limits to women's autonomy in River Yuman societies, but they appear to have been imposed not through pressure from kin or marriage obligations but through male violence. The rape of Masahai was described in chapter 4. Her conduct appears to have been tolerated until she blatantly attempted to seduce a man's wife for a second time. Devereux also reports that *kamalo:y* who told false and malign stories and taunted men in public might be subjected to punitive gang rapes and even genital mutilation, as might a promiscuous wife at the instigation of her husband.[149] The behavior cited to justify such attacks is similar to that of shamans who taunt the relatives of their victims because they wish to die (and join the souls they have captured through witchcraft).[150] Nonetheless, even in a sexually permissive culture in which, according to Devereux, the men "do not care to cohabit with involuntary or uninterested sex partners" and rape is extremely rare, the specter of sexual violence still cast its shadow on women's lives.[151]

The argument here, however, is not that sexual stratification was absent from River Yuman cultures, but that the sources of it in Collier's models—marriage politics, differential prestige accorded to men's food production, and limitation of women's influence to their kinship networks—were mitigated as a consequence of Yuman cultural evolution. Although women did not have the power to enforce their will on others, neither did most men. At the same time, both men and women had access to a range of social roles, lifestyles, and identities.

In sum, changes in subsistence patterns, which triggered transformations in the lineage system and marriage practices among River Yumans, resulted in a proliferation of not only genders but sexualities as well. In the domain of sex-as-play, *alyha:* and *hwame:* epitomized ideals of sexual variety, adventure, and humor. Since marriages were not crucial to men's adult status and prestige, it was not even important that a wife be female. Conversely, women could choose female husbands as well as male lovers. The Mohaves' flexible, extended families easily accommodated children, step-children, adopted children, and children conceived by lovers as well as spouses, along with relatives and even acquaintances.[152] The consequences of sexuality were two: the danger of sexual compulsion represented by witches and venereal disease—which *alyha:* and *hwame:*, the specialists in sexuality, had the power to cure.

The cultural domain in which the elaboration of sexuality and gender found its most complex expression was the warfare complex. Because of the leisure time afforded by the productivity of farming, River Yuman men were free to pursue a love of combat with little constraint, and by all accounts, they did so with extraordinary zest. For warriors (Mohave *kwanami*), success in battle "was the concrete expression of spiritual strength."[153]

If the stated goal of the warrior was the fulfillment of his dreams, the justification for warfare from a collective perspective was the benefits it brought to the tribe as a whole—namely, the stimulation of tribal fertility by the acquisition of powerful enemy scalps. This transformation of death into life was a collective endeavor, brought about through the victory dance. According to Fathauer, "The scalps were felt to bring good luck and power to the younger generation, and their display was attended by considerable euphoria and intensified courting activities." Indeed, "It was expected that the people would enjoy themselves sexually during the four days of the celebration."[154] The *kʷaxot* specifically instructed the young people to marry and have children—that is, to have sex during the ceremony.

The scalp ceremony juxtaposed two distinct forms of supernatural power— that of the warrior, represented by the enemy scalp, and that of postmenopausal women and *alyha:*, individuals whose sexuality was nonprocreative. It was the taunting of the old women and *alyha:* that served to transform the scalp's deadly power into sexual energy and fertility for the tribe. Metaphorically, they drained away the scalp's power and dispersed it to the participants in the ceremony. Stimulated by the displays of aggression, the euphoria of victory, and the pleasure of dancing, the celebrants paired off and retired to the brush for intercourse. Fertility was a tribal rather than a familial concern.[155]

Because *alyha:* were (symbolically) infertile, the scalp had no power over them. As threshold figures who both marked and bridged the boundaries of the Mohave universe, they could stand between the dangerous power of aliens and the tribe. Although this ability to domesticate scalps was related to their symbolic nonreproductivity, they were not viewed as being asexual. Rather, as we have seen, berdaches were regarded as being highly sexual. What has been subdivided as "heterosexual" and "homosexual" in Western societies was in River Yuman cultures linked into a single system. The nonprocreative sexuality of alternative genders contributed to the success of reproductive heterosexuality.

CONCLUSIONS

Although multiple genders were certainly present in earlier Yuman societies, they became prominent in the cultural innovations that accompanied the adoption by

River Yumans of a semi-sedentary horticultural lifestyle. These developments likely occurred between 1100, when the Amacava people began living on the Colorado River, and 1540, when Alarcón observed male berdaches with ritual roles. *Alyha:* and *hwame:* came to be associated with two key domains of the new cultural configuration—the emergence of a warfare-fertility complex and the elaboration of sexuality.

To borrow Lévi-Strauss's formulation, *alyha:* and *hwame:* were "good to think." They were likely the first instance of gender-based productive specialization. They confirmed beliefs in dream-power and in concepts of chance, luck, virtuosity, and transformation. Their presence in society increased the possibilities for sexual adventure and humor. At the same time, as highly sexual individuals who did not (normally) reproduce they represented and implemented the conceptual and ritual mediation between death and fertility that was central to the warfare complex.

The result of this examination of Yuman societies suggests that the multiplication of genders to encompass the emergence and/or growth of social and economic specialization is a potential of any division of labor based on gender (but not those based on sex). In fact, as chapter 10 shows, similar roles were widespread in the ancient societies of the Mediterranean and Near East, and exist in Asian and Oceanic societies to the present day. This analysis also demonstrates the importance of replacing heterosexist assumptions about human society with detailed models of how gender is produced in a given social formation. Of course, few theorists today presume that male and female social roles are "natural," but many still accept the naturalness of gender dichotomy. Collier's thesis that marriage politics are universally relevant as a diagnostic of gender relations in nonclass societies, for example, is plausible only as long as assumptions about the naturalness of heterosexuality and gender dualism are not questioned. Simply because opposite-sex intercourse is a requirement of human reproduction does not justify the expectation that every human culture will have its "version" of "marriage." Describing the casual partnerships of River Yumans with the same term as the arranged and culturally freighted unions of bridewealth and brideservice societies reduces the significance of the term "marriage" to little more than "occurrence of heterosexual intercourse."

Beyond this, centering analysis on heterosexual marriage practices automatically consigns multiple genders to a marginal status. If heterosexual desire is a given, then there really is no reason to discuss berdaches—they are merely incidental features of a larger system that, to be understood, must be studied in terms of how it *normally* works rather than in terms of its occasional failures. If, on the other hand, we do not presume heterosexual desire to be natural or given then two questions become relevant: How do gender systems instill, foster, and ensure heterosexual behavior, and how do some systems consistently produce individuals who are non-heterosexual and/or occupy statuses not male or female?

AFTERWORD: SEXUAL DIVERSITY IN CONTEMPORARY YUMAN SOCIETIES

Devereux speaks of the *alyha:* as a lapsed tradition, and he describes his more recent cases as instances of "homosexuality." Whereas alternative genders (or memory of them) survived in such neighboring tribes as the Navajo and Pueblos, the last known *alyha:* and *hwame:* lived in the generation of the parents of Devereux's informants. Perhaps the break with traditional roles was sharper among the Mohave because of the lapse of the *alyha:* initiation rite. Without the rite, many Mohaves would be uncertain whether to call an individual an *alyha:,* even if he manifested all the expected traits, and such individuals themselves would be unwilling to claim the label. It is also possible, however, that the history of sexual and gender diversity among Yuman groups is more complex than has been assumed. It may be that not only casual but committed homosexual relationships were a viable option in traditional Mohave culture—alongside that of being an *alyha:* or a partner of an *alyha:.* If so, then this pattern may have survived even though *alyha:* and *hwame:* roles did not.

That such relationships existed is suggested by a passage in Devereux's 1937 article in which he describes three men "accused of" "active and passive homosexuality"—none of whom cross-dressed or had undergone the *alyha:* initiation. All three men lived together; two were half-brothers. According to Devereux, "They are usually referred to as each other's wives and are said to indulge in rectal intercourse."[156] What's striking here is the indefiniteness of the role attributions. Devereux invokes the distinction between active and passive homosexuality, but he fails to indicate *who* is active and *who* is passive. In his discussion of *alyha:,* this distinction is crucial. One of these men would have to be a husband and another a "wife," and the "wife" would be expected to insist on the distinction.

Although Devereux reports that casual homosexual relations were "frequent" in traditional times (as they reportedly were among the Quechan[157]), because they do not fit his preconceived notion of "homosexuality" as sexual inversion he does not explore the extent to which same-gender relationships may have existed in earlier times. Kroeber, for example, identified two Mohave men who lived in the nineteenth century as "friends and partners," and both Mohave and Quechan census records from the late nineteenth century reveal households comprised of unrelated individuals of the same sex.[158] Especially intriguing are entries such as that for household #223 in the census Harrington took at Fort Mohave in 1911: Patrick Gilmore (Ichiyely) is listed as never married because he "did not like women."[159]

In 1965, *ONE* magazine published an interview with a gay-identified Mohave, Elmer Gates (called Elmer Gage in the article).[160] Gates reported being teased by other Mohave but considered himself accepted by the tribe. Like *alyha:* in the past, he specialized in crafts and knew traditional Mohave dances. He told the interviewer, "It seems like I'm the only one that's keeping these traditions alive"—although he made no mention of the *alyha:* role.

In the 1990s, memory of the role and traditional terms for it among the Mohave are all but forgotten. When two people of the same sex are thought to be having an affair, others simply say, "They're queer for each other."[161] Even so, despite the lapse of traditional roles, individuals with alternative sexual and gender identities have become increasingly visible in Yuman-speaking communities. In 1976, psychiatrist Robert Stoller described a member of one Yuman tribe in his thirties who was seeking sex reassignment surgery. Although this individual was unaware of historic berdache roles in his tribe, he reported that he was well-accepted. He was the best basketmaker and dressmaker in the tribe, having been trained by his mother.[162] He was seeking transsexual surgery at the urging of his male lover, who wanted to get legally married.

A few years after this, a member of the Havasupai tribe reported that there were three gay males in his community and another six who were bisexual. One of the homosexuals cross-dressed and had earned a reputation as the best basketmaker in the tribe. Another nonmasculine male was responsible for organizing, supervising, and designing clothes for the annual Miss Havasupai beauty pageant.[163] A decade later these individuals were still active in the community, and they had been joined by others. Between 1991 and 1992, Daniel Benyshek met five Havasupai whom he describes as "transgendered" on the basis of their dress, interpersonal style, speech and communication patterns, occupations and interests, and primary social groups. The Havasupai generally used the terms "gay" and "homosexual" in describing them. In fact, although two had considerable experience cross-dressing, Benyshek reports that all five wore men's clothes, albeit in an "androgynous" manner, during the time he worked in the community. Both elders and anthropologists familiar with the tribe told him that such persons "are as common and conspicuous today as they were rare in the 1950s and 1960s."[164]

In yet another Yuman-speaking community, a social network of lesbians became visible in the 1980s. An estimated 40 to 60 women on the reservation adopted committed lesbian lifestyles, and the network of women who are their friends or have had affairs with them is much larger. Tribal gossip traces this to the arrival in the 1970s of a non-Yuman Indian woman who became a local athletic star and to a female coach, both of whom had affairs with women. On the other hand, gay male members of the community are much less visible, most live off the reservations in nearby urban areas, and many have died from AIDS or alcohol-related causes. Nonetheless, several regularly return to the reservation for important tribal and family events, and their adoption of urban gay styles makes them increasingly visible.[165]

The Yuman-speaking people have an ancient history in the Colorado River region that includes a prominent place for multiple genders. Today, their communities may be small, located on the fringes of the urban centers of southern California and Arizona, but they nonetheless continue to foster complex and creative identities incorporating sexual and gender difference. When Elmer Gates was interviewed in 1965 he spoke more like an activist of the 1990s than a rural Indian whom history had passed by. "I guess I'm just on my own personal little warpath," he said, "not against whites but against heterosexuals who think everyone should be like them. I'm not always happy, but I'm always me. And they can like it or lump it. Life's too short to spend your time being something you don't want to be."[166]

CLOSE ENCOUNTERS:
A MODEL OF NATIVE SURVIVANCE

THE QUESTION OF TRANSMISSION

Until recently, the greatest challenge in studying North American gender diversity has been the problem of translation—finding the right concepts and terminology for describing social roles so unlike any found in contemporary Western societies. The multiple gender paradigm outlined in the previous chapters represents one answer to this problem. At the same time, a second question has arisen that deserves equal attention. It has less to do with translation and more with the problematics of transmission—assessing what novelist Gerald Vizenor refers to as "survivance," the capacity of native North Americans, against overwhelming odds, to pass on ideas, symbols, identities, and cultural forms from one generation to the next. The study of transmission raises questions of authenticity, authority, and interpretation. What is the true third and fourth gender tradition? Do berdaches exist today? Are contemporary gay, lesbian, and transgender natives their descendants? Is the two-spirit movement described in chapter 5 involved in the recovery of an important, overlooked dimension of native history or is it based on romantic constructions of an idealized past?

The answers to these questions that have been offered so far tend to be overly simplistic, even dogmatic. Both scholars and natives have relied on models of historical change that are no less reductionist than the categories "homosexual" and "transvestite." Consider, for example, the statement that "berdaches began to disappear soon after European or American control was established," or that their behavior became "vestigial," and that they "faded from view shortly after contact."[1] One anthropologist has concluded that "the cultural reality of the berdache has been destroyed, the victim of broader historical and material changes that could no longer sustain and reproduce the conditions of social recruitment and self-selection necessary."[2] Such invocations of the "vanishing berdache" have prompted some to ask, with sociologist Kenneth Plummer, "Why should one even begin to contemplate the notion that the *berdache* has anything at all to do with homosexuality in our terms?" But as chapter 5 showed, "our terms"—presumably those of European descent—are not the ones being used by many contemporary native people, who are drawing on terms from their own cultures to define sexual and gender diversity.[3]

Underlying this debate is a model of cultural change that opposes "tradition" to "assimilation." Western culture, in this view, is imposed on and replaces native culture in a process Ralph Linton once termed "directed culture change." The result is detribalization, the replacement of tribal traditions with Anglo-American culture.[4] Relying on this model, some have propounded rules limiting the use of terms such as "berdache," "gay," "homosexual," and so forth in reference to Native Americans. Fulton and Anderson state, "Imposing Western labels (such as 'male' and 'homosexual') on the aboriginal 'man-woman' imbues the role with Westernized meanings for which, we suggest, there was no context in aboriginal society. The word homosexual, for example, has its roots in the medical literature of mid-19th-century Germany."[5] The assumption here is that "aboriginal" and "Western" are discrete categories and that cultures have clear-cut boundaries and contents.

Officially, anthropologists have abandoned the view of cultures as holistic, discrete, and closed systems.[6] Ethnographies in the second half of the twentieth century often have documented the permeability of cultural borders and the wide range of circumstances in which cultural forms are transmitted and transformed. Anthropologists interested in political economy, such as Eric Wolf, have shown how even small, isolated societies are linked to international markets and world systems.[7] Still, the view of cultures as bounded entities continues to influence popular and academic discourse. As Renato Rosaldo observes, "Although the official view holds that all cultures are equal, an informal filing system more often found in corridor talk than in published writings classifies cultures in quantitative terms, from a lot to a little, from rich to poor, from thick to thin, and from elaborate to simple."[8] Rosaldo has shown how such assumptions marginalize what occurs at the interfaces of cultures using the Philippines and Mexico as examples, societies with multiple cultural zones and permeable borders. He concludes, "The view of an authentic culture as an autonomous internally coherent universe no longer seems tenable in a postcolonial world."[9] Rosaldo's observations apply equally well to native North America. In fact, I would argue that a model of cultures as self-contained systems does not apply to any period of North American history.

Native North American history has been periodized in terms of four phases: symbiosis, conflict, the reservation period, and reemergence or revivalism.[10] Today when anthropologists and native people use the word "traditional" what they usually have in mind is the culture of the symbiotic phase, that period of mutual interdependence between Europeans and natives that prevailed in many areas before the rise of North American nation-states. In truth, we know very little about native societies before the disruptions caused by contact and conquest. In the 1600s, the lifestyle of Northeastern and Canadian Indians was dramatically altered by the adoption of hunting, trapping, and trading, which linked their destinies to European markets. In the Plains, nomadic hunter-warrior lifestyles do not date back before the seventeenth century. Perhaps the best example of a traditional culture that is a highly creative synthesis is that of the Navajos. Within the course of a few centuries, the tribe absorbed the successive influences of the Anasazi (acquiring from them farming and religious practices), the Spaniards (source of horses and sheep), and the Americans (whose trading posts fostered the commercialization of weaving). Yet today the Navajos are recognized as sustaining to a remarkable extent their traditional culture, language, and religion.

Native North American survivance challenges analytical distinctions between history and structure, stability and change. As Marshall Sahlins shows in *Islands of History*, these are not exclusive alternatives. It often happens that a set of historical relationships reproduces traditional categories but at the same time gives them new values and new referents. Sahlins calls this the "structure of the conjuncture."[11] Change is both inevitable, yet inevitably constrained. "For even as the world can easily escape the interpretive schemes of some given group of mankind, nothing guarantees either that intelligent and intentional subjects, with their several social interests and biographies, will use the existing categories in prescribed ways." This is "the risk of the categories in action," the risk that, once deployed, especially in intercultural settings, categories will be changed; and invariably they are. Even so, Sahlins argues, "Things must preserve some identity through their changes or else the world is a madhouse," and he quotes the semiotician Ferdinand de Saussure, "The principle of change is based on the principle of continuity."[12]

The integration of synchronic (social-structural) and diachronic (historical) analysis enables Sahlins to reinterpret key episodes in native Hawaiian history. The actions of Hawaiian commoners eager to trade goods with Europeans; of royalty who assumed that Europeans, like themselves, were deities; and of women who sought intercourse with Europeans in order to bear the child of a god all served to reproduce the traditional stratification of Hawaiian society, confirming Sahlins's proposition that "the transformation of a culture is a mode of its reproduction." At the same time, Europeans presented new opportunities for forms of opposition between commoners and royalty. In taking advantage of these opportunities, Hawaiians transformed the functional values of their traditional categories. Eventually, as the relationship between categories changed, the structure of Hawaiian society itself was transformed.

Alternative gender roles were no less cultural syntheses than native cultures in general during the symbiotic phase of North American history. A review of the contact literature—writings by European explorers, travelers, traders, missionaries, and others—shows that the cultural exchange around white and native concepts of sexuality proceeded much as Sahlins's model predicts. Multiple genders were both reproduced *and* transformed. The rest of this chapter documents this "conjuncture of the structure" in two distinct settings: the North American frontier, where Europeans and third gender individuals met face-to-face; and Europe, where accounts of North American gender diversity were cited in ongoing discourses on gender and sexual difference. These discourses eventually gave rise to the modern conception of homosexuals as a category of persons, which ultimately fostered the formation of homosexual identities, communities, and politics in the twentieth century.

CLOSE ENCOUNTERS OF THE THIRD KIND

Before considering the evidence of frontier discourse it is helpful to review the contexts in which it occurred. Balboa's slaughter of berdaches in Panama in 1513 represents only one of the outcomes of the encounters between Europeans and North American multiple genders. A brief review reveals that other, less violent, outcomes occurred as well.

Symbiosis. In 1564, René Goulaine de Laudonnière and Jacques Le Moyne arrived in Florida to assert French claims to the region, which was the home of the Timucua, populous village dwellers with a complex, stratified society. Not long after Laudonnière's arrival, while marching through the dense Florida woodlands on a hot afternoon, his party found itself exhausted and nowhere near its destination. At that moment,

> We met an Indian woman of tall stature, which also was an Hermaphrodite, who came before us with a great vessell full of cleere fountaine water, wherewith she greatly refreshed us. For we were exceeding faint by reason of the ardent heate which molested us as we passed through those high woods. And I beleeve that without the succour of that Indian Hermaphrodite, or rather, if it had not bene

for the great desire which we had to make us resolute of our selves, we had taken up our lodging all night in the wood. Being therefore refreshed by this meane, wee gathered our spirits together, and marching with a cheerefull courage, wee came to the place which wee had chosen to make our habitation in.[13]

Later he encountered another "hermaphrodite" serving as an emissary from a Timucua king.[14]

The circumstances of Laudonnière's encounters with Floridian berdaches are common for the symbiotic phase of native-European relations. He does not denounce the "hermaphrodite" who aids him; he is grateful for "her" assistance. The berdache, for her part, seems to have actually sought out contact with the French. Accounts of Osh-Tisch and Hastíín Klah create similar impressions of berdaches as assertive, independent, and curious individuals who sought encounters with outsiders.[15] The Kutenai female berdache Qánqon also had extensive contacts with whites, and Woman Chief of the Crow tribe was "well known to all whites and Indians."[16] In each of these cases, the willingness of Europeans and Americans to interact with third and fourth gender natives reflects their reliance on native aid and alliances.

Accommodation. At the beginning of the twentieth century, a Klamath berdache known as White Cindy (Muksamse´lapli) was a familiar figure to local whites. "Old timers of Klamath Falls, Oregon, remember her well, as I do," one recalled, "for I well remember that as a child I always crossed the street when I saw her coming, being afraid of her from stories that I heard."[17] Those stories had largely to do with Muksamse´lapli's powers as a medicine person, which her tribespeople had learned to respect, and her reputation for fierce outbursts when she drank. Nonetheless, the stories did not stop local residents from regularly buying baskets and trading with the berdache, taking pictures of her, or telling ribald stories about her love affairs long after her death.

Klamath Falls was not the only western town in which whites regularly interacted with third and fourth gender natives. As Americans began settling the frontier, they frequently encountered—and accommodated—native gender diversity.[18] As related in chapter 2, the memories of the daughter of a Crow Indian agent illustrate how one Anglo-American family invented rationalizations for alternative gender behavior that made it understandable and acceptable within their cultural expectations and values. Others resolved the tension between Judeo-Christian mores and their friendship with berdaches by simple denial. As Matilda Stevenson wrote regarding her Zuni friend We'wha, "Some declared him to be an hermaphrodite, but the writer gave no credence to the story, and continued to regard We'wha as a woman." When finally confronted with evidence of We'wha's sex, she wrote, "As the writer could never think of her faithful and devoted friend in any other light, she will continue to use the feminine gender when referring to We'wha."[19]

Collaboration. Hastíín Klah's life illustrates another outcome of contact between berdaches and Euro-Americas—cooperation, collaboration, and friendship. Like We'wha, he formed close personal relationships with non-Indians (primarily women) and collaborated with them in producing a permanent legacy of his cultural expertise. Both individuals had an impact on how non-Indians thought about sexuality and gender. Hastíín Klah's status as a *nádleehí* was a frequent subject of discussion among the artists, writers, and intellectuals of Santa Fe who met him as the guest of Mary Wheelwright.[20] Similarly, Ruth Benedict was so impressed by the stories she heard about We'wha that she cited the famous Zuni *lhamana* in her groundbreaking discussion of homosexuality in *Patterns of Culture.*[21]

Attraction. Margaret Mead observed another kind of encounter between Euro-Americans and third gender natives while she was conducting fieldwork among the Omaha in the 1930s—attraction. "We were visited by a male friend who had been living an avowed homoerotic life in Japan, who was not transvestite but who had a complete repertoire of homosexual postures. Within an hour of his arrival, the single berdache in the tribe turned up and tried to make contact with him."[22] John Tanner, in his account of life on the frontier in the early nineteenth century, relates the determined efforts of the Ojibway berdache Ozaw-wen-dib to seduce him. "Not being discouraged with one refusal," Tanner complained, "she repeated her disgusting advances until I was almost driven from the lodge."[23] Other reports of same-sex contact between Europeans and natives include the Lutheran "sodomite" who pursued an affair with the son of a Yamasee chief, and a German suspected of "corrupting" a "lusty" and "effeminate" young Chickasaw.[24]

Resistance. When attempts to suppress gender diversity did occur, the outcome was not always as one-sided as Balboa's massacre. The Franciscan missionary Francisco Palou related events in California in the 1780s that show how third gender natives effectively resisted such efforts:

> Among the gentile women (who always worked separately and without mixing with the men) there was one who, by the dress, which was decorously worn, and by the heathen headdress and ornaments displayed, as well as in the manner of working, of sitting, etc., had all the appearances of a woman, but judging by the face and the absence of breasts, though old enough for that, they concluded he must be a man. . . . Taking off his aprons they found that he was more ashamed than if he really had been a woman. They kept him there three days, making him sweep the plaza, but giving him plenty to eat. But he remained very cast down and ashamed. After he had been warned that it was not right for him to go about dressed as a woman and much less thrust himself in with them, as it was presumed that he was sinning with them, they let him go. He immediately left the Mission and never came back to it, but from the

converts it was learned that he was still in the villages of the gentiles and going about as before, dressed as a woman.[25]

Rather than submitting to the will of the missionaries, the berdache ran away and resumed his preferred lifestyle beyond their jurisdiction. Given this episode, it is clearly a mistake to interpret the absence of multiple genders from historical records and ethnographies as evidence of the absence of such roles altogether.

These examples should dispel the notion that berdaches "faded from view" whenever Europeans appeared. Suppression was only one possible scenario and not necessarily the most frequent. But what was the impact of these contacts on how natives and Europeans thought about sexuality and gender? To answer this question we need to examine the evidence of discourse on the frontier itself and, in particular, the categories natives and Europeans used when communicating with each other.

THIRD/FOURTH GENDERS IN FRONTIER DISCOURSE

Although most frontier discourse was never written, there is some record of the terminology used to refer to third/fourth gender persons, summarized in Table 8.1. Three terms derive from European words: the French "berdache," the Spanish *mujer,* and the English "hermaphrodite." Two, *joya* and *schupans,* may be based on native words. The variations in their spelling is evidence that writers were transcribing terms they had heard but not read. I refer to them as "contact" rather than pidgin terms since, technically speaking, they do not belong to a pidgin language (although a tendency toward simplification, a typical pidginizing process, is apparent—*mojaro* from *Amugereado,* Morphy from hermaphrodite).[26] They are akin to terms such as *sachem, papoose,* and *pow-wow,* which were originally from the Algonkian language but were adopted by English colonists and then applied on a pantribal basis. Such borrowings typically occur soon after initial contact and then remain relatively stable.[27]

The complex history of the word "berdache" was related in chapter 1. Its first written use in the New World is in a text by Deliette from 1704. It does not appear again in writing until the early nineteenth century diaries of the fur trader Alexander Henry (as "berdashe") and the journals of Lewis and Clark (as "Birdashe").[28] It also was used in reference to the Kutenai female berdache Qánqon, who was called "Bundosh" in an 1825 journal and "Bowdash" in an 1837 journal.[29] In 1839 Prince Maximillian of Weid referred to *bardaches* in his account of his travels in North America.[30] The term occurs in various forms in writings by Catlin (1841), Tixier (1844), Stewart (1846), Kurz (1851), and Denig (1856).

Mujerado and its cognates are based on a verbalized form of the Spanish noun "woman," with the literal meaning of "woman-ed" in the sense of "made" or "artificial

TABLE 8.1.

Contact Terms for Multiple Genders

Term	Provenance	Date	Source
BERDACHE (FRENCH)			
Bardache	Illinois	1693	Deliette 1947: 124
La Berdach (PN),ᵃ ber-dash	Ojibway	1800	Henry 1897: 53
Birdashes	Hidatsa	1805	DeVoto [1904] 1953: 74
Bundosh/Bowdash (PN)	Kutenai	1825, 1837	Elliot 1914: 190; Gray 1913: 46
bardache	Northern Plains	1839	Maximillian 1841, 2: 133
Berdashe	Sauk and Fox	1841	Catlin 1973, 2: 214-15
La Bredache (PN), bre-daches	Osage	1844	Tixier 1940: 197
Broadashe (PN)	Blackfoot	1846	Stewart 1846: 54
berdache	Crow	1851	Kurz 1851: 211
Berdêches	Crow	1856	Denig 1953: 58
burdash	Tulalip	1889	Holder 1889: 623
bird-ash	Sioux	early 1900s	Powers 1963: 31
bredache, bardache, ber-dashe	Mississippi Valley French	1673-1850	McDermott 1941: 22-23
MUJERADO (SPANISH)			
hombres mugeriegosᵇ	Mexico/Peru	1607	García 1729: 297
hombres amugerados	Florida/Texas	1737	Arlegui 1737: 144
Amejerado (PN)	Tesuque	1823	Olmstead 1975: 156
mujerado	Acoma-Laguna	1851	Hammond 1887: 164
Mojara (PN)	Santa Clara	1860	Territorial Censusᶜ
Amugereado (PN)	Acoma	1882	Bandelier 1966: 326
mojaro	Acoma	1900	Casagrande and Bourns 1983: 229

woman," or perhaps "used (sexually) like a woman."[31] Although its use in Spain occurred primarily in the seventeenth and eighteenth centuries, in the Americas it has continued to be used to the present day in Mexico and the American Southwest.[32]

Schupan(s) originated as a contact term used by Russians and natives in Siberia to refer to gender transformed shamans. It appears to have been derived

Term	Provenance	Date	Source
mujerero/mujerota	New Mexico-Colorado	1983	Cobos 1983: 115

JOYA (SALINAN?)

Term	Provenance	Date	Source
joyas	Chumash	1775	Fages [1844] 1972: 33
Joyas	California missions	1780s	Palou [1787] 1977: 246
joyas	California missions	1791	Galbraith 1924: 229
Joya (PN)	Yokuts	1819	Gayton 1936: 81
Coias	So. California	1820s	Boscana 1846: 284
Joya	Chumash	1823	Beeler 1967: 52
joyas	California	1840s	Duflot de Mofras [1844] 1937: 192

SCHUPANS (KAMCHADAL?)

Term	Provenance	Date	Source
schupan	Kamchadal, Siberia	1740s	Stellers 1774: 351
schoopans	Koniag (Pacific Eskimo)	1803-1806	Lisiansky [1812] 1814: 199
schopans	Aleut	1805	Langsdorff [1812] 1813: 48
shúpans	Koniag, Aleut	1860s	Dall [1870] 1897: 402
Supan (PN)	Russian, Yukaghir (Siberia)	1880s	Bogoraz 1904: 455

HERMAPHRODITE (ENGLISH)

Term	Provenance	Date	Source
Morphy (PN)	Hopi	1892	Fewkes 1892: 11
morphodites	Navajo	1897	Matthews 1897: 217
murfidai	Pomo	1942	Essene 1942: 65
morphdites	Chugach (Pacific Eskimo)	1953	Birket-Smith 1953: 94

a. PN = personal name.

b. García lived in Mexico and Peru from 1592 to 1604. He uses this phrase in comparing berdaches in the New World to ancient Scythian enarees.

c. Jonathan Batkin, personal communication with the author, 1991.

from a Kamchadal word.[33] In the 1880s Bogoraz found it still in use in Siberia as both a personal name and as a category label. Meanwhile, Russians carried the word with them to Alaska. By the early nineteenth century, its use was so commonplace that the explorers Lisiansky and Langsdorff reported it as a native term for "men . . . living with men, and supplying the place of women" on Kodiak

Island and among the Aleuts.[34] In fact, the respective languages (Yupik and Aleut) are only remotely related, and the actual native terms for alternative genders have since been recorded (see Glossary).

The origin of *joya* is less certain. Palou reported that at San Antonio Mission in the 1780s the Salinan Indians called men who lived as women "with the name of Joya (which is what they call such ones in their native language)."[35] Most Spanish authors considered *joya* a native term.[36] In a bilingual confessional from 1823, however, *joya* is used as the Spanish translation of the Chumash term for male berdache, *'axi.*[37] *Joya* also appears as a notation next to the names of certain natives in mission records.[38] In 1819, Estudillo observed a "hermaphrodite" among the Yokuts "whom they called Joya."[39] Whether native or Spanish in origin, *joya* became a part of the intercultural vocabulary of colonial California. Its appearance in official records illustrates how such terminology could function within colonial systems of social control. In the Chumash confessional it occurs as part of a series of questions on sexual behavior. (Interestingly, male penitents were queried as to whether they had had intercourse with *either* an *'axi*/Joya or another man, which underscores the distinct gender status of the *'axi.*[40]) Similarly, in New Mexican census records of the early nineteenth century native males identified as potters, normally women's work, have names like "Juan Amejerado."[41]

The employment of contact terms in colonial systems of surveillance may have had the unintended consequence of increasing the visibility of alternative genders. Even if berdaches did not cross-dress, the use of these terms as personal names made them readily identifiable. Perhaps this practice developed when missionaries began assigning Christian names to natives. Should multiple gender natives be given male or female names? Calling them "Joya" or "Amejerado" would be one solution.[42]

The kind of social conditions that produced creole languages in the Caribbean, where a small, powerful, monolingual group dominated a larger, multilingual population, did not exist in contact zones north of Mexico. It is not surprising, therefore, that North American jargon for multiple genders reflects negotiation and compromise. In European texts, "sodomite" was the most common label used to refer to alternative genders in the New World. Why were "berdache" and *mujerado* preferred on the frontier itself? I believe the answer lies in the problem Europeans faced whenever they encountered sexual and gender difference. "Sodomites" were avatars of evil who must be denounced. Calling natives with alternative genders *mujerados,* "hermaphrodites," or "berdaches" alleviated some of the cognitive dissonance their presence provoked. As the Spanish chronicler Morfi reported of Texas Indians, "In this nation there are many boys whom the Spaniards of Béjar call hermaphrodites; but it is not known whether they are actually hermaphrodites or not."[43] Nonetheless, the citizens of this frontier community chose to assume they were, and in using "hermaphrodite" instead of "sodomite" they made a concession to native sensibilities.

The occurrence of these terms as personal names is also evidence that natives themselves were using them. When the fur trader Alexander Henry recorded the names of the Indians who joined his Red River Brigade in 1800, he listed them variously in French, English, and Ojibway, and sometimes all three. The berdache Ozaw-wen-dib is listed only by his "French" and "English" names—"La Berdash" and "Berdash."[44] Since Henry recorded Ojibway names in other cases, it appears that "Berdash" was the name that Ozaw-wen-dib was known by among Indians as well as whites. Indeed, in the 1880s the Turtle Mountain Chippewas still remembered him by this name.[45]

What were the implications of this terminology? One consequence would have been to foster the perception that distinct tribal instances of gender diversity were part of a universal "Indian" phenomenon. Europeans, of course, routinely lumped tribal cultures into generic categories such as "Indian" and "savage." But a native precedent for pantribal cultural categories existed before contact in the sign or gesture languages used in large areas of North America. These were, in effect, pidgin languages, but ones formulated in precontact conditions. In fact, one reason pidgins did not develop in North America was because Europeans found it easier to learn these gesture languages.[46] In Plains sign language the gesture for "berdache" combined the sign for "half" with those for "male" and "female" (an erect finger and a hair-combing gesture, respectively).[47] The concept is, literally, "half-man, half-woman." This is a fairly direct rendering of some native terms for third genders, which can be translated as "man-woman" (Shoshone *tainna'-wa'ippe*), but not *all* (for example, the Sioux *winkte* or Crow *boté*).[48] Nonetheless, when natives began to communicate with Europeans many of them already had a pantribal concept for alternative gender status. (Indeed, some natives assumed that multiple genders were universal, and they looked for, and found, counterparts in the white world).[49]

Sign language and contact terms contributed to the construction of an intercultural subject called "berdache," *mujerado,* and so forth. For the non-Indians who used these terms, their implication was primarily "men dressed as women, doing women's work." The religious dimensions of multiple genders, which are much more variable from tribe to tribe, are not reflected in these generic terms. Consequently, tribal terms and concepts remained current throughout the contact period, just as Europeans retained their categories of sexuality and gender. Rather, contact terms supplemented the categories of each group and, by creating cross-references between them, expanded their meanings.

Mujerado, "hermaphrodite," and "berdache" were also used, at various points in their history, to refer to homosexual or gender-variant men in Euro-American societies as well as on the frontier. "Berdache," of course, had been widely used this way in Europe before the nineteenth century. In the Southwest, variants of *mujerado* were used to refer to nonmasculine men and nonfeminine women. A dictionary of New Mexican and Colorado Spanish defines *mujerero* as a man "fond of women or given to spending his time gossiping in the kitchen with the women," and *mujerota* as a "hard-working or brave female."[50] Similarly, in the late nineteenth and early twentieth centuries, "hermaphrodite" was the basis of slang terms for non-masculine homosexuals in American urban settings.[51]

Current debates over appropriate labels and categories for describing North American gender diversity recapitulate frontier discourse in many respects. The need to translate multiple genders remains. The outcome, then and now, will always be hybrid, multicultural, multilingual signifieds whose ontological status is grounded in neither native nor Euro-American reality, but in the specific circumstances of the contact zone. The present denomination, "two-spirit," in this regard follows *mujerado*, "burdashe," "murfidai," and *joya*—and before these, the sign-language gesture for "half-man/half-woman,"—as a symbolization created for intercultural communication, which elaborates and complicates but does not replace existing categories.

GENDER DIVERSITY AND EUROPEAN DISCOURSE

The encounter between native and European gender and sexuality unfolded in a second, very different, context—the discourse of Europeans who read and cited the accounts of explorers, conquerors, and travelers. Texts such as those of Peter Martyr (1516), which reported Balboa's slaughter of berdaches; Oviedo (1526, 1535), which exhaustively cataloged sodomy among natives throughout Central America and the Caribbean; and Cabeza de Vaca (1542), which reported berdaches in Texas, were published in numerous editions and translations. They appeared in the collections of Ramusio (Italian), Hakluyt (English), Purchas (English), Thévenot (French), Harris (English), Pinkerton (English), Barcia (Spanish), Ternaux-Compans (French), and others. This literature was read not only by those who enjoyed narratives of exotic people and places but by also scholars in those disciplines (before the rise of the social sciences) concerned with the study of "man"—philosophy and history.[52] Subsequent explorers and travelers also read this literature, arriving in the New World with images and words formulated for perceiving, categorizing, and narrating what they would see.

A secondary literature on gender diversity in the Americas soon developed. Authors such as Oviedo and Herrera summarized and cataloged reports of sodomy and gender variance, while historians such as García and Torquemada speculated on their origins. In the early seventeenth century, Lescarbot, writing in French, and Ens and de Laet, in Latin, cited contact accounts of berdaches in their histories of the New World. By the end of that century, reports of alternative genders from Central America, Florida, and the Mississippi Valley were routinely quoted as if they all referred to the same phenomenon. Some authors called this subject "sodomite," others "hermaphrodite," but in either case the same sources were cited.

I have identified some 57 secondary sources published between 1500 and 1900 that refer to gender and sexual diversity in the Americas. These are all texts based on the written reports of others, which were, in turn, subsequently cited by at least one other author. An analysis of this intertext (to borrow a term from deconstructive criticism) reveals that the dissemination of contact accounts of North American gender diversity cut across several discursive domains: berdaches were invoked first and longest in a moral discourse, then in historical discourse and a discourse on prodigies, and finally, in the nineteenth century, in the discourses of the social sciences and medicine.[53]

Christian morality mandates moral discourse, what Guy Poirier has termed a "rhetoric of abomination," whenever it encounters the violation of biblical injunctions against cross-dressing or same-sex intercourse.[54] This was especially true for the devoutly religious and legalistic Spaniards, who sought to justify conquest by proving that the natives of the Americas were inferior to European Catholics. They were not alone, however, in translating native practices into categories of prohibited sexuality. In the early collection of travel accounts edited by Samuel Purchas, terms describing berdaches in texts by Cabeza de Vaca, Alarcón, and others are translated (and indexed) as "sodomy," even though the original texts do not use that word.

The clash of the Spaniards and French in Florida in the 1560s led to the citation of multiple genders in another European discourse, one concerning the existence of monsters and prodigies. The Frenchmen Laudonnière and Le Moyne matter-of-factly reported that "hermaphrodites" were common in Florida (while the Spaniard Torquemada wrote of *mariones* [sic] *impotentes* [impotent, nonmasculine homosexuals] committing the *pecado gravisimo*).[55] Europeans had long believed that the nether reaches of the world were occupied by fabulous beings such as hermaphrodites. Historian Margaret Hodgen has traced these beliefs back to classical times and attributes their survival to the desire of the Church "to distort all alien beliefs and customs."[56] However, as Poirier points out, neither Laudonnière nor Le Moyne link Floridian "hermaphrodites" to the sin that so preoccupied the Spaniards. Rather, discourse on prodigies suspended moral discourse. This no doubt reflected practical concerns of the Protestant French colonists in Florida, who were eager to win support for their enterprise back home. Rather than dwelling on the moral turpitude of the American natives, their interests were better served by projecting an Arcadian image of the New World.[57]

Laudonnière's and Le Moyne's widely disseminated reports spawned a long-lived debate among French authors over the nature of North American gender diversity. Observers of the Illinois in the late seventeenth century, for example, credited them with numerous hermaphrodites but also "hommes destinez dès leur enfance, à cet usage détestable" ("men destined from childhood for that detestable use") and men with "un malheureux penchant pour la Sodomie" ("an unfortunate desire for Sodomy").[58] Here, moral discourse has caught up with the discourse on prodigies. Even so, throughout the eighteenth century, travelers and historians continued to debate the discrepancy between reports of "hermaphrodites" and "sodomites."

The discourse on cultural differences also evolved. The straightforward question of whether natives were immoral became a much more complex issue of whether cultural differences in and of themselves were immoral, and what caused people to deviate from the culture dictated by Christian dogma (that is, "civilization"). Some scholars began to formulate theories, often fantastic, to account for diverse gender patterns in the Americas. Eventually, moral discourse became historical and comparative discourse. García and Torquemada, for example, resolved the problem of cultural differences by arguing that New World natives were immigrants from the Old World—lost tribes of Israelites or, perhaps, Scythians or Phrygians, as suggested by the apparent similarity between berdaches and the *enarees* and *galli,* religious figures from Old World cultures known to European scholars from classical sources.[59]

The transition from historical inquiry to sociological and anthropological inquiry involved less of a break than has been imagined. As Hodgen pointed out some years ago, instead of historical origins, nineteenth-century sociologists and anthropologists sought natural and social origins; and natives, instead of representing a literal survival of some biblical or classical people, came to represent a metaphoric survival of the primitive past of "mankind" (that is, Europeans), and evidence for the Victorian theory of the stages of civilization.[60]

The continuity between premodern moral and historical discourses and the discourse of nineteenth-century medicine and social sciences is evident in two texts dealing with the subject of multiple genders in North America published in 1768 and 1779 by the Dutchman Cornelius de Pauw (writing in French) and the German Christian Heyne (writing in Latin, respectively).[61]

Both authors, in true Enlightenment fashion, begin by debunking earlier reports of hermaphrodites in the New World. De Pauw, who devotes most of a chapter in his *Recherches philosophique sur les Américains* to the subject, takes special delight in ridiculing theories of berdaches as descendants of *galli* who somehow had made their way to the New World: "A more improbable, absurd or ludicrous explanation would be impossible to conceive."[62] After a digression on hermaphroditism in the plant world, he relates cases of alleged hermaphrodites in Europe who, on examination, were discovered not to be prodigies with two sets of sexual organs but females with enlarged clitorises. De Pauw speculates whether the same phenomenon might account for the reports of hermaphrodites in America, and he considers two possible causes of such characteristics: warm climate and the effects of female circumcision, reported to have been practiced by Florida natives. For de Pauw, Native American gender diversity was more evidence for his controversial thesis concerning the degeneration and inferiority of everything in the New World. His hermaphrodite was a monster, not a prodigy, and his text harkens back to a medieval view of change (and cultural difference, which is change or deviation from biblical precepts) as degeneration and decline.

Heyne's essay "De maribus inter Scythas morbo effeminatis et de Hermaphroditis Floridae," published in the prestigious *Commentationes* of the Royal Scientific Society of Göttingen, more clearly anticipates nineteenth-century medical discourse. In this text, discussion of North American berdaches occurs in the context of an inquiry into the conditions under which the male body might be feminized (thus inversely mirroring de Pauw's text, which is concerned with the masculinized female body). After a long review of the ancient and modern literature on *thēlia nosos,* or the "female disease," which was the presumed cause of Scythian men becoming *enarees* (cross-dressing priests), Heyne turns to reports of hermaphrodites in Florida. These prodigies are, he claims, men who, having been broken in spirit and body, give up manhood.[63] Even though Heyne, like de Pauw, refutes Lafitau's historical theories, he still makes use of the same parallel between North American multiple genders and the Scythian *enarees.* What he believes these two cases share, however, is not a common historical origin but a physiological cause—"morbo nervoso" ("nervous disease")—etiology instead of genealogy. Enfeebled by this disease, men adopt female dress. This "muliebris ille corporum habitus infami" ("shameful cross-dressing"), in turn, makes their bodies susceptible to "Veneris ludibrio" ("uncontrolled desire"). And from this, Heyne concludes, the custom arises whereby any man afflicted with effeminacy (*muliebria*) will don women's clothes and engage in sex with men in a passive role (*marium flagitiis pathicis infamium*).[64]

Although both texts anticipate medical discourse, they do not make the modern distinction between sexual identity and sexual orientation. For Heyne, male homosexuality is inseparable from gender variance, although he is uncertain whether effeminization (which he conceives of in primarily physiological terms) causes homosexual acts or homosexual acts cause effeminization. In either case, the object of knowledge—the male who varies in terms of gender and/or sexuality—now has a body. The cause of his behavior is to be sought there. Although this body is no longer imagined as being literally hermaphroditic, it is still seen as somehow different from that of the normal male. Instead of the distinct ontological status of the hermaphrodite, a third sex, we now have the defective body of a male viewed in terms of a dichotomous sex/gender system. Here we can detect the beginnings of the Foucaultian shift from homosexual acts to homosexual persons.

The origins of modern discourse on homosexuality have been traced to the writings of the early activists Karl Heinrich Ulrichs and Karl Maria Kertbeny, who began arguing for the reform of German laws against male homosexuality in the 1860s.[65] Their publications were soon followed by those of the medical authorities Karl Westphal, Richard von Krafft-Ebing, Albert Moll, and others, who often cited Ulrichs in particular, but insisted on pathologizing any condition involving same-sex desire or gender difference.[66] Nearly all these authors, however, were aware of Native American gender diversity, and many of them—including Lombroso, Mantegazza, Burton, Symonds, and Ellis—made extensive use of ethnographic reports. When Westphal reported at a meeting of the Berlin Medical-Psychological Society in 1868 "on several cases of persons who in a more or less high degree had a perverse inclination to individuals of the same sex or at least behaved in dress, actions, and the like in a way not corresponding to their sex," Adolf Bastian, the "father" of German ethnography, readily offered the information that "perverse sexual inclinations are often found in uncivilized tribes, that in some the individuals afflicted with it are even treated as a special caste, as more highly placed personalities, as sacred and the like."[67]

Of course, North America was not the only region where Europeans encountered homosexuality and gender diversity. Historian Rudi Bleys has reviewed writings by European travelers throughout the world and found that descriptions of whole peoples as sodomites or addicts of sodomy are typical of the premodern period. Beginning in the Enlightenment, however, as the texts of de Pauw and Heyne show, authors began to dwell on the perceived femininity of sodomites (that is, males who were receptive in sex with other males). Eventually, a discourse developed "that represented same-sex praxis as the exclusive behaviour of a distinct minority."[68] In the nineteenth century, this model was reified further and made to conform with both evolutionary theory (homosexuality was part of humankind's primitive past) and degeneration theory (homosexuality was a disease of overadvanced civilizations). Bleys argues that the feminization of sodomy and the minoritization of sodomites paralleled similar constructions of other races as feminine and femininity as inferior to masculinity, projects linked to the colonial and domestic goals of European states. Ultimately, Bleys concludes, racial, gender, and sexual others were all defined as essential, biological types.

The construction of the medical model of inversion (and, later, homosexuality) *required* historical and cross-cultural examples. If sexual variations were indeed diseases, natural not cultural phenomena, then cases of them surely occurred in other societies. Consequently, as one historian notes, many of the medical writers included "entire chapters attempting to demonstrate the presence of these diseases throughout history."[69] Although the epistemological break between medical categories and earlier taxonomies is now apparent to us, the authors of these texts themselves emphasized continuities between Western cases and those found in other times and places.

The most significant break between Victorian medical discourse and earlier texts was in their rules of evidence—in particular, the use of the case study. Now the "other," that instance of difference that must be explained, is found at home, among the mentally ill, the poor, the female, the criminal, and so forth. By the end of the nineteenth century, detailed case histories of Europeans had become the primary source of data, displacing Scythian *enarees* and North American berdaches to footnotes or separate chapters. Still, cross-cultural surveys remained prominent features of sexological texts. Iwan Bloch's *Beiträge zur Aetiologie der Psychopathia sexualis* (1902) has some twenty pages of ethnographic evidence, while the opening comments of Westermarck's chapter on "Homosexual Love," published in 1906, include the assertion, "In America homosexual customs have been observed among a great number of native tribes."[70] Cross-cultural data were especially prominent in the writings of early homosexual rights activists. Magnus Hirschfeld's *Die Transvestiten* (1910) includes a chapter devoted to ethnographic examples, while Ferdinand Karsch-Haack's *Das Gleichgeschlechtliche Leben der Naturvölker* (1911) and Edward Carpenter's *Intermediate Types among Primitive Folk* (1914) are exhaustive surveys of the literature on worldwide sexual and gender diversity.

The medical discourse on homosexuality inherited something from all the earlier discourses in which North American gender diversity had been cited. From moral discourse it received the equation of difference with defect. From the discourses on prodigies and the historical origins of cultural diversity it inherited concepts of the origin point and causation. Indeed, the hermaphrodite returns in nearly all the works of the Victorian theorists, alternately as monster and prodigy, in the form of *psychic* hermaphrodism and inversion—in Ulrichs's concept of a female soul in a male body, in Carpenter's "intermediate type," in Freud's view of the homosexual as a mother-identified male.

TRADITIONAL INNOVATIONS

Now we can answer Plummer's rhetorical question—whether berdaches have "anything at all to do with homosexuality in our terms." The answer is: yes, a good deal. The history of the discourses in which modern homosexuality was constructed cannot be told without reference to the role played by citation of cross-cultural gender and sexual diversity, any more than the history of North American berdaches in five hundred years of contact can be told without reference to European ideas and actions. Although the exact impact of this cultural exchange can and will be debated, as well as the extent to which Europeans accurately represented multiple genders in their texts, the extensive citation of them is incontestable. Knowledge of cross-cultural gender diversity has been an important point of reference for Western discussions of sexuality and gender since the sixteenth century.

The analytical distinction between the "homosexual role" of Western societies and the third/fourth gender roles found in native North America remains the starting point for research on this subject. At the same time, the error of the statements quoted at the beginning of this chapter should now be apparent. The assertion that "Westernized meanings" have no context in aboriginal society overlooks the long history of discourse on the frontier and in Europe in which native and European meanings influenced each other. As the preceding survey has shown, there is no "pure" native berdache tradition and there is no "pure" Western category of homosexuality. After five centuries of contact, both refer to each other.

An overly rigid application of social constructionism in the field of history can lead to the neglect of topics like transmission, exchange, and contamination. Fulton and Anderson base their comments on what has become a truism of social constructionist history, that "the word 'homosexual' . . . has its roots in the medical literature of mid-19th-century Germany."[71] But that literature, as we have seen, included at its inception references to North American multiple genders and related roles throughout the world. Further, the predominant self-conceptualization of mid- to late-nineteenth-century Europeans and North Americans who desired sex with their own gender was not that represented by the term "homosexual," but that of Ulrichs's *Urning*, a third-sexed being, and its predecessors, such as the "Molly" of eighteenth-century England.[72]

Gender difference was the original mode of modern homosexuality, not self-definition based on the choice of sexual object. Gender difference was the basis of the identities of those who launched the early homosexual emancipation movement, including Ulrichs, Hirschfeld, and Carpenter, and the men and women who frequented those furtive urban settings that eventually gave rise to lesbian and gay communities. When Ulrichs wrote in *Vindex*, his original broadside, "The Uranian is not male, but a hermaphrodite man-woman with a female sexual orientation," he used the same term, *Mannweib*, that German ethnographers routinely used to refer to North American alternative genders.[73] The reduction of lesbian and gay history to philology—the origin and dissemination of the term "homosexual"—foreshortens the history of these gender-based identities and elides their place in the genealogy of contemporary queer culture and politics.

Sociologist Mary McIntosh, for example, in her seminal essay on the "homosexual role," notes that in the modern era, "There seems to be no distinction at first between transvestism and homosexuality," but then formulates her central thesis in terms of a unitary pattern: "A distinct, separate, specialized role of 'homosexual' emerged in England at the end of the seventeenth century."[74] Similarly, in his early writings historian Jeffrey Weeks made note of "popular notions" that "invariably associated male homosexual behaviour with effeminacy and probably transvestism as well," but then he characterized nineteenth-century history in a way that excludes these "notions" and the identities based on them:

> The latter part of the nineteenth century . . . saw the clear emergence of new conceptualisations of homosexuality, although the elements of the new definitions and practices can be traced to earlier periods. The sodomite, as Foucault

has put it, was a temporary aberration. The 'homosexual,' on the other hand, belonged to a species, and it is this new concern with the homosexual person, both in legal practice and in psychological and medical categorisation, that marks the critical change, both because it provided a new subject of social observation and specialization and because it opened up the possibility of new modes of self-articulation.[75]

But what of the self-articulations of the Mollies and Uranians who stand between the sodomite of the premodern era and the gay man of the late twentieth century?

As historian George Chauncey Jr. observed in his 1983 review of early medical literature, "Sexual inversion, the term used in most of the nineteenth century, thus had a much broader meaning than our present term, homosexuality, which denotes solely the sex of the person one sexually desires. Sexual inversion, rather, connoted a total reversal of one's sex role."[76] He dated the transition period between the two terms as "the turn of the century."[77] In his more recent book, *Gay New York,* Chauncey moves this watershed forward even more, writing of a "transition from an *early twentieth-century* culture divided into 'queers' and 'men' on the basis of gender status to a *late twentieth-century* culture divided into 'homosexual' and 'heterosexuals' on the basis of sexual object choice."[78] More research will be necessary before definitive conclusions about the dissemination of medico-psychiatric concepts of homosexuality can be made. My own hypothesis is that notions of gender difference continued to dominate the self-conceptions of significant numbers of "homosexuals" well into the 1960s. If so, then the history of "homosexuality" may be significantly *less* than one hundred years. It may encompass only those decades following Stonewall; and if the renewed interest in gender on the part of today's queer-identified generation is any indication, it soon may be over.

Too often the discourse of elites has been taken to represent what happened in the lives of average people. David Halperin, in his essay "One Hundred Years of Homosexuality," singles out the year 1892 as marking a watershed in the history of sexuality because that is when the term "homosexual" was introduced into the English language. "Before 1892 there was no homosexuality, only sexual inversion."[79] This is an important modification to Foucault's formulation, which counterposed homosexuality to sodomy, assimilating inversion to the former. But, like Foucault, Halperin defines the identities constructed under the sign of "homosexuality" in such sharp distinction to earlier identities so as to place the latter outside the genealogy of contemporary lesbians and gay men altogether. "Being a womanish man, or a mannish woman, after all, is not the same thing as being a homosexual."[80] But this again begs the question: what *is* the subjectivity of the men and women who are called, or call themselves (a distinction many constructionists fail to make), "homosexual"? Halperin seems to assume that it does not include self-perceptions of gender difference.

The notion of the "epistemological break," although borrowed from Foucault, has been applied in ways that tend to reperiodize history into discrete phases, the hallmark of the conventional historiography Foucault strenuously critiqued. As an alternative, I propose Sahlins's model of historical process, which recognizes that the transformation of a culture is a mode of its reproduction. My point is that there have been *two* modern homosexualities—the type exemplified by the Molly and the Uranian, roles in which gender difference and homosexuality were imbricated, and the type defined by object-choice alone without special reference to gender. Both rightly can be characterized as "modern" in that both are understood as psychological phenomena characterizing types of persons.[81] The drawing of an arbitrary line between them overlooks their historical relationship and their coexistence; the way in which homosexual identity was produced both from *within* as well as *against* earlier identities.

When it comes to the history of native North America we can no longer cling to a pre-Foucaultian idea of power flowing in only one direction and always from the top down, for we will end up characterizing native people as passive victims of white conquest and culture. As the history of native survivance shows, European signs and symbols were actively incorporated into native cultural systems and Europeans absorbed accounts of gender diversity into theirs. The term "berdache" and the role itself, to the extent that we know it, was always-already a hybrid, a creative product of complex interactions over an extended period of contact.

The question of how contemporary lesbian, gay, and two-spirit native people are related to traditional berdaches remains open. What I have tried to show here is that it cannot be answered with either "yes" or "no," or with a model of history that counterposes "pure" or "indigenous" meanings to Western meanings. In evaluating claims concerning transmission we must consider at least three distinct elements of historical process:

- How and by whom were third and fourth gender identities, roles, and symbols transmitted in the past five centuries?
- How were these identities, roles, and symbols transformed in the process of being reproduced?
- And how were these changes intellectually and symbolically mediated—by, for example, the employment of contact terms—so as to maintain a "principle of continuity" in the midst of change?

Native history is not a fall from grace, a tragic decline from cultural integrity to disintegration and assimilation in which the present is always somehow less authentic, less interesting, less "traditional" than the past. It would be ironic, indeed, if the postmodern critique of essentialism made it impossible for contemporary natives to recognize themselves in traditional third and fourth gender persons. The alternative to self-effacement, as Clyde Hall (M. Owlfeather) argued in Living the Spirit, is cultural revival. "There is a need for a resurgence of that old pride and knowledge of place," he wrote. "Traditions need to be researched and revived. If traditions have been lost, then new ones should be borrowed from other tribes to create groups or societies for gay Indians that would function in the present."[82] Such a call is consistent with the history of Native American survivance, of transforming traditions to preserve them, of negotiating symbols and meanings in multicultural contact zones whose borders have grown to encompass us all.

NARRATIVES OF DOMINATION
OR THE CANT OF CONQUEST?:
COMPETING VIEWS OF ALTERNATIVE GENDERS

While the view presented in the previous chapters of North American berdache roles as normative social statuses is in agreement with that of most anthropologists and native people, two historians have offered sharply different perspectives. In 1989, in an article in *Out/Look* magazine, Ramón Gutiérrez, a professor of ethnic studies and former McArthur fellow, challenged my characterization of the Zuni berdache role. Far from occupying an accepted social status, he argued, *lhamana* were the objects of degrading subjugation. They truly were berdaches in the old Persian sense of the term—sexual slaves. "The men who were pressed into berdache status," Gutiérrez wrote, "were there primarily to service and delight the chiefs." The origins of the institution, he claimed, lay in the practice of routinely humiliating prisoners of war through "homosexual rape, castration, the wearing of women's clothes, and performing women's work."[1]

As one of his sources, Gutiérrez cited a forthcoming study by historian Richard Trexler, which was published in 1995 as *Sex and Conquest*. In this work,

Trexler states his goal to be the analysis of the relationship between "eros and power." He argues that throughout the Americas berdaches were "young men forced to dress as women, who served as offerings to the gods when, in religious rites, they were anally raped by the tribal big men or priests." According to Trexler, "A picture of the berdaches emerges that was, at the time of the conquests and in these first centuries of colonialism, one of degradation."[2]

Trexler and Gutiérrez's interpretations of North American gender diversity and sexuality challenge most work on the subject in the past twenty years. What is interesting about their analyses, especially Trexler's, is the attempt to apply the theories of Michel Foucault. Foucault, of course, was interested in how power worked through knowledge and discourse to produce subjectivity, identity, and agency. He understood power as being productive as much as inhibitive or repressive. No scholar has influenced recent work in history and cultural studies more than Foucault, but despite the breadth of his theories, his own research was substantially limited to the modern era. He had virtually nothing to say about non-Western societies and very little about women.

Foucaultian models of power can certainly be used to investigate native North American gender systems. When this is done, however, what becomes immediately apparent is that, contrary to Gutiérrez and Trexler's accounts, social and juridical power (laws, police, religious enforcement, and so forth) are largely absent in native societies. Instead, social control, even more than in modern Western societies, is achieved because individuals internalize the social order in the process of acquiring a sense of self and subjectivity. At the same time, the kind of power described in native discourse is of an entirely different order than the material and economic forms recognized in Western societies. Power in native societies is first and foremost spiritual and supernatural. This is why "wealth," in the form of goods and possessions, can be disposed of in extravagant displays such as the Northwest Coast potlatch, or give-away—because goods are considered merely a symbol of power, a sign that the individual has supernatural aid. That being the case, individuals can afford to give away their wealth, knowing that their spiritual power eventually will bring them more.[3]

One motivation for the use of Foucault is Gutiérrez's and Trexler's desire to challenge what they see as romanticizing tendencies in recent work on native gender diversity.[4] Certainly, the idea that social life in tribal societies was free of coercion or that individual freedom was unconstrained is erroneous. However, the notion of identities and roles being imposed by native rulers and enforced with violence and sexual assault is no less of a distortion of native realities.

The models of power that Gutiérrez and Trexler actually employ have little in common with Foucault's ideas. Neither attempt to identify or analyze native discourses through which berdache subjectivity was constructed. Foucault wrote of the confessional and the consulting room, of institutions and surveillance. These are not instances of the application of brute force but rather social spaces and practices by which knowledge is produced and used to make behavior intelligible (or, as Foucault describes it, "implanted in bodies, slipped in beneath modes of conduct, made into a principle of classification and intelligibility, established as a *raison d'être* and a natural order"[5]). What Gutiérrez and Trexler describe is slavery, a mode of hegemony that (in Europe) long preceded the modern forms of power Foucault was interested in.

The misapplication of Foucaultian precepts is compounded by flawed evidence. Gutiérrez, for example, states that Pedro de Castañeda's chronicle of the Coronado expedition describes a "berdache initiation in New Mexico" that culminates in the "berdache" entering a state of permanent prostitution.[6] The passage under question occurs near the beginning of Part II, Chapter I of the chronicle, which is headed "Concerning the province of Culiacán, its ceremonies and customs." Culiacán is on the west-central coast of Mexico, over a thousand miles south of New Mexico. Further, when the paragraph is read as a whole, it becomes clear that the rite described has nothing to do with berdaches at all. It begins, "There were among them men dressed as women, who married other men and served them as women. They used to canonize, with great solemnity, the women who wanted to remain unmarried in a great ritual or dance at which all the dignitaries of the district gathered. . . . [Gutiérrez's quote begins here]."[7] Clearly, a change in subject occurs from "men dressed as women" to "women who wanted to remain unmarried," although, typical of printing in this period, there is no paragraph break to signal the change. Had Castañeda written "they used to canonize *these* women," the reader might be justified in assuming the entire passage deals with "men dressed as women," but the wording clearly indicates two distinct subjects.[8]

To support his contention that Zunis ridiculed third gender males, Gutiérrez cites an article by Elsie Parsons. According to Gutiérrez,

> During one of the *sha'lko* [Sha'lako—*author*] dances Parsons saw at Zuñi, the audience "grinned and even chuckled" at U'k; "a very infrequent display of amusement during these *sha'lko* dances," Parsons confided. After the dance ended, Parsons' Cherokee hostess asked her: "Did you notice them laughing at her [U'k]? . . . She is a great joke to the people."

The full passage from Parsons, however, reveals an entirely different situation:

> When U'k fell out of line the audience, an audience mostly of women with their children, girls, and a few old men, grinned and even chuckled, a very infrequent display of amusement during these *sha'lako* dances. "Did you notice them laughing at her?" my Cherokee hostess [Margaret Lewis—*author*] asked me on my return. "She is a great joke to the people—*not because she is a* lha'mana, *but because she is half-witted.*"[9]

U'k was developmentally disabled—a "simpleton," according to another informant—and a bad dancer to boot. Margaret Lewis's comment clarifying the reasons
for the laughter couldn't be clearer; it had nothing to do with U'k's berdache status.

Both Gutiérrez and Trexler rely on a particular reading of an episode of the
Zuni origin myth in which a berdache kachina (along with two other gods) is
captured by enemy gods. These enemies are hunters, while the Zunis are farmers.
In *The Zuni Man-Woman* I argued that this passage is best understood as an
account of an initiation in which the leader of the enemy gods, Cha'kwen 'Oka
(literally, Warrior Woman), inducts Ko'lhamana into berdache identity (the other
two captives undergo transformations, as well). The episode is followed by the
resolution of the war, which entails the unification of the two people and,
symbolically, the mediation of hunting and farming, male and female. The
Ko'lhamana kachina bore the symbols of these opposites in a dance held to
commemorate these events.

In Trexler's reading, "The conquering Kia'nakwe [Kan'a:kwe] people prepare
a thanksgiving dance in which the imprisoned enemy gods were supposed to take
part in celebrating their own capture. But being macho, the god Ko'lhamana
refused, until, that is, the Cha'kwena forced him to dress up as a woman and
dance."[10] The actual passage as recorded by Stevenson reads, "Kor'kokshi
[henceforth known as Ko'lhamana], the first-born, was so angry and unmanageable that Ku'yapāli'sa [another name for Cha'kwen 'Oka] had him dressed in
female attire previous to the dance, saying to him 'You will now perhaps be less
angry.'"[11] Certainly, the passage lends itself to a reading that credits the *lhamana*
role to an act of coercion (although "had him dressed" is not quite as strong as
Trexler's "forced him to dress up"). However, this is not the origin of the *lhamana*
role. In two recorded versions of the myth the birth of the first berdache occurs
in the episode immediately preceding the war of the gods.[12] The encounter with
Cha'kwen 'Oka merely represents a transformation of this figure—as I have
argued, a rite of passage into adult berdache identity.

What caused me to look more closely at this episode was the word "angry."
Being "angry and unmanageable" was not "macho" behavior in Zuni terms, it was
antisocial behavior, the opposite of the ideal represented by the term *k'okshi*,
which has been translated as "be good, be obedient, be attractive" (and in the
form *'an-k'okshi,* it means "be tame").[13] Although Gutiérrez and Trexler both read
this episode as one of enslavement and ritual degradation, the only motivation for
Cha'kwen 'Oka's actions given in the text is to make Ko'lhamana "less angry"—
that is, more *k'okshi,* more like an ideal Zuni. The taming of anger is an important
theme of boys' initiation rites, as well. It is, indeed, a cultural obsession in all
Pueblo communities, which stress cooperation and harmony.

In other cases, Gutiérrez's reporting of Zuni practices is faulty. He writes,
"The person who personified Kor'kokshi [i.e., Kokk'okshi] during ceremonials
not only wore female clothes, but also had blood smeared between his thighs,"

which signifies "blood . . . coming from a torn anus due to homosexual rape or castration."[14] In fact, the Kokk'okshi kachinas, considered the oldest and most sacred of the Zuni gods, appear in sets and dance for rain. They are not cross-dressed and there is no smearing of blood. According to Stevenson, the berdache kachina Ko'lhamana was originally a Kokk'okshi kachina, but this is the only connection between them.[15] The ceremony Gutiérrez refers to is a ritual rabbit hunt, in which neither Kokk'okshi nor Ko'lhamana, but rather Cha'kwen 'Oka appears. As Stevenson, who witnessed the ceremony, reported, blood from the first rabbit killed was rubbed on the legs of the Warrior Woman to simulate menstruation.[16] When she ran through the brush this blood rubbed off onto the plants and encouraged the fertility of rabbits and other small game. As for homosexual rape of tribal members among the Zunis or any other North American tribe, there is simply no evidence.[17] Heterosexual rape is itself nearly nonexistent among the Zunis.[18]

Gutiérrez claims that *lhamana* only seem to have been respected because of their own self-interested reports. "As marginalized and low status individuals in the male political world, they were quite eager to tell their story to anyone willing to listen. Matilda Coxe Stevenson, Ruth Benedict and Elsie C. Parsons—all women who were themselves marginalized in the male academic world—listened to We'wha. As a result, We'wha was elevated greatly in social status in the eyes of all those who subsequently read about him."[19] In fact, We'wha had been dead for nearly twenty years before Parsons first visited Zuni in 1915, and over thirty years in the case of Benedict. Although Parsons and Benedict did report that *lhamana* were respected (as have anthropologists Ruth Bunzel, John Adair, and Triloki Pandey) this was based on what non-*lhamana* Zunis told them.

Once the errors in Gutiérrez's reporting have been corrected (several of which are repeated in his 1991 book, *When Jesus Came, the Corn Mothers Went Away*), there is little left to support his case.[20] Trexler, on the other hand, cites many more sources and makes sweeping conclusions about "the native American sexual universe" in general. Yet, again, close examination shows that the sources do not support his argument.

Nearly all the evidence Trexler cites comes from early contact accounts by Spaniards in the Aztec and Incan cultural spheres. Although he admits that most of these reports make no mention of coercion, he finds it "easy to imagine" that "the more characteristic reality was that their lords first raped these boys, and then 'punished' them, at least in Christian eyes, by dressing them as women."[21] The early Spanish historian Oviedo, he suggests, provides evidence of this, and he proceeds to quote a long passage relating how Cueva youth who become *camayao* put on ("*se ponen*") skirts like those of the women and "involve themselves in common household services" ("*se ocupan en el servicio comun de las casas*"). There is no mention of rape or force, however, and the wording clearly indicates that the acts were voluntary. Indeed, Trexler himself backtracks at this point, admitting that "Oviedo does not, it is true, provide the most detailed description of the sodomistic dynamics between *Herr und Knecht*," and he turns to the obscure Martín de Murúa, a sixteenth-century friar, who wrote of the Cuzceñans that "the one among them who got the job of being a woman or doing [a woman's] task in that bestial and excommunicated act was then put in women's dress, and was thereafter treated like one."[22] Ultimately, this single citation is the best evidence Trexler offers to support his thesis. The word "imagine," on the other hand, appears a disconcerting number of times in his text. "What can we imagine," he asks, "to have been the context within which Oviedo's 'lords' first raped and then dressed young boys as females?" His answer: "A boys' harem"![23] (And the next sentence begins, "The sources *suggest*. . . ." [emphasis added].)

When Trexler actually cites ethnographic literature, he does so randomly, without regard for geographic or historic context. In one paragraph he begins by describing seventeenth-century Columbia and ends by citing twentieth-century reports on the Kaska of Canada. In the case of the occasional reports of non-berdache men being threatened (or teased?) with imposed cross-dressing as a means of shaming them into more appropriate male gender behavior, Callender and Kochems showed some years ago that "this form of cross-dressing lacked the supernatural validation often attached to berdaches, was a mark of disgrace, and was temporary or potentially subject to change. The status it denoted was thus clearly distinct from that of the berdache." They also concluded that "statements that male war captives were forced to become berdaches seem mostly an anthropological myth."[24]

Trexler lingers on the case of the Delaware (or Lenni Lenape) Indians who were presumably made into "women" after their defeat by the Iroquois sometime in the sixteenth century. Mary Cappello has recently reviewed the historical and anthropological literature on this subject and found that the story is "almost entirely reconstructed out of the records of early American missionaries and explorers who lacked any adequate knowledge of Delaware or Iroquois sex/gender systems."[25] In fact, it has never been determined if, when, or how the Iroquois actually conquered the Delaware. At least one reason the Delaware may have been described as "women" was because the role of mediators and peacekeepers assigned to them by the Iroquois was thought of as female, based on the role of clan matrons in Iroquois politics.[26] In any case, in the long-standing debate over these reports, Cappello has found one constant: "a certitude about the negativity implicit in 'woman' lingers in spite of an admission of the multiple meanings ascribed to the term by the Native Americans themselves."

Ultimately, the arguments of Gutiérrez and Trexler depend upon a literal reading of the texts of European conquerors and missionaries. To accept their position requires accepting that these source texts are unbiased and accurate reports of native practices. This is expecting a lot of Renaissance Catholic Spaniards bent on conquest and gold. A more careful approach would begin by asking why this information was collected and written down, and what discourse (and rules of discourse) was it a part of.

As I argued in the previous chapter, sixteenth-century Spanish writings on North American gender diversity were part of a moral discourse in which the justification for Spanish conquest came to hinge on the question of the "rationality" of the natives. By rationality, the legalists meant a combination of reason, intelligence, and morality—as defined in Catholic terms. If the natives were rational, then conquering them was not just. If they were irrational, however, then conquering and Christianizing them was no more objectionable than domesticating animals.[27] In this debate, the practice of "sodomy" by natives was taken as irrefutable evidence of their "irrationality." Consequently, Spanish authors insisted on construing natives in alternative gender roles as "sodomites." Here is the reason why reports of sodomy began to pile up in the Spanish archives—the conquerors were collecting evidence to justify their conquest.

In 1540, Fernando Alarcón dutifully noted sexual irregularities among the Yuman-speaking tribes of the Colorado River, while Casteñeda, the chronicler of Coronado's expedition undertaken the same year, inventoried sexual particulars for each tribe encountered.[28] In Florida and California, Spanish missionaries were armed with confessionals that directed the rigorous questioning of natives on sexual matters—not whether they knew about alternative gender roles or what the meaning of such roles was, but only whether they had had sex with other males, animals, women not their wives, relatives, and so forth.[29] As this information flowed back to Spain, historians reiterated it in their texts. In 1535, Oviedo asserted that sodomy was universal in the Americas.[30] Bernal Díaz del Castillo referred to sodomy no less than nine times in his narrative of the conquest of Mexico.[31] López de Gómara mentioned it at least ten times; Cieza de León, twelve times; Herrera, sixteen times; Garcilasso de la Vega, three times; and Torquemada, five times.[32]

Some of the evidence Trexler treats as reliable was likely extracted by torture. When we read the term "confess" in the statement of the genocidal conquistador Nuño de Guzmán in reference to a berdache he captured in 1530—"He confessed that from boyhood he had that habit and earned his living from men by that sin"—we must recall that it was part of the technical language of the Inquisition, in which admissions under torture were considered equivalent to sacramental confessions.[33]

In 1550, Charles V ordered a halt to conquest in the Americas so that religious and political leaders could resolve the debate over just conquest. In a convocation at Valladolid, the jurist Juan Ginés de Sepúlveda was well-armed with references to sodomy when he argued that the American natives were irrational and that conquest was just.[34] The views of the reformist missionary Bartolomé de Las Casas won out, however (although he defensively denied evidence of native sexual diversity), and policies eventually were enunciated that recognized the natives' humanity and called for their incorporation into colonial society.[35] No other European or North American nation articulated equivalent principles until the late nineteenth century.

Gutiérrez and Trexler would re-stage the Valladolid debates, however, and have Sepúlveda win. Conquerors' reports of sexual abominations, in their view, are reliable evidence. The natives are guilty of "sodomy," an act that in European societies was usually understood as a rape of a younger man by an older man. In fact, Europeans never sympathized with berdaches as victims, but were infuriated by them precisely because they appeared to willingly engage in sodomy. One detects the same horror in the subtext of Gutiérrez's and Trexler's writings.

The more contact literature one reads, the more apparent it becomes how stereotypical its language is. This is the second reason early contact accounts of berdaches cannot be read literally. Their standardized language signals the operation of tropes in what amounts to a cant of denunciation.[36] Whether or not berdache status was coercively imposed, the rules of European discourse required that berdaches be described as if it were and that the possibility of an individual choosing or desiring an alternative gender identity never be represented.

The cant of denunciation employs three syntactic devices: *passive* constructions, in which berdaches are the objects of actions by unspecified others; *transitive* constructions, in which others act upon the berdache; and *reflexive* constructions, in which the berdache renders himself an object. A passage from Coreal illustrates all three: "the boys that *abandon themselves* [reflexive] thus *are excluded* [passive] from the society of men. . . . *They employ them* [transitive] in all the diverse handiworks of women."[37] In the early seventeenth century, Deliette also used a series of passive constructions to characterize the Illinois berdache: "There are men who *are bred* for this purpose from their childhood. . . . They *are girt* with a piece of leather or cloth. . . . Their hair *is allowed* to grow and *is fastened* behind the head. . . . They *are tattooed* on their cheeks like the women."[38] In narratives no less than literature, the device of repetition imputes significance to repeated elements regardless of their truth value. Here, the repetition of passive constructions elevates a grammatical convention—the subject who is always-already an object—into a canonical description of the male berdache.[39]

These formulas have remained surprisingly consistent over several centuries and arguably are continued in the twentieth century by psychological and sociological theories that similarly preclude the agency of berdaches. When theory reinforces grammar, the figure that results can be ludicrously overdetermined. According to Hassrick, "The role of the *winkte* suggests that certain Sioux boys were victims either of actual biological homosexuality or of parental overprotection."[40] Having covered the spectrum of twentieth century thinking about homosexuality, Hassrick can be certain that the berdache was a "victim." Similarly, Opler wrote of the Apache, "In this setting, the transvestite was more often physically aberrant than functionally disordered; in the latter event, the person was universally regarded as demented, and in either case, occupied a disgraceful position in society. Such people were avoided and kept hard at work at tasks reserved for women."[41] In phrases such as " kept hard at work" and "tasks reserved for women" one hears the unmistakable echoes of the contact literature and its passive and transitive constructions.

What cultural imperative guided Europeans when they wrote about North American gender diversity? It was the same imperative that led them to assume, whether they argued that the Delaware had been "made women" or had not, that such a condition was degrading. The berdache "debases himself" with "those occupations proper to that sex," the "employments of women," the "low drudgery to which the savage women are condemned," and the "menial tasks imposed upon a squaw."[42] Like women, the berdache must "submit to the duties of a wife," perform "all the labors and duties of that condition," and "please men."[43] Here is the template for how male Europeans and Americans wrote about the berdache—how they wrote about native women. They, too, were objects, the recipients of actions, and sometimes victims—condemned to and damned by "low drudgery."

The cant of the conquerors and scattered reports of imposed cross-dressing do not add up to the drastic reinterpretations Gutiérrez and Trexler propose. Hypermasculine and military values did prevail in some tribes (although not the Pueblos), but they coexisted with beliefs in supernatural power without counterparts in Western culture. Landes, for example, has described how some young men among the eastern Sioux "dreaded" warfare and fled the village in groups when war parties were organized. They were "not desired for marriage and were generally belittled. . . . However, the berdache, as my informants put it, 'had a dream to be like a woman, so he had to act like one or die.'"[44]

In native North American belief systems, a man who wore a dress because of a vision was the equal of the hypermasculine warrior whose visions gave him success against the enemy. Thus, in the following account, the famous chief Four Bears meets his match when he comes across a Sioux *winkte* one day on the plains. I think Gutiérrez and Trexler would be hard pressed to explain the outcome of this encounter in terms of their paradigm of subjugation.

> One day the Hidatsa war party found two women and a berdache digging wild
> turnips on the prairie. Until they were near they thought they were women, for
> all three Sioux were dressed alike. Before making the attack, Four Bears told his
> party that they would strike coups on the women but spare their lives. Four Bears

got ahead of the others and struck both but the berdache was brave, saying, "You can't kill me for I am holy. I will strike coups on you with my digging stick."

Then the berdache sang a sacred song and chased them. Four Bears shot an arrow at the berdache but it would not penetrate the robe. Then he knew that the berdache had great supernatural powers. Since he had been successful on all other military expeditions and did not want to spoil his luck, he called his party back. The expedition was successful, for they got the horse. Four Bears used good judgment, for it was hard to kill a berdache since they were holy.[45]

Not all third and fourth gender persons were remarkable individuals like this *winkte,* or like Hastíín Klah, Osh-Tisch, and Woman Chief. Nor are the circumstances that gay, lesbian, and two-spirit natives face today the same as those of their predecessors. In many cases traditional roles have lapsed and virulent homophobia has taken hold. Contemporary natives are right to complain about the antiquarian interests of anthropologists and historians when they face pressing problems now and have few means to broadcast their cause. At the same time, history is not an armchair pursuit when it provides the models and language for lesbian and gay natives to open dialogues about homophobia and (re)claim a place in their communities.

PREFERENCE OR SELECTION?

In a recent essay anthropologist Arnold Pilling argues that "the emergence of a cross-dresser in a Zuni household was nearly always a response to the lack of a sister or female matrilateral cousin in the household."[46] Although the problem Pilling describes is a real one within a matrilineal/matrilocal social structure—that is, the occasional lack of a daughter to inherit a house—the process he infers by which individual males became *lhamana* seems counterintuitive. In fact, Pilling offers no explication of exactly how such a process would work. One is left to imagine a family meeting at which it is decided that little Johnny must now wear a dress so that he can inherit a house twenty or more years later. Such procedures are unheard of among the Zunis, and, indeed, Pilling offers no evidence other than his inferences based on the composition of households as reported in U.S. census records.[47] Pilling does not cite or report this data in his essay. He reviews this evidence instead in a manuscript that remained unpublished at the time of his death in 1994,[48] which analyzes the household composition of several known *lhamana* as documented in censuses from 1900 to 1910.

The first case Pilling considers, that of Kasinelu, fits his hypothesis to the extent that Kasinelu does not appear to have had any sisters, nor did his mother's younger sister have any daughters (who would have been next in line to inherit). At the time that Kasinelu began cross-dressing (in 1896, according to Stevenson, at the age of sixteen), both women were in their forties and unlikely to have more children. Stevenson, however, witnessed Kasinelu's transformation and makes no reference to the inheritance issue. Nor does there appear to have been any family consensus or decision regarding the matter. According to Stevenson, while Kasinelu's mother and grandmother "were quite willing that the boy should continue in the work *in which he seemed interested*," his grandfather "endeavored to shame him out of his determination."[49]

The next case Pilling examines is that of Kwiwishdi, who did have sisters and whose status as a *lhamana,* Pilling admits, "was apparently not correlated with a lack of sisters." His third example, Lasbeke, also had an older sister.[50]

Next, he discusses Tsalatitse, who, Pilling concludes, was an only child living alone with his father in 1900. In 1910, however, Tsalatitse was reported to be living with a man with a different name, identified as his father, and the man's wife, identified as Tsalatitse's mother. Of this woman's six children, only Tsalatitse and another son had survived. If Tsalatitse's *lhamana* status was based on a lack of sisters, then we would want to know why he was selected for this function and not his brother.

Finally, Pilling analyzes the household of the *lhamana* Yuka (or U'k), who also does not fit the sisterless pattern, since by 1910 his older sister had inherited their house.[51]

In sum, only Kasinelu and Tsalatitse conform to Pilling's scenario; Kwiwishdi, Lasbeke, and Yuka do not. The other case we know about, that of We'wha, also disproves Pilling's hypothesis. Both of We'wha's parents died in a smallpox epidemic, and he was raised by an aunt. This woman, however, had a daughter who took over the household. Yet, in his 1997 essay, Pilling claimed that "all cross-dressers except U'k . . . lacked an elder sister."[52]

At least one source—not cited by Pilling—offers some support for his hypothesis. Gifford, in a 1940 culture element list, reported that Zuni parents might bring up a boy as a girl if there was no girl in the family.[53] Although there is still no confirmed case of this, there is no reason to rule it out either. In a matrilineal descent system, the presence of a male berdache in a household lacking a female descendent would be a happy occasion. Berdaches who became heads of households would be more visible in the community and, thus, an impression might arise that the two facts—lack of a female descendent and presence of a male berdache—were linked. What Pilling's own data makes clear, however, is that kinship selection was not the normal reason individuals became *lhamana,* and that his hypothesis, therefore, cannot be used to explain the presence of berdaches in general. As we saw in the case of Hastíín Klah (see chapter 3), Navajo families considered a *nádleehí* such a boon that they often concentrated resources to provide them specialized training. But this happened after clear evidence of inclinations and skills. More prominent families had more resources for such purposes, and therefore *nádleehí* from those families were likely to be more visible. However, if berdaches such as

Kasinelu could insist on alternative gender behavior despite opposition from some family members, then certainly boys *not* inclined to be berdaches would resist suddenly being dressed as girls.

As is so often the case, the missing evidence that might resolve the questions Pilling has raised are the voices of *lhamana* themselves. Only one text that I am aware of records the words of an actual *lhamana* explaining his reasons for entering that role, and it supports the conclusion I have argued here—that the large majority of those who became berdaches did so entirely of their own volition.

In a letter written some years after the fact, a former school teacher at Zuni recalled her conversation in the late 1880s with a young *lhamana* named Kwiwishdi. Why had he adopted women's clothing? she asked. Because he did women's work, he replied. "But I often do a man's work, Quewishty," she retorted, "and I do not put on a man's clothes to do it." Her interpreter spoke to Kwiwishdi in Zuni for several minutes and then explained, "He say[s] you do not love all peoples in the world as much as he do[es], and that's why he do[es] that." Exasperated, the teacher concluded, "This accounts for a kind of spiritual arrogance that is peculiar to those creatures."[54]

CONCLUSION:
THE PAST AND FUTURE OF GENDER DIVERSITY

North America was not unique in its diverse gender roles and identities. Examples of gender diversity can be found throughout the world. Indeed, at each horizon where we might begin to tell the human story—whether we are contemplating archaeological evidence; the earliest examples of writing; or humankind's oldest social pattern, that of the hunter-gatherer—we find evidence of alternative genders and identities, of individuals who were notmen and notwomen, of gendered skills, roles, and characteristics mixed in symbolic and practical ways.

On the western outskirts of Albuquerque a series of extinct volcanic cones dots the horizon. Their eruptions millennia ago left behind flows of pyrocrastic rubble and black volcanic tufa that today form a long, low mesa overlooking the floodplain of the Rio Grande. Tucked away in a natural shelter at the base of the mesa is an ancient campsite once frequented by prehistoric hunters and travelers. The evidence of their presence remains in the form of hundreds of petroglyphs covering the surrounding rocks. Many of the carvings amount to little more than the prehistoric equivalent of graffiti. Others evoke the mythical and ceremonial world of the ancestors of the Pueblo Indians.

One carving is particularly intriguing. Scratched on to the side of a large boulder halfway up the mesa is a crude depiction of a human head with long straight hair indicated on the right side.[1] This convention—asymmetrical hairstyle—occurs again a few dozen miles to the west, at a site called Pottery Mound. Painted on the wall of a kiva used between 1400 and 1500 C.E. is a figure with long, straight hair, the historic style of Pueblo men, on the right side of the head, and the hairstyle of a maiden, in which the hair is wrapped around a wooden form to create a whorl in the shape of a butterfly wing, on the left side. (The petroglyph at Albuquerque lacks any indication of hairstyle on the left.) In its right hand, the Pottery Mound figure also holds a quiver of arrows and a bow, men's implements, and in the left, a woven basket plaque, an object still made and used by Hopi women.[2]

All these traits have corresponding features in the Zuni kachina Ko'lhamana (literally, Supernatural Berdache)—the half-male and half-female hairstyle, the juxtaposition of men's and women's objects (which symbolize hunting and agriculture respectively). As described in the previous chapter, this kachina has a pivotal role in a mythical war between the gods. This myth, as Claude Lévi-Strauss has shown, centers around the opposition of hunting (the taking of life) and growing (the creation of life).[3] The people of Acoma and Laguna pueblos (midway between Zuni and Pottery Mound) also tell stories of a war between the gods, only in their tellings the entire population of enemies, the Storoka, are identified as berdaches, or *kokwimu*. Instead of a bifurcated male/female hairstyle, however, the Storokas' alternative gender status is indicated by a blanket robe worn in the women's fashion, with one shoulder exposed, over a pair of men's pants or leggings. The same convention is used in the costuming of the Hopi kachinas known as Korosta (First Mesa), Ota (Second Mesa), and Kwasaitaka, "Skirt Man" (Third Mesa).[4]

These kachinas and their precursors are evidence of a prehistoric ceremonial complex. Although its origin and dissemination remain conjectural, the cultural significance of multiple genders in this region cannot be doubted. Additional evidence for the prehistoric presence of these roles can be found in burial sites in which human remains typed as one sex are found in association with objects of the other sex. At the Zuni site of Hawikku and in excavations at Chaco Canyon male skeletons have been found interned with women's objects and implements.[5] Archaeologists such as Sandra Hollimon and Robert Schmidt are now beginning to develop methods for identifying multiple genders from archaeological remains.[6]

When ethnographic reports from Central and Latin America are analyzed, the conclusion that alternative gender statuses have a long history in the western hemisphere undoubtedly will be confirmed.[7] When this evidence is further augmented by the reports of such roles worldwide, basic assumptions about humans and human history may have to be altered. Although the number of individuals who occupied alternative gender roles may not have been large, the roles themselves were widespread and culturally significant.

The Siberian Chuckchi "soft man" (*yirka´ᵋ-la´ul*), or "transformed" shaman, known primarily from the reports of Vladimir Bogoraz, has been frequently cited as a parallel to the North American berdache. (Bogoraz also mentions women called *qa´čɪkɪčhɛča,* "similar to a man.") According to Bogoraz, "transformation takes place by the command of the *ke´let* [spirits], usually at the critical age of early youth."[8] He goes on to describe various "degrees of transformation," of which only the third and final stage is that of the soft man. In language reminiscent of that used by natives and anthropologists to describe berdaches, Bogoraz reports that "a young man who is undergoing it leaves off all pursuits and manners of his sex, and takes up those of a woman. He throws away the rifle and the lance, the lasso of the reindeer herdsmen, and the harpoon of the seal-hunter, and takes to the needle and the skin-scraper. He learns the use of these quickly, because the 'spirits' are helping him all the time."[9] Like North American berdaches, soft men did not cross genders from man to woman, literally or figuratively. They retained their male names, and the use of the label "soft man" precluded their complete assimilation into the category of women.[10]

At the same time, there is an important difference between Siberian and North American roles. Soft men represented a "branch of shamanism" in the words of Bogoraz.[11] Their cross-dressing, preference for women's work, and marriages to non-transformed men were not described as the motivations for their role change, nor were these the defining traits of their status. Soft men were shamans first, alternatively gendered second.[12] In North America, shamans or medicine people were distinct from berdaches; berdaches were sometimes shamans, but separate terms distinguished the roles.

Alternative gender statuses also have been documented for Polynesia and Oceania. The best known example is the *māhū* of Hawai'i and Tahiti, but there are counterparts in Samoa (the *fa'afafine*), Tonga (the *fakaleitī/fakafefine*), Tuvalu (the *pinapinaaine*), and other Polynesian islands. In the historical and anthropological literature *māhū* and their counterparts are identified as male (although in contemporary Hawai'i the term is applied to females as well).[13] As in North America, these roles are defined primarily in terms of labor contribution. As Niko Besnier reports, "The gender-liminal person in Polynesia is commonly thought to excel in women's tasks: his mats are said to be particularly symmetrical and regular in shape, his domestic chores singularly thorough, and he is more resilient to tedium than the average woman."[14] Other traits of (male) *māhū* and their counterparts are variable. Generally, their self-presentation includes nonmasculine characteristics, and they sometimes cross-dress, especially for festive occasions. However, Besnier found no reports of permanent cross-dressing anywhere in Polynesia.[15] Homosexuality, on the other hand, is consistently reported. Polynesian roles are distinct from those in Siberia and North America, however, in their lack of a religious dimension. The exception appears to be Hawaiian *māhū* who are credited with important functions in relation to the hula dance. As in the case of North American roles, *māhū* identity is now the subject of a revival movement.[16]

Beyond Oceania, social roles based on gender difference have been observed throughout Southeast Asia.[17] In Borneo, *manang bali* (among the Iban) and *basir* (among the Ngaju of Kalimantan), and in Sulawesi, *bajasa* (among the Toradjas) and *bissu* (of the Makasserese), are male cross-dressing shaman-priests who function as healers, ritual leaders, and religious performers. They receive their powers from female spirits and commune with the spirit world by entering trance states. They have sex and form relationships with men. These roles are similar to those of Siberia in that they are defined primarily as religious occupational statuses, rather than secular third gender roles that may or may not have a religious dimension. Other aspects of these roles reflect the differences between Siberian and North American societies and those of Southeast Asia. With their agrarian mode of production, large populations, social stratification, and high levels of specialization, Asian societies are able to support true priesthoods. *Manang bali, basir, bajasa,* and *bissu* are all described as functioning in groups to conduct rituals and fulfill other duties.

Additional examples of gender-transformed males specializing in shamanic religious roles can be cited from the Philippines, Korea, Vietnam, Cambodia, and Burma.[18] An early sixteenth-century religious manuscript from Thailand relates how three sexes—female, male, and *napumsaka* ("not male")—were conjured from four elements.[19]

Here we are in the much larger world-historical region that Toynbee (following classical Greek usage) termed the Oikoumene—that area of agrarian city-state societies, from Southeast Asia to the Mediterranean basin, long linked by trade, conquest, and cultural diffusion. In the western region, contact between the Near East and the Mediterranean predates the Greek and Roman empires. This sphere of influence was extended eastward by the spread of Islam. Throughout this region are instances of shaman-priests and priesthoods with similar core traits—gender transformation induced by female deities or spirits, the adoption of distinctive clothing and/or cross-dressing, and same-sex relations. The religious practices of these priests typically entail ecstatic dancing and trance states during which blessings are bestowed or prophecies uttered.

One of the most visible of these cults today is that of the *hijra* of Pakistan and northern India. *Hijra* (an Urdu term) are males and intersexed individuals devoted to Bahucharā Mātā, one of the many Indian mother goddess figures.[20] They live with gurus in collectives that are linked into transnational networks. Sometimes serving as temple functionaries, *hijra* appear most often in bands with established territories. Their primary religious role is to bless newlywed couples and newborn males by "calling down the blessings" of their goddess, fertility being foremost. Their performances incorporate bawdy dancing accompanied by the music of flutes and drums. Under British rule their traditional economic base was undermined, and today most *hijra* live a marginal existence as beggars or prostitutes.

Unlike the other examples considered so far, *hijra* are often castrated. In the course of the procedure, the initiate metaphorically dies and is reborn as a *sannyasi,* or saint, who embodies the power of the goddess. In practice, many *hijra* postpone the operation, and some forgo it altogether, despite pressure from other cult members and severe ridicule if they are discovered in public to have a penis. Castration does not transform *hijra* into women, however. As Serena Nanda's informants explain, "We are neither men nor women."[21]

Evidence of such roles occurs in Sanskrit literature as early as the first millennium B.C.E. *Hijra* often cite the episode in the fourth book of the *Mahābhārata* as an origin myth: The hero Arjuna disguises himself as a eunuch and lives in a harem for a year, teaching the arts of dance. An even older text, the *Śatapatha Brāhmaṇa* specifies the use of a "long-haired man" in one of its rites because he is "neither man nor woman" (5.1.2.14). Sanskrit terms for such individuals include *tr̥tīyā prakr̥ti* or "third nature," *strīrūpini/strīpumān,* "woman-man," and *napuṃsaka,* "not male."[22]

Elsewhere I have documented the parallels between *hijras* and the Greco-Roman priests of Cybele and Attis called *galli.*[23] Although *galli* were originally temple priests in the theocratic city-states of Anatolia, in Hellenistic times they became itinerant devotees, sometimes organized in collectives. Like the *hijra,* they danced accompanied by flutes and drums and entered trance states during which they cut themselves with knives and swords and uttered prophecies. In fact, their performance was often described as a war dance, related to (or the same as) that of the Corybantes. (The sword dance itself survived in European folk traditions as the Morris or Moresca.[24]) *Galli* dressed in a flamboyant and unique (neither male nor female) style. Like *hijra,* they were castrated, although details of the procedure are few, and they were still assumed to be sexually active with men. Also like *hijra, galli* were explicitly described as a *medium genus,* or third gender.

Even more ancient representatives of gender diversity can be found in the societies of Mesopotamia. From Sumerian times on, a significant number of the personnel of both temples and palaces—the central institutions of Mesopotamian city-states—were individuals with the gender identity of neither men nor women. These include the Sumerian *gala,* specialists in singing lamentations (which originally may have been a woman's occupation), and the *kur-gar-ra* (Akkadian *kurgarrû*) and *assinnu,* who are typically identified as servants of the goddess Inanna/Ishtar. Like *galli,* they performed a war dance, perhaps while in a trance state, with swords, clubs, and blood-letting, accompanied by the music of flutes, drums, and cymbals. Various texts allude to their homosexual practices. The conceptual basis for these roles is provided by an early Sumerian myth known as "The Creation of Man" (ca. 2000 B.C.E.). The goddess Ninmah fashions seven special types of persons, including the "Woman-who-is-not-giving-birth" and the "Man-in-the-body-of-which-no-male-and-no-female-organ-was-placed." Enki finds each one an occupation and position in society.[25] There is no clear evidence that any of the Mesopotamian priests described were actually castrated, however. The use of eunuchs to fill bureaucratic roles did not develop until Assyrian times.[26]

All this evidence suggests that the link between alternative genders and administrative and religious roles in Mesopotamian societies was archaic.[27] Whether these roles evolved from shaman-priest statuses comparable to those of Asia and North America, becoming institutionalized priesthoods as villages grew into cities, remains purely speculative. On the one hand, shamanic elements are clearly evident in the rites performed by *kurgarrû* and *assinnu.* On the other hand, these individuals appear to have filled functions in temples and palaces unique to an urban society. Unlike North American berdaches, they did not occupy a distinct gender role. Although they were conceptualized as gender-different, individuals were not *gala, kurgarrû,* or *assinnu* unless they were fulfilling official theocratic positions.

Nonetheless, there are at least three areas of similarity shared by all the roles I have described here. First is a component of economic specialization. In the horticultural and hunting-gathering societies of North America this took the form of crafts specialization, especially on the part of male berdaches. In the citied, agrarian societies of the Oikoumene, the economic dimension of alternative gender statuses lie in the realm of services rather than production, including healing, religious performances, prognostication, and so forth. A second common element are techniques and patterns of shamanism (with the apparent exception of Polynesian roles). A third is gender difference and homosexuality, although it is not always possible to identify whether these traits were the function of cultural expectations or individual motivations or both.

Nonprocreation is a common association of sexual and gender difference. From this perspective, homosexuality (involving relations between individuals of the same sex and same gender) and alternative gender roles (involving relations between individuals of the same sex but different genders) are equivalent—neither produces children. In the patriarchal agrarian societies of the Mediterranean and the Near East, nonprocreation was most often personified by the eunuch. In ancient India, any individual not manifesting heterosexual desire might be defined as "impotent."[28] Early Christians achieved nonprocreation (and thereby transcended gender) through various forms of asceticism. In North America, however, there was no expectation that berdaches did not desire or were incapable of sex. Their sexuality was viewed in terms of a contrast between sex for reproduction and sex for pleasure (which includes homosexuality), rather than between reproductive sexuality and the absence of sexuality altogether (which precludes homosexuality).

The nonprocreativity of alternative genders is frequently associated with concepts of death. To be nonprocreative (especially in patriarchal Old World cultures) was to be dead in a social sense, since the possibility of living on by passing one's name to subsequent generations was foreclosed. At the same time, nonprocreative sexuality can be a kind of defiance of death—a way of clinging to youth and refusing to age or, more drastically, a way of detaching oneself from ordinary physical existence to establish a special relationship to the realm of the spiritual and immortal.

Underlying the different ways in which other-gendered individuals serve as mediators is this special association with death. Thus berdaches in native California were undertakers because they could engage in contact with the dead, which for others would be harmful. In Siberia, Chuckchi soft men "died" when they entered trances, and their souls traveled to the spirit world. In Mesopotamia, the figures created to rescue Inanna/Ishtar in the story of her descent to the underworld can enter the land of the dead because as "sexless" beings they are, metaphorically, already dead. In India, *hijra* bestow blessings of fertility because, as castrated males, their own desire has been drained away, rendering them conduits for the fertility of the goddess herself. And in all these cultures—in the Greco-Roman world, Mesopotamia, southern Asia, and North America—other-gendered individuals performed war-related dances and rituals.[29]

This search for parallels to North American multiple genders has taken us to the threshold of history and culture. Clearly, sexual and gender diversity are an original part of the human heritage. It is not necessary to turn to theories of genetics and human biology to account for this. The model outlined in chapter 6 predicts the presence of multiple genders based on social and cultural factors related to gendered divisions of labor and non-dichotomous sex/gender cultural systems. These factors are widespread features of human societies, past and present.

Another reason multiple genders are so widespread may have to do with certain inherent properties of symbolic communication. As Lévi-Strauss has sought to demonstrate, structural oppositions and mediations are elemental to human thought. This would explain not only the widespread occurrence of binary gender categories but also the presence of mediating symbols and categories. Wherever there are two, a third cannot be far behind; and if there are three the possibility exists that the system will be stabilized not by repressing the third and unifying the two into one, but by adding a fourth. In the case of categories of humans, this would mean that multiple genders would be a fairly common occurrence.

Even though Lévi-Strauss analyzed Zuni mythology, in which the third gender figure Ko'lhamana is prominent, he never explored this implication of his theory.[30] For him it was always a matter of "bridging the gap between two and one."[31] The essentialism of binaries in structuralist theory means that the androgyne can never be the ontological basis for a social identity, but only an unstable admixture of male and female, a "mediating device" to be replaced by others in series of permutations that, as far as one can judge from Lévi-Strauss, unfold strictly on an intellectual level. What disappears in this infinite regression is what might be called the materiality of the third—the actual social roles, identities, and lifestyles based on these "mediating devices," of which no better example exists than North American multiple genders. Ultimately, structuralism remains grounded in a dualism unable to question its own assumptions—that binaries are natural and that nature (and the cultures founded on the binaries it gives) can never include such unnatural, nonbinary phenomena as gender diversity and homosexuality. Yet this is exactly what berdaches represent, identities distinct from male and female, combinations of the two plus everything the binary excludes.

Deconstruction shows how binaries are always covert hierarchies. A term such as "female" is invariably subordinated to a superior term such as "male" and represented as an inferior version of it. Semiotic analysis shows as well that the meaning of the terms of a binary resides in their unstable relationship to each other, not in their reference to a "transcendental signified"—a fixed, specifiable object or state of being self-evident to all observers. "Male" and "female" are no less unstable terms than the mediations they generate.

We do not have to embrace the precepts of structuralism and its successors, however, to agree that mediating practices and symbols are commonplace in human cultural endeavors, and that individuals seen as bridging genders are often elected to perform other mediations as well. Whether in the form of symbols or identities, gender difference is frequently endowed with special meaning; rarely is it viewed indifferently. Mediations can take many shapes, however, and be valued in many different ways. Third terms can be represented as androgynous blendings of male and female or as that which is neither male nor female. They can be prodigies or monsters.

The methods of deconstruction and poststructuralism have profoundly influenced scholars working within postmodern cultural studies and, especially, queer theory. Queer theorists have sought to demonstrate the inherent instability of not only male and female gender categories but the heterosexual/homosexual dichotomy, as well, and the human identities based on these categories. Once all binaries and identities have been deconstructed and their inherent instability, arbitrariness, and cultural relativity exposed, all that is left in the view of many current theorists is desire, conceptualized as prelinguistic, inherently antagonistic to categorization, and autonomous (that is, independent of social or linguistic determination).[32]

The weak link in this chain of reasoning is the lack of evidence for it. If postmodern theorists cite any empirical cases to support their arguments they invariably come from a single society and a single historical period—that of western Europe and North America within the past 150 years. Modern gay identity (but not homosexual behavior itself or other identities) has indeed had a very short history. At present it is bound to appear fluid and conditional. But is the novelty of gay identity a reflection of the inherent instability of all identities everywhere? Or can it be explained in historical terms, in relation to specific social factors that may or may not make identities unstable in other cultures and periods?

Many alternative gender roles occur in societies whose beliefs regarding sexuality and gender are explicitly constructionist. In such societies, cross-gender and mixed-gender symbols, ritual experiences, work, and sexuality are a part of many people's lives, not just members of multiple genders. As we saw in chapter 3, all initiates in the Navajo Yeibichai ceremony look through the eyes of the female Yé'ii mask and symbolically acquire a female perspective. At the same time, the presence of fluid concepts of sex, gender, and identity does not preclude the construction of stable social roles. Rather, fluidity leads to the diversification of identities, not their elimination. Identities, of course, are subject to the constructive forces of the societies they are part of—but (and this has not been appreciated enough in cultural studies) social organizations, cultural systems of meaning, and historical events can also provide the basis for longevity as well as fluidity. If "marriage," "family," "motherhood," "work," "play," and "art" can be used as categories of cross-cultural analysis, then gender mediation (encompassing enacted roles as well as symbols and meanings) can and should be included among them.

Perhaps the greatest value of a multiple gender paradigm is heuristic. On the one hand, it helps us see the cultural and historical coherency of roles that until recently have been treated in isolation. On the other hand, thinking about third and fourth genders helps break the cycle of projection in which Western observers constantly replicate heterosexual binarism wherever they turn their gaze. It requires us to suspend the assumption that heterosexuality and gender dualism is universal, that behind every gender lurks a sex, pulling difference back to one of two versions. As long as the language for talking about gender is confined to mutually exclusive, binary terms, lesbians, gay men, and other sexual minorities are bound to come off looking bad—as defective, counterfeit, or imitation men and women. The only alternative in a dichotomous system of gender is androgyny, a mixture of the two. But the mixture is only more of the same. Androgyny is intrinsic to a heterosexist imaginary. Third and fourth genders, on the other hand, help us to perceive all that is left over when the world has been divided into male and female—the feelings, perceptions, and talents that may be neither.

Of course, queer theorists seek not only to reveal the instability of identities, many exalt fluidity as a political goal. Native North American gender diversity, however, shows that "fluidity" does not always constitute a disruptive force. Only in patriarchal cultures does gender difference become gender transgression. And only in modern societies has an ideology of dichotomous and fixed sexes become the basis of comprehensive state interventions that make third and fourth genders unfeasible. When one believes that sex is given by nature in two incommensurable forms, the attitude toward that which is non-binary shifts from ambivalence and awe to horror and condemnation.

Native North American third and fourth genders represent something ultimately more radical than the politics of gender transgression. The cultural distance between third gender deities such as the Navajo Begochidíín and the Bella Coola Sxints, and Western constructions of homosexuality is breathtaking. Apparently, homophobia is no more natural than heterosexuality. Societies can accept and integrate sexual and gender difference. But that alone—tolerance, respect for the individual—is not foreign to Western concepts. It is the fact that native societies positively linked these behaviors to their highest religious and spiritual beliefs that poses the greatest challenge to us today. It is not merely a matter of different judgments of the same phenomenon, but completely different perceptions of what that phenomenon is. The native cultural consciousness perceived something in third and fourth gender individuals that Western societies have been oblivious to for millennia.

Indeed, a century and a half of social scientific study has had almost nothing to say about why gender difference, homosexuality, and religious and artistic aptitude are linked in so many individuals and societies. Not even lesbian, gay, bisexual, and transgender activists claim more than that their behavior is morally neutral in and of itself and not a threat to society. Only a few voices, rejected by many on both the left and right of the lesbian/gay movement, assert that (some) lesbians, gays, and other sexual minorities (might) have traits that are socially, culturally, and spiritually valuable.[33] Nonetheless, this is precisely what the lives of Osh-Tisch, Klah, and Woman Chief attest. Theirs was a difference that served.

The subject of North American gender diversity might be of little more than antiquarian interest except for two things. First, as chapter 8 shows, the citation of accounts of multiple genders in European discourse played a role in the construction of the first mode of modern homosexuality, the alternative gender identity of the Uranian (and his counterparts). Second is the presence of native people today who continue or have resumed defining themselves in terms of traditional roles. This fact alone challenges the exceptionalism attributed to modern homosexuality in social constructionist accounts, which describe it as the unique product of uniquely modern social and historical factors. The social context and beliefs underlying third and fourth gender roles could hardly be more different from those of industrialized, capitalist societies. But constructions can be constructed as either related or disparate. The phenomenon of native survivance as described in chapter 8 means that new signifiers and labels are attributed essential, consistent meanings—especially concepts of spirituality. At the same time, historic signifiers of gender difference are being freed to migrate across time and space and find new iterations in modern discourse and social practice. By producing creative syntheses of traditional and modern social roles, by reminding us that our desires represent not only needs but visions and aspirations as well, one of North America's most beleaguered minorities-within-a-minority—lesbian, gay, and two-spirit natives—may one day change how we all think about our sexual and gender identities.

As I reflect on the stories in this book, one image stands out: that of the Floridian "hermaphrodite" in 1564 bringing Laudonnière and his men "a great vessell full of cleere fountaine water, wherewith she greatly refreshed us." So many of the third and fourth gender natives described in this book actively reached out to Europeans and Anglo-Americans—out of a desire to learn about them, a desire to teach them the benefits of their own cultures, a desire to barter for their goods, and sometimes out of pure desire itself. In so doing they followed a principle native people had been applying for centuries in their dealings with each other in a continent that has always been multicultural: affirm the other who affirms you.[34]

And so native people came to the encounter with the newcomers with gifts, eager to showcase their culture—their food, their dances, their acumen, their powers. They expected that the Europeans would return the gesture. But instead of affirmation they were judged and denounced, their culture and identities negated, their lands stolen. Affirming the other who affirms you remains an excruciating exercise for many Euro-Americans, whose Judeo-Christian heritage for so long has allowed them only to affirm those who look, act, and signify as they do. The debt owed native North Americans cannot be considered paid as long as this mindset prevails and the negation of the Other continues.

The gestures of outreach by third and fourth gender natives speak not only of their goodwill, but of their self-assurance and confidence, as well. Little did they know, although they often found out soon enough, that the very source of their assurance, an accepted social identity based on gender difference, would threaten some of the most deeply held beliefs and values of the Europeans. From that misunderstanding has come untold tragedy. And yet, in the innocence of that expectation—that the other would indeed affirm them—there is the hope that some day yet they will. And why not? Gender and sexual diversity in North America and elsewhere were once differences that served. If we can remember the stories told here, they may yet serve again.

GLOSSARY OF NATIVE TERMS FOR ALTERNATIVE GENDER ROLES AND SEXUALITY BY LANGUAGE FAMILY[1]

	Male	Female	Source
ALEUT-ESKIMO			
Inuit	*sipiniq* infant whose sex changes at birth		Saladin d'Anglure 1986: 42
Aleut	*aijahnhuk*		Jacobi 1937: 122
	ayagígux‘ man transformed into a woman	*tayagígux‘* woman transformed into a man	Jochelson 1933: 71
Pacific Eskimo/ Yup'ik	*akhnuchik, aranu:tiq* "man-woman"		Davydov 1977: 166; Birket-Smith 1953: 94
		Tyakutyi "what kind of people are those two"	Birket-Smith 1953: 94, 136
Kuskokwim River	*aranaruaq* "woman-like"	*angut"guaq* "man-like"	Angukcuaq, pers. comm. 1997
St. Lawrence Island	*yuk allakuyaaq* "different, distinct person"		Angukcuaq, pers. comm. 1997
ALGONQUIAN			
Arapaho	*haxu'xan, hoxux* (sg.), *hoxuxunó* (pl.) "rotten bone"(?)		Kroeber 1902: 19; Terry Tafoya, pers. comm. 1992
Blackfoot			
	ake:ṡkassi "acts like a woman"		Schaeffer 1965: 221
		sakwo'mapi akikwan "boy-girl"	Schultz 1919: 38

1. Terms in this table refer to male and female alternative gender roles unless otherwise noted. Key variants are included, separated by commas, with the most current form last. Original transcriptions have been simplified following the orthography of the Handbook of North American Indians. Names of mythical figures are capitalized. Literal translations of terms appear in quotes.

	Male	Female	Source
		ninauposkitzipxpe, *ninawaki* "manly-hearted woman"	Lewis 1941: 143; Seward 1946: 120
		matsaps "crazy" woman	Seward 1946: 120
Cheyenne			
	he´eman (sg.) *he´emane'o* (pl.) fr. *hée,* "woman"	*hetaneman* (sg.) *hatane´mane'o* (pl.) fr. *hetan,* "man"	Petter 1915: 1116; Grinnell 1923, 2:39; Winfield Coleman 1997, pers. comm.
		heemanèvo ehazistoz "acts of sapphism" *heeo zetaomeaeuowa-thaazess* "sapphism, Lesbian love"	Petter, Newberry Library
Cree			
	ayekkwe, a:yahkwew "split testicles," i.e., sterile		Lacombe 1874: 164, 326; Skinner 1911: 151; Mandelbaum 1940: 256
Fox-sauk			
	i-coo-coo-a, i-coo-coo-ah, äyä'kwä´		Catlin 1973, 2:214; Owen 1902: 54; Michelson 1925: 256
Gros Ventre	*athúth*		Schaeffer 1965: 232
Illinois			
	ikoueta		La Salle 1880: 368
		ickoue ne kioussa "hunting women"	Lahontan 1905: 463
Miami			
	waupeengwoatar "the white face"		Trowbridge 1938: 68
Micmac			
	geenumu gesallagee "he loves men"		Williams 1986: 227
Ojibwa			
	agokwa		Tanner 1956: 89
		okitcitakwe "warrior woman"	Skinner 1914: 486

	Male	Female	Source
Potawatomi			
	m´nuhtokwae fr. *m´nuhto* "supernatural, extraordinary" + female suffix		Landes 1970: 195-96
ATHAPASKAN			
Apache			
	ńdé'sdzan "man-woman"		Farrarr 1997: 237
	Na-yénnas-ganné man-woman warrior		Porter 1986: 195
Navajo			
	nutlys, nátli, nu´tle, nádle, nadle, nádleeh, nádleehí "he changes," "being transformed," "that which changes," "one who changes time and again"	(same)	Stephen 1930: 98; Matthews 1897: 217; Franciscan Fathers 1910: 292; Hill 1935: 273; O'Bryan 1956: 7; Young and Morgan 1980: 525; Haile 1978: 166
	Békotsidi, Begochiddy, Begochidi, Bego chi-dii, Begochidíín		Matthews 1897: 86, 226; Klah 1942: *passim*; Luckert 1975: *passim*; Parrish 1982: [7]
Ingalik			
	nok'olhanxodelea:n(e) "woman pretenders"	*che:lxodelea:n(e)* "man pretenders"	Osgood 1940: 460; 1958: 261
CARIBAN			
Karankawa			
	monaguía		De Solís 1931: 44
HOKAN-SIOUAN/CADDOAN			
Arikara	*kᵘxa't, skᵘxa't*		Hollimon 1999, pers. comm.
Pawnee	*ku'saat, eku'saat*		Hollimon 1999, pers. comm.
HOKAN-SIOUAN/CALIFORNIAN			
Atsugewi			
	ya:wa:	*brumaiwi*	Voegelin 1942: 228

	Male	Female	Source
Chumash			
	agí, 'aqi, 'axi		Applegate 1966: 155; Beeler 1967: 52; Hudson 1979: 40
Pomo			
Northern	*dass, das, da* fr. *da*, "woman"	(same)	Powers 1976: 132; Gifford 1926: 333; Gifford and Kroeber 1937: 195; Essene 1942: 65
Southern	*t!um, chum*		Gifford 1926: 333; Gifford and Kroeber 1937: 195
Salinan			
	joya		Palou 1977: 246
Shasta			
	gituk'uwahí		Holt 1946: 317
Yana			
	lô´ya		Sapir and Spier 1943: 275
HOKAN-SIOUAN/SIOUAN			
Dakota			
Assiniboin	*wi^{n}kta^n´, wi^n´ya^n* *i^{n}kenu´ze*		Lowie 1909: 42
Teton/Lakota (Eastern)	*wingkte, wing´kte, winkte* "would-be woman"		Riggs 1890: 577; Dorsey 1890: 467; Buechel 1970: 587; Powers 1977: 58; DeMallie 1983: 243
	wingktépi sodomy [sic]		Riggs 1890: 577; Dorsey 1890: 467
		lila witkowin "crazy woman"	Walker 1980: 165
Santee/Dakota (Western)	*winktah, wing´kta, wingkta, wi:ngkta*		Snelling 1971: 27, 238; Riggs 1890: 577; Dorsey 1890: 467; Weitzner 1979: 228; Landes 1968: 57
		winox:tca' akitcita "women police"	Landes 1968: 57, 69

	Male	Female	Source
Dhegiha			
Kansas	*mi^{n}quge*		Dorsey 1890: 379, 517
Omaha	*mi^{n}quga*		Dorsey 1890: 378
Osage	*mixu´ga* "moon instructed"		Fletcher and La Flesche 1911: 132
Ponca	*mi^{n}quga*		Dorsey 1884: 266; Dorsey 1890: 379
Missouri River			
Crow	*bote, bate, bate´, badé*		Holder 1889; Lowie 1912: 226; Lowie 1935: 48; Voget 1964: 490; Williams 1986a: 81
Hidatsa	*biatti, miáti, miati* "woman-compelled"		Maximilian 1839-1841, 2: 564; Matthews 1877: 191; Dorsey 1890: 516-17
Mandan			
	mih-dacka, mihdeke		Maximilian 1839-1841, 2: 132; Will and Spinden 1906: 210
Winnebago			
Oto	*mixo´ge*		Whitman 1969: 50
Winnebago	*shiángge* eunuch, unmanly man		Lurie 1953: 709
HOKAN-SIOUAN/YUMAN			
Cocopa			
	elha	*waʀhameh*	Gifford 1933: 294
Maricopa			
	i̇lyaxai´ related to "girlish" *yĕsa'a´n* "barren person"	*kwi̇ ʀaxamĕ´*	Spier 1933: 6, 242
Mohave			
	alyha, alyha:	*hwami, hwame:*	Kroeber 1976: 748-49; Devereux 1937: 500

	Male	Female	Source
Tipai			
		Warharmi	Gifford 1931: 12
Yuma/Quechan			
	elxa'	*kwe'rhame*	Forde 1931: 157
KIOWA-TANOAN			
Tewa			
	kwidó "old woman/old man"		Jacobs and Cromwell 1992: 56, 66
Tiwa			
	lhunide		Parsons 1932: 245
MUSKOGEAN			
Chickasaw/Choctaw			
	hoobuk eunuch		Adair 1968: 143,199
NADENE			
Tlingit			
	gatxan "coward"; halfman-halfwoman		De Laguna 1954: 178
	wⁿcitc boy whose sex changes at birth		De Laguna 1954: 183
PENUTIAN			
Klamath			
	tuinikhátko, *tw!inna'ek*	(same)	Gatschet 1890: 581 Spier 1930: 51
Miwok			
	osabu, osa, 'oshá'pu fr. *osa,* "woman"		Gifford 1926: 333; Berman 1982: 129
Nisenan			
	osha'pu, 'osa:pu		Faye 1923: 45; Uldall and Shipley, 1966: 249
	suku	(same)	Loeb 1933: 183
	Bo'hem kül'leh "Road Woman"		Powers 1976: 345

	Male	Female	Source
Nomlaki			
	walusa, tôhkêt		Goldschmidt 1951: 387
Sahaptian			
	waxlha		Terry Tafoya, pers. comm. 1992
Takelma			
	xa-wisa		Andrew Lisac, pers. comm. 1995
Tsimshian			
	Kanâ´ts		Boas 1895: 201
Wishram			
	ik!ê´laskait		Spier and Sapir 1930: 221
Yokuts			
	tongochim, tunosim, tono´chim		Kroeber 1976: 497, 500; Gayton 1948: 46
	Tuyuyu		Gayton and Newman 1940: 72
Tulare Yokuts	*lokowitnono*		Gayton 1948: 31
RITWAN			
Yurok			
	wergern		Kroeber 1976: 46
SALISHAN			
Bella Coola			
	Sxînts, Sxints		Boas 1898b: 40; McIlwraith 1948: 45
	Alha'ya´o		Boas 1898b: 40
Flathead			
	ma'kalí, mé'mi "berdache" *tcin-mámalks* "to be a berdache" *tcinés-koeumísti-l- isnkuskaltemíg"* "homosexualism between men"	*ntalhá* "lesbianism" *tcinés-koeumísti-l- isnksmé'em* "homosexualism between women"	Turney-High 1937: 156-57

	Male	Female	Source
Quinault			
	keknatsaʹnxwixʷ "part woman"	*tawkxwaʹnsixʷ* "man-acting"	Olson 1936: 99
Sanpoil			
	st'aʹmia hermaphrodite *sinlhispsiwiʹxᵘ* male homosexuality	*sinta'xlauʹwam* female homosexuality	Ray 1932: 148
UTO-AZTECAN			
Hopi			
	hoʹvo, hoʹva, hova		Stephen 1929: 34; Stephen 1936: 276; Titiev 1972: 214-15
	Kwasaitaka ("Skirt Man"), *Korosta/Korowista*		Titiev 1972: 214-15
Kawaiisu			
	hu'yupĭz (also PN)		Zigmond 1977: 74
Luiseño			
	cuit, kwit, cuut (San Juan Capistrano) *uluqui, uluki, yuliki* (mountain area) *coia* (i.e., *joya*) (elsewhere)		Boscana 1846: 284; Kroeber 1976: 647; White 1963: 186
Monache			
	taiʹyap, taiʹʹup		Gayton 1948: 236, 274
Paiute			
Northern	*t'übás, t'übáse mogóʹne, tubázanthnᵃ, tüvasa, tuvaʹsa, dü:baʹs* "sterile," fr. *vasap* "dry"	(same)	Lowie 1924b: 283; Stewart 1941: 440; Kelly 1932: 157; Steward 1943: 385
		moroni noho	Stewart 1941: 440
Owens Valley			
	tŭdayapⁱ, tuyayap "dress like other sex"		Steward 1933: 238; Steward 1941: 253
Southern	*tawanaverim*		Kelly 1964: 100

	Male	Female	Source
	Ma:aiʹpots		Lowie 1924b: 282
	kwiʻtuʹ-nnaigi-ri "anus-copulator"		Sapir 1931: 576
Pima-Papago			
	wi:k'ovat "like a girl"		Hill 1938a: 339
	ge kuhkunaj male homosexual		Saxton and Saxton 1969: 11
Shoshone			
Western Shoshone	*tangwuwaip, tangowaip, tanggowaipü, tainna'-wa'ippe,* "man-woman"	(same)	Steward 1941: 253; Hall 1997: 273
	taikwahni tainnapa'	*taikwahni wa'ippena'*	Hall 1997: 273
	tubasaʹ, waip: singwa "half," "woman-half"	*nuwŭdŭka*	Steward 1941: 253
Northern Shoshone	*tŭbasa* "sterile"	(same)	Steward 1943: 385
	tubasa waip:	*waip:ŭ sungwe* "woman-half"	Steward 1943: 385
	tenanduakia	(same)	Steward 1943: 385
Gosiute	*tuvasa*		Steward 1943: 385
Tubatulabal			
	huiy		Voegelin 1938: 47
Ute			
	tuwásawits, tuwusuwi-ci		Lowie 1924b: 282; Smith 1974: 149-50
YUKIAN			
Wappo			
	sóte' male homosexual *wós* hermaphrodite		Sawyer 1988: 11, 12
Yuki			
	í-wa-musp, iwop-naiip, íwap-náip, ipnaip (abbr.) "man-woman," "man-girl"	*musp-íwap náip* "woman man-girl"	Powers 1976: 132; Kroeber 1976: 180: Foster 1944: 1986

Male	Female	Source
LANGUAGE ISOLATES		
Keresan (Acoma-Laguna)		
qoqoymo, koquima, kokwimu, kokwi´ma, kok'we´'ma		Bandelier 1966: 326; Gunn 1916: 173; Parsons 1918: 180; 1923: 166; Stirling 1942: 70
Storoka, Shtorok'a, Storoka (a.k.a *Kurret-tiku, Tcai´nok'ana:tca*); *K'omutina, Kumootina*		Gunn 1916: 173; Parsons 1920: 98; Stirling 1942: 70; White 1943: 310
Kutenai		
kupalhke:tek "to imitate a woman"	*títqattek* "pretending to be a man"	Schaeffer 1965: 217-18, 224
stámmiya "acts like a woman"		
Zuni		
lhamana, lha'ma; *Kol-hama(na)*	*katsotse* "girl-boy"	Parsons 1916, 1939a; Roscoe 1991: 22, 27, 230
lhajmana (v.) "be a transvestite, behave like a woman, be awkward"		Newman 1958: 27

TRIBAL INDEX OF
ALTERNATIVE GENDER ROLES AND SEXUALITY[1]

Tribe and Sources	Area	Male Role	Other male	Female role	Other female	Myth/ tale
1. "California Indians"	California					
Galbraith [1791] 1924: 229		•				
Duflot de Mofras [1844] 1937: 192-93		•				
Cook [1811-] 1976: 111,102, 153		•	•			
2. "Virginia Indians"	Southeast					
Purchas 1614: 768			•			
Strachey [1612] 1953: 113, 206			•		•	
3. Achumawi	California					
Powers [1877] 1976: 133		•				•
Stewart 1941: 405, 421		•		•		
Voegelin 1942: 134-35,228		•		•		
4. Acoma	Southwest					
Hammond [1851] 1887: 166-67		•				
Bandelier [1882] 1966: 326		•				
Casagrande and Bourns [1900] 1983: 82, 229		•				
Parsons 1918: 181		•				
Stirling 1942: 70		•				•

1. Primary and key secondary sources are cited (additional sources for many tribes are cited in footnotes to the text). Date in brackets is original publication date or, if italicized, date of event or observation (if significantly different from publication date). Sources for each tribe appear in chronological order of earliest publication or observation date. Tribes are listed by their most commonly accepted names; alternative names appear in parentheses, followed by the cultural area traditionally occupied by the tribe. A bullet under the headings "Male role" or "Female role" indicates documentation of an alternative gender status. A bullet under "Other male" or "Other female" indicates reports of other alternative gender behavior and/or homosexuality. A bullet under "Myth/tale" indicates a myth or tale involving alternative genders.

Tribe and Sources	Area	Male Role	Other male	Female role	Other female	Myth/tale
White 1943: 310, 324-25		•				
5. Aleut	Alaska					
Masterson and Brower [1768] 1948: 59		•				
Jacobi (Merck) [1790-91]: 122		•				
Sauer 1802: 160		•				
Langsdorff [1812] 1813: 47-48		•				
Dall 1897: 402		•				
Jochelson 1933: 71		•		•		
6. Apache (Indeh)	Southwest					
Porter [1885] 1986: 195, 197			•		•	•
Gifford 1936: 296		•				
Gifford 1940: 66,163		•		•		
Opler [1941] 1965: 79-80, 415-16		•			•	
Opler 1969: 101-2		•				
Buchannan 1986: 24-37				•		
Robinson 1997				•		
7. Arapaho (Inuna-ina)	Plains					
Kroeber 1902: 19-20		•				•
Dorsey and Kroeber 1903: 261-62					•	•
Steward 1943: 385		•				
8. Arikara (Tanish)	Plains					
Maximilian 1839-1841, 2: 133		•				
Holder 1889: 623		•				
9. Assiniboine (Nakoda)	Plains					
Maximilian 1839-1841, 2: 133		•				
Kurz [1851] 1937: 211, 214		•				

Tribe and Sources	Area	Male Role	Other male	Female role	Other female	Myth/ tale
Denig [1856] 1930: 434					•	
Lowie 1909: 42, 223		•			•	•
10. Atsugewi	California					
Voegelin 1942: 134-35, 228		•		•		
11. Baffinland Eskimo	Arctic					
Kemp 1984: 470-72		•		•		
12. Bella Bella	Northwest					
McIlwraith 1948, 1:45		•				
13. Bella Coola	Northwest					
Boas 1898a: 28, 48, 53-54		•				•
Boas 1898b: 38-40		•				•
McIlwraith 1948, 1: 45-46, 53, 265; 2: 148, 179, 188-94		•				•
14. Bering Strait Eskimo (Inupiaq)	Alaska					
Dall [1870] 1897: 139		•		•		
Dall 1878: 5-6				•		
15. Blackfoot (Siksika, Piegan, Blood)	Plains					
Schultz [1840s] 1916: 12-20					•	
Maximillian 1839-1841, 2: 133		•				
Stewart 1846: 53-55		•				
Schultz [1840s] 1919: 11, 38, passim					•	
Schultz [1870s] 1962: 228-30, 348-50					•	
Schultz [1870s] 1926: 100-102, 117, 140					•	
Lewis 1941: 173-87					•	
Goldfrank 1951: 82-83			•		•	
Schaeffer 1965: 221-23		•				
Hungry Wolf 1980: 62-68					•	

Tribe and Sources	Area	Male Role	Other male	Female role	Other female	Myth/tale
16. Caddo	Southeast					
NAA Ms. #2932 [1880s]		•				
Newcomb 1961: 301		•				
17. Cahto (Kato)	California					
Driver 1939: 347		•				
Essene 1942: 31,65		•				
18. Carrier	Subarctic					
McIlwraith 1948, 1: 45-46					•	
19. Cheyenne (Suhtai, Tsistsistas)	Plains					
Powell [1866] 1981: 134, 455, 666		•		•		
Grinnell [1866] 1956: 237-38, 336		•		•		
Grinnell 1910: 306-7		•				
Petter 1915: 1116		•		•		
Grinnell 1923, 1: 157; 2: 39-47, 287		•			•	•
Hoebel 1960: 77-78, 96-97		•				
Schwartz 1989: 88-89		•				•
20. Cherokee	Southeast					
Williams 1986a: 4		•				
21. Chickasaw	Southeast					
Romans [1775] 1961: 56				•		
Swanton [1776] 1928b: 364				•		
Adair [1776] 1968: 143, 163-64, 199				•		
Swanton 1928a: 697, 700		•		•		
22. Chilula	California					
Driver 1939: 347		•				
23. Chipewyan	Subarctic					
Crowe [1715] 1974: 77-78, 89-90					•	

Tribe and Sources	Area	Male Role	Other male	Female role	Other female	Myth/ tale
van Kirk [1715] 1974					•	
24. Choctaw	Southeast					
Bossu [1768] 1962: 169		•				
Adair [1775] 1968: 143, 199			•			
Romans [1775] 1961: 56		•	•			
Swanton 1928a: 697, 700		•	•			
25. Chumash	California					
Costanso [1769] 1910: 46, 47		•				
Fages [1775] 1972: 33		•				
Palou [1787] 1913: 215		•				
Beeler [1823] 1967: 52-53		•	•			
Hudson [1890s] 1979: 40		•				
Harrington 1942: 32, 45		•				
Applegate 1966: 128, 155		•				
26. Coastal Algonkians	Northeast					
Drake 1884: 105, 187-90, 239-40, 244, 248-57					•	
Lincoln 1913: 12, 25, 34, 44-45, 48, 55, 96, 105, 125, 130, 150					•	
27. Coahuiltec	Southwest					
De Vaca [1542] 1625: 1519		•				
28. Cocopa	Southwest					
Gifford 1933: 294		•		•		
Druck er 1941: 163, 218		•		•		
29. Coeur d'Alene	Plateau					
Ray 1932: 148		•				
30. Comanche (Niuam)	Plains					
NAA Ms. #2932 [1880s]		•				
31. Costanoan	California					
Palou [1787] 1913: 214-15		•				

Tribe and Sources	Area	Male Role	Other male	Female role	Other female	Myth/ tale
Harrington 1942: 32, 45		•				
32. Cree	Subarctic					
Lacombe 1874: 164, 326		•				
Skinner 1911: 151-52		•				
33. Cree (Natimiwiyiniwuk)	Plains					
Mandelbaum 1940: 256-57		•				
Skinner 1914: 486					•	
34. Creek	Southeast					
Romans [1775] 1961: 56			•			
Adair [1746] 1968: 25					•	
Swanton 1922: 373		•				
Swanton 1928a: 697, 700		•	•			
35. Crow (Apsáalooke)	Plains					
Henry [1806] 1897: 399			•			
Maximilian 1839-1841, 1: 401; 2: 133, 564		•				
De Smet [1840] 1905: 1017-18		•				
Kurz [1851] 1937: 211, 213-14		•			•	
Beckwourth [1854] 1931: xxiv, 133-44					•	
Denig [1856] 1930: 433-34					•	
Denig [1856] 1953: 58-59, 64-68		•			•	
Denig [1856] 1961: 187-88, 195-200		•			•	
Holder 1889: 623-25		•				
Simms 1903: 580-81		•				
Lowie 1912: 226		•				
Lowie 1935: 48, 312-13		•				
Ford and Beach 1951: 133		•				

Tribe and Sources	Area	Male Role	Other male	Female role	Other female	Myth/tale
36. Delaware (Lenni Lenape)	Northeast					
Loskiel [1789] 1794: 14			•			
Brinton [1884] 1969: 109-22			•			
Flannery 1939: 129			•			
Goddard 1978: 223, 231		•				
37. Eyak	Northwest					
Birket-Smith and De Laguna 1937: 206		•				
38. Flathead (Salish)	Plateau					
Holder 1889: 623		•				
Teit 1930: 384		•				
Turney-High 1937: 85, 156-57		•	•	•	•	
Turney-High 1941: 128		•				
39. Fox (Musquakie, Mesquaki)	Northeast					
Catlin [1832] 1973, 2: 214-15		•				
Owen 1902: 54-55		•				
Jones 1907: 150-53, 314-33, 354-55			•		•	•
Michelson 1925: 256-57		•				
40. Gabrielino	California					
Harrington 1942: 32, 45		•				
41. Gosiute	Great Basin					
Steward 1943: 385		•				
42. Greenland Eskimo (Godthab/Nuuk)	Arctic					
Kent 1935: 29-30, 131, 294-97			•			
43. Gros Ventres (Atsina) (Haaninan)	Plains					
Holder 1889: 623		•				
44. Haida	Northwest					

Tribe and Sources	Area	Male Role	Other male	Female role	Other female	Myth/tale
McIlwraith 1948, 1: 46		•		•		
45. Haisla	Northwest					
Olson 1940: 199, 200		•		•		
McIlwraith 1948, 1: 45		•		•		
46. Hare	Subarctic					
Broch 1977: 95-101			•			
47. Havasupai	Southwest					
Witham and Mathy 1986: 84			•			
48. Hidatsa (Minitari)	Plains					
Jackson [1804] 1978: 531		•				
Henry [1806] 1897: 348		•	•			
Maximilian 1839-1841, 2: 133, 564		•				
Matthews 1877: 191		•				
Holder 1889: 623		•				
Dorsey 1890: 516-17		•				
Weitzner [1906-1918] 1979: 226-29		•				
Beckwith 1937: 233		•				
Bowers 1950: 298-99		•				•
Bowers 1965: *passim*		•				
49. Hopi	Southwest					
Fewkes 1892: 11		•				
Stephen [1893] 1929: 34-35			•			•
Stephen [1893] 1936: 276, 1222		•				
Beaglehole and Beaglehole 1935: 65		•	•		•	
Talayesva 1942: 38, 39, 40, 103, 108, 117, 186, 259, 294			•			
Eggan 1943: 368			•		•	
Titiev 1944: 205			•		•	

Tribe and Sources	Area	Male Role	Other male	Female role	Other female	Myth/ tale
Duberman [1965] 1982: 12, 46			•		•	
Titiev 1972: 153, 214-15, 225		•				•
Malotki 1995: 49-64					•	•
50. Hupa	California					
Driver 1939: 347		•				
51. Illinois	Northeast					
Bossu [1768] 1962: 82			•			
La Salle [1662] 1880: 368		•				
Marquette [1681] 1900: 128, 129		•				
La Salle [1681] 1901: 145, 146		•				
Membré [1691] 1903: 155		•				
Hennepin [1697] 1903: 167- 68, 653		•				
"Tonti" [1697] 1814: 237-38		•				
Lahontan [1703] 1905: 462- 63		•		•		
Deliette [1704] 1934: 329- 30, 343		•	•			
Raudot [1710] 1940: 388-89		•	•			
Barcia [1723] 1951: 306		•				
Charlevoix 1744, 3: 303		•				
52. Ingalik	Alaska					
Osgood 1940: 460		•		•		
Osgood 1958: 219, 261-63		•		•		
Snow 1981: 611		•				
53. Inuit (Canadian Eskimo)[2]	Arctic					
Poncins 1941: 135-38			•			

2. Includes Central Arctic (Copper Eskimo, Netsilik), Caribou (and Sallirmiut), Eastern (Iglulik), and Quebec Inuit.

Tribe and Sources	Area	Male Role	Other male	Female role	Other female	Myth/ tale
Saladin d'Anglure 1984: 494, 497		•		•		
Saladin d'Anglure 1986		•		•		
Saladin d'Anglure 1992		•		•		
54. Ipai (Diegueño)	California					
Drucker 1937: 27, 49		•				
55. Iroquois	Northeast					
Bacqueville 1722: 41		•				
Loskiel [1789] 1794: 14			•			
56. Isleta	Southwest					
Parsons 1932: 245-47		•				
Parsons 1939a: 38					•	
57. Kalispel (Pend d'Oreille)	Plateau					
Buckley [1842] 1989: 252, 260, 284-86					•	
Point [1842-46] 1967: 158, 192					•	
De Smet [1846] 1905: 578					•	
De Smet [1846] 1906: 332					•	
58. Kansa (Hutanga)	Plains					
James [1822] 1972: 82-83		•				
Dorsey 1890: 379		•				
59. Karankawa	Southwest					
De Vaca [1542] 1625: 1519		•				
De Solís [1767-68] 1931: 44		•				
Morfi [1770s] 1932: 55		•				
60. Kaska	Subarctic					
Honigmann 1949: 164-65			•			
Honigmann 1954a: 129-30			•	•	•	
Goulet 1997			•		•	
61. Kawaiisu	Great Basin					

Tribe and Sources	Area	Male Role	Other male	Female role	Other female	Myth/ tale
Driver 1937: 90, 99, 109		•				
Zigmond 1977: 74		•				•
Zigmond 1986: 406		•				
62. Kiowa (Gaigwa)	Plains					
NAA Ms. #2932 [1880s]		•				
63. Kitanemuk	California					
Harrington 1942: 32, 45		•				
64. Klamath	Plateau					
Holder 1889: 623		•				
Gatschet 1890: 581		•				
Spier 1930: 51-53		•		•		•
Voegelin 1942: 134-35		•		•		
McLeod 1953: 32-34		•				
Stern 1965: 20, 24, 114		•				
65. Koso (Panamint)	Great Basin					
Driver 1937: 90		•				
66. Kutenai	Plateau					
Elliott [1825] 1914: 190				•		
Gray [1837] 1913: 46-47				•		
Spier 1935: 26-27				•		
Turney-High 1941: 128				•		
Schaeffer 1965: 193-236		•		•		
67. Kwakiutl (Kwagulth)	Northwest					
Ford 1941: 68-69, 129-32		•				
68. Laguna	Southwest					
Hammond [1851] 1887: 163-66		•				
Gunn 1916: 173-75		•				•
Parsons 1918: 181-82		•				
Parsons 1920: 98-99, 101		•				•

Tribe and Sources	Area	Male Role	Other male	Female role	Other female	Myth/ tale
Parsons 1923: 166, 237, 248, 272		•				
Bunzel [1929] 1972: 57		•				
Parsons 1932: 246		•				
69. Lassik	California					
Essene 1942: 31, 65		•				
70. Lillooet	Plateau					
Teit 1906: 267		•		•		
71. Luiseño	California					
Boscana 1846: 283-84		•				
72. Maidu	California					
Voegelin 1942: 134, 228		•				
73. Mandan (Numakiki)	Plains					
DeVoto [1805] 1953: 74		•				
Maximilian 1839-1841, 2: 132-33		•				
Catlin [1841] 1973, 1: 112-14			•			
Holder 1889: 623		•				
Will and Spinden 1906: 128, 210		•				
Beckwith 1916: 233		•				
Bowers 1950: 270, 272, 289, 296, 298-99		•				•
Bowers 1965: 315, 325		•				
74. Maricopa	Southwest					
Spier 1933: 6, 242-43, 254		•		•		•
Drucker 1941: 163, 218		•		•		
75. Mattole	California					
Driver 1939: 347		•				
76. Menominee	Northeast					
Skinner 1913: 34		•				

Tribe and Sources	Area	Male Role	Other male	Female role	Other female	Myth/ tale
77. Miami	Northeast					
Trowbridge 1938: 68		•				
78. Micmac (Mi'kmaq)	Northeast					
Williams 1986a: 227			•			
79. Miwok	California					
Gifford 1916: 163		•				
Gifford 1926: 333		•				
Beals 1933: 376		•				
Aginsky 1943: 430		•				
80. Modoc	California					
Meachem 1876					•	
Ray 1963: 43		•				
81. Mohave	Southwest					
Hrdlic#kla 1908: 184		•		•		
Kroeber [1925] 1976: 748-49		•		•		•
Devereux 1937: 498-527		•	•	•		•
Drucker 1941: 163		•		•		
Devereux [1961] 1969a: *passim*		•	•	•	•	•
82. Monache (Western Mono)	California					
Gifford [1915] 1932: 44		•				
Driver 1937: 90, 99, 109		•				
Gayton and Newman 1940: 73		•				•
Aginsky 1943: 430		•				
Gayton 1948: 236, 274		•				•
83. Naskapi	Subarctic					
McKenzie [1808] 1960: 414			•			
84. Natchez	Southeast					

Tribe and Sources	Area	Male Role	Other male	Female role	Other female	Myth/tale
Dumont de Montigny 1753: 247-[49]		•				
85. Navajo (Navaho, Diné)	Southwest					
Stephen [1885] 1930: 98, 100		•				•
Matthews 1897: 70-72, 77, 86-87, 217, 220, 226		•				•
Matthews 1907: 58-60						•
Franciscan Fathers 1910: 178, 292, 350		•				•
Reichard [1928] 1969: 150		•				
Haile [1930] 1978: 82-90, 161-68, 171-72		•	•	•		•
Haile [1932] 1981: 11, 18-32		•				•
Goddard 1933: 128-29		•				•
Hill 1935: 272-79		•		•		•
Gifford 1940: 66, 163		•		•		
Reichard 1944a: 16-25		•				•
Spencer 1947: 20, 25-26, 28-30, 36, 73, 75, 98-100, 124		•				•
Spencer 1957: 81, 101-4, 107, 149, 226, 228-30		•				•
Reichard [1974] 1983: 140-42, 309-10, 386-90, 433		•				•
Luckert 1975: *passim*						•
Medicine 1983: 278					•	
86. Nez Perce	Plateau					
Holder 1889: 623		•				
Mandelbaum 1938: 119		•				
87. Nisenan	California					
Powers [1877] 1976: 345						•
Faye 1923: 45		•				
Loeb 1933: 183		•			•	

Tribe and Sources	Area	Male Role	Other male	Female role	Other female	Myth/tale
Beals 1933: 376		•				
Uldall and Shipley 1966: 249		•				
88. Nisqually (Southern Coast Salish)	Northwest					
Warner [1847] 1972: 84, Index 79, A-59		•				
89. Nomlaki	California					
Goldschmidt 1951: 387		•				
90. Nootka (Nuu-chah-nulth)	Northwest					
Drucker 1951: 331		•		•		
Cameron 1981: 129-38					•	
91. North Alaska Eskimo (Inuit)	Alaska					
Spencer 1959: 246-47			•		•	
92. Ojibwa	Subarctic					
Skinner 1911: 151-52		•				
Hallowell 1939: 193-94			•		•	
Hallowell 1955: 294-95, 303-4, 425			•		•	•
93. Ojibwa	Northeast					
Henry [1801] 1897: 53-54, 163-65		•				
Grant [1804] 1960: 357		•				
McKenney 1827: 315-16		•				
Tanner [1830] 1956: 89-91		•				
McKenney and Hall [1838] 1933: 120-21		•				
Landes [1937] 1969: 54-55			•		•	
Landes 1938: 179-80, 182, 184, 187			•		•	
94. Ojibwa	Plains					
Skinner 1914: 485-86					•	
95. Okanagon	Plateau					

Tribe and Sources	Area	Male Role	Other male	Female role	Other female	Myth/ tale
Cline 1938: 137		•				
Mandelbaum 1938: 119		•		•		•
96. Omaha	Plains					
James [1822] 1972: 180			•			
Dorsey 1890: 378-79		•				
Mead 1932: 188-89		•				
Mead [1932] 1961: 1452		•				
Mead [1930] 1963: 256, 293, 294-95, 304-5		•				
Weitzner 1979: 229		•				
97. Osage (Wazhazhe)	Plains					
Tixier [1840] 1940: 182, 197, 234		•	•			
McCoy 1840: 360-61		•				
Fletcher and La Flesche 1911: 132-33		•				•
98. Oto (Otoe, Chiwere)	Plains					
Irving, Jr. [1835] 1955: 93-95		•				
Whitman [1937] 1969: 22, 29, 30, 50		•				•
99. Ottawa	Northeast					
Duggan [1793] 1887: 108					•	
100. Pacific Eskimo/Yup'ik (Koniag, Chugach)	Alaska					
Sarytschew [1790] 1806: 16		•				
Merck [1790] 1937: 122		•				
Sauer 1802: 176		•				
Pierce [1804] 1978: 121, 135		•		•		
Davydov [1810] 1977: 166		•				
Langsdorff [1812] 1813: 64		•				
Lisiansky 1814: 199		•				

Tribe and Sources	Area	Male Role	Other male	Female role	Other female	Myth/ tale
Choris 1822: (VII)8		•				
Dall [1870] 1897: 402-3		•				
Birket-Smith 1953: 94, 136-37		•		•		•
101. **Paiute, Northern**	Great Basin					
Lowie 1924b: 283		•				
Kelly 1932: 157-58		•		•		
Stewart 1941: 405, 421, 440		•		•		
Steward 1943: 338, 385		•				
102. **Paiute, Owens Valley (Eastern Mono)**	Great Basin					
Steward 1933: 238		•				
Driver 1937: 90		•				
Steward 1941: 253, 312		•				
Fowler and Dawson 1986: 732		•				
103. **Paiute, Southern (Chemehuevi)**	Great Basin					
Lowie 1924b: 282		•				•
Sapir 1931: 576			•			
Steward 1941: 253, 312		•		•		
Drucker 1941: 163		•				
Stewart 1944: 298, 332		•				
Kelly 1964: 100-1		•			•	
104. **Papago (Tohono O'odham)**	Southwest					
Lumholtz 1912: 352-53		•	•			
Underhill [1936] 1979: 64, 67-68, 74		•				
Underhill [1939] 1969: 186-87		•				
Gifford 1940: 66,163		•		•		
Drucker 1941: 163, 218		•		•		
Joseph et al. 1949: 227		•				

Tribe and Sources	Area	Male Role	Other male	Female role	Other female	Myth/tale
Saxton and Saxton 1969: 11, 73			•			
105. Patwin	California					
Kroeber 1932: 272		•				
Gifford and Kroeber 1937: 153		•				
106. Pawnee (Chahiksichahiks)	Plains					
Dorsey 1906: 138-39		•				•
Murie 1914: 640		•				
Dorsey and Murie 1940: 108		•				
Weltfish 1965: 29			•		•	
107. Pima	Southwest					
Hill 1938a: 338-40		•		•		
Drucker 1941: 163, 218		•				
Saxton and Saxton 1969: 11, 73			•			
108. Pomo	California					
Powers [1877] 1976: 132		•				
Gifford and Kroeber 1937: 153, 195-96		•		•		
Gifford 1926: 333		•				
Essene 1942: 31, 65		•				
109. Ponca	Plains					
Dorsey 1884: 266		•				
Dorsey 1890: 379		•				
Howard 1965: 142-43		•				
110. Potawatomi	Northeast					
Landes 1970: 26, 36-37, 41, 183, 190-91, 195-202, 316		•			•	
111. Quapaw	Plains					
St. Cosme [1699] 1917: 360		•				
112. Quechan (Yuma)	Southwest					

Tribe and Sources	Area	Male Role	Other male	Female role	Other female	Myth/tale
Alarcón [1540] 1940: 130, 148		•				
Font [1775] 1931: 105		•				
Gibbs 1853: 115		•				
Forde 1931: 157		•		•		
Gifford 1931: 56		•		•		
Spier 1933: 6, 242-43, 254		•		•		•
Drucker 1937: 27		•		•		
Devereux 1937: 506, 522						
113. Quileute	Northwest					
Olson 1936: 99		•		•		
114. Quinault (Southwestern Coast Salish)	Northwest					
Olson 1936: 99		•		•		
115. Salinan	California					
Palou [1787] 1977: 245-46		•				
Mason 1912: 164		•				
Harrington 1942: 32, 45		•				
116. San Felipe	Southwest					
Parsons 1932: 247		•				
117. San Juan	Southwest					
Parsons 1926: 191-92					•	•
Jacobs 1983: 460		•				
Jacobs and Cromwell: 54-56		•	•			
118. Sanpoil	Plateau					
Ray 1932: 148			•		•	
119. Santa Ana	Southwest					
Gifford 1940: 66, 163		•				
120. Santo Domingo	Southwest					
Bandelier [1882] 1966: 326		•				
Curtis [1910] 1926: 134-35					•	

Tribe and Sources	Area	Male Role	Other male	Female role	Other female	Myth/tale
121. Sauk	Northeast					
Keating 1825: 221-22		•				
Catlin [1832] 1973, 2: 214-15		•				
122. Shasta	California					
Voegelin 1942: 134-35, 228		•		•		
Holt 1946: 317		•				
123. Shoshone, Eastern (Wind River)	Great Basin					
Shimkin 1947: 298		•				
124. Shoshone, Western	Great Basin					
Miller [1837] 1951: 90, 137					•	
De Smet [1840] 1905: 1017-18					•	
Holder 1889: 623		•				
Steward 1941: 252-53, 312		•		•		
125. Shoshone-Bannock, Northern	Great Basin					
Steward 1943: 338, 385		•		•		
126. Sinkyone	California					
Driver 1939: 347		•				
127. Sioux (Lakota, Santee, Yankton)	Plains					
La Salle [1662] 1880: 368		•				
Marquette [1681] 1900: 128, 129		•				
Hennepin [1697] 1903: 653		•				
Perrin du Lac 1805: 318, 352		•				
Snelling [1830] 1971: 27, 238		•				
Maximillian 1839-1841, 2: 133		•				
Hyde [1866] 1937: 147		•				
Fletcher 1887: 281		•				

Tribe and Sources	Area	Male Role	Other male	Female role	Other female	Myth/tale
Holder 1889: 623		•				
Dorsey 1890: 467		•				•
Riggs 1890: 577			•			
Weitzner [1906-1918] 1979: 228-29		•				
Walker [1910s] 1980: 165-166					•	•
Walker [1910s] 1982: 127, 147		•				
Wissler 1912: 92-3		•				
Lowie 1913: 118-19		•			•	
Mirsky 1937: 416-7		•			•	
Erikson 1945: 329-30		•			•	
Hassrick 1964: 50, 121, 133-35, 313-20		•			•	•
Landes 1968: 31-9, 49, 57, 66, 112-3, 123, 127-8, 206-7		•			•	
Dyck 1971: 106-7					•	
Fire/Lame Deer and Erdoes 1972: 149-50		•				
Laubin and Laubin 1977: 365-67		•				
Powers 1977: 38, 58-59		•			•	•
Medicine 1983: 272, 274					•	
DeMallie 1983: 243-48		•			•	•
128. Siuslaw	Northwest					
Barnett 1937: 185		•				
129. Spokane	Plateau					
Cox [1832] 1957: 190-92		•				
130. Squamish (Central Coast Salish)	Northwest					
Barnett 1955: 128, 149		•				

Tribe and Sources	Area	Male Role	Other male	Female role	Other female	Myth/tale
131. Takelma	Northwest					
Barnett 1937: 185		•				
132. Tesuque	Southwest					
Olmstead [1823] 1975: 156		•				
133. Thompson	Plateau					
Teit 1900: 321		•		•		
134. Timucua	Southeast					
Laudonniere [1565] 1904, 8: 453; 9: 16, 56, 69		•	•			
Le Moyne [1565] 1965: 69, 81		•				
Pareja [1613] 1972: 39, 43, 75-76			•		•	
Coréal 1722: 33-34		•				
Charlevoix 1744, 1: 27		•				
135. Tipai (Kamia)	California					
Gifford 1931: 12, 56, 79-80		•		•		•
Drucker 1937: 27, 49		•				
Drucker 1941: 163		•				
136. Tlingit	Northwest					
Fleurieu [1798] 1801: 370			•			
Holmberg 1855: 121		•				
Knapp and Childe 1896: 35-36					•	
De Laguna 1954: 178, 183		•		•		
137. Tolowa	California					
Barnett 1937				•		
Driver 1939: 347		•				
Gould 1978: 131, 134		•				
138. Tsimshian	Northwest					
Boas 1895: 201						•
139. Tubatulabal	California					

Tribe and Sources	Area	Male Role	Other male	Female role	Other female	Myth/ tale
Driver 1937: 90, 99, 109		•				
Voegelin 1938: 47		•				
140. Tulalip (Southern Coast Salish)	Northwest					
Holder 1889: 623		•				
141. Tuscarora/Nottaways	Northeast					
Boyce 1978: 285		•				
142. Tututni	Northwest					
Barnett 1937: 185		•				
143. Ute	Great Basin					
Lowie 1924b: 282-83		•				
Gifford 1940: 66, 163		•		•		
Steward 1943: 385		•				
Stewart 1944: 298, 332		•		•		
Opler 1963: 147		•				
Smith 1974: 149-50		•				
144. Walapai	Southwest					
Drucker 1941: 163, 218		•				
145. Wappo	California					
Willoughby 1963: 59, 62		•		•		
Sawyer 1988: 10-12		•			•	
146. Washo	Great Basin					
Stewart 1941: 405, 421		•		•		
147. Winnebago (Hocak)	Northeast					
Lurie 1953: 708-12		•				
148. Wintu	California					
Du Bois 1935: 50-51		•	•	•	•	
Voegelin 1942: 134		•		•		
149. Wishram	Plateau					
Spier and Sapir 1930: 220-21		•				

Tribe and Sources	Area	Male Role	Other male	Female role	Other female	Myth/ tale
150. Wiyot	California					
Driver 1939: 347		•		•		
Elsasser 1978: 159		•		•		
151. Yamasee (Guale)	Southeast					
Barcia [1566] 1951: 117-18			•			
Solís de Merás [1566] 1923: 180-81			•			
152. Yana	California					
Gifford and Klimek 1936: 84		•		•		
Sapir and Spier 1943: 275		•				
153. Yavapai	Southwest					
Devereux [1961] 1969a: 313				•		
154. Yokuts	California					
Gayton [1819] 1936: 81		•				
Mayfield [1850] 1993: 107		•				
Kroeber [1925] 1976: 497, 500-501		•				
Driver 1937: 90, 99, 109		•				
Gayton and Newman 1940: 34, 72, 73, 86-87, 96		•			•	•
Aginsky 1943: 430		•				
Gayton 1948: 31, 46, 106-7, 236		•				•
155. Yuki-Huchnom	California					
Powers [1877] 1976: 132-33		•				
Kroeber [1925] 1976: 180		•				
Gifford and Kroeber 1937: 195		•				
Driver 1939: 347		•				
Essene 1942: 31, 65		•				
Foster 1944: 183, 186		•		•		
156. Yurok	California					

Tribe and Sources	Area	Male Role	Other male	Female role	Other female	Myth/ tale
Kroeber [1925] 1976: 46		•				
Driver 1939: 347		•				
Erikson 1945: 338-39					•	
157. Zuni (A:shiwi)	Southwest					
Stevenson 1904: 37-38		•				•
Parsons 1916: 521-28		•		•		
Parsons 1939b: 338-39		•				
Gifford 1940: 66, 163		•				
Stewart 1960: 13-14		•				

NOTES

CHAPTER 1

1. 1961: 187, 199.
2. [1542] 1625: 1519.
3. 1594: pl. 22, see also pp. [109]-110. The episode, which occurred in 1513, was first reported by Peter Martyr [1516] 1966: 106.
4. Antonio de la Calancha, quoted in Guerra 1971: 189.
5. The act was introduced in the House by Bob Barr and signed into law by President Bill Clinton on September 21, 1996.
6. Williams 1986a: 57.
7. *American Heritage Dictionary,* 3d ed., p. 2132. The Sanskrit *vadhri,* "eunuch" (fr. *vadh,* "strike"; Penzer 1925: 319; Saletore 1974: 43) appears to be another related term, perhaps deriving from the practice of crushing the testicles. It occurs in the Atharvaveda (c. 500 B.C.E.), in which it is used in reference to gender ambivalent figures performing functions similar to those of modern hijras (6.138.3).
8. Courouve 1982: 18.
9. In regional Italian *bardassa* came to mean simply "boy" (Diez 1887: 42).
10. *Bardaje* was used occasionally in Central America as well. See Guerra 1971: 43; Alonso 1958: s.v. "Bardaj," "Bardaja," and "Bardaje."
11. 1947: 124.
12. While used primarily in reference to alternative gender roles, among French speakers in Missouri it came to be used generally to mean "coward" (McDermott 1941: 22).
13. 1877: 191.
14. 1890: 378, 516.
15. Whitehead 1981: 97; Clemmer in Eggan, Clemmer, and Duberman 1980: 182. Other examples: Seward, "Some may be homosexual, but the majority are not" (1946: 118); and Linton, the "majority" of berdaches are not homosexual (1936: 480).
16. Hill 1935: 278.
17. Catlin [1841] 1973: 214-15; Owen 1902: 54-55
18. Erickson 1945: 329-30.
19. Carter 1939: rev. of 44.
20. Weitzner 1979: 229.
21. Murie 1914: 640; Batkin 1995: 66; Whitman [1937] 1969: 22, 29, 30, 50.
22. Ford 1941: 129-30.
23. See Tafoya 1989.
24. Osage: Fletcher and La Flesche 1911: 132-33, Tixier [1844] 1940: 234; Oto: Irving [1835] 1955: 93-94; Crow: De Smet 1905: 1017. The reverse could happen, too, berdaches becoming men, as in the cases of the Klamath Lɛleʹks (Spier 1930: 52) and Hidatsa Poor Wolf (Weitzner 1979: 226-28). For other cases of berdaches in opposite-sex relationships, see Olson 1940: 200; 1936: 99; McIlwraith 1948, 1: 45-46; Hill 1935: 276; Spier 1930: 52. However, some examples of berdache heterosexuality that have been cited are questionable: for example, a

sentence in Deliette (1947: 113) that suggests that Illinois women and girls "prostituted" themselves to berdaches (unconfirmed by other reports); an equally confusing claim by Perrin du Lac (1805: 352) that berdaches were used to satisfy the "brutal passion of both sexes" (followed by a description of how berdaches regularly had sex with men on hunting parties); Devereux's account of the Mohave female berdache Masahai, who engaged in limited heterosexual prostitution (see chapter 4); an account by Fletcher and LeFlesche of an adult warrior, already married heterosexually, who began cross-dressing as a result of a dream (1911: 132-33); and Stevenson's (1904: 38) report of "rumors" that the Zuni berdache We'wha fathered "several" children. In *The Zuni Man-Woman* I suggested that these reports may have been based on the use of fictive kinship terms, in which an individual who functioned as a mother or father might be called such, regardless of actual blood relation. A berdache who adopted or raised children (see, for example, Reichard 1969: 150) would very likely be called by a parental kinship term. In fact, some Zunis I have spoken to identify themselves as relatives of We'wha, but this is based on clan membership, not direct descent. These conclusions have been criticized, however (see Clemmer [1994]), and consequently I have made additional inquiries on the subject at Zuni. My questions elicited a great deal of laughter. "How could he be a father?" my traditional hosts responded teasingly. "He was a woman!"

25. Klamath: Spier 1930: 52; Ingalik: Osgood 1958: 261; Flathead: Teit 1930: 38, Turney-High 1937: 85; Pima: Hill 1938: 339; Bella Coola: McIlwraith 1948, 1: 45-46; Plains Cree: Mandelbaum 1940: 256; Apache: Opler 1965: 111. In Mandelbaum and Opler it is said that a particular male berdache "never married," but it is not clear if this means they never married anyone, or never married women but married men (or had sex with them).

26. Examples include Linton 1936: 480; Mirsky 1937: 417; Hoebel 1960: 97; Driver 1961: 535; Hassrick 1964: 133-34; Mead 1961: 1452; Hurdy 1970: 48-49; Forgey 1975. With little or no evidence, authors of the more recently published *Handbook of the North American Indian* continue to rehash this cliche (e.g., Wallace 1978: 689). La Barre makes the failed masculinity hypothesis the basis of a full-fledged psychoanalysis of berdaches (1970).

27. 1968: 207. See also DeMallie 1983: 245; Callender and Kochems 1983: 448.

28. Callendar and Kochems 1983: 448-49; Greenberg 1988: 44-45.

29. Henry 1897: 163-65; McKenney and Hall [1838] 1933: 120-21; Schaeffer 1965: 223; Hyde 1937: 147.

30. Apache: Porter 1986: 195; Acoma-Laguna: Gunn 1916: 172-75; San Juan: as told to me by Tony García in 1983. See chapter 7 for Yuman examples.

31. See Greenberg 1986.

32. Drucker 1937: 49. On "jote," see chapter 8.

33. See Greenberg 1988: 77-88; Williams 1986a: chapter 7 and *passim*; and the useful discussion of the problems of interpretation in Kessler and McKenna 1985: 29-41.

34. Bowers 1965: 167; Powers [1877] 1976: 132.

35. 1983: 269.

36. 1984: 29.

37. Le Moyne de Morgues 1591: plates 17, 23 and 1965: 69, 81. Laudonnière also reported that they "beare the victuals when they goe to warre" ([1586] 1904, 8: 453, 9: 56). See also Coreal 1722: 33-34.

38. Morfi [1770] 1932: 55; Arlegui 1737: 143.

39. [1542] 1749: 29a.

40. 1753: 247-[49].

41. [1681] 1900: 129. See also Hauser 1990.

42. Landes 1970: 195-96.

43. I do not, however, find the evidence for berdache roles among Iroquois and Coastal Algonkian tribes in Greenberg's sources (1988: 40-41): Charlevoix describes Illinois berdaches but only vaguely refers to the Iroquois having lost their reputation for "chastity" as a result of their contact with the Illinois (*"Les Iroquois en particulier étoient assez chastes, avant qu'ils eussent*

Commerce avec les Illinois, & d'autres Peuples voisins de la Louysiane") (1744, 3: 303); Loskiel also vaguely accuses the Delaware and Iroquois of "unnatural crimes" (1794: 14); Charbonneau makes no reference to the Iroquois at all ("Charbonneau behauptete sogar, dass in dieser Hinsicht die Bardaches den Weibern vorgezogen würden") (Maximilian 1839-1841, 1: 401); and the citations in Ferdinand Karsch-Haack (1911: 328-30) fail to provide the evidence Greenberg suggests. The Handbook of North American Indians reports "indications of the presence of berdaches" among the Delaware (citing Loskiel [Goddard 1978: 231]) and among the southern coastal Iroquoians (Boyce 1978: 285), but of the historical sources only Bacqueville de la Potherie (1722: 41) indicates that an alternative gender existed among the Iroquois.

44. Fletcher and La Flesche 1911: 132.

45. [1934] 1959: 264.

46. Powers 1977: 38, 58.

47. Winfield Coleman; personal communication with the author. The creator god, for example, has both a man's and a woman's name.

48. 1984: 495, 497; 1986; 1992.

49. 1992: 42.

50. McIlwraith 1948, 1: 45; De Laguna 1954: 183.

51. Goulet 1997: 59-64.

52. 1814: 199. See also Sarytschew 1806, 2: 16.

53. Birket-Smith 1953: 94; Holmberg 1855: 120.

54. Davydov 1977: 166; Choris 1822, VII: 8; Langsdorff [1812] 1813: 47-48, 64.

55. Olson 1940: 199, 200; McIlwraith 1948, 1: 45-46, 53, 265, 2: 148:179, 188-94.

56. Birket-Smith and De Laguna 1937: 206.

57. Teit 1930: 384; Spier 1930: 51-53.

58. Spier 1930: 52; McCleod 1953: 32-34. See also Gogol 1983: 13, 15.

59. Shimkin 1947: 298.

60. For the Chumash 'axi as undertakers, see Hollimon 1996.

61. Monache: Gifford 1932a: 44; Aginsky 1943: 430; Pomo: Gifford and Kroeber 1937: 195; Miwok: Aginsky 1943: 430; Achumawi, Atsugewi, Shasta: Voegelin 1942: 134.

62. Zigmond 1986: 406.

63. Clemmer has claimed that "there is no berdache role" among the Hopis (in Duberman, Eggan, and Clemmer 1980: 182-83) and, more recently, that "Hopis themselves deny the existence of a role that would correspond to the Zuni lhamana," although he describes two historic Hopi males who "did women's work and donned female attire" in the late nineteenth century (1994). In fact, a Hopi term for berdaches, hova, was reported by anthropologists a century ago (Stephen 1929: 34, 1936: 276; see also Fewkes 1892: 45; Beaglehole and Beaglehole 1935: 65), which Titiev translated as "homosexual or transvestite" (1972: 215), along with dances by kachinas that are considered to be hova (Titiev 1972: 153, 214-15, 225). I have not done research at Hopi, but contemporary Hopis I have spoken to affirm the existence of the term and its use in reference to nonmasculine and/or homosexual males. Apparently there was no Hopi equivalent to the famous Zuni lhamana, We'wha, but that hardly means the role was absent. Various factors may account for differences in how Hopis and Zunis have remembered traditional roles. In the late nineteenth century, at a time when populations at both Hopi and Zuni were at an all-time low (under 2000), the Zunis lived in a single village. The opportunities for a given individual to encounter one of the few individuals in an alternative gender status would be much greater than among the Hopi, who lived (and live) in some twelve scattered villages, several of which probably did not have a single hova. Given these factors it seems somewhat disingeneous to deny that the Hopi had an equivalent status to the Zuni lhamana or that the Hopi gender system was somehow so different as not to produce gender diversity. Stephen, for example, in a journal entry for 1892, made such an equation when he noted that the Zuni We'wha "is a man, but of the abominable sort known to the Hopi

as *ho´va*, to the Navajo as *nû'tlehî*, to the Zuñi as *lah´ma* i.e. hermaphrodite" (1936: 276). See also Jacobs and Cromwell 1992:

64. See Roscoe 1991.

65. Hill 1938: 338-40; Underhill [1939] 1969: 186-87.

66. Native Hawai'ian culture also has a social status comparable to the North American alternative genders (see chapter 10).

67. See Fausto-Sterling 1993.

68. Jacobs and Thomas 1994.

69. See Courouve 1982; *Oxford English Dictionary*, s.v. "bardash."

70. 1955: 121.

71. 1897: 217.

72. 1889: 623.

73. 1980. The critics of Boswell's alleged essentialism are legion. See especially Halperin (1990) and Boswell's responses (1982-1983, 1990).

74. Since most of the published literature cited in this book comes from the field of anthropology, it can be assumed that the authorities I refer to are anthropologists unless otherwise noted.

75. Herdt 1994: 61, 72.

CHAPTER 2

1. 1928: 32.

2. For background on Scott's career, see Scott 1928 and Harper 1968.

3. Harper 1968: 101.

4. 1928: 628.

5. Ibid.: 461. Tribal members refer to themselves as the Apsáalooke, which means "large-beaked bird" (Frey 1987: 27).

6. Scott 1928: 31, 32, 56-57.

7. Ibid.: 50.

8. 1970: 51, 21-22.

9. This is Williams's spelling (1986a: 68) based on the pronunciation of contemporary Crows. A more accurate transcription might be *ó:tsikyap dapés* (Lowie 1960: 240, 272, 398). In agency census counts, he appears as Otsekap-Napes, Otse Kap Napes, Oche-cap-dupays, Odup-dah-pace, Odup dapace, O chay cup duppace, and O che cup dupays (NA, CAR, Census Rolls).

10. [1839-1841] 1906, 22: 354.

11. 1953: 58, 64-68.

12. Lowie 1918: 28-30.

13. 1953: 58.

14. In Crow census rolls, Finds Them and Kills Them is consistently recorded as a male, with one exception. In the 1929 census, which records his death, a small letter "F" has been written above the letter "M" as the entry for sex (NA, CAR, File 111-3 Census, 1928, Numerical Correspondence).

15. NAA, Ms. #2932.

16. Voget 1964: 490; Simms 1903: 580.

17. Curtis 1970: 67. Williams erroneously states that nineteenth-century Crow berdaches did not have a ceremonial role (1986a: 80). The *boté* role in the sun dance is documented in Lowie 1915: 32; Nabokov 1967: 83; and Voget 1984: 94-95.

18. 1889: 624.

19. 1977: 177. See also Hoxie 1991.

20. NAA, Ms. #2932. Scott's notes refer to berdaches among the Arapaho, Caddo, Comanche, Dakota, Flathead, Kiowa, Nez Percé, and Southern Cheyenne.

21. U.S. Board of Indian Commissioners 1920: 24.

22. Scott uses feminine pronouns throughout his interview notes. Whether this was a preference expressed by Osch-Tisch is not clear. The Crow language lacks gendered pronouns (Frey 1987: 25).

23. The following passages are from NAA, Ms. #2932.

24. NAA, Crow #4720, Asbury to Scott, 16 July 1928.

25. Williams 1986a: 80.

26. Clyde Hall, personal communication with the author, March 1990, May 1997. The lodge appears in a photograph in Galante 1980: 54.

27. 1889: 624, 623; see also Voget 1964: 490.

28. 1951: 133. According to one informant, seventeen of his adolescent friends had had sex with *boté*. This practice continues today (Clyde Hall, pers. comm., May 1997).

29. Vaughn 1956: ix.

30. "Stand-off" is the general assessment, but one officer who was present insisted "we had been most humiliatingly defeated" (Mills 1918: 409).

31. Vaughn 1956: 21; Linderman 1930: 155.

32. Finerty 1955: 101.

33. Gender difference on the frontier was not limited to natives. Crook's detachment had "unintentionally employed" Calamity Jane, dressed as a man, as a teamster. When she was discovered, she was "placed in improvised female attire under guard," as one officer recalled (Mills 1918: 401).

34. De Barthe 1958: 117, 120; Vaughn 1956: 58, 62, 76, 115.

35. 1932: 227-31. The full account by Pretty Shield is reprinted in Roscoe 1995a. Plenty Coups did mention "Finds and Kills Him" in the late 1920s, when listing surviving Crow veterans of the Rosebud engagement (Hayne 1929: 109).

36. Finerty 1955: 134.

37. Linderman 1930: 166, 171; cf. Vaughn 1956: 150.

38. NAA, Ms. #2932.

39. Nickerson in Schmitt 1946: 197.

40. Linderman 1932: 231.

41. Brust 1992 and pers. comm., 20 January 1991.

42. Linderman 1930: 311; 1932: 10.

43. NA, CAR, Williamson to Commissioner, July 1, 1887, Press Copies of Letters Sent to the Commissioner of Indian Affairs; Holder 1889: 625.

44. Wyman 1892: 287; Reynolds 1905: 226; Bradley 1977: 177; Petzoldt 1928: 1490. In fact, as Hoxie has shown, Crow marriage patterns typically entailed a period of youthful experimentation and serial monogamy followed by the establishment of quite stable, long-term relationships (1991: 306).

45. 1912: 226; see also Simms 1903: 581.

46. 1986a: 179. Williamson was agent from December 1885 until May 1888. Briscoe succeeded him, serving until June 1889. Williamson resigned amidst controversy over his handling of grazing permits and the events of the Swordbearer uprising, the only occasion of armed conflict between Crows and Americans (see Upton 1973: 117-67, 166-67). According to the *Billings Gazette,* "Charges of a personal nature were also made, that Williamson is loud, profane and quick tempered" (10 December 1887). Briscoe was also removed after attempting to bribe railroad officials (Bradley 1977: 153).

47. Bowers 1965: 315.

48. Bradley 1977: 90; Holder 1889: 624.

49. Hayne 1929: 90.

50. Williams 1986a: 183. Cf., Hayne 1929: 93-94; Petzoldt 1932: 29.

51. Judd 1927: 105; Bradley 1977: 91.

52. Voget 1984: 16, 19, 22.

53. Williams 1986a: 183.

54. NA, CAR, Census Rolls, 1886-1904, 1887 Census, Press Copies of Miscellaneous Letters Sent, Lists of Bands.

55. Lowie 1912: 226.

56. Carter 1939: rev. of 32, 46.

57. Riebeth 1985: 88-89; NAA, Ms. #2932; NAA, Crow #4720, Asbury to Scott. Cf. *bi:aka:te* in Lowie 1960: 149, 249. "M" is an alternate for "B" when used as an initial letter.

58. Riebeth 1985: 88-89.

59. NA, CAR, Files 129 and 130, State Fairs, Numerical Correspondence.

60. Martha Beckwith, who conducted fieldwork among the Hidatsa-Mandan in 1929-1932, reported that "a hermaphrodite among the Crow died here. He wore the dress of a woman, but earlier had been a great warrior" (1937: 233). Possibly Osch-Tisch died while visiting the Fort Berthold reservation.

CHAPTER 3

1. Newcomb 1964: 47; McNitt 1962: 304.

2. Newcomb 1966: 3-6.

3. WMAI, Ms. #1-1-128, p. 27.

4. Newcomb 1964: 4; Faris 1990: 86.

5. "Klah" means "Lefthanded," a descriptive name with no reference to berdache status. It is more accurately transcribed as *tl'ah*. "Hastíín" is the Navajo equivalent of "Mr." or "Sir" (Wyman 1983: 295). Although his Anglo contemporaries referred to him as "Klah" in their writings, Navajos today generally use the more formal form, "Hastíín Klah," when speaking of him. Faris also gives the name Azaethlin (1990: 86).

6. Newcomb 1964: xvi, 47, 116-17.

7. Ibid.: 115-16.

8. *Gallup Independent,* 3 March 1937.

9. Newcomb 1964: xxi.

10. Ibid. 1940; 1964.

11. 1944a: 19.

12. Hill 1935: 275; Newcomb 1964: 110.

13. Haile 1981: 19.

14. Hill 1935: 275.

15. 1969: 150.

16. Hill 1935. See also James 1937: 85-86.

17. 1978: 164.

18. 1897: 217.

19. 1943: 12.

20. 1978: 164.

21. Ibid.: 274; Leighton and Kluckhohn 1969: 78.

22. Leighton and Kluckhohn 1969: 78; Hill 1943: 12; Reichard 1968: 161.

23. Young and Morgan 1980: 525.

24. 1933: 39. On Haile, see Lyon 1987.

25. 1978: 164-65.

26. 1935: 276.

27. Haile 1978: 161; Fishler 1953: 25. The *nádleehí* in this account is addressed as "beautiful-one-who-is-both-ways," which Haile considers his/her "true," esoteric name (1978: 162).

28. 1935: 273.

29. Gifford 1940: 163; Medicine 1983: 278.

30. Haile 1978: 164.

31. 1992. Jeff King's telling has two male *nádleehí*, both of whom perform domestic tasks (King 1943: 6). Frank Goldtooth mentions four *nádleehí*, who join the men and have sex with them (Fishler 1953: 25).

32. 1935: 274; see also Haile 1978: 162.

33. A series of photographs by James Mooney from 1893 reveal a *nádleehí* in just such a role (see Roessel [1980: 95, 96, 152, 207]). The location is identified as "the camp of Charlie the Weaver," and the photographs show adults and children as well as Charlie.

34. Stephen 1930: 98.

35. Thomas 1992.

36. 1977: 24.

37. See Witherspoon 1977.

38. Faris 1990: 120, 132.

39. Witherspoon 1977: 26.

40. Haile 1950: 137-38.

41. Haile 1978: 162. Ultimately, the question for Haile was whether the *nádleehí* is "a homosexual male in the garb of a woman, a transvestite" or "a true hermaphrodite to whom abnormal sex activities are not attributed" (162)—a distinction more relevant to his Catholic background than views held by Navajos. He repeatedly invokes the "better traditions of the tribe" and the "saner element in the tribe," which insist that true *nádleehí* were asexual, and he condemns those Navajos who claim the name of *nádleehí* and engage in "sodomitical practices" (166).

42. Hill 1935: 274; Haile 1978: 163.

43. Cf. Reichard 1977: 78.

44. For this reason, Epple argues that the Navajo conceptualization of *nádleehí* is not equivalent to a third gender (1997). Thomas, however, describes female and male *nádleehí* as third and fourth genders, respectively, and provides supporting linguistic evidence (1997).

45. Young and Morgan 1980: 525; Thomas 1992; Epple 1991. According to Haile, *nádleehí* is the relativized form, meaning "the one who changes time and again," and is used in reference to mythical figures, while *nádleeh* is the normal noun form (1978: 166).

46. Witherspoon 1977: 29.

47. 1935: 273.

48. Matthews 1902: 119; Witherspoon 1994: 367-70.

49. Newcomb 1964: 84-85.

50. Ibid.: 93-95.

51. Ibid.: 97; Reichard 1944a: 23.

52. Reichard 1983: 141.

53. Newcomb 1964: 97. More recent writers have perpetuated the confusion. See, for example, McGreevy 1982: [11], Wyman 1983: 264, 295, and Dockstader 1987: 24. In fact, I've been told a story about Father Haile, who participated in a sweat ceremony with Klah and was able to observe him in the nude. Haile reportedly said, "This business about Klah being an hermaphrodite is nonsense. He has balls like everyone else." The *nádleehí* Kinábahi was also reported to be a hermaphrodite by Hill, but Haile's informants considered "her" male, and one remarked "he has testicles like we have" (1978: 165).

54. 1944a: 23.

55. 1964: 97.

56. Ibid.: 103.

57. Witherspoon 1981.

58. See McNitt 1962; Volk 1988.

59. McNitt 1962: 261; Kent 1985: 90; Rodee 1982: 70.

60. 1977: 141, 145.

61. 1964: 113.

62. See Badger 1979: 104-5. Apparently, the Bureau of Ethnology's exhibits included "a portrait of one of the most celebrated blanket-makers in the Navajo tribe. While costumed as a *woman*, this figure really represents a man belonging to a peculiar class of 'women-men'" (SWM, Envelope #38, "Monthly Report of Frank Hamilton Cushing, September, 1893").

63. Truman 1893: 260.

64. 1964: 116

65. Quoted in Kahn 1990: 11.

66. Reichard 1944a: 23.

67. Nightway, Blessingway, Hailway, Navajo Windway, Mountainway, Big Star Way, Apache Windway, and Beautyway (Faris 1990: 87).

68. 1964: 108.

69. Ibid.: 117.

70. Ibid.: 135.

71. Ibid.: 147. This was his niece. Klah adopted her two daughters (Newcomb 1964: 71; 1966: 199), who later collaborated with him in weaving sandpainting tapestries.

72. 1944a: 23.

73. 1964: 198-99.

74. 1964: 157.

75. For discussions and illustrations of early sandpainting weavings, see Wheat 1976a: 220, 223 and 1976b: 48 (cf. Parezo 1983: 46); McNitt 1957: 249-51; Maxwell 1984: 48; and Campbell 1987: 33.

76. 1951: 81. Aleš Hrdlička also reported Klah's presence in the Chaco area (1908: 238-39; cf. Brugge 1980: 166).

77. Newcomb 1966: 138; 1964: 115. According to Newcomb, the fragment was copied in 1910. However, the Hyde Expedition disbanded in 1903 and Wetherill was killed in July 1910. The Coolidges also report that Klah copied an ancient blanket, but at a much earlier date, which Newcomb disputes (Coolidge and Coolidge 1930: 106).

78. Newcomb 1964: 115. According to the Coolidges, this occurred in 1910 (1930: 104, 106).

79. 1968: 158-59.

80. Newcomb, Fishler, and Wheelwright 1956: 111.

81. 1964: 115.

82. These nieces were Hanesbah, who married Sam Manuelito and was known as "Mrs. Sam," and Althbah, who married Sam's brother, Jim Manuelito, and was known as "Mrs. Jim" (Newcomb 1966: 200).

83. Rodee 1982: 73; McGreevy 1981: 55-61, 85.

84. A fairly complete catalog of these can be found in the file "Hosteen Klah Sandpainting Tapestries" (WMAI, Ms. #4-1-26, copy of an original from the Museum of Northern Arizona). See also WMAI, Ms. #1-3-1, Newcomb to Wheelwright, 23 January 1951; Wyman 1983: 264-72, appendix B.

85. 1981: 103.

86. 1983: 22; see also Parezo 1982.

87. 1964: 162; Parezo 1982: [22]. After Klah's death, one of these nieces continued weaving sandpaintings while the other returned to the Two Gray Hills style (Wyman 1983: 266).

88. 1981: 104.

89. See Rushing 1995.

90. Parezo 1983: 110.

91. David P. McAllester in McGreevy 1987, n.p.

92. Ibid. 1965: 206.

93. Howe 1965: 207.

94. Parrish 1982: [3]; McGreevy 1987b.
95. WMAI, Ms. #1-1-128, p. According to Howe, Wheelwright was working on this memoir ("Journey Towards Understanding") in her last summer and reading Jung's *Psychology and Religion* (1965: 216).
96. This is the date Newcomb provides (1964: 159); see also WMAI, "Mary Cabot Wheelwright (1878-1958): Short Biography." In a letter written in 1931, Wheelwright refers to her first meeting with Klah "11 years ago" [i.e., 1920] at a Fire Dance after purchasing one of his sandpainting tapestries (WMAI, Ms. #1-3-6, Wheelwright to Kidder, 3 December 1931). See also Newcomb, Fishler, and Wheelwright (1956: 3). Accurate dates for Wheelwright's early visits to New Mexico and her initial meeting with Klah are elusive. Both Wheelwright and Newcomb wrote late in their lives, and both had difficulty remembering dates.
97. WMAI, Ms. #1-1-128, pp. 18-19.
98. WMAI, Alice Corbin Henderson Correspondence, MCW to "Folks," 15 October [1932].
99. Klah 1942: 11-13.
100. WMAI, Ms. #1-3-6, MCW to Kidder, 3 December 1931.
101. Wheelwright in Newcomb et. al. 1956 3; Newcomb 1964: 159-62, 167; Parrish 1982: [5].
102. WMAI, Ms. #1-1-128, pp. 47ff.; Parrish et al. 1985.
103. Reichard 1944b; Hoijer, Wheelwright, and McAllester 1950.
104. 1964: 172.
105. Parrish 1982: [7].
106. Newcomb 1964: 180-81.
107. Ibid.: 37-38, 203-6.
108. Faris lists several medicine men reported to have been informally taught by Klah (1990: 86, 95).
109. Lincoln 1970: 214.
110. WMAI, Ms. #1-1-128, p. 92.
111. See Ford 1990 and 1991.
112. WMAI, Ms. #1-1-128, pp. 91-92; Ford 1991: 10.
113. Bruce Bernstein, pers. comm., 18 November 1987.
114. 1964: 192.
115. Ibid.: 194.
116. The first being the Zuni We'wha, who met President Cleveland in 1886 (Roscoe 1991).
117. 1964: 193-94.
118. *Gallup Independent,* 21 July 1934.
119. 1964: 201.
120. In Navajo terms, such a gesture would signify a close and long-term relationship (Thomas, pers. comm., December 1992).
121. 1902. For a study of the ceremony and its documentation, see Faris 1990.
122. Matthews 1902: 176.
123. See Spencer 1957.
124. 1975: 169, 176-77.
125. Haile 1978: 161.
126. Ibid.: 161.
127. Ibid.: 83.
128. Ibid.: 85.
129. Schneider 1961: 13.
130. Haile 1978: 88.
131. See also Haile 1978: 161.
132. Ibid.: 161.
133. Klah 1942: 112.
134. Ibid.: 39; 1951: 1; Reichard 1983: 387.
135. Klah 1946: 15-16. Cf. Reichard 1944b: 47-49.

136. 1944b: 21.
137. Sandner 1979: 78, 38.
138. In Radin 1972: 203.
139. 1968: 19.
140. 1944a: 21-24; Hill 1935: 279; Bailey 1943; Wyman 1943 and 1947; Kluckhohn 1979: 72.
141. WMAI, Ms. #1-1-128, p. 38.
142. Eliade 1965: 116-17.
143. 1983: 142.
144. Witherspoon 1982: 30.
145. Kluckhohn and Leighton 1962: 240.
146. WMAI, Ms. #1-1-128, p. 37.
147. 1944a: 24.
148. 1979: 78, 38.
149. Repatriation of Klah's artifacts began in 1976 (McGreevy 1987: n.p.), with subsequent transfers (Faris 1990: 251, 254).
150. My view of Klah contrasts with that of Faris, who writes of the "'socialization' of Hosteen Klah to Wheelwright's requests, and to the narrative style" and refers to the tellings by him that Wheelwright recorded as "artificial" documents (1990: 176-77). If there is no "unified, single, authoritative, and original 'version' of the Nightway 'myth,'" as Faris argues, then there is certainly no version unshaped by the context of its telling—and the distinction between "artificial" and "natural" contexts in the long period of interaction between Navajos, Pueblos, Hispanics, and Anglos can have little or no analytical value.
151. 1944a: 19, 23.
152. 1991, 1996, 1997.
153. 1997: 181. Harry Hay recalls a similar conversation with Tony García of San Juan Pueblo and a former associate of Mary Wheelwright in 1967, in which the former insisted that Klah was both male and female and the latter argued that he was "neither," and thus "he could talk about women to men and about men to women" (pers. comm., 10 October 1986).
154. Interview with the author, 19 July 1985.

CHAPTER 4

1.   Fleming 1968: 6-7. See also le Corbeiller 1961.
2.   Smits 1982.
3.   *Las sergas de Esplandian* (translated as *The Labors of the Very Brave Knight Esplandian* [1992]) written around 1500 by Garci Rodriguez de Montalvo.
4.   Segal and Stineback 1977: 50. The English were no less vigilant in regard to homosexuality among their own. The earliest laws of Virginia included a prohibition against sodomy (Strachey 1969: 12).
5.   Fleming describes this transformation (1968: 6-9). See also Fleming 1965.
6.   Sauer 1971: 166-67; Niethammer 1977: 142.
7.   See Grumet 1980.
8.   Lincoln 1913: 25.
9.   Ibid.: 150.
10. Grumet 1980: 51; Williams 1880: 105, 187-90, 239-40; Thatcher 1900: 306; Niethammer 1977: 140-41; Foreman 1954: 21-23.
11. 1980: 257, 266. See also Green 1975.
12. See Fiedler 1968.
13. For a recent review of the history, legend, and literature of Pocahontas, see Tilton 1994.
14. Jones 1988: 51.

15. Collier and Yanagisako 1987: 39. More recently, Collier and Yanagisako have sought to transcend reliance on analytical dichotomies such as public/private, although they still premise universal inequality (1987).

16. 1983: 276.

17. 1983: 260-61.

18. See, for example, Etienne and Leacock 1980; Schlegel 1977. See also the recent collection edited by Klein and Ackerman (1995).

19. See Allen 1986.

20. See, for example, Weist 1980: 258, 259.

21. See, for example, Landes's pioneering study of Ojibway women, in which she concludes that a lack of socialization of women makes a "wide range of developments in their personalities and careers" possible, but characterizes this variability as "spontaneous and confused behavior" in contrast to men's more structured lives ([1938] 1969: vii).

22. 1981: 90, 86.

23. 1984: 40-41; Callender and Kochems 1983: 455-56.

24. See, for example, Collier 1988: 260 n. 12.

25. 1986: 16-17. Ten years earlier, Niethammer at least included a subheading on lesbianism in her survey of Native American women, although she failed to distinguish gender-based female homosexuality (i.e., female berdaches) and same-sex relations between non-berdache women.

26. Homosexual behavior: Hallowell 1955, 1939; Landes [1937] 1969: 54-55; Opler 1965: 415. Relationships: Weltfish 1965: 29; Schultz 1926: 100-1 (see also Hanna 1986: 50, 95, 115); Dyck 1971: 106-7. Tales and myths: Lowie 1909: 223; Jones 1907: 150-53; Malotki 1995: 49-64; Gayton and Newman 1940: 34-35.

27. Cromwell 1997.

28. 1988: 168-69.

29. The name of the female doctor suggests that she is a leader more than just a shaman or healer. The four females represent the oppositions of procreative sexuality/non-procreative sexuality and intellect/emotion (Michael Tsosie, personal communication with the author).

30. See Devereux 1939: 107; 1950c: 206-8.

31. Devereux 1937: 504; 1948a: 434. The name of the *kamalo:y* in the myth means "Girl who has a big heart" (Kroeber 1972: 17; Michael Tsosie, pers. comm.). There are parallels to *kamalo:y* in several tribes. Among the Cocopa, such girls are called "crazy hearts" (Kelly 1977: 61). Among the Papago, "light women" have "wandering hearts" and refuse to settle down with one man (Underhill [1939] 1969: 184). The Lakota call such women *witkowin*, a term used in the sense of "prostitute." *Witkowin* are believed to be under the influence of the same goddess who inspires males to become berdaches (DeMallie 1983: 245-56; Powers 1977: 58-59).

32. Kroeber mentions the presence of a fifth woman but no role is assigned her (1972: 17 n. 2). According to contemporary Mohave, she was present "just in case" and "because things change," a figure who can be assigned functions pertaining to future events that may require mythological explanation (Michael Tsosie, pers. comm.).

33. Kroeber 1972: 13; translation in brackets by Dr. Tsosie.

34. Grumet 1980: 49; Strachey 1953: 206.

35. Quoted in Grumet 1980: 49.

36. Russell 1980; Flannery 1939: 114-25, 122-23. Similar practices were followed by the Powhatans of Virginia (see Rountree 1989).

37. Grumet 1980: 49. White Rose (Nancy Ward), who was named the *ghighau* or head beloved-woman for her village in 1755 after taking her husband's place in a battle, also fits this pattern (see Niethammer 1977: 143; Foreman 1954: 73-86).

38. Williams 1880: 188; Thatcher 1900: 305.

39. Flannery 1939: 115; Grumet 1980: 52.

40. Grumet 1980: 50; Foreman 1954: 23-24.

41. Grumet 1980: 50-52; Williams 1880: 248-56; Foreman 1954: 26-30, 32-33; Thatcher 1900: 305.

42. 1905: 463.

43. 1915: 1116.

44. Coleman, 25 April 1997, pers. comm.

45. Reproduced in Powell 1981: 78, 84. Coleman disputes Powell's identification of this woman (pers. comm.).

46. Winfield Coleman, pers. comm.

47. I am indebted to Mike Cowdry for providing me a copy of Petter's notes. Petter's annotated dictionary is in the Newberry Library, Chicago, Illinois.

48. See sources cited in Weist 1980: 263 and Schaeffer 1965: 224-35.

49. Warrior societies: Landes 1968: 69; Skinner 1914: 485-86. Auxillaries: Lowie 1935: 106; Powers 1986. See also Landes [1938] 1969: 135-77 and *passim,* and Niethammer 1977, chap. 7.

50. Ravalli in Garraghan 1938: 377. On the history of the mission to the Flatheads, see Ewers 1948: 14-22; Peterson and Peers 1993.

51. Ewers 1948: 22.

52. 1906: 332.

53. Peterson and Peers 1993: 73.

54. Buckley 1989: 252; cf. Point 1967: 158; Peterson and Peers 1993: 73.

55. Buckley 1989: 284-85; Point 1967: 192; De Smet 1906: 332.

56. Point 1967: 156; see the line drawing version in Peterson and Peers 1993: 72.

57. Point 1967: 158.

58. 1905: 578. *Voyages* was published in English as *Letters and Sketches, with a Narrative of a Year's Residence among the Indians of the Rocky Mountains.*

59. 1930: 433-34; Denig 1953, 1961.

60. 1961: 196-97

61. Ibid.: 198.

62. Ibid. 1930: 433-34.

63. Ibid.: 433.

64. Ibid. 1961: 199.

65. Kurz 1937: 213-14; Denig 1930: 433.

66. Denig 1961: 200. Woman Chief's name was used some fifty years later. In an 1890 tribal census, "Mea-Muchatese, Woman Chief" is listed as a forty-year-old husband engaged in farming (CAR, Press Copies of Letters Sent to the Commissioner of Indian Affairs, 1883-1910, box 3 [1890-92; 1894-95], "Enumeration of Crow Indians for 11th Census U.S. by M. Wyman. September 18th 1890," p. 178, no. 913).

67. [1854] 1931: 133.

68. Ibid.: 134.

69. Thompson 1916: 520.

70. On Schultz, see Hanna 1986.

71. Schultz 1916: 13.

72. According to Hungry Wolf she was also invited to join the Braves Society of young warriors (1980: 67).

73. Schultz 1916: 16-17.

74. Elsewhere, Schultz says the enemies were Kutenais (1962: 348).

75. Schultz 1916: 20.

76. Ibid. 1919: 11, 38.

77. Ibid.: 86.

78. Ibid.: 79.

79. Ibid.: 294.

80. Ibid.: 101-2.

81. Hungry Wolf places her death around 1850 (1980: 63).

82. Ewers 1965: 12-13.

83. 1980: 66. Hungry Wolf provides yet another version of Running Eagle's demise: she was killed in hand-to-hand combat while leading a war party on a revenge attack against the Flathead (1980: 68).

84. Seward 1946: 120; Ewers 1958: 100. Kehoe (1976) challenges this view.

85. 1941: 176.

86. Ibid.: 175.

87. Seward 1946: 120; Schultz 1926: 117.

88. 1941: 185, 178, 181.

89. Ibid.: 176-80, 185.

90. Hungry Wolf 1980: 63.

91. Ewers 1958: 11-12.

92. Medicine 1983: 269-70; Liberty 1982: 10-19; Blackwood 1984: 36.

93. 1906: 244.

94. 1962: 229, 348. Woman Chief also inspired an imitator—an Assiniboine woman joined a war party dressed as a man, but she was subsequently killed (Denig 1930: 434).

95. 1926: 140.

96. 1941: 184.

97. See Medicine 1983: 270.

98. The skew in the documented frequency of female berdache roles in the West can be partly attributed to Kroeber's culture element surveys in the 1930s and early 1940s, when, for the only time in the history of anthropological research, questions about gender diversity were systematically asked. On the surveys, see T. Kroeber 1970: 163-67 and Stewart 1960: 13-14.

99. Honigmann 1954: 130. Cf. Goulet 1997, who questions the accuracy of Honigmann's report and its interpretation as evidence of a female berdache role. His point that cultural beliefs concerning the malleability of gender do not always result in the presence of a named alternative gender role is well-taken. However, his claim that the females Honigmann described were, in fact, engaging in standard behavior for Northern Athapaskan women is less convincing, and he provides no evidence that might resolve the question of whether a Kaska female berdache role existed (his own examples come from the linguistically-related but distinct Dene Tha).

100. 1878: 5-6.

101. 1951: 331; see also Cameron 1981.

102. Knapp and Childe 1896.

103. Hill 1935: 273.

104. Ball 1970: 15.

105. See Robinson 1997; Buchanan 1986: 24, 27-38; Stockel 1993: 152, 156; Opler 1965: 415; Ball 1970: *passim*.

106. Ball 1970: 14; Boyer and Gayton 1992: 34, 54-55, 70, 111; cf. Robinson 1997: 52. In the 1880s, John Bourke interviewed an Western Apache woman named Na-tzilā-chingân, or Captain Jack, who was a medicine person and chief of a band (Porter 1986: 197).

107. Collier and Rosaldo 1981: 284.

108. Callender and Kochems 1983: 446.

109. 1905: 3, 1,017-18.

110. Schaeffer 1965: 196-97.

111. Devereux's informants were Hivsu: Tupom(a) (Dan Lamont) and "Old Mrs. Tcatc" (Chach Cox), the granddaughter of chief Irataba, then in her eighties, who was related to Masahai through her mother.

112. Stewart 1983: 57.

113. This and subsequent translations of Mohave terms have been provided by Michael Tsosie. Dr. Tsosie, a descendant of Masahai's brother, has generously shared with me the results of his

interviews with Masahai's relatives and other research. In his 1937 article Devereux refers to her as Sahaykwisa but later clarifies that this is a contraction of her longer name (1969:550).

114. Devereux 1937: 509. Hrdlička's Mohave informant reported a case of a female "hermaphrodite" within his memory—possibly Masahai (1908: 184).

115. Michel Tsosie, pers. comm.

116. Devereux 1935: 150-51; Devereux 1969: 416-17.

117. Ibid. 1937: 523; 1969: 417. A Walapai informant in the late 1920s reported a Mohave woman at Needles who "slept with other women and masturbated them with her hands." Another Walapai mentioned a Mohave woman (dressed as a woman) who "came to Kingman with a Mohave prostitute and also had relations with a Walapai woman" (Kroeber 1935: 146-47).

118. Devereux 1937: 523; 1969: 417.

119. Ibid. 1937: 523.

120. According to contemporary Mohave, such a rebuff is a sure sign that the individual being courted actually loves the suitor. A true rejection would have been to completely ignore the the *hwame:*'s attentions (Michael Tsosie, pers. comm.).

121. Devereux 1969: 419.

122. Ibid.

123. NAA, Entry #29, Box 7, "1911 census at Forth Mohave," household #173.

124. 1937: 525; 1969: 417, 419.

125. Ibid. 1948: 436.

126. Ibid. 1969: 419; 1948: 436.

127. Ibid. 1948: 435.

128. Michael Tsosie, pers. comm.

129. Devereux 1969: 420; 1948: 436.

130. Ibid. 1937: 526.

131. See Kelly 1977.

132. 1977: 76-77.

133. Devereux 1969: 424.

134. Given her active love life and the much shorter life span of Mohave in the late ninteenth century, Dr. Tsosie believes Masahai actually may have been in her 30s at the time of her death.

135. 1969: 420-21.

136. Ibid.: 421.

137. Ibid.: 420.

138. Ibid.: 530; see also Fathauer 1951: 234.

CHAPTER 5

1. On the history of GAI, see Gengle 1976; Roscoe 1987b.

2. Roscoe 1987b. All quotes in this and the following paragraph are from this article, unless otherwise noted.

3. Robles 1992: 43.

4. Roscoe 1991: 199.

5. Ibid. 1987b: 72.

6. James Abrams, personal communication with the author, 14 February 1997. The American Indian AIDS Institute ceased operation in 1996.

7. Anguksuar, pers. comm., 26 April 1997.

8. See Harris and Lone Dog 1993.

9. See Rowell 1997: 91.

10. See Tafoya 1989; Harris 1991.

11. Freiberg 1991: 12; Rowell 1997: 87.

12. Patron 1991: 58-60. On native bisexuality, see Tafoya 1989: 288; 1992: 257-58. On the social service needs of lesbian/gay/two-spirit natives in general, see Brown, ed. 1997.

13. Hanson 1992: 65.

14. James Abrams, pers. comm., 14 February 1997.

15. See Rowell 1997: 88.

16. Patron 1991: 60.

17. Edwards 1997b: 5.

18. Bettelyoun 1991: [2-4]; see also Rowell 1991: n.p.; Hayes 1992: n.p.

19. Day 1990: n.p.

20. See Asetoyer, Beaulieu, and Rush 1992: 77-81.

21. The retention statistics are from NNAAPC-funded case management programs.

22. See National Native American AIDS Prevention Center 1995.

23. Duran 1997: 6.

24. Calvin 1993: 12.

25. Anon. 1995; Rowell 1997: 89-91.

26. 1991: n.p.

27. Harnum 1995: n.p.

28. Anon. 1994: [2].

29. Anon. 1993.

30. Rowell 1997: 87-88.

31. Edwards 1997a: 1.

32. Day 1990: n.p.

33. Freiberg 1991: 13. See also Rowell 1997: 93.

34. Carole LaFavor is the subject of a documentary, *Her Giveaway: A Spritual Journey with AIDS*, produced by the Minnesota American Indian AIDS Task Force.

35. Quoted in Patron 1991: 60.

36. Quoted in anon. 1990: 4. On the impact of epidemics on native populations, see also Rowell 1997: 86.

37. Decisions to exclude substance use and individuals who are under the influence of substances have been controversial. Many of the organizers of these events are former or recovering substance abusers who strongly believe that the sobriety of those in recovery and the goals of the events they are organizing are threatened by the presence of alcohol and drugs. On the other hand, others have argued that such criteria discourage many community members from attending, and, being exclusionary, contradict traditional native values. GAI in San Francisco, for example, rarely specified its events as alcohol-free in its early years (and has been criticized for that). Having attended many of its events, I have observed that intoxicated individuals were handled much as children are managed and integrated into Indian events—with a great deal of patience, gentle boundary-setting, and, if they have drunk too much, care-taking. In the end, few events I have attended were actually derailed by the presence of an inebriated participant. In the 1990s, public events in the San Francisco urban Indian community are increasingly alchohol-free.

38. Scott 1988: 8; Little Thunder 1997: 206.

39. See Lang 1997.

40. Anguksuar, pers. comm., 6 May 1997, and 1997: 221. In an article published in 1986, Williams quoted a self-identified Lakota *winkte* who said, "A winkte is two spirits, man and woman, combined into one spirit" (1986b: 196). I have found no evidence, however, that the proponents of "two-spirits" were aware of this statement. That oral transmission has been a primary vehicle of the term's dissemination is evident in the variant accounts now given of its origins. For the founders of WeWah and BarCheeAmpe in New York City, "two-spirit" "came from a group of people in the Midwest who had heard that term used in some of the communities in that part of the country" (Harris and Lone Dog 1993: 156). In an article

published in 2-Spirited People of the 1st Nations' newsletter, the term was said to be from "the Lakota dialect" (Ahneen/Sgene 1995: 8).

41. Hammond 1992: n.p.

42. Jacobs and Thomas 1994.

43. This article (Roscoe 1988b), written for a popular magazine, was one of my first published works on the subject, and it is the only one in which I used the phrase "a traditional gay role" in reference to berdaches. Nonetheless, the article is frequently cited as representative of my work in general by authors who fail to cite any of my subsequent articles and books (for example, Fulton and Anderson 1992; Cromwell 1997; Califia 1997). At a time when social constructionism has become hegemonic in several disciplines (see chapter 10), my article has become a convenient whipping boy for those seeking examples of essentialism to criticize. However, none of these critics has taken the care to note that in using the phrase "a traditional gay role" I was actually *quoting* (and attempting to explicate) the native cultural experts that I had interviewed.

44. Tafoya 1992: 258.

45. Harris and Lone Dog 1993: 156, 158.

46. Ibid.: 157.

47. 1992: 254, 258.

48. The term is still not universally known or accepted, hence the circumlocution "lesbian, gay, and two-spirit" is now frequently used. See the roundtable discussion by gay/bisexual/two-spirit native men in Rowell (1996).

49. Harris and Lone Dog 1993: 157.

50. Anguksuar [LaFortune] 1990: 59.

51. Roscoe 1991: 202-3.

52. Jacobs 1983: 460.

53. Ibid. 1996: 297.

54. Williams 1986a: 217, 224, 226. See also Williams 1986b.

55. Epple 1996.

56. Allen 1986: 259. On Kenny and others see also Roscoe 1995b.

57. Brant 1993: 946-47.

CHAPTER 6

1. 1722: 33-34 (my trans.). Concerning the authorship and reliability of this text, see Jaramillo 1953.

2. Even those with firsthand experience in America reiterated earlier texts, for example, Hennepin ([1698] 1903: 167-68) and Lahontan ([1703] 1705: 144), who paraphrased Marquette's 1681 description of Illinois berdaches.

3. 1986: 4.

4. Actually, "hermaphrodite" has long carried erotic connotations. As Pliny wrote, "Individuals are occasionally born who belong to both sexes: such persons we call Hermaphrodites. . . . at present they are employed for sexual purposes (*deliciis*)" (*Nat. Hist.* 7.3.34). The fixing of "hermaphrodite" as a physical condition and its relegation to the jargon of medical and biological science did not occur until the twentieth century. The *Oxford English Dictionary*, for example, gives figurative as well as zoological and botanical definitions: "an effeminate man or virile woman," "a catamite," and "a person or thing in which any two opposite attributes or qualities are combined." The sense of "hermaphrodite" for the early chroniclers of Native American sexual diversity may not be so different than that of "berdache." Both words could refer to "pretty" or "non-masculine" youth as erotic objects.

5. 1931: 105.

6. [1703] 1905: 462.
7. Tonti [1697] 1814: 238.
8. 1753: 247-[49].
9. 1953: 58.
10. 1884: 266.
11. 1890: 581. Some medical doctors eagerly examined berdaches to resolve just this question—and found them to be anatomically normal males (Hammond 1887: 164-65; Holder 1889: 624; Powers [1877] 1976: 132).
12. James [1822] 1972: 82-83.
13. Kroeber 1940; Benedict 1959; Devereux 1937.
14. 1955: 125. See also Mead 1963: 294-95; Munroe et al. 1969; Forgey 1975: 2-3; Greenberg 1988: 40.
15. Kroeber's use of the term reflects his early contact with psychiatry. After a pilgrimage to Vienna in 1915 he briefly practiced psychoanalysis (Kroeber, T. 1970: 98, 101-7).
16. Reichard 1944a: 23; McDermott 1941: 22.
17. Recent studies of native North American gender diversity remain mired in debates over definition and terminology (see, for example, Jacobs, Thomas, and Lang 1997), which perpetuate the exoticism of multiple genders and the invisibility of their contributions to native cultures and history. Although tribal differences in the construction of social roles should by no means be overlooked, to deny the interconnections between North American cultures, including their gender roles, is to subscribe to the "container" model of culture criticized in Chapter 5.
18. Beaglehole and Beaglehole 1935: 65.
19. 1940: 200.
20. 1948: 107.
21. 1967: 252.
22. Roscoe 1988a. The concept of multidimensional models is similar to Needham's polythetic categories (1993) and Wittgenstein's notion of family resemblance. I also proposed the concept of "sociosexual specialization" as a culturally neutral term defining a field of study concerned with homosexuality in the broadest sense—that is, encompassing its associations with gender difference as well as sexuality. This etic term helps avoid reliance on ethnocentric categories such as "the sexual" or "the erotic," which may not be universally relevant.
23. 1975: 86.
24. [1978] 1985: 29. Wikan used "third gender" in reference to Omani *khanith* in a 1978 article.
25. 1983: 459-60. See also Jacobs and Cromwell 1992.
26. 1988: 170-71.
27. See Murray 1996: 161-66. Murray argues that determining if a third gender is present requires the elicitation of native contrast sets that consistently distinguish a third category in relation to other genders, or explicit statements from natives to the effect that there are three genders. The use of pronouns other than those for women and men would also be strong evidence of a distinct gender. While Murray's points are well taken, I would not pin determinations about the presence of multiple genders strictly on linguistic evidence. We need to determine generally how men and women are defined in a given culture, then compare these sets of traits to those attributed to alternative statuses before determining if these statuses are gender constructions. We unnecessarily limit our analysis when we insist that only native concepts, categories, models, and terminology are valid for discussing a given culture. While instances that meet Murray's linguistic criteria can be cited, I also believe that there are cases in which use of the descriptor "third/fourth gender" is justified even though the people concerned might not use that precise terminology, because that concept is still closer to their understanding of gender difference—closer, for example, than the terms "homosexual," "transvestite," or "transsexual." However, Murray's point that categories like "sex" and "gender" may not be universally relevant is important, and I am mindful of his concern that a reliance on gender

CHANGING ONES

alone as an analytic category fosters a tendency to discount the sexual dimension of berdache roles.

28. Haraway 1991: 133. See also Kessler and McKenna [1978] 1985: 7; Scott 1986; Lamphere 1987.

29. 1981: 83

30. 1986: 166. See also Jacobs and Cromwell 1992: 45, 62.

31. Whitehead 1981: 85; cf. Greenberg 1988: 40.

32. 1990: 39. See the criticism of Schlegel in Jacobs and Cromwell 1992: 67.

33. See Rubin 1975.

34. 1981: 107.

35. Ibid.: 108-9; cf. Lang 1990.

36. Callender and Kochems 1983: 456.

37. 1981: 90, 91.

38. 1990. See also Trumbach 1994.

39. 1975.

40. 1993: 10. See also Butler 1990.

41. 1994: x.

42. Roscoe 1991, chap. 5.

43. See Shapiro 1991.

44. Roscoe 1991, chap. 6; Haile 1981: 11, 18-32; Kroeber 1972.

45. 1981: 111.

46. Whitehead's model represents an advance over that of Munroe, Whiting, and Hally, who link the presence of "institutionalized male transvestism" to a lack of sex distinctions—which they define as the use of sex as a discriminating factor in prescribing behavior and membership (Munroe, Whiting, and Hally 1969: 87-91). However, they make no attempt to relate sex distinctions to the division of labor, so that "degree of sexual differentiation" remains a subjective judgment. In some societies certain activities or behaviors may not be coded for gender, but this does not mean that distinctions between gender roles were unclear in the minds of natives or that these differences, wherever they were perceived, were not defended and maintained. In a subsequent article, Munroe and Munroe (1977) report a higher incidence of male transvestism in societies in which males contribute 50 percent or more of subsistence. Again, no allowance is made for the role of native belief systems. The relative cultural value placed on women's work and their role in distributing their goods and products are likely to be more reliable correlates of male berdache roles.

47. Collier and Yanagisako 1987: 44.

48. 1959: 87.

49. 1983: 460. See also Jacobs and Cromwell 1992: 56.

50. 1983: 456.

51. Of course, many of the tribes most strongly associated with the Plains warrior stereotype were sedentary and horticultural prior to the acquisition of horses and guns.

52. Bowers 1965: 166-68; Williams 1986a: 81; Holder 1889: 623; cf. Hassrick 1964: 133; Hoebel 1960: 77-78.

53. Northwest Coast tribes with berdache roles include Eyak, Tlingit, Haida, Haisla, Bella Bella, Bella Coola, Kwakiutl, Nootkans, Quileute, Central Coast Salish (Squamish), Southwestern Coast Salish (Quinault), Southern Coast Salish (Nisqually), Siuslawans, Athapaskans (Tututni), Takelma, Tolowa, Hupa, and Yurok. Sources are cited in the tribal index.

54. Boas 1898b: 38-40; McIlwraith 1948, 1: 45-46, 53; 2: 148, 179, 188-94; Boas 1898a: 48.

55. 1948, 1: 265.

56. Berdache status was also incorporated into the social system of the Tlingit, who believed that the "half-man, half-woman" was a reincarnation of a particular clan's ancestor. According to De Laguna, only members of this clan became berdaches (1954: 178, 183). (She also reports that "institutionalized berdaches or transvestites" were denied. However, historical sources

clearly describe Tlingit berdaches [Fleurieu 1801: 370; Holmberg 1855: 120-21].) Comparative studies will be important in identifying the relationship between prestige differentiation and the elaboration of gender categories. The *hijras* of India, for example, represent an alternative gender role in a large-scale, ranked society (Nanda 1990). A similar example is provided by the Greco-Roman *galli,* priests of Cybele and Attis (Roscoe 1996a).

57. This summary is based on Brugge 1983.

CHAPTER 7

1. Although the conclusions (and any errors) are mine, this chapter could not have been written without the assistance of Dr. Michael Tsosie, who generously shared his field notes, research, feedback, and knowledge of the Mohave language.

2. Devereux obtained a slightly different account. According to his informant, Nyahwera (probably the same individual Kroeber calls Nyavarup), the god Matavilye, Mastamho's predecessor, first declared that there would be berdaches while on his deathbed (1937: 503). This is not inconsistent, however, with Mastamho's role in subsequently establishing the initiation rite for *alyha:*.

3. Translations appearing in brackets have been provided by Michael Tsosie. Figures in mythological accounts are typically given names incorporating terms for pre-adults as a reflection of the new and unfinished nature of the world in those times.

4. Kroeber 1972: 18.

5. Ibid.: 19-20.

6. Kroeber translates *mat'ara* as "playground" (1976: 752), but Dr. Tsosie argues that "party place" or "party zone" better convey the connotations of the term (personal communication with the author). Miawka'orve has been identified with a site in the northern Mohave Valley (Kroeber 1972: 20).

7. For example, Avikwame, or High Mountain, the sacred site located within traditional Mohave territory, is cited in the origin myths of all other Yuman-speaking tribes. See Kroeber 1920: 152-53); 1976: 781, 799; Castetter and Bell 1951: 40.

8. Devereux 1969: 2.

9. Ibid. 1937: 503.

10. Devereux 1937: 503; 1935: 71-72.

11. 1935: 110; 1937: 503, 518.

12. Kroeber 1976: 754.

13. Devereux 1948b: 104.

14. Ibid. 1937: 503.

15. Ibid. 1935: 508; 1935: 71.

16. Castetter and Bell 1951: 246.

17. Turner 1969.

18. Devereux 1935: 99.

19. Ibid. 1937: 510-11.

20. Ibid.: 513, 517; 1939: 102.

21. 1937: 513-14; 1947: 532-33; 1935: 71; 1951b: 205.

22. 1935: 72.

23. 1937: 514.

24. Ibid.: 511-13; 1935: 72-73; 1947: 537.

25. Ibid. 1937: 503.

26. Ibid.: 510. In subsequent articles Devereux says they did (1947: 541; 1948a: 436).

27. 1937: 507, 509, 516.

28. Ibid.: 515.

29. Ibid. 1939: 102; 1935: 73.

30. 1937: 519.

31. Ibid.: 515.

32. Ibid.: 502; Devereux 1950b: 56.

33. Ibid. 1935: 80.

34. 1950b: 56.

35. Kroeber 1972: 19.

36. Devereux 1937: 516.

37. Kroeber 1972: 20.

38. Ibid. 1948: 28.

39. Ibid. 1976: 752; Stewart 1947: 270; Fathauer 1951; 1954: 99, 108, 109.

40. Kroeber reports Yakatha'alya simply as the name of the dance itself (1976: 752). Devereux transcribes it as *yakkisaalyk* (1937: 517) and *yakhatha'alyk* (n.d., 7). It appears as "Yakatha Alye" in notes by H. Davidson (UCLA, Sherer Collection, Box 95, "Fort Mojave Tribal Records").

41. The *yakatha:alya* played a role on one other occasion. When a *kʷaxot* died, all the scalps in his possession were destroyed. The *yakatha:alya* sang while they were carried about a final time (Fathauer 1954: 108).

42. Devereux 1937: 517; Kroeber 1948: 28. Male berdaches also taunted enemy scalps among the neighboring Papago (Underhill [1939] 1969: 186).

43. 1937: 517; 1935: 74-75.

44. 1935: 74-75.

45. 1947: 270.

46. According to Devereux, *alyha:* were considered cowards, and he cites the term *malyhaek*, which he translates as "thou are a coward" (1937: 517, 518). The words for coward and *alyha:* are, in fact, unrelated (Michael Tsosie, pers. comm.).

47. 1948: 28-34; summarized in Kroeber [1925] 1976: 761.

48. Kroeber 1948: 34. The translations are Kroeber's, who speculated that the names refer to dance steps. However, Dr. Tsosie believes the common denominator is references to styles of walking, possibly with the implication of flirting, which were considered characteristic of *alyha:* (pers. comm.). Kroeber refers to them as "chiefs," although they are not termed such in the narrative proper.

49. Kroeber 1948: 34.

50. Ibid.: 28.

51. [1556] 1940: 130.

52. Kelly 1977: 4.

53. [1556] 1940: 148.

54. 1937: 502.

55. Over two hundred years later, Pedro Font also observed berdaches in the Colorado River area:

> Among the women I saw some men dressed like women, with whom they go about regularly, never joining the men. The commander called them *americados*, perhaps because the Yumas call effeminate men *maricas*. I asked who these men were, and they replied that they were not men like the rest, and for this reason they went around covered this way. From this I inferred they must be hermaphrodites, but from what I learned later I understood that they were sodomites, dedicated to nefarious practices. (Font 1931: 105)

The term *marica* is actually derived from the Spanish *maricón*, at present a derogatory term for male homosexuals (see Murray and Dynes in Murray 1995: 186).

56. Forde 1931: 157. Drucker 1937: 27 and Kroeber 1976: 749 report both male and female berdaches.

57. *Pluchea sericea.* In Quechan and Mohave origin myths, arrowweed is the first plant to grow.

58. Bee 1989: 25.

59. Forde 1931: 157.

60. Drucker 1937: 27; but not female berdaches (Kroeber 1976: 749).

61. Gibbs 1853: 115.

62. Forde 1931:157.

63. Kelly 1949: 86.

64. Gifford 1931: 56.

65. Spier 1933: 242. See also Drucker 1941: 163.

66. 1933: 242.

67. See Spier 1933: 242-43; Harwell and Kelly 1983: 75.

68. Harwell and Kelly 1983: 71.

69. Spier 1933: 242.

70. Ibid.: 253. Róheim reports the dream of a Quechan shaman who visited two mountains, both called Sakupaj, one male and the other female (1932: 192).

71. NAA, entry #29, box 650, file 5. Mohave tales frequently conclude with the main character turning into a rock or other geographic feature. An abstract of Maricopa mythology published by Culin is harder to evaluate. Four original offspring (two of the Earth and Sky, and two of the Sun and Moon) are all identified as "hermaphrodites"—Kokmat, Spider (his brother), Coyote, and Fox (1907: 201, 204). "Each of these four were both male and female, but the female side of Spider became the wife of Kokmat, who alone married." Coyote and Fox play a gambling game with Kokmat. (Spier 1933: 345).

72. Gifford 1933: 294.

73. Drucker 1941: 163, 218.

74. Gifford 1933: 294.

75. Ibid. 1936: 296, 298; Drucker 1941: 163; Devereux 1969: 313.

76. Kroeber 1935: 146.

77. Drucker 1941: 163, 218.

78. Ibid. 1937: 27.

79. Havasupai: Smithson and Euler 1964: 32-35; Qua-kuiña-haba/Kwa'akuya-inyohave: Bourke 1889: 186, Kroeber 1976: 764; Sinyaxau: Waterman 1910: 339, Luomala 1978: 605.

80. There may have been a Quechan counterpart to Nyohaiva since the Quechan Av'alyunu songs are said to be the same as those of the Nyohaiva cycle (Kroeber 1976: 786-87; 1948: 29). A Warharmi-like figure also may lie behind a report from Don Juan de Oñate's expedition in 1605. Oñate learned of an island in the sea called Ziñogaba, and that

> the mistress or chieftainess of it was a giantess, and that she was called Ciñacacohola, which means chieftainess or mistress. They pictured her as the height of a man-and-half of those of the coast, and like them very corpulent, very broad, and with big feet; and that she was old, and that she had a sister, also a giantess, and that there was no man of her kind, and that she did not mingle with anyone of the island. The mystery of her reigning on that island could not be solved, whether it was by inheritance, or tyranny by force of arms. And they said that all on the island were bald, having no hair on the head. (Zárate-Salmerón [1626] 1916: 276)

In fact, several Yuman goddesses are said to live in the ocean, usually in the west: the Mohave Catheña/Qua-kuiña-haba/Kwa'akuya-inyohave, or Old Woman of the West (Bourke 1889: 186; Sherer Collection Box 95; Kroeber 1976: 764); the Havasupai goddess

(Smithson and Euler 1964: 32-35); and the Yavapai Widapokwi/Komwida-pokuwia/ Komwida-pokuma (Gifford 1932: 243; 1936: 307-9; 1936: 308). Kroeber speculated that the name Ziñogaba is a contraction of the Mohave terms *thenya'aka* (or *thinyaak*), "woman," and *ava*, "house," while Ciñaca-cohota is "woman-kahota" or chief (1976: 803).

81.　Luomala 1978: 600.

82.　1937: 5.

83.　Gifford 1931: 77.

84.　Spier 1933: 143.

85.　Kelly 1977: 118-19.

86.　This is Kroeber's translation of the term, which also encompasses the sexual couplings that occur during dances and tribal celebrations (Kroeber 1948: 63), although Dr. Tsosie suggests a better rendering is "pleasurable activity" (pers. comm.).

87.　1937: 501-2.

88.　See Herdt 1991.

89.　For background on these informants, see Devereux 1969: 5-6.

90.　Devereux 1937: 522. Kuwal himself was highly atypical. His family line is said to have died off because of incest (Michael Tsosie, pers. comm.).

91.　1937: 511.

92.　Ibid.: 513.

93.　See, for example, Bolin 1988. This appears to be changing. The term "transgender" is replacing transsexual, and many who undergo surgical sex reassignment now acknowledge their previous lives in another gender and, in the case of male-to-females, reject traditional images of femininity (see Stone 1991).

94.　Devereux 1935: 72.

95.　Cf. the story of Cane (Kroeber 1948: 8-9).

96.　Devereux 1937: 510.

97.　Kroeber 1972: 20.

98.　Ibid. 1976: 730, fig. 60a; Taylor and Wallace 1947: fig. 6a.

99.　Martin and Voorhies 1975: 98-99.

100.　1935: 99.

101.　On fuzzy categories, see Murray 1983.

102.　Devereux 1937: 518.

103.　Ibid.: 514.

104.　1935: 61. Devereux reports this statement as an exception to the flexibility and cooperation typical of the Mohave division of labor.

105.　See Devereux 1951a.

106.　Devereux 1935: 403; Kroeber 1972: 5. See Morris 1977.

107.　Devereux 1948a: 439.

108.　In the origin myth of the neighboring Quechan, the culture hero has to instruct the people to have vaginal, not anal intercourse; later he saves them from a flood by hiding them in his anus (Harrington 1908).

109.　1935: 14; 1937: 514.

110.　1966.

111.　1937: 520.

112.　Schroeder 1979: 100-1.

113.　Ibid.: 103.

114.　Hicks 1974: 135; Bee 1989: 17.

115.　Hicks 1974: 138.

116.　Schroeder 1979: 106-7.

117.　Stewart 1983: 2-3.

118.　See White 1974: 119.

119.　Castetter and Bell 1951: 254-55.

120. Castetter and Bell estimate that River Yumans obtained thirty to fifty percent of their food supply from agriculture (1951: 74).
121. See Hicks 1974; Fathauer 1954: 112.
122. Bee 1981: 4; 1983: 87; Stewart 1983: 57-59; Kroeber 1976: 736.
123. Bee 1981: 9.
124. Gifford 1932b: 233.
125. 1951: 276.
126. Harrington 1908: 327.
127. Fathauer 1954: 110; 1951: 273.
128. Devereux 1937: 501.
129. 1951: 276.
130. Luomala 1978: 602; Spier 1928: 222; Gifford 1932b: 195-96; 1936: 296-97.
131. Kroeber 1935: 140-41.
132. Gifford 1932b: 197; 1936: 292.
133. 1939: 101.
134. Stewart 1983: 64; Devereux 1950a: 88. Spanish and American authorities alike denounced the sexual freedom of the Mohaves and their relatives. See Pedro Font 1931: 105; Department of the Interior 1898: 112, 1896: 359.
135. Kroeber 1948: 64; cf. Nyohaiva myth summarized above.
136. Spier 1931: 224-25; Kelly 1977: 61, 63.
137. Castetter and Bell 1951: 251.
138. 1947: 260.
139. Devereux n.d.: 8; 1951b: 202.
140. 1939: 97.
141. 1950a: 90.
142. 1988.
143. Ibid.: 2.
144. Devereux 1942a: 304.
145. Collier and Rosaldo 1981: 281.
146. Kroeber 1948: 65.
147. Mohave: Stewart 1947: 267; Devereux n.d.: 12. Quechan: Forde 191: 168; Bee 1989: 31. Cocopa: Gifford 1933: 300; Kelly 1977: 134; 1949: 86. Yavapai: Gifford 1932b: 185; 1936: 298. Women were prominent in the Mohave, Quechan, Maricopa, and Yavapai scalp ceremonies.
148. 1939: 101-2.
149. 1948a: 453-54.
150. The extent to which any of these behaviors were an aspect of pre-contact Mohave life is open to question. Alcohol consumption appears to have played an important role in the cases Devereux reported.
151. Devereux n.d.: 18.
152. Ibid. 1939: 98-101.
153. Forde 1931: 134.
154. 1954: 108, 100.
155. Fathauer 1951: 275.
156. 1937: 498-99.
157. Forde 1931: 157.
158. Kroeber 1973: 9. Mohave: Michael Tsosie, pers. comm.; Quechan: U.S. Census Office 1900, Fort Yuma Agency.
159. NAA, entry #29, box 7, 1911 census at Fort Mohave.
160. Waltrip 1965.
161. Michael Tsosie, pers. comm.
162. Stoller 1976: 530-33.
163. Whitam and Mathy 1986: 84.

164. 1992: 50-51.
165. Michael Tsosie, pers. comm.
166. Waltrip 1965: 10.

CHAPTER 8

1. Callender and Kochems 1983: 443; Hauser 1990: 57.
2. Herdt 1991: 489.
3. 1981: 48.
4. Linton 1940: 501; see also Spicer 1961.
5. 1992: 608.
6. See Ortner 1984.
7. See Wolf 1982.
8. 1989: 197.
9. Ibid.: 87; see also Roscoe 1996b.
10. Leacock and Lurie 1971: 11.
11. 1985: 125.
12. Ibid.: 145, 153.
13. Laudonnière [1586] 1904, 9: 16.
14. Ibid.: 69.
15. Innovation and intercultural communication may have been expected of alternative genders in some tribes. As Bowers reported concerning Hidatsa *miáti*: "Not being bound as firmly by traditional teachings coming down from the older generations through the ceremonies, but more as a result of their own individual and unique experiences with the supernatural, their conduct was less traditional than that of the other ceremonial leaders" (1965: 167).
16. Denig 1930: 434.
17. McCleod 1953; Gogol 1983: 13, 15; Spier 1930: 52.
18. Gay movement pioneer Harry Hay recalls a photograph of his mother and her siblings as children in Virginia City, Nevada, posing with their housekeeper: a native man known as Indian Jack, who wore a woman's dress over a pair of men's pants (personal communication with the author, January 1985). Steward also reported a male berdache from this area who kept house for local whites (but did not cross-dress) (1941: 253).
19. Stevenson 1904: 310.
20. Based on conversations with Harry Hay and Bruce Bernstein.
21. Other natives who worked with non-Indians to record native cultural knowledge and may have been berdaches were Bernard Second (d. 1988), an Apache spiritual leader (Farrer 1997); Henry Azbill (d. 1973), a Chico Maidu artist (Craig Bates, pers. comm., July 1994); and possibly Kitsepawit (Fernando Librado) (d. 1915), a Chumash traditionalist who worked with John Harrington (Hudson 1979).
22. 1961: 1452.
23. 1956: 90. See also Henry 1897: 163-65; McKenney and Hall 1933: 120-21.
24. Yamasee: Barcia [1723] 1951: 117-18; Solís de Merás [1893] 1923: 180-81. Chickasaw: Adair [1775] 1968: 163-64.
25. Palou [1787] 1913: 214-15.
26. See Mühlhäuser 1980: 21.
27. See Tuttle in Chiappelli 1976, 2: 595-611.
28. Henry 1897: 163; Jackson 1978: 531. Jacobs and Cromwell credit the dissemination of "berdache" to "Jesuit missionary influences" (1992: 65) and cite the *Jesuit relations* edited by Thwaites and volumes 6 to 9 of the 1810-1811 edition of the *Lettres édifiantes et curieuse,* the "Jesuit Letters," but they do not provide page references. In fact, I do not find "berdache" in

either of these works. Thwaites uses "berdache" in a footnote to Marquette's discussion of the Illinois third gender role, but Marquette himself does not use it. I also fail to find any use of "berdache" in the 1780 edition of the *Lettres* (documents relating to North America appear in vol. 6 and the first part of vol. 7).

29. Elliott 1914: 190; Gray 1913: 46.

30. Maximillian 1839-1841, 2: 133.

31. See Hay 1963.

32. See Alonso (s.v. "*Amujerado, -da*") and Santamaria (s.v. "*Amujerado*"). Another term applied by Spaniards to berdaches, *amarionado/amaricado/marica/maricon,* appears to have a distinct etymology from *mujerado.* Guerra derives it from "Mary/Maria" (43; Cabeza de Vaca [1542] 1749: 29a; Font 1931: 105).

33. Stellers 1774: 289, 351; Krasheninnikov [1755] 1972: 213; Bogoraz 1904: 455.

34. Lisiansky 1814: 199.

35. "... *con el nombre de Joya (que dicen llamarlos así en su lengua nativa)*" ([1787] 1977: 245). *Joya* is "jewel" in Spanish, which has led some to assume that its origin is in that language. Although it can be used in reference to the male genitals in the same sense as the English phrase "family jewels," I am not aware of a precedent for its application to gender-variant or homosexual men.

36. See Malspina (in Galbraith 1924: 229) and Boscana 1846: 284.

37. Applegate 1966: 155; also rendered *agí* (Beeler 1967: 52) and *'aqi* (Hudson 1979: 40).

38. Hollimon 1997: 176.

39. Gayton 1936: 81.

40. Beeler 1967: 52-53.

41. Olmstead 1975: 156.

42. Another word that might be considered here is *joto/jote,* a term of uncertain origin used in Mexico for nonmasculine homosexual men. In some areas of northern Mexico, *jotos* are fully integrated members of their communities with the social and sexual status of ersatz women, although they are "neither wholly male nor wholly female" (Alonso and Koreck 1989: 111). In the 1930s, Drucker's Tipai informants insisted that berdaches, whom they called "jotes," were to be found "only among Mexicans" (1937: 49; see Alonso 1958 and Morínigo 1985, s.v. "Joto").

43. 1932: 55. This text is based on De Solís (1931: 44; see Newcomb 1961: 64).

44. 1897: 53.

45. Carter 1935: rev. 45; see also Erikson 1945: 329-30.

46. On the origins of pidgin languages, see Stoller 1979: 78. On sign language, see Hymes 1980: 408.

47. NAA, Ms. #2932.

48. Miller 1972: 136, 146; Clyde Hall, pers. comm.; Jacobs and Cromwell 1992: 66.

49. See Bossu for an Illinois Indian's impressions of nonmasculine European men ([1768] 1962: 84) and see chapter 3 for the comments of Navajos regarding *nádleehí* among whites.

50. Cobos 1983: 115; see also entries on *mujerengo, mujerero,* and *mujeriego/-ga* in Alonso 1958 and in Santamaria 1959.

51. *Gay Talk* reports "morph" and "morphdite" as colloquialisms of "hermaphrodite" referring to the "stereotype homosexual" (Rodgers 1979: 105-6).

52. For an overview of the incunabula of the New World, see Gerbi (in Chiappelli 1976, 1: 37-44) and Hirsch (in Chiappelli 1976, 2: 537-62). Hand characterizes the readership of this literature as "the clergy, educated laymen, and the entrepreneurial classes who stood to gain by commerce with the New World and its peoples" (in Chiappelli 1976, 1: 46).

53. See the bibliography and table published in Roscoe 1995c.

54. Poirier 1993a: 223.

55. [1615] 1943: 427; see Lestringant 1982.

56. 1964: 88.

57. See Poirier 1993b.

58. La Salle 1901: 146; Lahontan 1705: 144.

59. Even earlier, Las Casas, in his *Historia de las Indias* (not published until 1875), argued that native men who dressed like women did not do so "*para el detestable sin*" but in "*la manera que refiere Hipócrates y Galeno, que hacen algunas gentes cithias* [Scythians]" (3: 479). One finds the same parallel in Lafitau [1724] 1974: 56-58, Kraft 1766: 207, and Heriot [1805] 1807: 278. The sources on the *enarees* are Herodotus 4.67 and the Hippocratic author of *Peri aerōn* 17-22. For the *galli*, see Roscoe (1996a).

60. See Berkhofer 1978: part 2. Hodgen traces this theory back to medieval notions of the Great Chain of Being.

61. Heyne (1729-1812) inaugurated the lectures on archaeology and mythology in 1763 that made the University of Göttingen a center of classical studies. The writings of the Abbé de Pauw (1739-1799) have been judged less kindly. Historian Preserved Smith characterized *Recherches philosophiques sur les Américains* as "a work every whit as prejudiced and untrue to fact as is the gaudy picture of the savage by Rousseau" (145-46; see also White in Chiappelli 1976, 1: 128). For the criticism of a contemporary of de Pauw's, see Clavigero [1780-81] 1979: 359-60.

62. 1769: 100, trans. mine.

63. 1779: 39, 41.

64. Ibid. 44.

65. On Ulrichs, see Kennedy 1988; on Kertbeny, see Herzer 1985; Féray and Herzer 1990.

66. See Hekma 1994: 222-29.

67. Quoted in Kennedy 1988: 128.

68. Bleys 1995: 136.

69. Davidson 1990: 316-17.

70. [1906] 1931: 529.

71. 1992: 608.

72. See Trumbach 1994.

73. "*Denn nach dem Ausgeführten ist der Urning nicht Mann, sondern zwitterartiges Mannweib mit weiblicher Richtung der Geschlechtsliebe*" (Ulrichs 1975: 49). Other writers who use *Mannweib* include Maximilian, Müller, and Bastian.

74. McIntosh 1981: 37, 38. See also Murray 1996.

75. 1981: 101-2.

76. 1982-1983: 119.

77. Ibid.: 115.

78. 1994: 22, emphasis mine.

79. Halperin 1990: 15.

80. Ibid.: 24.

81. Davidson 1990: 309.

82. Hall (M. Owlfeather) 1988: 104. See also the interviews with Hall by Thompson (1994: 117-30) and Young (1997). For a useful model of the reconstitution of cultures and identity around core symbols, see Spicer 1971.

CHAPTER 9

1. 1989: 63, 62, 66.

2. 1995: 9.

3. For a useful discussion of native concepts of power, see Bean 1976.

4. Of this work, however, Gutiérrez cites only my article (1988b), and Trexler discusses only Williams 1986a.

5. 1980: 44.

6. 1989: 63.

7. Hammond and Rey 1940: 248.

8. Perhaps these women occupied roles similar to Mohave *kamalo:y* and Papago "light women" (see chapter 4).

9. 1916, 528; emphasis mine.

10. 1995: 73.

11. Stevenson 1904: 37.

12. Cushing 1896: 401; Stevenson 1904: 32, 37.

13. Newman 1958: 23.

14. 1989: 65.

15. 1904: 37.

16. See Bunzel 1932: 931-35; Parsons 1939a: 464, 758-61; 1915: 380-81; Stevenson 1904: 89-94.

17. Gutiérrez cites the report of the Army surgeon Hammond concerning practices at Acoma pueblo (Hammond 1887: 163-67), where individuals were supposedly "made" into berdaches. This was purportedly accomplished not through rape, but through excessive masturbation. Hay analyzed this report some years ago (1963). Hammond's account may be a garbled version of a recruitment procedure used by a (possibly berdache) medicine society (see Hay 1996: 275-83). The one report of homosexual rape of non-tribal members that I am aware of is Tixier (1940: 182).

18. See, for example, Smith and Roberts 1954.

19. 1989: 66.

20. 1991: 33-36.

21. 1995: 90-91.

22. Ibid.: 91.

23. Ibid.: 94.

24. 1983: 444, 451. Examples they discuss include Yuki (Powers 1877: 132); Illinois: punishment for desertion (Bossu [1768] 1972: 82); Winnebago: punishment for desertion or claiming false honors (Lurie 1953: 712); Santee Dakota: public humiliation at dances for youths who had not joined a war party (Landes 1968: 206-7).

25. Forthcoming.

26. Goddard summarizes the sources and concludes that refering to the Delaware as "women" was a rhetorical ploy of the Iroquois and was applied for a fairly short period of time (1978: 223).

27. On this debate, see Hanke 1949; 1970.

28. Alarcón [1556] 1940: 130, 147-48. Castañeda [1838] 1940: 248, 249, 253, 256.

29. See, for example, Pareja [1613] 1972: 39, 76; Señán in Beeler 1967: 52-53.

30. [1535] 1959: 1: 118-19; 4: 377; 5:9.

31. [1632] 1982: 8, 96, 97, 99, 115, 158, 163, 182, 646-47.

32. López de Gómara [1552] 1922, 1: 69, 104, 106, 113, 119, 128, 163, 171, 177, 2: 218; Cieza de León [1553] 1924: 96, 164, 166, 171, 190, 205-7, 253-54, 294, 324; Herrera [1601-15] 1991: *passim*; Garcilasso de la Vega [1609] 1943, 1: 155, 2: 29-30, 236; and Torquemada [1615] 1943: 12, 380, 392-94, 427.

33. "*Confesó que desde chiquito lo havia acostumbrado y ganava su bida con los hombres al aficio.*" Quoted in Trexler 1995: 217; my trans. On the role of torture in the production of texts by the Spaniards, see Tedlock 1993: 142.

34. Sepúlveda 1941: 113, 117.

35. See Hanke 1949.

36. I have in mind here the subtitle of Francis Jennings's classic work, *The Invasion of America: Indians, Colonialism, and the Cant of Conquest.*

37. Coreal 1722: 33-34, emphasis mine.

38. Deliette 1947 [1699]: 112-13, emphasis mine. The "De Gannes Memoir" (1934: 329-30) is believed to have been plagiarized from Deliette.

39. For other examples, see Langsdorff [1812] 1813: 47-48; Lisiansky 1814: 199; Hennepin [1698] 1903: 167-68; Denig 1953: 58; Marquette [1681] 1900: 128; Charlevoix 1744, 3: 303; Morfi [1770] 1932: 55; Tanner [1830] 1956: 89.

40. 1964: 121.

41. 1963: 147.

42. Charlevoix 1744, 3: 303; Tanner [1830] 1956: 99; Powers [1877] 1976: 132.

43. Jackson 1978: 531; De Smet 1905: 1017; Langsdorff [1812] 1813: 48.

44. 1968: 206-7.

45. Bowers 1965: 256.

46. Pilling 1997: 72.

47. I have sent copies of Pilling's manuscript to consultants at Zuni who likewise fail to confirm his inferences.

48. Pilling 1993. Dr. Pilling generously provided me with a copy of this manuscript.

49. Stevenson 1904: 37, emphasis mine.

50. In fact, Lasbeke had two sisters, who were still alive in 1993.

51. Pilling also makes the observation that "Yuka, like most of the other men-women, was living in a small household." In fact, many Zuni households were reduced in size in this period due to a series of epidemics and low infant survival rates.

52. 1997: 72.

53. 1940: 66, 163.

54. Roscoe 1991: 23.

CHAPTER 10

1. See fig. 7 in Roscoe 1991

2. Adams has speculated that a migration from Hopi to Pottery Mound occurred around the beginning of the fifteenth century and was instrumental in spreading the rain-oriented kachina cult to the Rio Grande (1991: 142). However, there is no direct equivalent of the figure depicted at Pottery Mound in the historic Hopi kachina pantheon. Instead, it appears most developed at Zuni. In fact, the distribution of this figure and its conventions more closely coincides with Hopi traditions that tell of a migration of people *from* the Rio Grande who stopped for a time at Zuni and then settled at prehistoric Hopi villages of Sikyatki and Awatovi (Adams 1991: 55, 72-73). Prominent among the kachinas associated with this group is the warrior woman called Chakwen 'Oka at Zuni and Tsa'kwayna at Hopi. A related kachina, the Hopi He'e'e, has the half-male, half-female hairstyle of Ko'lhamana and the Pottery Mound figure.

3. See Lévi-Strauss [1955] 1965.

4. Roscoe 1991: 251 n. 2.

5. Ibid.: 24, 230.

6. Hollimon 1996, 1997. Schmidt's dissertation, "Beyond the missionary (im)position: Variation in sex, gender, and sexuality in prehistory," is forthcoming.

7. See Murray 1995: 80-87, 273-92; Williams 1986a, chap. 7; Foster 1985.

8. Bogoraz in Murray 1992: 297. This account has been so casually cited that misconceptions about the transformed shaman have developed, which Murray corrects (1992: 309-10).

9. In Murray 1992: 298.

10. Bogoraz's account of Chuckchi soft men is unique in defining them strictly as shamans. Other reports describe them almost entirely in sexual terms—as cross-dressing concubines (see Wrangel [1839: 227] on the Chuckchi, Krasheninnikoff [in Murray 1992: 333] and Stellers [1774: 289, 350-51] on the Kamchadal, and Jochelson [in Murray 1992: 313-14] on the Koryak). Jochelson argued that "the most important feature of the institution of the koe'kčuč

lay, not in their shamanistic power, but in their position with regard to the satisfaction of the unnatural inclinations of the Kamchadal." If the emphasis in these reports on nonspiritual motivations are valid, it may be that many cases of Siberian gender transformation are, indeed, similar to the North American pattern, in which personal inclinations beginning in childhood motivate adoption of berdache identity, which is merely confirmed by subsequent dreams and visions.

11. In Murray 1992: 297.

12. In fact, Siberian shamans routinely employ symbolic forms of gender-crossing as part of their technical repertoire (see Jochelson in Murray 1992: 321-24), which led Czaplicka some years ago to argue that shamans were a "third class" distinct from the "classes" of males and females (in Murray 1992: 329-39).

13. Robertson 1989: 314.

14. 1994: 296. See also Watts in Murray 1992: 171-84 and Murray 1992: 151-63.

15. 1994: 297.

16. See Robertson 1989: 313-26.

17. For surveys of these roles, see Murray 1992: 273-92.

18. Philippines, *bayoc* (Murray 1992: 187-89); Korea, *paksu mudang* (Murray 1992: 261-62); Vietnam, *bong lai cai/bong lo* (Heimann and Cao 1975: 91); Cambodia, *chucus* (San Antonio 1914: 45); Burma, *acault* (Spiro 205-6, 219-26; Coleman, Colgan, and Gooren 1997); south India, *jogappa* (Bradford 1983).

19. Peltier 1991: 203.

20. For a detailed account of the contemporary *hijra*, see Nanda 1990.

21. 1990: 15.

22. *Tṛtfiyā prakṛti: Kāmasūtra* 2.9, *Mahābhārata* 4.59 [northern variant], *Ubhayābhisārikā* v. 21. *Strī rūpini/strī pumān: Kāmasūtra* 2.9, *Mahābhārata* 5.189.5, *napuṃsaka: Nāṭya-śāstra* 24.68-69.

23. The following discussion of Greco-Roman and Mesopotamian examples is based on Roscoe 1996a.

24. See Hay 1996: 47-50, 110-12.

25. Jacobsen 1987: 151-66.

26. See Roscoe 1996a: 217.

27. The element -ar in the Sumerian term *kurgarrū*, for example, dates it as far back as the pre-Sumerian, early Chalcolithic period of 5600-5000 B.C.E. (Henshaw 1994: 284).

28. The *Nārada Smṛti*, for example, defines fourteen categories of "impotent men," including those "naturally impotent," men who have been castrated, those cursed by a supernatural being, those afflicted by jealousy, those who spill their seed, and those who are shy (12.11-19).

29. Evidence exists of alternative gender statuses in African societies as well, to be presented in a forthcoming collection, *African Homosexualities*, edited by Stephen O. Murray and Will Roscoe.

30. Regarding this oversight, see Roscoe 1995d.

31. Lévi-Strauss 1965: 102.

32. See Morton 1996: 1-33.

33. See Roscoe 1995a and Hay 1996.

34. Drinnon 1987: 108.

BIBLIOGRAPHY OF
NATIVE LESBIAN/GAY LITERATURE

ANTHOLOGIES AND COLLECTIONS

Allen, Paula Gunn, ed. 1989/1990. *Spider Woman's granddaughters: Traditional tales and contemporary writing by Native American women*. Boston: Beacon Press; New York: Fawcett Columbine. (Includes Paula Gunn Allen, Vickie Sears, Janice Gould [Misha Gallagher].)

Brant, Beth. 1984/1988/1991. *A gathering of spirit: Writing and art by North American Indian women*, 2d ed. Rockland, Md.: Sinister Wisdom; Ithaca, N.Y.: Firebrand Books.

Bruchac, Joseph. 1987. *Survival this way: Interviews with American Indian poets*. Tucson: Sun Tracks/University of Arizona Press. (Interviews with Paula Gunn Allen, Maurice Kenny.)

———, ed. 1994. *Returning the gift: Poetry and prose from the first North American Native Writers' Festival*. Tucson: University of Arizona Press. (Includes Judith Volborth, Janice Gould).

Corinne, Tee A., ed. 1991. *Riding desire: An anthology of erotic writing*. Austin: Banned Books. (Includes Beth Brant, Vickie Sears.)

Fife, Connie, ed. 1993. *The colour of resistance: A Native women's anthology*. Toronto: Sister Vision Press. (Includes Beth Brant, Janice Gould, and others.)

Green, Rayna, ed. 1984. *That's what she said: Contemporary poetry and fiction by Native American women*. Bloomington: Indiana University Press. (Includes Paula Gunn Allen, Judith Mountain Leaf Volborth.)

Lerner, Andrea, ed. 1990. *Dancing on the rim of the world: An anthology of contemporary Northwest Native American writing*. Tucson: Suntracks/University of Arizona Press. (Includes Chrystos, Vickie Sears.)

Lesley, Craig and Katheryn Stavrakis, eds. 1991. *Talking leaves: Contemporary Native American short stories*. New York: Laurel. (Includes Beth Brant, Vickie Sears, Maurice Kenny.)

Moraga, Cherríe and Gloria Anzaldúa, eds. 1981. *This bridge called my back: Writings by radical women of color*. Watertown, Mass.: Persephone Press. (Includes Chrystos, Barbara Cameron.)

Morse, Carl and Joan Larkin, eds. 1988. *Gay and lesbian poetry in our time: An anthology*. New York: St. Martin's Press. (Includes Beth Brant, Vickie Sears, Chrystos, Maurice Kenny.)

Moses, Daniel D. and Terry Goldie, eds. 1992. *An anthology of native Canadian literature in English*. Toronto: Oxford University Press. (Includes Beth Brant, Daniel Moses.)

Silvera, Makeda, ed. 1991. *Piece of my heart: A lesbian of color anthology*. Toronto: Sister Vision.

SINGLE-AUTHOR WORKS

Allen, Paula Gunn. 1981. "Lesbians in American Indian cultures." *Conditions* 7: 65-87.

———. 1982. *Shadow country*. Native American Series. Los Angeles: American Indian Studies Center, University of California.

———. 1983/1986. *The woman who owned the shadows*. San Francisco: Spinsters; Spinsters/Aunt Lute.

———. 1986. *The sacred hoop: Recovering the feminine in American Indian traditions*. Boston: Beacon Press.

———. 1988. *Skins and bones: Poems 1979-87*. [Albuquerque, N.M.]: West End Press.

———. 1991. *Grandmothers of the light: A medicine woman's sourcebook*. 1991. Boston: Beacon Press.

Brant, Beth (Degonwadonti).1985. *Mohawk trail*. Ithaca, N.Y.: Firebrand.

———. 1991. *Food & spirits: Stories*. Ithaca, N.Y.: Firebrand Books.

———. 1994. *Writing as witness: Essay and talk*. Toronto: Women's Press.

———, ed. 1995. *I'll sing 'til the day I die: Conversations with Tyendinaga elders*. Toronto: McGilligan Books.

Chrystos. 1988. *Not vanishing*. Vancouver, B.C.: Press Gang.

———. 1991. *Dream on*. Vancouver, B.C.: Press Gang.

———. 1993. *In her I am*. Vancouver, B.C.: Press Gang.

Day, Sharon. 1983. *Drink the winds, let the waters flow free*. Minneapolis: Johnson Insitute.

Fife, Connie. 1992. *Beneath the naked sun*. Toronto: Sister Vision.

Gould, Janice. 1990. *Beneath my heart*. Ithaca, N.Y.: Firebrand Books.

Grieves, Catron. 1987. *Moonrising*. Oklahoma City: Red Dirt Press.

Kenny, Maurice. 1958. *Dead letters sent and other poems*. New York: Troubador Press.

———. 1977. *North: Poems of home*. Chapbook no. 4. Marvin, S.D.: Blue Cloud Quarterly.

———. 1979/1981. *Only as far as Brooklyn*. Boston: Good Gay Poets.

———. 1979/1981. *Dancing back strong the nation: Poems. Blue Cloud Quarterly* 25 (1). Marvin, S.D.: Blue Cloud Quarterly Press; Buffalo, N.Y.: White Pine Press.

———. 1981. *Kneading the blood*. New York: Strawberry Press.

———. 1982. *The smell of slaughter. The Blue Cloud Quarterly* 28 (1). Marvin, S.D.: Blue Cloud Quarterly Press.

———. 1982/1986. *Blackrobe: Isaac Jogues, b. March 11, 1604, d. October 18, 1646*. Saranac Lake, NY: North Country Community College Press; Saranac Lake, N.Y.: Chauncy Press.

———. 1984. *The mama poems*. Buffalo, N.Y.: White Pine Press.

———. 1985. *Is summer this bear*. Saranac Lake, N.Y.: Chauncy.

———. 1985/1990. *Rain and other fictions. The Blue Cloud Quarterly* 31 (4). Marvin, S.D.: Blue Cloud Quarterly Press; Fredonia, N.Y.: White Pine Press.

———. 1987. *Between two rivers: Selected poems*. Fredonia, N.Y.: White Pine Press.

———. 1988. *Humors and/or not so humorous*. Buffalo, N.Y.: Swift Kick.

———. 1988. *Greyhounding this America: Poems and dialog*. Chico, Calif.: Heidelberg Graphics.

———. 1990. *The short and the long of it: New poems*. Little Rock: American Native Press Archives, University of Arkansas at Little Rock.

———. 1991. *Last mornings in Brooklyn*. Renegade 24. Norman, Okla.: Point Riders Press.

———. 1992. *Tekonwatonti, Molly Brant, 1735-1795: Poems of war*. Fredonia, N.Y.: White Pine Press.

———. 1995. *On second thought: A compilation*. Norman: University of Oklahoma Press.

Midnight Sun, ed. 1986. *Fireweed: A Feminist Quarterly* (Native Women's Issue) 22.

Sears, Vickie L. 1990. *Simple songs*. Ithaca, N.Y.: Firebrand Books.

Tafoya, Terry. 1982. "A Legend of the Hellers." In *Sword of chaos*, edited by Marion Z. Bradley, 35-39. New York: DAW Books.

———. 1984. *Change!: Northwest Native American legends*. Acoma, N.M.: Pueblo of Acoma Press.

———. 1986. "Tupilak." In *Sword and sorceress III*, edited by Marion Z. Bradley, 201-210. New York: DAW Books.

———. 1989. "Why Ant Has a Small Waist" and "Dancing with Dash-Kayah." In *I become part of it: Sacred dimensions in Native American life*, edited by D. M. Dooling and Paul Jordan-Smith, 88-91, 92-100. New York: Parabola Books.

Volborth, J. Ivaloo [Judith Mountain Leaf]. 1978. *Thunder-Root: Traditional and contemporary Native American verse*. Los Angeles: American Indian Studies Center, UCLA.

White, Kevin. 1993. *Where eagles dare to soar: Indians, Politics and AIDS*. Kahnawake, Quebec: Owera Books.

BIBLIOGRAPHY

Relevant page numbers for primary sources appear in parentheses at the end of the entry.

ARCHIVAL SOURCES

National Anthropological Archives, Smithsonian Institution, Washington, D.C. [NAA].
    Crow #4720. Source Print Collection.
    Entry #29. John Peabody Harrington Papers. Mohave linguistic and ethnographic notes.
    Ms. #2932. Hugh Lenox Scott, "Berdache," "Notes on Sign Language and Miscellaneous
        Ethnographic Notes."
National Archives, Seattle, Wash. Crow Agency Records, Records of the Bureau of Indian Affairs,
        Record Group 75 [CAR].
    1887 Census
    Census Rolls, Lists of Bands and Adult Crow Indians, and Tract Books.
    Census Rolls, 1886-1904.
    Files 129 and 130, State Fairs, Numerical Correspondence.
    Lists of Bands
    Press Copies of Letters Sent to the Commissioner of Indian Affairs
    Press Copies of Miscellaneous Letters Sent
Southwest Museum, Los Angeles. Hodge-Cushing Collection [SWM].
    Envelope #38. Monthly Reports of Frank Hamilton Cushing.
University of California, Los Angeles. Sherer Collection [UCLA].
Wheelwright Museum of the American Indian, Santa Fe, New Mexico [WMAI].
    Alice Corbin Henderson Correspondence.
    Mary Cabot Wheelwright (1878-1958): Short Biography, by Amy S. Ford. Ms.
    Ms. #1-1-128. Mary C. Wheelwright. Journey Towards Understanding. Ms.
    Ms. #1-3-1. Correspondence, MCW, 1930-1957.
    Ms. #1-3-6. Correspondence, Laboratory of Anthropology.
    Ms. #4-1-26. Wyman Collection, Hosteen Klah Sandpainting Tapestries.

OTHER SOURCES

Adair, James. [1775] 1968. *Adair's history of the American Indians*. Ed. Samuel Cole Williams. New
    York: Promontory Press. (25, 109, 143, 163-64, 199).
Adams, E. Charles. 1991. *The origin and development of the Pueblo katsina cult*. Tucson: University of
    Arizona Press.
Aginsky, Burt W. 1943. "Culture element distributions 24: Central Sierra." *University of California
    Anthropological Records* 8(4). (430).
Ahneen/Sgene. 1995. "A life of denial." *The Sacred Fire* (January): 8.

Alarcón, Hernando de [1556] 1940. "Report of Alarcon's expedition." In *Narratives of the Coronado expedition 1540-1542*, ed. George P. Hammond and Agapito Rey, 124-55. Albuquerque: University of New Mexico Press. Originally published as "Relatione della navigatione & scoperta che fece il Capitano Fernando Alarcone," in *Terzo volume delle navigationi et viaggi...*, ed. Giovanni Battista Ramusio, 363-70. Venice: Giunti. (130, 148).

Allen, Paula Gunn. 1981. "Lesbians in American Indian cultures." *Conditions* 7: 67-87.

———. 1986. *The sacred hoop: Recovering the feminine in American Indian traditions.* Boston: Beacon Press.

Alonso, Ana M. and Maria T. Koreck. 1989. "Silences: 'Hispanics,' AIDS, and Sexual Practices." *differences: A Journal of Feminist Cultural Studies* 1(1): 101-24.

Alonso, Martín. 1958. *Enciclopedia del idioma.* Madrid: Aguilar.

Amsden, Charles A. 1964. *Navaho weaving: Its technic and history.* Chicago: Rio Grande Press.

Angelino, Henry and Charles L. Shedd. 1955. "A note on berdache." *American Anthropologist* 57: 121-26.

Anguksuar [Richard LaFortune]. 1990. "Vision". In *Twin Cities gay & lesbian celebration 1990 official pride guide,* 58-59. Minneapolis: Twin Cities Lesbian-Gay Pride Committee.

———. 1997. "A postcolonial perspective on Western (mis)conceptions of the cosmos and the restoration of indigeneous taxonomies." In *Two-spirit people: Native American gender identity, sexuality, and spirituality,* ed. Sue-Ellen Jacobs, Wesley Thomas, and Sabine Lang, 217-22. Urbana: University of Illinois Press.

Anon. 1990. *Two Eagles* [AIGLA/Minneapolis newsletter] (fall): 4.

Anon. 1993. *Positively Native Newsletter* 1(1) (summer).

Anon. 1994. *In the Wind: American Indian/Alaska Native/Hawaiian Native Community AIDS Network Newsletter* 5(2) (May): [2].

Anon. 1995. *In the Wind,* 6(4) (July/August).

Applegate, Richard B. 1966. "Ineseño Chumash grammar." Ph.D. diss. University of California, Berkeley. (128, 155).

Arlegui, Jose. 1737. *Crónica de la provincia de N. S. P. S. Francisco de Zacatecas.* Mexico: José Bernardo de Hogal. Reprinted 1851. (143-44).

Asetoyer, Charon, Lori Beaulieu, and Andrea G. Rush. 1992. "Women and HIV." In *HIV prevention in Native American communities,* comp. Andrea G. Rush, 77-81. Oakland: National National American AIDS Prevention Center.

Bacqueville de la Potherie. 1722. *Histoire de l'Amerique septentrionale.* Vol. 3. Paris: Jean-Luc Nion and François Didot. (41).

Badger, Reid. 1979. *The great American fair: The World's Columbian Exposition and American culture.* Chicago: Nelson Hall.

Bailey, Flora L. 1943. Review of *Navajo Creation Myth. American Anthropologist* 45: 125-26.

Ball, Eve. 1970. *In the days of Victorio: Recollections of a Warm Springs Apache.* Tucson: University of Arizona Press.

Bandelier, Adolph F. 1966. *The Southwestern journals of Adolph F. Bandelier.* Ed. Charles H. Lange and Carroll L. Riley. Albuquerque and Santa Fe: University of New Mexico Press, Musuem of New Mexico Press. (326).

Barcia, Andres Gonzalez de. [1723] 1951. *Barcia's chronological history of the continent of Florida....* Trans. Anthony Kerrigan. Gainesville: University of Florida Press. (117-18, 306).

Barnett, H. G. 1937. "Culture element distributions 7: Oregon coast." *University of California Anthropological Records* 1(3). (185).

———. 1955. *The Coast Salish of British Columbia.* Eugene: University of Oregon Press. (128, 149).

Bastian, Adolf. 1860 [1968]. *Der Mensch in der Geschichte: Zur Begründung einer psychologischen Weltanschauung.* Vol. 3. Reprint. Osnabrück: Biblio-Verlag.

———. 1878. *Die Culturländer des Alten America.* Vol. 2. Berlin: Weidmannsche.

Batkin, Jonathan, ed. 1995. *Splendid heritage: Masterpieces of Native American art from the Masco Collection.* Santa Fe, N.M.: Wheelwright Museum of the American Indian.

Beaglehole, Ernest and Pearl Beaglehole. 1935. "Hopi of the Second Mesa." *American Anthropological Association Memoir* 44. (65).

Beals, Ralph L. 1933. "Ethnology of the Nisenan." *University of California Anthropological Records* 31(6). (376).

Bean, Lowell J. 1976. "Power and its applications in native California." In *Native Californians: A theoretical retrospective*, ed. Lowell J. Bean and Thomas C. Blackburn, 407-20. Ramona, Calif.: Ballena Press.

Beckwith, Martha W. 1937. "Mandan-Hidatsa myths and ceremonies." *Memoirs of the American Folklore Society* 32. (233).

Beckwourth, James P. [1854] 1931. *The life and adventures of James P. Beckwourth*. Ed. T. D. Bonner. New York: Alfred A. Knopf. (xxiv, 133-44).

Bee, Robert L. 1981. *Crosscurrents along the Colorado: The impact of government policy on the Quechan Indians*. Tucson: University of Arizona Press.

———. 1983. "Quechan." In *Handbook of the North American Indian*. Vol. 10 , ed. Alfonso Ortiz, 86-98. Washington, D.C.: Smithsonian Institution.

———. 1989. *The Yuma*. New York: Chelsea House Publishers.

Beeler, Madison S., ed. 1967. *The Ventureño Confesionario of José Señán, O.F.M.* University of California Publications in Linguistics 47. Berkeley: University of California Press. (52-53).

Benedict, Ruth. [1934] 1959. *Patterns of culture*. Boston and New York: Houghton Mifflin. (262-65).

Bennett, Emerson. 1850. *The Prairie Flower; or, adventures in the far west*. Cincinnati: U. P. James.

———. 1851. *Leni Leoti; or, adventures in the far west*. Cincinnati: J. A. and U. P. James.

Benyshek, Daniel C. 1992. "Native American female ascendancy, traditional conceptualizations of gender, and atypical male gender-role behavior." M.A. thesis, Arizona State University.

Berkhofer, Robert F., Jr. 1978. *The white man's Indian: Images of the American Indian from Columbus to the present*. New York: Knopf.

Berlant, Anthony and Mary H. Kahlenberg. 1977. *Walk in beauty: The Navajo and their blankets*. Boston: New York Graphic Society.

Berman, Howard. 1982. "Freeland's Central Sierra Miwok myths." *Reports from the Survey of California and Other Indian Languages* 3. (115, 129).

Besnier, Niko. 1994. "Polynesian gender liminality through time and space." In *Third sex, third gender: Beyond sexual dimorphism in culture and history*, ed. Gilbert Herdt, 285-328. New York: Zone.

Bettelyoun, Willie. 1991. "Survivorship." *Seasons: The National Native American AIDS Prevention Center* (spring): [2-4].

Birket-Smith, Kaj. 1953. *The Chugach Eskimo*. Copenhagen: Nationalmuseets Publikationsfond. (94, 136-37).

Birket-Smith, Kaj and Frederica De Laguna. 1937. *The Eyak Indians of the Copper River delta, Alaska*. Kobenhavn: Levin and Munksgaard. (206).

Blackwood, Evelyn. 1984. "Sexuality and gender in certain American Indian tribes: The case of cross-gender females." *Signs: The Journal of Women in Culture and Society* 10(1): 27-42.

———. 1988. Review of *The spirit and the flesh: Sexual diversity in American Indan culture* by Walter L. Williams. *Journal of Homosexuality* 15(3-4): 165-76.

Bleys, Rudi C. 1995. *The geography of perversion: Male-to-male sexual behaviour outside the West and the ethnographic imagination, 1750-1918*. New York: New York University Press.

Bloch, Iwan. 1902. *Beiträge zur Aetiologie Psychopathia sexualis*. Vol. 1. Dresden: H. R. Dohrn. (42-49).

Bloomfield, Maurice, trans. 1897. *Hymns of the Atharva-Veda*. Vol. 42, *Sacred Books of the East*. Oxford: Clarendon Press.

Boas, Franz. 1895. "Sagen der Indianer an der Nordwest-Küste America's." *Zeitschrift für Ethnologie* 27: 189-234. (201).

———. 1898a. "Facial paintings of the Indians of northern British Columbia." *Memoirs of the American Museum of Natural History* 2(1). (28, 48, 53-54).

———. 1898b. "The mythology of the Bella Coola Indians." *Memoirs of the American Museum of Natural History* 2(2). (38-40).

Bogoraz, Vladimir G. [Waldemar Bogoras]. 1904. The Chukchee. *American Museum of Natural History Memoir* 11(2).

Bolin, Anne. 1988. *In search of Eve: Transsexual rites of passage*. South Hadley: Bergin and Garvey.

Boscana, Geronimo. 1846. *Chinigchinich: A historical account of the origin, customs, and traditions of the Indians at the missionary establishment of St. Juan Capistrano, Alta California. . . .* New York: Wiley and Putnam. (283-84).

Bossu, Jean-Bernard. 1768. *Nouveaux voyages aux Indes Occidentales*. Paris: Le Jay.

———. 1962. *Jean-Bernard Bossu's travels in the interior of North America 1751-1762*. Trans. and ed. Seymour Feiler. Norman: University of Oklahoma Press. (82, 84, 169).

Boswell, John. 1980. *Christianity, social tolerance, and homosexuality: Gay people in Western Europe from the beginning of the Christian era to the fourteenth century.* Chicago: University of Chicago Press.

———. 1982-1983. "Revolutions, universals and sexual categories." *Salmagundi* 58-59: 89-113.

———. 1990. "Concepts, experience, and sexuality." *differences: A Journal of Feminist Cultural Studies* 2(1): 67-87.

Bourke, John G. 1889. "Notes on the cosmogony and theogony of the Mojave Indians of the Rio Colorado, Arizona." *Journal of American Folk-lore* 2(6): 169-89.

Bowers, Alfred. 1950. *Mandan social and ceremonial organization.* Chicago: University of Chicago Press. (270, 272, 289, 296, 298-99).

———. 1965. "Hidatsa social and ceremonial organization." *Bureau of American Ethnology Bulletin* 194. (105, 115, 132, 159, 166-68, 256, 259-60, 267, 315, 325-27, 330, 427, 438).

Boyce, Douglas W. 1978. "Iroquoian tribes of the Virginia-North Carolina coastal plain." In *Handbook of North American Indians.* Vol. 15, ed. Bruce Trigger, 282-95. Washington, D.C.: Smithsonian Institution. (285).

Boyer, Ruth M. and Narcissus D. Gayton. 1992. *Apache mothers and daughters: Four generations of a family.* Norman: University of Oklahoma Press.

Bradford, Nicholas. 1997. "Transgenderism and the cult of Yellamma: Heat, sex, and sickness in South Indian Ritual." In *Que(e)rying religion: A critical anthology,* ed. Gary D. Comstock and Susan E. Henking, 294-310. New York: Continuum.

Bradley, Jr., Charles C. 1977. *After the buffalo days: An account of the first years of reservation life for Crow Indians, based on official government documents from 1880 to 1904 A.D.* Vol. 1. N.p.

Brant, Beth. 1993. "Giveaway: Native Lesbian writers." *Signs* 18(4): 944- 47.

Brinton, Daniel G. [1884] 1969. *The Lenape and their legends.* Reprint. New York: AMS Press. (109-22).

Broch, Harold B. 1977. "A note on berdache among the Hare Indians of northwestern Canada." *Western Canadian Journal of Anthropology* 7: 95-101.

Brown, Lester, ed. 1997. *Two spirit people: American Indian lesbian women and gay men.* New York: Harrington Park Press.

Brugge, David M. 1980. *A history of the Chaco Navajos.* Reports of the Chaco Center 4. Albuquerque: National Park Service, Division of Chaco Research.

———. 1983. "Navajo prehistory and history to 1850." In *Handbook of the North American Indian.* Vol. 10, ed. Alfonso Ortiz, 489-97. Washington, D.C.: Smithsonian Institution.

Brust, James. 1992. "Into the face of history." *American Heritage* 43(7): 104-13.

Buchanan, Kimberly M. 1986. *Apache women warriors.* Southwestern Studies Series no. 79. El Paso: Texas Western Press. (24-37).

Buckley, Cornelius M. 1989. *Nicolas Point, S.J.: His life and Northwest Indian chronicles.* Chicago: Loyola University Press. (252, 260, 284-86).

Buechel, Eugene. 1970. *A dictionary of the Teton Dakota Sioux language.* Ed. Paul Manhart. Pine Ridge, S.D.: Red Cloud Indian School. (449, 587).

Bunzel, Ruth L. [1929] 1972. *The Pueblo potter: A study in creative imagination in primitive art.* Reprint. New York: Dover Publications. (57).

———. 1932. "Zuñi Katcinas." *Bureau of American Ethnology Annual Report* 47, 837-1086.

Burton, Richard F. 1885. *The book of the Thousand Nights and a Night.* Vol. 10. Burton Club.

Butler, Judith. 1990. *Gender trouble: Feminism and the subversion of identity.* New York: Routledge.

———. 1993. *Bodies that matter: On the discursive limits of "sex."* New York: Routledge.

Buxton, L. H. Dudley. 1923. Some Navajo folktales and customs. *Folk-lore* 34(4): 293-308.

Cabeza de Vaca, Alvar Nuñez. [1542] 1749. "Naufragios de Alvar Nuñez Cabeza de Vaca." In *Historiadores primitivos de las Indias Occidentales.* Vol. 1, ed. Andres Gonzalez de Barcia Carballido y Zuniga, 1-43 (numbered separately). Madrid. Originally published as *La relación que dió . . . de lo acaescido en las Indias.* Zaragoza: Augustín de Paz y Juan Picardo. (21a, 29a).

———. [1542] 1625. "A relation of Alvaro Nunez . . . translated out of Ramusio, and abbreviated." In *Purchas his pilgrimes in five books,* part 4, ed. Samuel Purchas, 1499-1532. London: William Stansby for Henrie Fetherstone. (Book 8: 1519).

Califia, Pat. 1997. *Sex changes: The politics of transgenderism.* San Francisco: Cleis.

Callender, Charles and Lee M. Kochems. 1983. "The North American berdache." *Current Anthropology* 24(4): 443-70.

———. 1986. "Men and not-men: Male gender-mixing statuses and homosexuality." In *The many faces of homosexuality*, ed. Evelyn Blackwood, 165-78. New York: Harrington Park Press.

Calvin, Susan. 1993. "AIDS & the Navajo: An interview with an HIV-positive Navajo." *The Sacred Fire* (June): 12.

Cameron, Anne. 1981. *Daughters of Copper Woman*. Vancouver: Press Gang. (129-38).

Campbell, Tyrone D. 1987. *Historic Navajo weaving: Three cultures—one loom*. N.p.: Avanyu Publishing.

Cappello, Mary. forthcoming. *William Penn's treaty with the Indians: Improper relations in American cultural studies*.

Carpenter, Edward. 1914. *Intermediate types among primitive folk: A study in social evolution*. London: George Allen.

Carter, John G. 1935, 1939. "Documents on unfamiliar ceremonies, observances, and customs of the North American Indians." Unpub. ms.

Casagrande, Louis B. and Phillips Bourns. 1983. *Side trips: The photography of Sumner W. Matteson 1898-1908*. Milwaukee: Milwaukee Public Museum and the Science Museum of Minnesota. (82, 229).

Casteñeda, Pedro de. [1838] 1940. "Castañeda's history of the expedition." In *Narratives of the Coronado expedition 1540-1542*, ed. George P. Hammond and Agapito Rey, 191-283. Albuquerque: University of New Mexico Press. Originally published as "Relation du voyage de Cibola entrepris en 1540," in *Voyages, relations et mémoires originaux pour servir à l'histoire de la découverte de l'Amérique*. Ser. 1, vol. 9, ed. Henri Ternaux-Compans. Paris: Arthus Bertrand. (248-50).

Castetter, Edward F. and Willis H. Bell. 1951. *Yuman Indian agriculture: Primitive subsistence on the lower Colorado and Gila Rivers*. Albuquerque: University of New Mexico Press.

Catlin, George. [1841] 1973. *Letters and notes on the manners, customs, and condition of the North American Indians*. 2 vols. Reprint. New York: Dover. (1: 112-14; 2: 214-15).

Charlevoix, François Xavier de. 1744. *Histoire et description générale de la Nouvelle France avec le journal historique d'un voyage fait par ordre du Roi dans l'Amérique Septentrionnale*. Vols. 1 and 3 (includes *Journal d'un voyage fait par ordre du Roi dans l'Amérique Septentrionnale; Adressée a Madame la Duchesse de Lesdiguieres*). Paris: Nyon Fils. (1: 27; 3: 303).

Chauncey, George, Jr. 1982-1983. "From sexual inversion to homosexuality: Medicine and the changing conceptualization of female deviance." *Salmagundi* 58-59: 114-46.

———. 1994. *Gay New York: Gender, urban culture, and the making of the gay male world, 1890-1940*. New York: Basic Books.

Chiapelli, Fredi, ed. 1976. *First images of America: The impact of the New World on the old*. 2 vols. Berkeley: University of California Press.

Choris, M. Louis. 1822. *Voyage pittoresque autor du monde, avex des portraits de sauvages*. . . . Paris: Firmin Didot. (Part VII, 8).

Cieza de León, Pedro de. [1553] 1924. *La crónica general del Perú*. Vol. 1, ed. Horacio H. Urteaga. Lima: Libreria e Imprenta Gil. Originally published as *Parte primera de la chronica del Peru*. Seville: Casa de Martín de Montesdoca.

Clavigero, Franceso Saverio. [1780-81] 1979. *The history of Mexico*. Vol. 2. New York and London: Garland Publishing. Originally published as *Storia antica del Messico cavata da' migliori storici spagnuoli, e da' manoscritti, e dalle pitture antiche degl' Indiani*. . . . Cesena: Gregorio Biasini.

Clemmer, Richard O. 1994. Review of *The Zuni Man-Woman*. *American Indian Quarterly* 18(2): 275-77.

Clifford, James. 1986. "Introduction: Partial truths." In *Writing culture: The poetics and politics of ethnography*, ed. James Clifford and George E. Marcus, 1-26. Berkeley: University of California Press.

Cline, Walter. 1938. "Religion and world view." In *The Sinkaietk or southern Okanagon of Washington*, ed. Leslie Spier, 131-82. General Series in Anthropology 6. Menasha, Wisc.: George Banta. (137).

Cobos, Rubén. 1983. *A dictionary of New Mexico and Southern Colorado Spanish*. Santa Fe: Museum of New Mexico Press. (115).

Coleman, Eli, Philip Colgan, and Louis Gooren. 1997. "Male cross-gender behavior in Myanmar (Burma): A description of the acault." In Que(e)rying religion: A critical anthology, ed. Gary D. Comstock and Susan E. Henking, 287-93. New York: Continuum.

Coleman, Winfield. forthcoming. People of two spirits: The androgyne in Cheyenne art thought. N.p.

Collier, Jane F. 1988. Marriage and inequality in classless societies. Stanford: Stanford University Press.

Collier, Jane F. and Michelle Z. Rosaldo. 1981. "Politics and gender in simple societies." In Sexual meanings: The cultural construction of gender and sexuality, ed. Sherry B. Ortner and Harriet Whitehead, 275-329. Cambridge: Cambridge University Press.

Collier, Jane F., and Sylvia J. Yanagisako. 1987. "Toward a unified analysis of gender and kinship." In Gender and kinship: Essays toward a unified analysis, ed. Jane F. Collier and Sylvia J. Yanagisako, 14-50. Stanford: Stanford University Press.

Cook, Sherburne F. [1943] 1976. The conflict between the California Indians and white civilization. Berkeley: University of California Press. (102, 111, 153).

Coolidge, Dane and Mary R. Coolidge. 1930. The Navajo Indians. Boston: Houghton Mifflin Co.

Coréal, François. 1722. Voyages de François Coreal aux Indes Occidentales contenant ce qu'il y a vû de plus remarquable pendant son séjour de 1666 jusqu'en 1697. . . . Vol. 1. Amsterdam: J. Frederic Bernard. (33-34).

Costanso, Miguel. [1776] 1910. The narrative of the Portola expedition of 1769-1770. Ed. Frederick Teggard. Publications of the Academy of Pacific Coast History 1(4). (46, 47).

Courouve, Claude. 1982. "The word 'bardache.'" Gay Books Bulletin 8: 18-19.

Cox, Ross. [1832] 1957. The Columbia River. . . . Ed. Edgar I. Stewart and Jane R. Stewart. Norman: University of Oklahoma Press. (190-92).

Cromwell, Jason. 1997. "Traditions of gender diversity and sexualities: A female-to-male transgender perspective." In Two-spirit people: Native American gender identity, sexuality, and spirituality, ed. Sue-Ellen Jacobs, Wesley Thomas, and Sabine Lang, 119-42. Urbana: University of Illinois Press.

Crowe, Keith J. 1974. A history of the original peoples of northern Canada. Kingston: McGill-Queen's University Press. (77-78, 89-90).

Culin, Stewart. 1907. "Games of the North American Indians." Bureau of American Ethnology Annual Report 24.

Curtis, Edward S. 1970. The North American Indian. Vol. 4. New York: Johnson Reprint Corporation.

———. 1926. The North American Indian. Vol. 16. Johnson Reprint Corp. (134-35).

Cushing, Frank H. 1896. "Outlines of Zuñi creation myths." Bureau of Ethnology Annual Report 13, 321-447. Washington, D.C.: Government Printing Office.

Dall, William H. 1878. "Social life among our aborigines." American Naturalist 12(1): 1-10. (5-6).

———. [1870] 1897. Alaska and its resources. Boston: Lee and Shepard. (139, 402-3).

Davidson, Arnold I. 1990. "Closing up the corpses: Diseases of sexuality and the emergence of the psychiatric style of reasoning." Meaning and method: Essays in honor of Hilary Putnam, ed. George Boolos, 295-325. Cambridge: Cambridge University Press.

Davydov, G. I. [1810] 1977. Two voyages to Russian America, 1802-1807. Ed. Colin Bearne. Materials for the Study of Alaska History 10. Kingston, Ont.: Limestone. (166).

Day, Sharon. 1990. "AIDS and homophobia in American Indian communities: A vision for change." Seasons (summer): n.p.

De Barthe, Joe. 1958. Life and adventures of Frank Grouard. Norman: University of Oklahoma Press.

de Bry, Theodore, ed. 1594. Americae pars quarta: Sive, insignis & admiranda historia de reperta primum Occidentali India a Christophoro Columbo anno M.CCCCXCII, scripta ab Hieronymo Benzono. . . . Frankfurt: Theodore de Bry.

de Laet, Joannes. 1633. Novus Orbis seu descriptionis India Occcidentalis libri XVIII. Lugduni Batavorum: Elzevirios.

De Laguna, Frederica. 1954. "Tlingit ideas about the individual." Southwestern Journal of Anthropology 10: 172-89. (178, 183).

de Pauw, Cornelius. 1769. Recherches philosophiques sur les Américains, ou mémoires intéressants, pour servir à l'histoire de l'espèce humaine. Vol. 2. Berlin: George Jacques Decker.

De Smet, Pierre-Jean. 1905. Life, letters and travels of Father Pierre-Jean De Smet, S.J., 1801-1873. Vols. 2-3, ed. Hiram M. Chittenden and Alfred T. Richardson. New York: Francis P. Harper. (578, 1017-18).

————. 1906. "De Smet's Oregon missions and travels over the Rocky Mountains, 1845-1846." In *Early Western Travels, 1748-1846.* Vol. 29, ed. Reuben G. Thwaite. Cleveland: Arthur H. Clark. (332).

De Solís, Gaspar José de. 1931. "Diary of a visit of inspection of the Texas missions made by Fray Gaspar José de Solís in the year 1767-68." Ed. Margaret K. Kress. *Southwestern Historical Quarterly* 35(1): 28-76. (44).

Deliette, Pierre. 1934. "Memoir of De Gannes concerning the Illinois country." In *The French foundations, 1680-1693,* ed. Theodore C. Pease and Raymond C. Werner, 302-98. Collections of the Illinois State Historical Library 23, French Series 1. Springfield: Illinois State Historical Library: 302-98. (329-30, 343).

————. 1947. "The memoir of Pierre Liette." In *The western country in the 17th century: The memoirs of Lamothe Cadillac and Pierre Liette,* ed. Milo Milton Quaife, 87-174. Chicago: Lakeside Press. (112-13, 124).

DeMallie, Raymond. 1983. "Male and female in traditional Lakota culture." In *The hidden half: Studies of Plains Indian women,* ed. Patricia Albers and Beatrice Medicine, 237-65. Lanham, Md.: University Press of America. (243-48).

Denig, Edwin T. 1930. "Indian tribes of the upper Missouri." Ed. J. N. B. Hewitt. *Bureau of American Ethnology Annual Report* 46. (433-34).

————. 1953. "Of the Crow nation." Ed. John C. Ewers. *Bureau of American Ethnology Bulletin* 151. (58-59, 64-68).

————. 1961. *Five Indian tribes of the upper Missouri.* Ed. John C. Ewers. Norman: University of Oklahoma Press. (187-88, 195-200).

Devereux, George. n.d. "The place of sexuality in Mohave warfare." Unpubl. ms. in author's possession.

————. 1935. "Sexual life of the Mohave Indians: An interpretation in terms of social psychology." Ph.D. diss., University of California, Berkeley.

————. 1937. "Institutionalized homosexuality of the Mohave Indians." *Human Biology* 9: 498-527.

————. 1939. "Mohave culture and personality." *Character and Personality* 8(2): 91-109. (102, 104).

————. 1942a. "Social structure and the economy of affective bonds." *Psychoanalytic Review* 29(3): 303-14.

————. 1947. "Mohave orality: An analysis of nursing and weaning customs." *Psychoanalytic Quarterly* 16: 519-46.

————. 1948a. "The Mohave Indian kamalo:y." *Clinical Pscyhopathaology* 9(3): 433-57.

————. 1948b. "Mohave pregnancy." *Acta Americana* 6(1-2): 89-116.

————. 1950a. "Heterosexual behavior of the Mohave Indians." In *Psychoanalysis and the social sciences II,* ed. G. Róheim. New York.

————. 1950b. "Psychodynamics of Mohave gambling." *American Imago* 7(1): 55-65.

————. 1950c. "Mohave Indian autoerotic behavior." *Psychoanalytic Review* 37 (3): 201-220.

————. 1951a. "Cultural and characterological traits of the Mohave related to the anal stage of psychosexual development." *Psychoanalytic Quarterly* 20: 398-422.

————. 1951b. "Atypical and deviant Mohave marriages." *Samīkṣā: Journal of the Indian Psychoanalytical Society* 4(4): 200-15.

————. [1961] 1969. *Mohave ethnopsychiatry: The psychic disturbances of an Indian tribe.* Reprint. Washington, D.C.: Smithsonian Institution. (313, *passim*).

DeVoto, Bernard, ed. [1904] 1953. *The journals of Lewis and Clark.* Boston: Houghton Mifflin. (74).

Díaz del Castillo, Bernal. [1632] 1982. *Historia verdadera de la conquista de la Nueva España.* Vol. 1, ed. Carmelo Saenz de Santa Maria. Madrid: Instituto Gonsalo Fernández de Oviedo. Originally published Madrid, 1632. (8, 96, 97, 99, 115, 158, 163, 182, 646-47).

Diez, Friedrich. 1887. *Etymologisches Wörterbuch der Romanischen Sprachen,* 5th ed. Bonn: Adolph Marcus.

Dockstader, Frederick J. 1987. *The song of the loom: New traditions in Navajo weaving.* New York: Hudson Hills Press.

Dorsey, George A. 1906. "The Pawnee: Mythology, part I." *Publications of the Carnegie Institute* 59. (138).

Dorsey, George A. and Alfred L. Kroeber. 1903. "Traditions of the Arapaho." *Field Museum Anthropological Series* 5. (261-62).

Dorsey, George A. and James R. Murie. 1940. "Notes on the Skidi Pawnee society." *Field Museum Anthropological Series* 27(2). (108).

Dorsey, J. Owen. 1884. "Omaha sociology." *Bureau of American Ethnology Annual Report* 3. (266).

———. 1890. "A study of Siouan cults." *Bureau of American Ethnology Annual Report* 11. (378-79, 467, 516-17).

Douglas, Mary. 1966. *Purity and danger: An analysis of concepts of pollution and taboo.* London: Routledge and Kegan Paul.

Drinnon, Richard. 1987. "The metaphysics of dancing tribes." In *The American Indian and the problem of history*, ed. Calvin Martin, 106-13. New York: Oxford University Press.

Driver, Harold E. 1937. "Culture element distributions 6: Southern Sierra Nevada." *University of California Anthropological Records* 1(2). (90, 99, 109).

———. 1939. "Culture element distributions 10: Northwest California." *University of California Anthropological Records* 1(6). (347).

———. 1961. *Indians of North America.* Chicago: University of Chicago Press.

Drucker, Philip. 1937. "Culture element distributions 5: Southern California." *University of California Anthropological Records* 1(1). (27, 49).

———. 1941. "Culture element distributions 17: Yuman-Piman." *University of California Anthropological Records* 6(3). (163, 218).

———. 1951. "The northern and central Nootkan tribes." *Bureau of American Ethnology Bulletin* 144. (331).

Du Bois, Cora A. 1935. "Wintu ethnography." *University of California Publications in American Archaeology and Ethnology* 36(1). (50-51).

Duberman, Martin B. 1982. "1965 Native American transvestism." *New York Native*, June 21-July 4: 12, 46.

Duberman, Martin B., Fred Eggan, and Richard O. Clemmer. 1980. "Hopi Indians redux." *Radical History Review* 24: 177-87.

Duflot de Mofras, Eugene. [1844] 1937. *Duflot de Mofras' travels on the Pacific coast.* Vol. 2, ed. Marguerite Eyer Wilbur. Santa Ana, Calif.: Fine Arts Press. (192-93).

Duggan, Thomas. 1887. "Extracts from journal." In "Historical collections: Copies of papers on file in the Dominion Archives at Ottawa, Canada," 105-9. *Michigan Pioneer Historical Collections* 12. (108).

Dumont de Montigny, M. 1753. *Mémoires historiques sur la Louisiane.* . . . Vol. 1. Paris: J. B. Bauche. (247-[49]).

Duran, Betty E. S. 1997. "Traditional healing and spirituality in HIV-care services for American Indians, Alaska natives, and native Hawaiians." *In The Wind* 8(1): 6-7.

Dyck, Paul. 1971. *Brulé: The Sioux people of the Rosebud.* Flagstaff, Ariz.: Northland Press. (106-7).

Edwards, F. Thomas. 1997a. "AIDS deaths among Native Americans drops by 32%." *In the Wind* 8(1): 1-2.

———. 1997b. "Review of *Trends in Indian Health*." *In the Wind* 8(2-3): 5.

Eggan, Dorothy. 1943. "The general problem of Hopi adjustment." *American Anthropologist* 45: 357-73. (368).

Eliade, Mircea. 1965. *Mephistopheles and the androgyne: Studies in religious myth and symbol.* New York: Sheed and Ward.

Elliott, T. C. 1914. "Journal of John Work, Sept. 7th-Dec. 14th, 1825." *Washington Historical Quarterly* 5(3): 163-91. (190).

Ellis, Havelock and John A. Symonds. [1896] 1897. *Sexual inversion.* London: Wilson and MacMillan. Originally published as *Das konträre Geschlechtsgefühl.* Leipzig: G.H. Wigand.

Elsasser, Albert B. 1978. "Wiyot." In *Handbook of North American Indians.* Vol. 8, ed. Robert F. Heizer, 155-63. Washington, D.C.: Smithsonian Institution. (159).

Ens, Gaspar. 1612. *Indiae Occidentalis historia: In qua prima regionum istarum detectio, situs, incolarum mores, aliaque eo pertinentia, breuiter explicantur.* Coloniae: Gulelm. Lutzenkirchen. (163).

Epple, Carolyn. 1991. "Beyond berdache: Navajo nádleeh as becoming again." Paper presented at the 90th Annual Meetings of the American Anthropological Association, Chicago, Ill.

———. 1996. "'That would be like lesbians': Male Navajo *nadleehi* descriptions of sexual partners." Paper presented at the 95th Annual Meetings of the American Anthropological Association, San Francisco, Calif.

————. 1997. "A Navajo worldview and *nádleehí*: Implications for Western categories. In *Two-spirit people: Native American gender identity, sexuality, and spirituality*, ed. Sue-Ellen Jacobs, Wesley Thomas, and Sabine Lang, 171-91. Urbana: University of Illinois Press.

Erikson, Erik H. 1945. "Childhood and tradition in two American Indian tribes." *Psychoanalytic Study of the Child* 1: 319-50. (329-30, 338-39).

Essene, Frank. 1942. "Culture element distributions 21: Round Valley." *University of California Anthropological Records* 8(1). (31, 65).

Etienne, Mona and Eleanor Leacock. 1980. *Women and colonization: Anthropological perspectives.* New York: Praeger.

Ewers, John C. 1948. "Gustavus Sohon's portraits of Flathead and Pend d'Oreille Indians, 1854." *Smithsonian Miscellaneous Collections* 110(7).

————. 1958. *The Blackfeet: Raiders on the northwest plains.* Norman: University of Oklahoma Press. (93, 100).

————. 1965. Deadlier than the male. *American Heritage* 16(4): 10-13.

Fages, Pedro. 1844. "Voyage en Californie." In *Nouvelles annales des voyages et des sciences géographiques.* Vol. 1 [= vol. 101, ser. 4, year 5], 145-82. Paris: Arthus Bertrand. (173).

————. 1972. *A historical, political, and natural description of California by Pedro Fages, soldier of Spain,* trans. Herbert I. Priestly. Ramona, Calif.: Ballena Press. (33).

Faris, James C. 1990. *The Nightway: A history and a history of documentation of a Navajo ceremonial.* Albuquerque: University of New Mexico Press. (183, 195, 214, 227).

Farrer, Claire R. 1997. "A 'berdache' by any other name. . . . is a brother, friend, lover, spouse: Reflections on a Mescalero Apache singer of ceremonies." In *Two-spirit people: Native American gender identity, sexuality, and spirituality,* ed. Sue-Ellen Jacobs, Wesley Thomas, and Sabine Lang, 236-51. Urbana: University of Illinois Press.

Fathauer, George H. 1951. "Religion in Mohave social structure." *Ohio Journal of Science* 51(5): 273-76.

————. 1954. "The structure and causation of Mohave warfare." *Southwestern Journal of Anthroplogy* 10(1): 97-118.

Fausto-Sterling, Anne. 1993. "The five sexes: Why male and female are not enough." *Sciences* 33(2): 20-25.

Faye, Paul-Louis. 1923. "Notes on the southern Maidu." *University of California Publications in American Archaeology and Ethnology* 20. (45).

Féray, Jean-Claude and Manfred Herzer. 1990. "Homosexual studies and politics in the 19th century: Karl Maria Kertbeny." *Journal of Homosexuality* 19(1): 23-47.

Fergusson, Erna. 1951. *New Mexico: A pageant of three peoples.* New York: Alfred A. Knopf.

Fewkes, W. Walter. 1892. "A few Tusayan pictographs." *American Anthropologist* 5(1): 9-26. (11).

Fiedler, Leslie A. 1968. *The return of the vanishing American.* New York: Stein and Day.

Finerty, John F. 1955. *War-path and bivouac: The Big Horn and Yellowstone expedition,* ed. Milo Milton Quaife. Lincoln: University of Nebraska Press.

Fire/Lame Deer, John and Richard Erdoes. 1972. *Lame Deer: Seeker of visions.* New York: Simon and Schuster. (149-50).

Fishler, Stanley A. 1953. *In the beginning: A Navaho creation myth.* Anthropology Papers 1, Department of Anthropology, University of Utah.

Flannery, Regina. 1939. *An analysis of Coast Algonquian culture.* Catholic University of America, Anthropological Series no. 7. Washington, D.C.: Catholic University of America Press. (129).

Fleming, E. McClung. 1968. "Symbols of the United States: From Indian queen to Uncle Sam." In *Frontiers of American Culture,* ed. Ray B. Browne et al., 1-24. Purdue University Studies.

Fletcher, Alice C. 1887. "The Elk Mystery or festival of the Ogallala Sioux." *Reports of the Peabody Museum of American Archeaology and Ethnology* 3(3) (*Report* 16 [1882]): 276-88. (281).

Fletcher, Alice C. and Francis La Flesche. 1911. "The Omaha tribe." *Bureau of American Ethnology Annual Report* 27. (132-33).

Fleurieu, C. P. Claret. [1798] 1801. *A voyage round the world performed during the years 1790, 1791, and 1792, by Étienne Marchand.* Vol. 1. London: Longman, Rees, Cadell, Davies. (370).

Font, Pedro. 1931. *Font's complete diary: A chronicle of the founding of San Francisco.* Trans. Herbert E. Bolton. Berkeley: University of California Press. (105).

Ford, Amy S. 1990. "The hooghan Mary and Willie built: A documentation." *The Messenger* [Wheelwright Museum of the American Indian, Santa Fe] (autumn): 8-11.

————. 1991. "The hooghan Mary and Willie built: A narrative." *The Messenger* (spring): 6-7.

Ford, Clellan S. 1941. *Smoke from their fires: The life of a Kwakiutl chief*. New Haven: Yale University Press. (68-69,129-32).

Ford, Clellan S. and Frank Beach. 1951. *Patterns of sexual behavior*. New York: Harper and Row. (130-31).

Forde, C. Daryll. 1931. "Ethnography of the Yuma Indians." *University of California Publications in American Archaeology and Ethnology* 28(4). (157).

Foreman, Carolyn T. 1954. *Indian women chiefs*. Washington, D.C.: Zenger Publishing.

Forgey, Donald G. 1975. "The institution of the berdache among the North American Plains Indians." *Journal of Sex Research* 11(1): 1-15.

Foster, George M. 1944. "A summary of Yuki culture." *University of California Anthropological Records* 5(3). (183, 186).

Foster, Stephen W. 1985. "A bibliography of homosexuality among Latin-American Indians." *The Cabirion and Gay Books Bulletin* 12: 17-19.

Foucault, Michel. [1978] 1980. *History of sexuality, volume I: An introduction*. New York: Vintage.

Fowler, Catherine S. and Lawrence E. Dawson. 1986. "Ethnographic basketry." In *Handbook of North American Indians*. Vol. 11, ed. Warren L. d'Azevedo, 705-37. Washington, D.C.: Smithsonian Institution. (732).

Franciscan Fathers. 1910. *An ethnologic dictionary of the Navaho language*. St. Michaels, Ariz.: Franciscan Fathers. (178, 292, 350).

Freiberg, Peter. 1991. "'We consider ourselves Indian first, and then gay or lesbian.'" *Washington Blade* (9 August): 1.

Frey, Rodney. 1987. The *world of the Crow Indians as driftwood lodges*. Norman: University of Oklahoma Press.

Fulton, Robert and Steven W. Anderson. 1992. "The Amerindian 'man-woman': Gender, liminality, and cultural continuity." *Current Anthropology* 33(5): 603-10.

Galante, Gary. 1980. "Crow lance cases and sword scabbards." *American Indian Art Magazine* 6(1): 64-73.

Galbraith, Edith C. 1924. "Malspina's voyage around the world." *California Historical Society Quarterly* 3(3): 216-37. (229).

García, Gregorio. [1607] 1729. *Origen de los Indios de el Nuevo Mundo, e averiguado con discurso de opiniones*, 2nd ed. Madrid: Francisco Martinez Abad. Originally published as *Origen de los Indios de el Nuevo Mundo, e Indias Occidentales*. Valencia: Pedrio Patricio Mey. (297).

Garcilasso de la Vega, el Inca. [1609] 1943. *Comentarios reales de los Incas*. 2 vols. Ed. Ángel Rosenblat. Buenos Aires: Emecé Editores.

Garraghan, Gilbert J. 1938. *The Jesuits of the middle United States*. Vol. 2. New York: America Press.

Gatschet, Albert S. 1890. "Dictionary of the Klamath language." *U.S. Geological Survey Contributions to North American Ethnology* 2(2). (581).

Gayton, Ana H. 1936. "Estudillo among the Yokuts: 1819." In *Essays in anthropology presented to A. L. Kroeber in celebration of his sixtieth birthday*, ed. Robert H. Lowie, 67-85. Berkeley: University of California Press. (81).

————. 1948. "Yokuts and Western Mono ethnography." *University of California Anthropological Records* 10(1-2). (31, 46, 106-7, 236, 274).

Gayton, Ana H. and Stanley S. Newman. 1940. Yokuts and Western Mono myths. *University of California Anthropological Records* 5(1). (34, 72, 73, 86-87, 96).

Gengle, Dean. 1976. "Gay American Indians." In *Gay American history: Lesbians and gay men in the U.S.A.*, ed. Jonathan Katz, 332-34. New York: Thomas Y. Crowell.

Gibbs, George, comp. 1853. "Journal of the expedition of Colonel Redick M'Kee, United States Indian Agent, through north-western California, performed in the summer and fall of 1851." In *Historical and statistical information respecting the history, condition and prospects of the Indian tribes of the United States*. Vol. 3, ed. Henry R. Schoolcraft, 99-177, 634. Philadelphia: Lippincott, Grambo. (115).

Gifford, Edward W. n.d.. "Central Miwok shamans." Ethnological document CU-23.1, Manuscript #179. University Archives, Bancroft Library, Berkeley.

————. 1916. "Miwok moieties." *University of California Publications in American Archaeology and Ethnology* 12(4). (163).

———. 1926. "Clear Lake Pomo society." *University of California Publications in American Archaeology and Ethnology* 18(2). (333).

———. 1931. "The Kamia of Imperial Valley." *Bureau of American Ethnology Bulletin* 97. (12, 56, 79-80).

———. 1932a. "The Northfork Mono." *University of California Publications in American Archaeology and Ethnology* 31(2). (44).

———. 1932b. "The southeastern Yavapai." *University of California Publications in American Archaeology and Ethnology* 29(3): 177-252.

———. 1933. "The Cocopa." *University of California Publications in American Archaeology and Ethnology* 31(5). (294).

———. 1936. "Northeastern and western Yavapai." *University of California Publications in American Archaeology and Ethnology* 34(4): 247-354. (296, 298).

———. 1940. "Culture element distributions 12: Apache-Pueblo." *University of California Anthropological Records* 4(1). (66, 163).

Gifford, Edward W. and Stanislaw Klimek. 1936. "Culture elements distributions II: Yana." *University of California Publications in American Archaeology and Ethnology* 37(2). (84).

Gifford, Edward W. and Alfred L. Kroeber. 1937. "Culture element distributions IV: Pomo." *University of California Publications in American Archaeology and Ethnology* 37(4). (153, 195-96).

Goddard, Ives. 1978. "Delaware." In *Handbook of North American Indians*. Vol. 15, ed. Bruce Trigger, 213-39. Washington, D.C.: Smithsonian Institution. (223, 231).

Goddard, Pliny E. 1933. "Navajo texts." *Anthropological Papers of the American Museum of Natural History* 34(1). (128-29).

Gogol, John M. 1983. "Klamath, Modoc, and Shasta basketry." *American Indian Basketry* 3 (2): 4-17. (13, 15).

Goldfrank, Esther S. 1951. "Observations on sexuality among the Blood Indians of Alberta, Canada." *Pscyhoanalysis and the Social Sciences* 3: 71-98.

Goldschmidt, Walter. 1951. "Nomlaki ethnography." *University of California Publications in American Archaeology and Ethnology* 42(4). (387).

Gould, Richard A. 1978. "Tolowa." In *Handbook of North American Indians*. Vol. 8, ed. Robert F. Heizer, 128-36. Washington, D.C.: Smithsonian Institution. (131, 134).

Goulet, Jean-Guy A. 1997. "The Northern Athapaskan 'berdache' reconsidered: On reading more than there is in the ethnographic record." In *Two-spirit people: Native American gender identity, sexuality, and spirituality*, ed. Sue-Ellen Jacobs, Wesley Thomas, and Sabine Lang, 45-68. Urbana: University of Illinois Press.

Grant, Peter. [1890] 1960. "The Sauteux Indians about 1804." In *Les Bourgeois de la Compagnie du Nord-Ouest: Récits de voyages, lettres et rapports inédits relatifs au nord-ouest canadien*. Vol. 2 , ed. L. R. Masson, 306-66. New York: Antiquarian Press. (357).

Gray, William H. 1913. "The unpublished journal of William H. Gray from December, 1836, to October, 1837." *Whitman College Quarterly* 16(2): 1-79. (46-47).

Green, Rayna. 1975. "The Pocahontas perplex: The image of Indian women in popular culture." *Massachussetts Review* 16: 678-714.

———. 1980. "Native American women." *Signs* 6(2): 248-67.

Greenberg, David F. 1986. "Why was the berdache ridiculed?" In *The many faces of homosexuality*, ed. Evelyn Blackwood, 179-90. New York: Harrington Park Press.

———. 1988. *The construction of homosexuality*. Chicago: University of Chicago Press, 1988.

Grinnell, George B. 1910. "Coup and scalp among the Plains Indians." *American Anthropologist* n.s. 12(2): 296-310. (306-7).

———. 1923. *The Cheyenne Indians: Their history and ways of life*. 2 vols. New Haven: Yale University Press. (1: 157; 2: 39-47, 287).

———. 1956. *The fighting Cheyennes*. Norman: University of Oklahoma Press. (237, 336).

Grosz, Elizabeth. 1994. *Volatile bodies: Toward a corporeal feminism*. Bloomington: Indiana University Press.

Grumet, Robert S. 1980. "Sunksquaws, shamans, and tradeswomen: Middle Atlantic Coastal Algonkian women during the 17th and 18th centuries." In *Women and colonization: Anthropological perspectives*, ed. Mona Etienne and Eleanor Leacock, 43-62. New York: Praeger.

Guerra, Francisco. 1971. *The pre-Columbian mind: A study in the aberrant nature of sexual drives, drugs affecting behaviour and the attitude towards life and death, with a survey of psychotherapy, in pre-Columbian America.* London/New York: Seminar.

Gunn, John M. 1916. *Schat-Chen: History, traditions and narratives of the Queres Indians of Laguna and Acoma.* Albuquerque: Albright and Anderson. (172-75).

Gutiérrez, Ramón. 1989. "Must we deracinate Indians to find gay roots?" *Out/Look* (winter): 61-67.

———. 1991. *When Jesus came, the Corn Mothers went away: Marriage, sexuality, and power in New Mexico, 1500-1846.* Stanford: Stanford University Press.

Guzmán, Nuño de. [1556] 1625. "The relation of Nunno di Gusman." In *Purchas his pilgrimes in five books,* part 4, ed. Samuel Purchas, 1556-1559. London: William Stansby for Henrie Fetherstone. Originally published as "Relation di Nunno di Gusman," in *Terzo volume delle navigationi et viaggi. . . . ,* ed. Giovanni Battista Ramusio, 331-39. Venice: Giunti. (1558).

Haile, Berard. 1933. "Navaho games of chance and taboo." *Primitive Man* 6(2): 35-45. (39).

———. 1949. *Emergence myth according to the Hanelthnayhe or Upward-Reaching Rite.* Rewritten by Mary C. Wheelwright. Navajo Religion Series 3. Santa Fe: Museum of Navajo Ceremonial Art.

———. 1950. *A stem vocabulary of the Navaho language.* Vol. 1. St. Michaels, Ariz.: St. Michaels Press. (136-38).

———. 1978. *Love-magic and Butterfly People: The Slim Curly version of the Ajiłee and Mothway myths.* Ed. Karl W. Luckert. American Tribal Religions 2. (82-90, 161-68, 171-72).

———. 1981. *Women versus men: A conflict of Navajo emergence.* Lincoln: University of Nebraska Press. (11,18-32).

Hall, Clyde [M. Owlfeather]. 1988. "Children of Grandmother Moon." In *Living the spirit: A gay American Indian anthology,* ed. Will Roscoe, 97-105. New York: St. Martin's.

———. 1997. "You anthropologist make sure you get your words right." In *Two-spirit people: Native American gender identity, sexuality, and spirituality,* ed. Sue-Ellen Jacobs, Wesley Thomas, and Sabine Lang, 272-75. Urbana: University of Illinois Press.

Hallowell, A. Irving. 1939. "Sin, sex and sickness in Saulteaux belief." *British Journal of Medical Psychology* 18(2): 191-97. (193-94).

———. 1955. *Culture and experience.* Philadelphia: University of Pennsylvania Press. (294-95, 303-4, 425).

Halperin, David M. 1990. *One hundred years of homosexuality and other essays on Greek love.* New York: Routledge.

Hammond, Rick. 1992. "Two-spirited people." *The Sacred Fire* (winter): n.p.

Hammond, William A. 1887. *Sexual impotence in the male and female.* Detroit: George S. Davis. (163-67).

Hanke, Lewis. 1949. *The Spanish struggle for justice in the conquest of America.* Philadelphia: University of Pennsylvania Press.

———. 1970. *Aristotle and the American Indians: A study in race prejudice in the modern world.* Bloomington: Indiana University Press.

Hanna, Warren L. 1986. *The life and times of James Willard Schultz (Apikuni).* Norman: University of Oklahoma Press.

Hanson, Les. 1992. "Indian men who have sex with men: A case study of the American Indian AIDS Institute of San Francisco." In *HIV prevention in Native American communities,* comp. Andrea G. Rush, 65-71. Oakland: National National American AIDS Prevention Center.

Haraway, Donna. 1991. *Simians, cyborgs, and women: The reinvention of nature.* New York: Routledge.

Harnum, Betty. 1995. "Where did the name ASAPI come from?" *Positively Native Newsletter* 2(8): n.p.

Harper, James William. 1968. "Hugh Lenox Scott: Soldier-diplomat, 1876-1917." Ph.D. dissertation, University of Virginia.

Harrington, John P. 1908. "A Yuma account of origins." *Journal of American Folk-lore* 21: 324-48.

———. 1942. "Culture element distributions 19: Central California coast." *University of California Anthropological Records* 7(1). (32, 45).

Harris, Curtis. 1991. "All night ride: One perspective on the health care crisis in the Native community in New York City." *Seasons* (summer): n.p.

Harris, Curtis and Leota Lone Dog. 1993. "Two spirited people: Understanding who we are as creation." *New York Folklore* 19 (1-2): 155-64.

Harwell, Henry O. and Marsha C. S. Kelly. 1983. "Maricopa." In *Handbook of North American Indians*. Vol. 10, ed. Alfonso Ortiz, 71-85. Washington, D.C.: Smithsonian Institution.

Hassrick, Royal B. 1964. *The Sioux: Life and customs of a warrior society*. Norman: University of Oklahoma Press. (50, 121, 133-35, 313-20).

Hauser, Raymond E. 1990. "The *Berdache* and the Illinois Indian tribe during the last half of the seventeenth century." *Ethnohistory* 37(1): 45-65.

Hay, Henry [Harry]. 1963. "The Hammond report." *One Institute Quarterly* 18: 6-21.

———. 1996. *Radically gay: Gay liberation in the words of its founder*, ed. Will Roscoe. Boston: Beacon.

Hayes, Daris. 1992. "PWA profile." *Seasons* (winter): n.p.

Hayne, Coe. 1929. *Red men on the Bighorn*. Philadelphia: Judson Press.

Heiman, Elliott and Cao Van Lê. 1975. "Transsexualism in Vietnam." *Archives of Sexual Behavior* 4(1): 89-95.

Hekma, Gert. 1994. "'A female soul in a male body': Sexual inversion as gender inversion in nineteenth-century sexology." In *Third sex, third gender: Beyond sexual dimorphism in culture and history*, ed. Gilbert Herdt, 213-39. New York: Zone.

Hennepin, Louis. 1697. *Nouvelle découverte d'un très grand pays situé dans l'Amérique. . . .* Utrecht: G. Broedelet.

———. [1698] 1903. *A new discovery of a vast country in America*. Vol. 2, ed. Reuben G. Thwaites. Reprint. Chicago: A. C. McClurg. (167-68, 653).

Henry, Alexander. 1897. *New light on the early history of the greater Northwest: The manuscript journals of Alexander Henry and of David Thompson, 1799-1814*. Vol. 1, ed. Elliott Coues. New York: Francis P. Harper. (53-54, 163-65, 348, 399).

Henshaw, Richard A. 1994. *Male and female, the cultic personnel: The Bible and the rest of the ancient Near East*. Princeton Theological Monograph Series 31. Allison Park, Penn.: Pickwick Publications.

Herdt, Gilbert. 1991. "Representations of homosexuality: An essay on cultural ontology and historical comparison, Part I." *Journal of the History of Sexuality* 1(3): 481-504.

———. 1994. "Introduction: Third sexes and third genders." In *Third sex, third gender: Beyond sexual dimorphism in culture and history*, ed. Gilbert Herdt, 21-81. New York: Zone.

Heriot, George. [1805] 1807. *Travels through the Canadas, containing a description of the picturesque scenery on some of the rivers and lakes. . . .* London: Richard Phillips.

Herrera y Tordesillas, Antonio de. [1601-15] 1991. *Historia general de los hechos de los castellanos en las Islas i Tierra Firme del Mar Oceano o "Decades" de Antonio de Herrera y Tordesillas*, ed. Mariano Cuesta Domingo. 4 vols. Madrid: Universidad Complutense de Madrid. Originally published Madrid: Juan Flameco y Juan de la Cuesta.

Herzer, Manfred. 1985. "Kertbeny and the nameless love." *Journal of Homosexuality* 12(3/4): 1-26.

Heyne, Christian G. 1779. "De maribus inter Scythas morbo effeminatis et de Hermaphroditis Floridae." *Commentationes Societatis Regiae Scientiarum Gottingensis per Annum 1778, Historicae et Philologicae Classis*. Vol. 1, 28-44. Göttingen: Joan. Christ. Dieterich.

Hicks, Frederic. 1974. "The influence of agriculture on aboriginal socio-political organization in the Lower Colorado River Valley." *Journal of California Anthropology* 1(2): 133-44.

Hill, Willard W. 1935. "The status of the hermaphrodite and transvestite in Navaho culture." *American Anthropologist* 37: 273-79.

———. 1938a. "Note on the Pima berdache." *American Anthropologist* 40: 338-40.

———. 1938b. "The agricultural and hunting methods of the Navaho Indians." *Yale University Publications in Anthropology* 18. (99, 126).

———. 1943. *Navaho humor*. General Series in Anthropology 9. Menasha, Wisc.: George Banta. (8, 12).

Hirschfeld, Magnus. 1910. *Die Transvestiten: Eine Untersuchung über den erotischen Verkleidungstrieb*. Berlin: Alfred Pulvermacher and Co.

Hodgen, Margaret T. 1964. *Early anthropology in the sixteenth and seventeenth centuries*. Philadelphia: University of Pennsylvania Press.

Hoebel, E. Adamson. 1960. *The Cheyennes: Indians of the Great Plains*. New York: Holt, Rinehart and Winston. (77-78, 96-97).

Hoijer, Harry, trans., Mary C. Wheelwright, and David P. McAllester. 1950. *Texts of the Navajo creation chant*. Cambridge: Peabody Museum of Harvard University.

Holder, A. B. 1889. "The bote: Description of a peculiar sexual perversion found among North American Indians." *New York Medical Journal* 50(23): 623-25.

Hollimon, Sandra E. 1996. "Sex, gender and health among the Chumash: An archaeological examination of prehistoric gender roles." *Proceedings of the Society for California Archaeology* 9: 205-8.

——. 1997. "The third gender in native California: Two-spirit undertakers among the Chumash and their neighbors." In *Women in prehistory: North America and Mesoamerica*, eds. Cheryl Claassen and Rosemary Joyce, 173-88. Philadelphia: University of Pennsylvania Press.

Holmberg, H. J. 1855. *Ethnographische skizzen über die völker des Russischen Amerika*, pt. 1. Helsinfors: H. C. Friis. (120-21).

Holt, Catherine. 1946. "Shasta ethnography." *University of California Anthropological Records* 3(4). (317).

Honigmann, John J. 1949. "Culture and ethos of Kaska society." *Yale University Publications in Anthropology* 40. (164-65).

——. 1954a. "The Kaska Indians: An ethnographic reconstruction." *Yale University Publications in Anthropology* 51. (129-30).

Howard, James H. 1965. "The Ponca tribe." *Bureau of American Ethnology Bulletin* 195. (142-43).

Howe, Helen. 1965. *The gentle Americans, 1864-1960: Biography of a breed*. New York: Harper and Row.

Hoxie, Frederick E. 1991. "Searching for structure: Reconstructing Crow family life during the reservation era." *American Indian Quarterly* 15: 287-309.

Hrdlička, Aleš. 1908. "Physiological and medical observations among the Indians of southwestern United States and northern Mexico." *Bureau of American Ethnology Bulletin* 34. (47, 51, 184).

Hudson, Travis, ed. 1979. *Breath of the sun: Life in early California as told by a Chumash Indian, Fernando Librado to John P. Harrington*. Banning, Calif.: Malki Museum Press. (40).

Hungry Wolf, Beverly. 1980. *The ways of my grandmothers*. New York: William Morrow. (62-68).

Hurdy, John Major. 1970. *American Indian religions*. Los Angeles: Sherbourne Press. (48-49).

Hyde, George E. 1937. *Red Cloud's folk: A history of the Oglala Sioux Indians*. Norman: University of Oklahoma Press. (147).

Hymes, Dell. 1980. "Commentary." In *Theoretical orientations in creole studies*, ed. Albert Valdman and Arnold Highfield, 389-423. New York: Academic.

Irving, Jr., John Treat. [1835] 1955. *Indian sketches taken during an expedition to the Pawnee tribes, 1833*. Ed. John F. McDermott. Norman: University of Oklahoma Press. (93-95).

Jackson, Donald, ed. 1978. *Letters of the Lewis and Clark expedition with related documents 1783-1854*, 2nd ed. Urbana: University of Illinois Press. (531).

Jacobi, A. 1937. "Carl Heinrich Mercks ethnographische Beobachtungen über die Völker des Beringsmeers 1789-91." *Baessler-Archiv* 20(3-4): 113-37. (122).

Jacobs, Sue-Ellen. 1983. "Comment on 'The North American Berdache.'" *Current Anthropology* 24(4): 459-60.

Jacobs, Sue-Ellen and Jason Cromwell. 1992. "Visions and revisions of reality: Reflections on sex, sexuality, gender, and gender variance." *Journal of Homosexuality* 23(4): 43-69. (54-56).

Jacobs, Sue-Ellen and Wesley Thomas. 1994. "Native American two-spirits." *Anthropology Newsletter* (November): 7.

Jacobs, Sue-Ellen, Wesley Thomas, and Sabine Lang, eds. 1997. *Two-spirit people: Native American gender identity, sexuality, and spirituality*. Urbana: University of Illinois Press.

Jacobsen, Thorkild. 1987. *The harps that once . . . : Sumerian poetry in translation*. New Haven: Yale University Press.

James, Edwin, comp. [1822] 1972. *Account of an expedition from Pittsburgh to the Rocky Mountains under the command of Major Stephen H. Long*. Barre, Mass.: Imprint Society. (82-83, 180).

James, Marjorie. 1937. "A note on Navajo pottery-making." *El Palacio* 43(13-14-15): 85-86.

Jaramillo, Gabriel G. 1953. "Francisco Coreal y su viaje a las Indias Occidentales." *Boletin de la Sociedad Geografica de Colombia* 11(1): 27-62.

Jochelson, Waldemar [Vladimir Iakalson]. 1933. *History, ethnology and anthropology of the Aleut*. Carnegie Institution of Washington Publication no. 432. Washington, D.C. (71).

Jones, Eugene H. 1988. *Native Americans as shown on the stage, 1753-1916*. Metuchen, N.J.: Scarecrow.

Jones, William. 1907. "Fox texts." *Publications of the American Ethnological Society* 1. (150-53, 314-33, 354-55).

Joseph, Alice, Rosamond B. Spicer, and Jane Chesky. 1949. *The desert people: A study of the Papago Indians.* Chicago: University of Chicago Press. (227).

Judd, Bertha Grimmell. 1927. *Fifty golden years: The first half century of the woman's American Baptist Home Mission Society, 1877-1927.* New York: Woman's American Baptist Home Mission Society.

Jung, C. G. 1968. *Psychology and alchemy,* 2d ed. Princeton: Princeton University Press.

Kahn, Eunice. 1990. "The White Spirit land: Sandpainting reproduction from the Blessingway." *The Messenger* (autumn): 11-12.

Karsch-Haack, Ferdinand. [1911] 1975. *Das gleichgeschlechtliche Leben der Naturvölker.* Reprint. New York: Arno Press. (314-15, 320-27, 564-66).

Keating, William H. 1825. *Narrative of an expedition to the source of St. Peter's River, Lake Winnepeck, Lake of the Woods, etc., etc. performed in the year 1823 under the command of Stephen H. Long Major U.S.T.E..* Vol. 1. Philadelphia: H. C. Carey. (221-22).

Kehoe, Alice B. 1976. "Old woman had great power." *Western Canadian Journal of Anthropology* 6(3): 69-76.

Kelly, William H. 1949. "The place of scalps in Cocopa warfare." *El Palacio* 56(3): 85-91.

———. 1977. "Cocopa ethnography." *Anthropological Papers of the University of Arizona* 29.

Kelly, Isabel T. 1932. "Ethnology of the Surprise Valley Paiute." *University of California Publications in American Archaeology and Ethnology* 31(3). (157-58).

———. 1964. "Southern Paiute ethnography." *University of Utah Anthropological Papers* 69. (100-101).

Kemp, William B. 1984. "Baffinland Eskimo." In *Handbook of North American Indians.* Vol. 5, ed. David Damas, 463-75. Washington, D.C.: Smithsonian Institution. (470-72).

Kennedy, Hubert. 1988. *Ulrichs: The life and works of Karl Heinrich Ulrichs, pioneer of the modern gay movement.* Boston: Alyson.

Kent, Kate P. 1985. *Navajo weaving: Three centuries of change.* Santa Fe: School of American Research Press.

Kent, Rockwell. 1935. *Salamina.* New York: Harcourt, Brace and Co. (29-30, 131, 294-97).

Kessler, Suzanne J., and Wendy McKenna. [1978] 1985. *Gender: An ethnomethodological approach.* Chicago: University of Chicago Press. (24-41).

Khera, Sigrid and Patricia S. Mariella. 1983. "Yavapai." In *Handbook of North American Indians.* Vol. 10, ed. Alfonso Ortiz, 38-54. Washington, D.C.: Smithsonian Institution.

King, Jeff. 1943. *Where the two came to their father: A Navaho war ceremonial.* New York: Pantheon Books.

Klah, Hasteen [Hastíin Klah]. 1938. *Tleji or Yehbechai myth.* Museum of Navajo Ceremonial Art Bulletin 1. Santa Fe: Museum of Navajo Ceremonial Art.

———. 1942. *Navajo creation myth: The story of the emergence,* comp. Mary C. Wheelwright. Navajo Religion Series. Vol. 1. Santa Fe: Museum of Navajo Ceremonial Art. (39-49,67-69).

———. 1946. *Hail Chant and Water Chant,* ed. Mary C. Wheelwright. Navajo Religion Series 2. Santa Fe: Museum of Navajo Ceremonial Art.

———. 1951. "Myth of the Mountain Chant." In *Myth of the Mountain Chant and Beauty Chant,* ed. Mary C. Wheelwright. Museum of Navajo Ceremonial Art Bulletin 5. Santa Fe: Museum of Navajo Ceremonial Art.

Klein, Laura P. and Lillian A. Ackerman, eds. 1995. *Women and power in native North America.* Norman: University of Oklahoma Press.

Kluckhohn, Clyde. 1979. "Myths and rituals: A general theory." In *Reader in comparative religion,* ed. William A. Lessa and Evon Z. Vogt. New York: Harper and Row.

Kluckhohn, Clyde and Dorothea Leighton. 1962. *The Navajo,* rev. ed. Garden City, N.Y.: Anchor Books, Doubleday.

Knapp, Frances and Rheta L. Childe. 1896. *The Thlinkets of southeastern Alaska.* Chicago: Stone and Kimball. (35-36).

Krafft-Ebing, Richard von. [1886] 1892. *Psychopathia sexualis mit besonderer Berücksichtigung der conträren Sexualempfindung: Eine klinisch-forensische Studie,* rev. ed. Stuttgart: Ferdinand Enke.

Kraft, Jens. 1766. *Die Sitten der Wilden, zur Aufklärung des Ursprungs und Aufnahme der Menschheit.* Kopenhagen: Mummischen Buchhandlung.

Krasheninnikov, Stepan P. [1755] 1872. *Explorations of Kamchatka, north Pacific scimitar: Report of a journey made to explore eastern Siberia in 1735-1741, by order of the Russian imperial government.* Trans. E. A. P. Crownhart-Vaughan. Portland: Oregon Historical Society.

Kroeber, Alfred L. 1902. "The Arapaho." *American Museum of Natural History Bulletin* 18. (19-20).

———. 1920. "California culture provinces." *University of California Publications in American Archaeology and Ethnology* 17(2): 151-69.

———. [1925] 1976. *Handbook of the Indians of California.* Reprint. New York: Dover. (46, 180, 497, 500-1, 647, 748-49).

———. 1932. "The Patwin and their neighbors." *University of California Publications in American Archaeology and Ethnology* 29(4). (272).

———, ed. 1935. "Walapai ethnography." *Memoirs of the American Anthropological Association* 42.

———. 1940. "Psychosis or social sanction." *Character and Personality* 3(3): 204-15. (209-11).

———. 1948. "Seven Mohave myths." *Anthropological Records* 11(1).

———. 1972. "More Mohave myths." *Anthropological Records* 27.

———. 1973. "A Mohave war reminiscence, 1854-1880." *University of California Publications in Anthropology* 10.

Kroeber, Theodora. 1970. *Alfred Kroeber: A personal configuration.* Berkeley: University of California Press.

Kurz, Rudolph F. 1937. "Journal of Rudolph Friederich Kurz." Ed. J. N. B. Hewitt. *Bureau of American Ethnology Bulletin* 115. (211, 213-14).

La Barre, Weston. 1970. *The ghost dance: Origins of religion.* Garden City, N.Y.: Doubleday.

La Salle, Robert Cavalier de. [1879] 1880. "An account of Hennepin's exploration in La Salle's letter of August 22, 1682." In *A description of Louisiana,* by Louis Hennepin, trans. John G. Shea. New York: John G. Shea. (368).

———. [1867] 1901. *Relation of the discoveries and voyages of Cavalier de La Salle from 1669 to 1681: The official narrative,* trans. Melville B. Anderson. Chicago: The Caxton Club. Originally published in *Relations et mémoires inédits pour servir l'histoire de la France dans les pays d'outre-mer . . .* , ed. Pierre Margry. Paris: Challamel aîné. (145, 146).

Lacombe, Alb. 1874. *Dictionnaire de la langue des Cris.* Montreal: C. O. Beauchemin. (164, 326).

Lafitau, Joseph François. [1724] 1974. *Customs of the American Indians compared with the customs of primitive times.* Trans. W. N. Fenton and E. L. Moore. Vol. 1. Toronto: Champlain Society. Originally published as *Mours des sauvages Amériquains: comparées aux mours des premiers temps.* Paris: Saugrain l'aîné.

Lahontan, Louis Armand de. [1703] 1705. *Memoires de l'Amérique Septentrionale, ou la suite des voyages de Mr. Le Baron La Hontan.* Vol. 2. Amsterdam: Jonas L' Honoré. (144).

———. 1905. *New voyages to North-America by Baron de Lahontan.* Vol. 2, ed. Reuben G. Thwaites. Chicago: A. C. McClurg. (462-63).

Lambert, Claude Francois. 1750. *Histoire générale, civile, naturelle, politique et religieuse de tous les peuples du monde.* Vol. 14. Paris: David. (149).

Lamphere, Louise. 1987. "Feminism and anthropology: The struggle to reshape our thinking about gender." In *The impact of feminist research in the academy,* ed. Christie Franham, 11-33. Bloomington: Indiana University Press.

Landes, Ruth. [1937] 1969. *Ojibwa sociology.* Reprint. New York: AMS Press. (54-55).

———. [1938] 1969. *The Ojibwa woman.* New York: Columbia University Press. (135-77, 179-80, 182, 184, 187).

———. 1968. *The Mystic Lake Sioux.* Madison: University of Wisconsin Press. (31-39, 49, 57, 66, 112-13, 123, 127-28, 206-7).

———. 1970. *The Prairie Potawatomi.* Madison: University of Wisconsin Press. (26, 36-37, 41, 183, 190-91, 195-202, 316).

Lang, Sabine. 1990. *Männer als Frauen—Frauen als Männer: Geschlechtsrollenwechsel bei den Indianern Nordamerikas.* Hamburg: Wayasbah-Verlag.

———. 1997. "Various kinds of two-spirit people: Gender variance and homosexuality in Native American commnities." In *Two-spirit people: Native American gender identity, sexuality, and spirituality,* ed. Sue-Ellen Jacobs, Wesley Thomas, and Sabine Lang, 100-18. Urbana: University of Illinois Press.

Langsdorff, Georg H. von. [1812] 1813. *Voyages and travels in various parts of the world in the years 1803 to 1807.* London: Henry Colburn. (47-48, 64).

Laqueur, Thomas. 1990. *Making sex: Body and gender from the Greeks to Freud*. Cambridge: Harvard University Press.

Las Casas, Bartolomé de. 1875. *Historia de las Indias*. Vols. 3, 5, ed. Marqués de la Fuensanta del Valle and D. José Sancho Rayon. Madrid: Miguel Ginesta.

Laubin, Reginald and Gladys Laubin. 1977. *Indian dances of North America: Their importance to Indian life*. Norman: University of Oklahoma Press. (365-67).

Laudonnière, Rene Goulaine de. [1586] 1904. In *The principal navigations, voyages, traffiques, and discoveries of the English nation. . . .* Vols. 8: 446-86, 9: 1-100, ed. Richard Hakluyt. Glasgow: James MacLehose and Sons. Originally published as *L' Histoire notable de la Floride située en Indies Occidentales, contenant les trois voyages faits en icelle par certains capitaines & pilotes francois. . . .* Paris: G. Auray. (8: 453; 9: 16, 56, 69).

le Corbeiller, Clare. 1961. "Miss America and her sisters." *Metropolitan Museum of Art Bulletin* 19(8): 209-223.

Le Moyne de Morgues, Jacques. 1591. *Brevis narratio eorum quae in Florida Americae provicina Gallis acciderunt, secunda in illam navigatione, duce Renato de Laudoniere classis praefaecto anno MDLXIIII; quae est secunda pars Americae*. Ed. Theodore de Bry. Frankfurt: Theodore de Bry. (Plates 17, 23).

———. 1965. "Narrative of Le Moyne." In *The new world: The first pictures of America made by John White and Jacques le Moyne and engraved by Theodore de Bry . . .*, rev. ed. Ed. Stefan Lorant. New York: Duell, Sloan and Pearce. (69, 81).

Leacock, Eleanor B. and Nancy O. Lurie, eds. 1971. *North American Indians in historical perspective*. New York: Random House.

Leighton, Dorothea and Clyde Kluckhohn. 1969. *Children of the people*. New York: Octagon Books. (78).

Lestringant, Frank. 1982. "Les séquelles littéraires de la Floride française: Laudonnière, Hakluyt, Thevet, Chauveton." *Bibliothèque d'humanisme et renaissance* 44: 7-36.

Lettres. 1781. *Lettres édifiantes et curieuses, écrites des missions étrangeres*, rev. ed. Vols 6-9, Mémoires d'Amérique. Paris: J. G. Merigot.

Lévi-Strauss, Claude. [1955] 1965. "The structural study of myth." In *Myth: A symposium*, ed. Thomas A. Sebeok, 81-106. Bloomington, Ind.: Indiana Unversity Press.

Lewis, Oscar. 1941. "Manly-hearted women among the North Piegan." *American Anthropologist* 43: 173-87.

Liberty, Margot. 1982. "Hell came with horses: Plains Indian women in the equestrian era." *Montana: The Magazine of Western History* 32 (3): 10-19.

Lincoln, Charles H. 1913. *Narratives of the Indians wars, 1675-1699*. New York: Charles Scribner's Sons. (12, 25, 34, 44-45, 48, 55, 96, 105, 125, 130, 150).

Lincoln, Jackson S. 1970. *The dream in primitive cultures*. New York: Johnson Reprint.

Linderman, Frank B. 1930. *American: The life story of a great Indian*. New York: John Day Company.

———. 1932. *Red mother*. New York: John Day Company.

Linton, Ralph. 1936. *The study of man*. New York: Appleton-Century-Crofts. (480).

———, ed. 1940. *Acculturation in seven American Indian tribes*. Gloucester, Mass.: Peter Smith.

Lisiansky, Urey. 1814. *A voyage round the world in the years 1803, 4, 5, & 6, performed by order of His Imperial Majesty Alexander the First, emperor of Russia, in the ship Neva*. London: John Booth. (199).

Little Thunder, Beverly. 1997. "I am a Lakota womyn." In *Two-spirit people: Native American gender identity, sexuality, and spirituality*, ed. Sue-Ellen Jacobs, Wesley Thomas, and Sabine Lang, 203-9. Urbana: University of Illinois Press.

Loeb, E. M. 1933. "The eastern Kuksu cult." *University of California Publications in American Archaeology and Ethnology* 33(2). (183).

Lombroso, Cesare. 1889. *L'uomo delinquente in rapporto all'antropologia, alla giurisprudenza ed alle discipline carcerarie*, 4th ed. Vol. 1. Turin: Fratelli Bocca.

López de Gómara, Francisco. [1552] 1922. *Historia general de las Indias*. Madrid: Calpe. Originally published as *La historia general de las Indias y Nueuo Mundo. . . .* Zaragoza: Agustín Millán.

Loskiel, George H. [1789] 1794. *History of the mission of the United Brethren among the Indians in North America*, trans. Christian I. LaTrobe. London: Brethren's Society for the Furtherance of the Gospel. (14).

Lowie, Robert H. 1909. "The Assiniboine." *Anthropological Papers of the American Museum of Natural History* 4(1). (42, 223).

———. 1912. "Social life of the Crow Indians." *Anthropological Papers of the American Museum of Natural History* 9(2). (226).

———. 1913. "Dance associations of the eastern Dakota." *Anthropological Papers of the American Museum of Natural History* 11(2). (118-19).

———. 1915. "The Sun Dance of the Crow Indians." *Anthropological Papers of the American Museum of Natural History* 16(1).

———. 1918. "Myths and traditions of the Crow Indians." *Anthropological Papers of the American Museum of Natural History* 25(1).

———. 1924b. "Notes on Shoshonean ethnography." *Anthropological Papers of the American Museum of Natural History* 20(3). (282-83).

———. 1935. *The Crow Indians.* New York: Farrar and Rinehart. (48, 312-13).

———. 1960. *Crow word lists: Crow-English and English-Crow vocabularies.* Berkeley: University of California Press.

Luckert, Karl W. 1975. *The Navajo hunter tradition.* Tucson: University of Arizona Press.

Lumholtz, Carl. 1912. *New trails in Mexico.* New York: Charles Scribner's Sons. (352-53).

Luomala, Katharine. 1978. "Tipai and Ipai." In *Handbook of North American Indians.* Vol. 8, ed. Robert F. Heizer, 592-609. Washington, D.C.: Smithsonian Institution.

Lurie, Nancy O. 1953. "Winnebago berdache." *American Anthropologist* 55: 708-12.

Lyon, William H. 1987. "Ednishodi Yazhe: The Little Priest and the understanding of Navajo culture." *American Indian Culture and Research Journal* 11(1): 1-41.

Mackenzie, Alexander. [1801] 1802. *Reisen von Montreal durch Nordwestamerika nach dem Eismeer und der Süd-See in den Jahren 1789 und 1793.* Hamburg: Benjamin Gottlob Hoffmann. Originally published as *Voyages from Montreal, on the River St. Laurence, through the continent of North America, to the frozen and Pacific Oceans in the years 1789 and 1793.* London: T. Cadell, Jun. and W. Davies. (108).

Malotki, Ekkehart, trans. 1995. *The bedbugs' night dance and other Hopi sexual tales: Mumuspi'yyungqa tuutuwutsi.* Lincoln: University of Nebraska Press for Northern Arizona University. (49-64).

Mandelbaum, David G. 1940. "The Plains Cree." *Anthropological Papers of the American Museum of Natural History* 37(2). (256-57).

Mandelbaum, May. 1938. "The individual life cycle." In *The Sinkaietk or southern Okanagon of Washington,* ed. Leslie Spier, 101-29. General Series in Anthropology 6. Menasha, Wisc.: George Banta. (119).

Manfred, Frederick. [1975] 1985. *The manly-hearted woman.* Lincoln: University of Nebraska Press.

Mantegazza, Paolo. [1885-86] 1932. *Love—the gigantic force.* Trans. James Bruce. New York: Anthropological Press (Falstaff Press). Originally published as *Gli amori degli uomini: Saggio di una etnologie dell'amore.* Milano.

Marquette, Jacques. [1681] 1900. "Of the first voyage made by Father Marquette toward new Mexico, and how the idea thereof was conceived." In *Travels and explorations of the Jesuit missionaries in New France, 1610-1791,* ed. Reuben G. Thwaites, 86-163. The Jesuit relations and allied documents 59. Cleveland: Burrows Brothers. Originally published as "Découverte de quelques pays et nations de l'Amérique Septentrionale," in *Recueil de voyages de Mr. Thévenot,* ed. Melchisedec Thévenot. Paris: Estienne Michallet. (128, 129, 309-10).

Martin, M. Kay and Barbara Voorhies. 1975. *Female of the species.* New York: Columbia University Press.

Mason, J. Alden. 1912. "The ethnology of the Salinan Indians." *University of California Publications in American Archaeology and Ethnology* 10(4). (164).

Masterson, James R. and Helen Brower. [1781] 1948. *Bering's successors 1745-1780: Contributions of Peter Simon Pallas to the history of Russian exploration toward Alaska.* Seattle: University of Washington Press. (59).

Matthews, Washington. 1877. "Ethnography and philology of the Hidatsa Indians." *United States Geological and Geographical Survey, Miscellaneous Publications* 7. (191).

———. 1897. "Navaho legends." *Memoirs of the American Folklore Society* 5. (70-72, 77, 86-87, 217, 220, 226).

———. 1902. "The Night Chant, a Navaho ceremony." *American Museum of Natural History Memoir* 6.

————. 1907. "Navaho myths, prayers, and songs." *University of California Publications in American Archaeology and Ethnology* 5. (58-60).

Maximilian (Prince of Wied), Alexander P. 1839-1841, 1906. *Reise in das innere Nord-America in den jahren 1832 bis 1834.* 2 vols. Koblenz: J. Hoelscher. (1: 401; 2: 132-33, 564). Translated as "Travels in the interior of North America, 1832-1834," in *Early western travels,* vols. 22 and 23, ed. Reuben G. Thwaites. Cleveland: Arthur H. Clark. (22: 354; 23: 283-84).

Maxwell, Gilbert S. 1984. *Navajo rugs: Past, present and future,* rev. ed. Santa Fe: Heritage Art.

Mayfield, Thomas J. 1993. *Indian summer: Traditional life among the Choinumne Indians of California's San Joaquin Valley.* Berkeley: Heyday Books and the California Historia Society. (107).

McAllester, David. 1941. "Water as a disciplinary agent among the Crow and Blackfoot." *American Anthropologist* 43: 593-604. (597).

McCoy, Isaac. 1840. *History of Baptist Indian missions, embracing remarks on the former and present condition of the aboriginal tribes.* . . . Washington, D.C. and New York: William M. Morrison and H. and S. Raynor. (360-61).

McDermott, John F. 1941. *A glossary of Mississippi Valley French, 1673-1850.* Washington University Studies, Language and Literature, n.s., 12. (22-23).

McGreevy, Susan. 1981. "Navajo sandpainting textiles at the Wheelwright Museum." *American Indian Art* 7(1): 55-85.

————. 1982. "Woven holy people: Navajo sandpainting textiles." In *Woven holy people: Navajo sandpainting textiles,* [8-14]. Santa Fe: Wheelwright Museum of the American Indian.

————. 1987a. "Journey towards understanding: A museum evolving." *The Messenger* (third quarter): n.p.

————. 1987b. "Journey towards understanding: Mary Cabot Wheelwright and Hastiin Klah." *The Messenger* (special edition): n.p.

McIlwraith, T. F. 1948. *The Bella Coola Indians.* 2 vols. Toronto: University of Toronto Press. (1: 45-46, 53, 265; 2: 148, 179, 188-94).

McIntosh, Mary. 1981. "The homosexual role." In *The making of the modern homosexual,* ed. Kenneth Plummer, 30-49. London: Hutchinson.

McKenney, Thomas L. 1827. *Sketches of a tour to the lakes, of the character and customs of the Chippeway Indians, and of incidents connected with the treaty of Fond du Lac.* Baltimore: Fielding Lucas, Jr. (315-16).

McKenney, Thomas L., and James Hall. [1838] 1933. *The Indian tribes of North America with biographical sketches and anecdotes of the principal chiefs.* Vol. 1, ed. Frederick W. Hodge. Edinburgh: John Grant. (120-24).

McKenzie, James. [1890] 1960. "The King's posts and journal of a canoe jaunt through the King's domains." In *Les bourgeois de la Compagnie du Nord-Ouest: Récits de voyages, lettres et rapports inédits relatifs au nord-ouest canadien.* Vol. 2, ed. L. R. Masson, 405-54. New York: Antiquarian Press. (414).

McLeod, Edith R. 1953. "White Cindy, mystery figure." *The Siskiyou Pioneer in Folklore, Fact and Fiction* 2(3): 32-34.

McNitt, Frank. 1962. *The Indian traders.* Norman: University of Oklahoma Press.

————. 1957. *Richard Wetherill: Anasazi.* Albuquerque: University of New Mexico Press.

Meacham, A. B. 1876. *Wi-ne-ma (the woman-chief) and her people.* Hartford: American Publishing.

Mead, Margaret. 1932. *The changing culture of an Indian tribe.* New York: Columbia University Press. (188-89).

————. 1961. "Cultural determinants of sexual behavior." In *Sex and internal secretions,* 3d ed. Vol. 2, ed. William C. Young, 1433-79. Baltimore: Williams and Wilkins. (1451-53).

————. 1963. *Sex and temperament in three primitive societies.* New York: William Morrow. (256, 293, 294-95, 304-5).

Medicine, Beatrice. 1983. "'Warrior women'—sex role alternatives for Plains Indian women." In *The hidden half: Studies of Plains Indian women,* ed. Patricia Albers and Beatrice Medicine, 267-80. Lanham, Md.: University Press of America. (270-74, 278).

Membré, Zenobius. [1691] 1903. "Narrative of the adventures of La Salle's party at Fort Crevecœur in Ilinois, from February 1680 to June 1681." In *Discovery and exploration of the Mississippi Valley,* ed. John G. Shea, 151-68. Albany: Joseph McDonough. (155).

Merck, Carl H. 1937. "Carl Heinrich Mercks ethnographische Beobachtungen über die Völker des Beringsmeers 1789-1791." Ed. A. Jacob. *Baessler-Archiv* 20 (3-4): 113-37. (122).

Michelson, Truman. 1925. "The mythical origin of the White Buffalo Dance of the Fox Indians." *Bureau of American Ethnology Annual Report* 40. (256-57).

Miller, Alfred Jacob. 1951. *The West of Alfred Jacob Miller.* Ed. Marvin C. Ross. Norman: University of Oklahoma Press. (90, 137).

Miller, Wick R., comp. 1972. *Newe natekwinappeh: Shoshoni stories and dictionary.* University of Utah Anthropological Papers 94. Salt Lake City: University of Utah Press.

Mills, Anson. 1918. *My story.* Ed. C. H. Claudy. Washington, D.C.: Privately printed.

Mirsky, Jeannette. 1937. "The Dakota." In *Cooperation and competition among primitive peoples,* ed. Margaret Mead, 382-427. New York: McGraw-Hill. (416-17).

Moll, Albert. [1891] 1899. *Die konträre Sexualempfindung,* rev. ed. Berlin: Bischer's Medicin.

Morfi, Juan Agustin de. [1770] 1932. *Excerpts from the Memorias for the history of the Province of Texas.* . . . Trans. Frederick C. Chabot. San Antonio: Privately published. (55).

Morgan, Lewis H. 1877. *Ancient society or researches in the lines of human progress from savagery, through barbarism to civilization.* New York: Henry Holt.

Morínigo, Marcos A. 1985. *Diccionario de Americanismos.* N.p.: Muchnik Editores.

Morris, C. Patrick. 1977. "Heart and feces: Symbols of mortality in the dying god myth." In *Flowers of the wind: Papers on ritual, myth and symbolism in California and the Southwest,* ed. Thomas C. Blackburn, 41-57. Socorro, N.M.: Ballena Press.

Morton, Donald. 1996. *The material queer: A LesBiGay cultural studies reader.* Boulder, Col.: Westview Press.

Mühlhäuser, Peter. 1980. "Structural expansion and the process of creolization." In *Theoretical orientations in creole studies,* ed. Albert Valdman and Arnold Highfield, 19-55. New York: Academic.

Müller, J. G. 1867. *Geschichte der Amerikanischen Urreligionen.* 2nd ed. Basel: Schweighauser.

Munroe, Robert L. and Ruth H. Munroe. 1977. "Male transvestism and subsistence economy." *Journal of Social Pscyhology* 103: 307-8.

Munroe, Robert, John W. Whiting, and David Hally. 1969. "Institutionalized male transvestism and sex distinctions." *American Anthropologist* 71: 87-91.

Murie, James R. 1914. "Pawnee Indian societies." *Anthropological Papers of the American Museum of Natural History* 11(7). (640).

Murray, Stephen O. 1983. "Fuzzy sets and abominations." *Man* 19: 396-99.

———. 1992. *Oceanic homosexualities.* New York: Garland Publishing.

———. 1995. *Latin American male homosexualities.* Albuquerque: University of New Mexico Press.

———. 1996. *American gay.* Chicago: University of Chicago Press.

Nabokov, Peter. 1967. *Two Leggings: The making of a Crow warrior.* New York: Thomas Y. Crowell.

Nanda, Serena. 1990. *Neither man nor woman: The hijra of India.* Belmont, Calif.: Wadsworth.

National Native American AIDS Prevention Center. 1995. *HIV-care models for American Indians, Alaska Natives, and native Hawaiians: Community and provider perspectives.* Oklahoma City: NAAPC Research and Dissemination Unit.

Needham, Rodney. 1983. *Against the tranquility of axioms.* Berkeley: University of California Press.

Newcomb, Franc J. 1940. *Navajo omens and taboos.* Santa Fe: Rydal Press.

———. 1949. "'Fire lore' in Navajo legend and ceremony." *New Mexico Folklore Record* 3. Albuquerque: New Mexico Folklore Society.

———. 1966. *Navaho neighbors.* Norman: University of Oklahoma Press.

———. 1964. *Hosteen Klah: Navaho medicine man and sand painter.* Norman: University of Oklahoma Press. (97).

Newcomb, Franc J., Stanley Fishler, and Mary C. Wheelwright. 1956. "A study of Navajo symbolism." *Papers of the Peabody Museum of Archaeology and Ethnology* 32(3).

Newcomb, W. W., Jr. 1961. *The Indians of Texas from prehistoric to modern times.* Austin: University of Texas Press. (51, 74, 301).

Newman, Stanley. 1958. "Zuni Dictionary." *Indiana University Research Center in Anthropology, Folklore, and Linguistics Publication* no. 6 and *International Journal of American Linguistics* 24(1), pt. 2.

Niethammer, Carolyn. 1977. *Daughters of the earth: The lives and legends of American Indian women.* New York: Collier Books. (229-32).

Olmstead, Virginia, trans. 1975. *Spanish and Mexican colonial censuses of New Mexico: 1790, 1823, 1845.* Albuquerque: New Mexico Genealogical Society. (156).

Olson, Ronald L. 1936. "The Quinault Indians." *University of Washington Publications in Anthropology* 6(1). (99).

———. 1940. "Social organization of the Haisla of British Columbia." *University of California Anthropological Records* 2(5). (199, 200).

Opler, Marvin K. 1963. "The southern Ute of Colorado." In *Acculturation in seven American Indian tribes*, ed. Ralph Linton, 119-206. Gloucester, Mass.: Peter Smith. (147).

———. 1967. *Culture and social psychiatry*. New York: Atherton Press. (252-53).

Opler, Morris E. [1941] 1965. *An Apache life-way: The economic, social, and religious institutions of the Chiricahua Indians*. Reprint. New York: Cooper Square. (79-80, 415-16).

———. 1969. *Apache odyssey: A journey between two worlds*. New York: Holt, Rinehart and Winston. (101-2).

Ortner, Sherry B. 1984. "Theory in anthropology since the sixties." *Comparative Studies in Society and History* 26: 126-66.

Osgood, Cornelius. 1940. "Ingalik material culture." *Yale University Publications in Anthropology* 22. (460).

———. 1958. "Ingalik social culture." *Yale University Publications in Anthropology* 53. (219, 261-63).

Oviedo, Gonzalo Fernandez de. [1535] 1959. *Historia general y natural de las Indias*. Vols. 1, 4, 5, ed. Juan Perez de Tudela Bueso. Madrid: Ediciones Atlas. Originally published as *La historia general de las Indias*. Seville.

Owen, Mary A. 1902. "Folk-lore of the Musquakie Indians of North America." *Publications of the Folklore Society* (London) 51. (54-55).

Palou, Francisco. [1787] 1977. *Biografía de Fray Junípero Serra, O.F.M., apóstol y civilizador de los Indios Pames de la Sierra Gorda de Méjico y de los de la Alta California (1713-1784)*. Mallorca: Palma. Originally published as *Relacion historica de la vida y apostolicas tareas del venerable Padre Fray Junipero Serra*. México: Don Felipe de Zúñiga y Ontiveros. (244-45)

———. [1787] 1913. *Life and apostolic labors of the venerable Father Junipero Serra*. Trans. C. Scott Williams. Pasadena: George Wharton James. (214-15).

Pareja, Francisco de. [1613] 1972. *Francisco Pareja's 1613* Confessionario: *A documentary source for Timucuan ethnography*. Ed. Jerald T. Milanich and William C. Sturtevant. Tallahassee, Fl.: Division of Archives, History, and Records Management, Florida Department of State. Originally published as *Confessionario en lengua Castellan y Timuquana*. Mexico: Diego Lopez Davalos. (39, 43, 75-76).

Parezo, Nancy J. 1982. "Navajo singers: Keepers of tradition, agents of change." In *Woven holy People: Navajo sandpainting textiles*, [15-22]. Santa Fe: Wheelwright Museum of the American Indian.

———. 1983. *Navajo sandpainting: From religious act to commercial art*. Tucson: University of Arizona Press.

Parrish, Rain. 1982. "Hosteen Klah and Mary Cabot Wheelwright: The founders, the founding." In *Woven holy people: Navajo sandpainting textiles*, [1-7]. Santa Fe: Wheelwright Museum of the American Indian.

———, et al. 1985. *I̧I̧ KÁÁH: The paintings that heal* [exhibit brochure]. Santa Fe: Wheelwright Museum of the American Indian.

Parsons, Elsie C. 1915. "Zuñi conception and pregnancy beliefs." *Proceedings of the Nineteenth International Congress of Americanists*, 379-83.

———. 1916. "The Zuñi ła'mana." *American Anthropologist* 18: 521-28.

———. 1918. "Notes on Acoma and Laguna." *American Anthropologist*, n.s., 20: 162-86. (181-82).

———. 1920. "Notes on ceremonialism at Laguna." *Anthropological Papers of the American Museum of Natural History* 19(4). (98-99, 101).

———. 1923. "Laguna genealogies." *Anthropological Papers of the American Museum of Natural History* 19(5). (166, 237, 248, 272).

———. 1926. "Tewa tales." *Memoirs of the American Folk-lore Society* 19. (191-92).

———. 1932. "Isleta, New Mexico." *Bureau of American Ethnology Annual Report* 47. (245-47).

———. 1939a. *Pueblo Indian religion*. 2 vols. Chicago: University of Chicago Press. (38, 53, 540, 765).

———. 1939b. "The last Zuñi transvestite." *American Anthropologist* 41(2): 338-40.

Patron, Eugene J. 1991. "Native Americans with AIDS struggle with bureaucratic red tape and little access to care." *The Advocate* no. 584 (27 August): 58-60.

Peltier, Anatole-Roger. 1991. *Paṭhamamūlaūī: The origin of the world in the Lan Na tradition*. Chiang Mai, Thailand: Suriwong Book Centre.

Penzer, N. M., ed. 1925. "Indian eunuchs." In *The ocean of story, Being C. H. Tawney's translation of Somadeva's Katha Sarit Sagara*. Vol. 3, trans. C. H. Tawney, 319-29. Delhi: Motilal Banarsidass.

Perrin du Lac, François Marie. 1805. *Voyage dans les deux Louisianes, et chez les nations sauvages du Missouri, par les Etats-Unis, l'Ohio et les Provinces qui le bordent, en 1801, 1802 et 1803. . . .* Paris: Capelle et Renand. (318, 352).

Peter Martyr [Pietro Martire d'Anghiera]. [1516] 1966. "De Orbe Novo Petri Martyris ab Angleria, mediolanensis protonotarii Caesaris senatoris Decades." *Opera*. Facsimile edition. Graz: Akademische Druck and Verlagsanstalt. Originally published as *De rebus oceanis et Orbe Novo Decades tres. . . .* Alcalá de Henares: Arnaldi Guillelmi.

Peterson, Jacqueline and Laura Peers. 1993. *Sacred encounters: Father De Smet and the Indians of the Rocky Mountain West*. Norman: Washington State University in association with the University of Oklahoma Press. (72, 73).

Petter, Rodolphe C. 1915. *English-Cheyenne dictionary*. Kettle Falls, Wash. (1116).

Petzoldt, William A. 1928. "Crow Indian weddings." *Watchman-Examiner* 16(47) (November 22): 1490.

———. 1932. "From the war-path to the Jesus trail: Being a record of thirty years of missionary service among the Crow Indians in Montana." In *The moccasin trail*. Philadelphia: Judson Press.

Pierce, Richard A. 1978. *The Russian Orthodox religious mission in America, 1794-1837, with materials concerning the life and works of the Monk German, and ethnographic notes by the Hieromonk Gedeon*, trans. Colin Bearne. Materials for the Study of Alaska History 11. Kingston, Ont.: Limestone Press. (121, 135).

Pilling, Arnold R. 1993. "Zuni men-women and the U.S. Census." Unpubl. ms.

———. 1997. "Cross-dressing and shamanism among selected western North American tribes." In *Two-spirit people: Native American gender identity, sexuality, and spirituality*, ed. Sue-Ellen Jacobs, Wesley Thomas, and Sabine Lang, 69-100. Urbana: University of Illinois Press.

Plummer, Kenneth, ed. 1981. *The making of the modern homosexual*. London: Hutchinson.

Point, Nicolas. 1967. *Wilderness kingdom: Indian life in the Rocky Mountains, 1840-1847, the journals and paintings of Nicolas Point, S.J.* Trans. Joseph P. Donnelly. New York: Holt, Rinehart and Winston. (158, 192).

Poirier, Guy. 1993a. "French renaissance travel accounts: Images of sin, visions of the New World." *Journal of Homosexuality* 25: 215-29.

———. 1993b. "Marc Lescarbot au pays des Ithyphalles." *Renaissance and Reformation* 17: 73-85.

Polk, Earl. 1991. "Traditional teachings and the prevention of high risk behavior." *Seasons* (fall): n.p.

Poncins, Gontran de. 1941. *Kabloona*. New York: Reynal and Hitchcock. (135-38).

Porter, Joseph C. 1986. *Paper medicine man: John Gregory Bourke and his American West*. Norman: University of Oklahoma Press. (92-93, 195, 197).

Powell, Peter J. 1981. *People of the sacred mountain: A history of the northern Cheyenne chiefs and warrior societies, 1830-1879*. New York: Harper and Row. (134, 455, 666).

Powers, Marla N. 1986. *Oglala woman: Myth, ritual, and reality*. Chicago: University of Chicago Press. (16-17).

Powers, Stephen. [1877] 1976. *Tribes of California*. Berkeley: University of California Press. (132, 133, 345).

Powers, William K. 1963. "A winter count of the Oglala." *American Indian Tradition* 9(1): 27-37. (31, 35).

———. 1977. *Oglala religion*. Lincoln: University of Nebraska Press. (38, 58-59).

Radin, Paul. 1972. *The trickster: A study in American Indian mythology*. New York. Schocken.

Raudot, Antoine D. 1940. "Memoir concerning the different Indian nations of North America." In *The Indians of the western Great Lakes, 1615-1760*, ed. W. Vernon Kineitz, 339-410. Ann Arbor: University of Michigan Press. (388-89).

Ray, Verne F. 1932. "The Sanpoil and Nespelem." *University of Washington Publications in Anthropology* 5. (148).

———. 1963. *Primitive pragmatists: The Modoc Indians of Northern California*. Seattle: University of Washington Press. (43).

Reichard, Gladys A. [1928] 1969. *Social life of the Navajo Indians*. Reprint. New York: AMS Press. (150).

———. [1936] 1968. *Navajo shepherd and weaver*. Reprint. Glorieta, NM: Rio Grande Press. (161).

———. [1939] 1977. *Navajo medicine man sandpaintings*. Reprint. New York: Dover Publications.

———. 1944a. "Individualism and mythological style." *Journal of American Folkore* 57(223): 16-25.

———. 1944b. *The story of the Navajo Hail Chant*. New York: Gladys A. Reichard.

———. [1974] 1983. *Navaho religion: A study of symbolism*. Tucson: University of Arizona Press. (140-42, 309-10, 386-90, 433).

Reynolds, S. G. 1905. "Report of Crow Agency." *Annual Reports of the Department of the Interior for the Fiscal Year Ended June 30, 1904, Indian Affairs, Part I, Report of the Commissioner*. Washington: Government Printing Office.

Riebeth, Carolyn R. 1985. *J. H. Sharp among the Crow Indians 1902-1910: Personal memories of his life and friendships on the Crow Reservation in Montana*. El Segundo, Calif.: Upton and Sons.

Riggs, Stephan R. 1890. "A Dakota-English dictionary." Ed. J. Owen Dorsey. *U.S. Geologic Survey, Contributions to North American Ethnology* 7. (577).

Robertson, Carol E. 1989. The *māhu* of Hawai'i (an art essay). *Feminist Studies* 15(2): 313-26.

Robinson, Sherry. 1997. "Lozen: Apache woman warrior." *Wild West* (June): 52-56, 81-82.

Robles, Jennifer J. 1992. "Tribes and tribulations." *Advocate* 616 (November): 40-44.

Rockwell, Kent. 1935. *Salamina*. New York: Harcourt, Brace, and Company. (29-30, 131, 294-97).

Rodee, Marian E. 1981. *Old Navajo rugs: Their development from 1900 to 1940*. Albuquerque: University of New Mexico Press.

———. 1982. "Navajo ceremonial-pattern weaving and its relationship to drypainting." In *Navaho religion and culture: Selected views*, ed. David M. Brugge and Charlotte J. Frisbie, 68-74. Museum of New Mexico Papers in Anthropology 17. Santa Fe.

Rodgers, Bruce. 1979. *Gay talk: A (sometimes outrageous) dictionary of gay slang*. New York: Paragon.

Rodriguez de Montalvo, Garci. 1992. *The labors of the very brave Knight Esplandian*. Trans. William T. Little. Binghamton, N.Y.: Center for Medieval and Early Renaissance Studies, State University of New York at Binghamton.

Roessel, Jr., Robert A. 1980. *Pictorial history of the Navajo from 1860 to 1910*. Rough Rock, Ariz.: Navajo Curriculum Center, Rough Rock Demonstration School.

Róheim, Géza. 1932. "Psycho-analysis of primitive cultural types." *International Journal of Psycho-analysis* 13(1-2): 1-224.

Romans, Bernard. [1775] 1961. *A concise natural history of east and west Florida*. New Orleans: Pelican Publishing. (46, 47).

Rosaldo, Renato. 1989. *Culture and truth: The remaking of social analysis*. Boston: Beacon.

Roscoe, Will. 1987a. "A bibliography of berdache and alternative gender roles among North American Indians." *Journal of Homosexuality* 14(3/4): 81-171.

———. 1987b. "Living the tradition: Gay American Indians." In *Gay spirit: Myth and meaning*, ed. Mark Thompson, 69-77. New York: St. Martin's.

———. 1988a. "Making history: The challenge of lesbian and gay studies." *Journal of Homosexuality* 15(3/4): 1-40.

———. 1988b. "The Zuni man-woman: A traditional philosophy of gender." *Out/Look* 1(2): 56-67.

———, ed. 1988c. *Living the spirit: A gay American Indian anthology*. New York: St. Martin's.

———. 1991. *The Zuni man-woman*. Albuquerque: University of New Mexico Press.

———. 1994. "How to become a Berdache: Toward a unified analysis of multiple genders." In *Third sex, third gender: Beyond sexual dimorphism in culture and history*, ed. Gilbert Herdt, 329-72. New York: Zone.

———. 1995a. *Queer spirits: A gay men's myth book*. Boston: Beacon Press.

———. 1995b. "Maurice Kenny" and "Native North American literature." In *The gay and lesbian literary heritage: A reader's companion to the writers and their works, from antiquity to the present*, ed. Claude Summers, 419-20, 513-16. New York: Norton.

———. 1995c. "Was We'wha a homosexual?: Native American survivance and the two-spirit tradition." *GLQ: A Journal of Lesbian/Gay Studies* 2(3): 193-235.

———. 1995d. "'Strange Craft, Strange History, Strange Folks': Cultural Amnesia and the Case for Lesbian/Gay Studies." *American Anthropologist* 97(3): 448-53.

———. 1996a. "Priests of the goddess: Gender transgression in ancient religions." *History of Religions* 35(3): 295-330.

———. 1996b. "Writing queer cultures: An impossible possibility?" In *Out in the field: Reflections of lesbian and gay anthropologists*, ed. Ellen Lewin and William L. Leap, 200-11. Urbana: University of Illinois Press.

Rountree, Helen C. 1989. *The Powhatan Indians of Virginia: Their traditional culture.* Norman: University of Oklahoma Press.

Rowell, Ron. 1991. "Confidentiality is an essential ingredient in quality assurance: An editorial." *Seasons* (spring): n.p.

———. 1996. *HIV Prevention for gay/bisexual/two-spirit men: A report of the National Leadership Development Workgroup for Gay/Bisexual/Two-spirit Native American Men.* Oakland: National Native American AIDS Prevention Center.

———. 1997. "Developing AIDS services for Native Americans: rural and urban contrasts." In *Two spirit people: American Indian lesbian women and gay men*, ed. Lester Brown, 85-95. New York: Harrington Park Press.

Rubin, Gayle. 1975. "The traffic in women: Notes on the 'political economy' of sex." In *Toward an anthropology of women*, ed. Rayna R. Reiter, 157-210. New York: Monthly Review Press.

Rushing, W. Jackson. 1995. *Native American art and the New York avant-garde.* Austin: University of Texas Press.

Russell, Howard S. 1980. *Indian New England before the Mayflower.* Hanover, NH: University Press of New England.

Sabin, Joseph. 1868-1936. *Biblioteca Americana: A dictionary of books relating to America, from its discovery to the present time.* New York.

Sahlins, Marshall. 1985. *Islands of time.* Chicago: University of Chicago Press.

Saladin d'Anglure, Bernard. 1984. "Inuit of Quebec." In *Handbook of North American Indians.* Vol. 5, ed. David Damas, 476-507. Washington, D.C.: Smithsonian Institution. (494, 497).

———. 1986. "Du fœtus au chamane: la construction d'un 'troisième sexe.'" *Etudes Inuit/Inuit Studies* 10(1-2): 25-114. Reprinted in *Amerindian rebirth: Reincarnation belief among North American Indians and Inuit*, ed. Antonia Mills and Richard Slobodin, 82-106. Toronto: University of Toronto Press, 1994.

———. 1992. "Le 'troisième' sexe." *Ethnologie* 23: 836-44.

Saletore, R. N. 1974. *Sex life under Indian rulers.* Delhi: Hind.

San Antonio, Gabriel Quiroga de. 1914. *Breve et veridique relation des evenements du Cambodge, par Gabriel Quiroga de San Antonio, de l'Ordre de Saint Dominique.* Trans. Antoine Cabaton. Paris: E. Leroux.

Sanders, G. M. 1972. "Gallos." In Vol. 8, *Reallexikon für Antike und Christentum*, 984-1034. Stuttgart.

Sandner, Donald. 1979. *Navaho symbols of healing.* New York: Harcourt Brace Jovanovich. (38, 78, 114-17).

Santamaria, Francisco J. 1959. *Diccionario de Mejicanismos.* Mexico: Porrua.

Sapir, Edward. 1931. "Southern Paiute dictionary." *Proceedings of the American Academy of Arts and Sciences* 65(3). (576).

Sapir, Edward and Leslie Spier. 1943. "Notes on the culture of the Yana." *University of California Anthropological Records* 3(3). (275).

Sarytschew, Gawrila [Gavriil A. Sarychev]. 1806. *Account of a voyage of discovery to the north-east of Siberia, the frozen ocean, and the north-east sea.* Vol. 2. London: Richard Phillips. (16).

Sauer, Carl O. 1971. *Sixteenth century North America: The land and the people as seen by the Europeans.* Berkeley: University of California Press.

Sauer, Martin. 1802. *An account of a geographical and astronomical expedition to the northern parts of Russia . . . by Commodore Joseph Billings in the years 1785, &c. to 1794.* London: T. Cadell, Jun. and W. Davies. (160, 176).

Sawyer, Jesse O. 1988. "Were there Wappo berdache?" *Society of Lesbian and Gay Anthropologists Newsletter* 10(3): 10-12.

Saxton, Dean and Lucille Saxton. 1969. *Dictionary: Papago and Pima to English, English to Papago and Pima.* Tucson: University of Arizona Press. (11, 73).

Schaeffer, Claude E. 1965. "The Kutenai female berdache: Courier, guide, prophetess, and warrior." *Ethnohistory* 12(3): 193-236.

Schlegel, Alice. 1977. "Male and female in Hopi thought and action." In *Sexual stratification: A cross-cultural view*, ed. Alice Schlegel, 245-69. New York: Columbia University Press.

————. 1990. "Gender meanings: General and specific." In *Beyond the second sex: New directions in the anthropology of gender*, ed. Peggy R. Sanday and Ruth G. Goodenough, 23-41. Philadelphia: University of Pennsylvania Press.

Schmitt, Martin F., ed. 1946. *General George Crook: His autobiography*. Norman: University of Oklahoma Press.

Schneider, David M. 1961. "Introduction: The distinctive features of matrilineal descent groups." In *Matrilineal kinship*, ed. David M. Schnieder and Kathleen Gough, 1-29. Berkeley: University of California Press.

Schroeder, Albert H. 1979. "Prehistory: Hakataya." In *Handbook of North American Indians*. Vol. 9, ed. Alfonso Ortiz, 100-7. Washington, D.C.: Smithsonian Institution.

Schultz, James W. 1916. *Blackfeet tales of Glacier National Park*. Boston: Houghton Mifflin. (12-20).

————. 1919. *Running Eagle: The warrior girl*. Boston: Houghton Mifflin. (11, 38, *passim*).

————. 1926. *Signposts of adventure: Glacier National Park as the Indians know it*. Boston: Houghton Mifflin. (100-2, 117, 140).

————. 1962. *Blackfeet and buffalo*. Norman: University of Oklahoma Press. (228-30, 348-50).

————. 1984. *The story of Running Eagle: Pi'tamaka as told by Tail-Feathers-Coming-Over-the-Hill*. Ed. Jon Allan Reyhner, 1-12. Heart Butte, Mont.: Bilingual Education Program.

Schwartz, Warren E. 1989. *The last contrary: The story of Wesley Whiteman (Black Bear)*. Sioux Falls, S.D.: Center for Western Studies, Augustana College. (88-89).

Scott, Cynthia. 1988. "Historic conference for American Indians held locally." *Equal Time* (Minneapolis) (6 July): 8.

Scott, Hugh L. 1928. *Some memories of a soldier*. New York: The Century Co.

Scott, Joan W. 1986. "Gender: A useful category of historical analysis." *American Historical Review* 91: 1053-75.

Segal, Charles M. and David C. Stineback. 1977. *Puritans, Indians and manifest destiny*. New York: G. P. Putnam's Sons.

Sepúlveda, Juan Ginés de. 1941. *Tratado sobre las justas causus de la guerra contra los Indios*, trans. Marcelino Menendez y Pelayo. Mexico: Fonda de Cultura Economica.

Seward, Georgene H. 1946. *Sex and the social order*. New York: McGraw-Hill. (112-24).

Shapiro, Judith. 1991. "Transsexualism: Reflections on the persistence of gender and the mutability of sex." In *Body Guards: The cultural politics of gender ambiguity*, ed. Julia Epstein and Kristina Straub, 248-79. New York: Routledge.

Shimkin, Demitri B. 1947. "Childhood and development among the Wind River Shoshone." *University of California Anthropological Records* 5(5). (298).

Simms, S. C. 1903. "Crow Indian hermaphrodites." *American Anthropologist*, n.s., 5: 580-81.

Skinner, Alanson. 1911. "Notes on the eastern Cree and northern Saulteaux." *Anthropological Papers of the American Museum of Natural History* 9(1). (151-52).

————. 1913. "Social life and ceremonial bundles of the Menomini Indians." *Anthropological Papers of the American Museum of Natural History* 13(1). (34).

————. 1914. "Political organization, cults, and ceremonies of the Plains-Ojibway and Plains-Cree Indians." *Anthropological Papers of the American Museum of Natural History* 11(6). (485-86).

Smith, Anne M. Cooke. 1974. "Ethnography of the Northern Utes." *Museum of New Mexico Papers in Anthropology* 17. (149-50).

Smith, Preserved. 1962. *The Enlightenment, 1687-1776*. New York: Collier.

Smith, Watson and John M. Roberts. 1954. "Zuni law: A field of values." *Papers of the Peabody Museum of American Archaeology and Ethnology* 43(1).

Smithson, Carma L. and Robert C. Euler. 1964. "Havasupai religion and mythology." *University of Utah Anthropological Papers* 68.

Smits, David D. 1982. "The 'squaw drudge': A prime index of savagism." *Ethnohistory* 29(4): 281-306.

Snelling, William J. [1830] 1971. *Tales of the Northwest*. Minneapolis: Ross and Haines. (27, 238).

Snow, Jeanne H. 1981. "Ingalik." In *Handbook of North American Indians*. Vol. 6, ed. June Helm, 602-17. Washington, D.C.: Smithsonian Institution. (611).

Sobol, Rose. 1976. *Woman chief*. Pinebrook, N.J.: Laurel-Leaf Library, Dell Books.

Solís de Merás, Gonzalo. [1893] 1923. *Pedro Menéndez de Avilés, adelanto governor and captain-general of Florida: Memorial*. Trans. Jeannette T. Connor. Publications of the Florida State Historical Society 3. Deland, Fl.: Florida State History Society. (180-81).

Spencer, Katherine. 1947. "Reflection of social life in the Navaho origin myth." *University of New Mexico Publications in Anthropology* 3. (20, 25-26, 28-30, 36, 73, 75, 98-100, 124).

———. 1957. "An analysis of Navaho Chantway myths." *Memoirs of the American Folklore Society* 48. (81, 101-4, 107, 149, 226, 228-30).

Spencer, Robert F. 1959. "The North Alaska Eskimo: A study in ecology and society." *Bureau of American Ethnology Bulletin* 171.

Spencer, Robert F., Jesse D. Jennings, et al. 1965. *The Native Americans*. New York: Harper and Row. (373).

Spicer, Edward H. 1961. "Types of contact and processes of change." In *Perspectives in American Indian culture change*, ed. Edward H. Spicer, 517-44. Chicago: University of Chicago Press.

———. 1971. "Persistent cultural systems: A comparative study of identity systems that can adapt to contrasting environments." *Science* 174: 795-800.

Spier, Leslie. 1928. "Havasupai ethnography." *Anthropological Papers of the American Museum of Natural History* 29(3).

———. 1930. "Klamath ethnography." *University of California Publications in American Archaeology and Ethnology* 30. (51-53).

———. 1933. *Yuman tribes of the Gila River*. Chicago: University of Chicago Press. (6, 242-43, 254).

———. 1935. *The Prophet Dance of the Northwest and its derivatives: The source of the Ghost Dance*. General Series in Anthropology 1. Menasha, Wisc.: George Banta. (26-27).

Spier, Leslie, and Edward Sapir. 1930. "Wishram ethnography." *University of Washington Publications in Anthropology* 3(3). (220-21).

Spiro, Melford. 1978. *Burmese supernaturalism*, rev. ed. Philadelphia: Insitute for the Study of Human Issues.

St. Cosme, J. F. Buisson de. [1861] 1917. "The voyage of St. Cosme, 1698-1699." In *Early narratives of the Northwest*, ed. Louise P. Kellogg, 335-62. New York: Charles Scribner's Sons. (360).

Stellers, Georg W. 1774. *Beschreibung von dem Lande Kamtschatka*. Frankfurt and Leipzig: Johann George Fleischer.

Stephen, Alexander M. 1929. "Hopi tales." *Journal of American Folklore* 42: 1-72. (34-35).

———. 1930. "Navajo origin legend." *Journal of American Folklore* 43: 88-104. (100).

———. 1936. *The Hopi journals of Alexander M. Stephen*. 2 vols. Ed. Elsie Clews Parsons. New York: Columbia University Press. (276, 1222).

Stern, Theodore. 1965. *The Klamath tribe: A people and their reservation*. American Ethnological Society Monograph 41. Seattle: University of Washington Press. (20, 24, 114).

Stevenson, Matilda C. 1904. "The Zuñi Indians: Their mythology, esoteric societies, and ceremonies." *Bureau of American Ethnology Annual Report* 23. (37-38).

Steward, Julian H. 1933. "Ethnography of the Owens Valley Paiute." *University of California Publications in American Archaeology and Ethnology* 33(3). (238).

———. 1941. "Culture element distributions 13: Nevada Shoshoni." *University of California Anthropological Records* 4(2). (252-53, 312).

———. 1943. "Culture element distributions 23: Northern and Gosiute Shoshoni." *University of California Anthropological Records* 8(3). (265, 338, 385).

Stewart, Kenneth M. 1947. "Mohave warfare." *Southwestern Journal of Anthropology* 3(3): 257-78.

———. 1983. "Mohave." In *Handbook of North American Indians*. Vol. 10, ed. Alfonso Ortiz, 55-70. Washington: Smithsonian Institution.

Stewart, Omer C. 1941. "Culture element distributions 1: Northern Paiute." *University of California Anthropological Records* 4(3). (405, 421, 440).

———. 1944. "Culture element distributions 28: Ute-Southern Paiute." *University of California Anthropological Records* 6(4). (298, 332).

———. 1960. "Homosexuality among the American Indians and other native peoples of the world." *Mattachine Review* 6(2): 13-19. (13-14).

Stewart, William George Drummond [anon.]. 1846. *Altowan: Or, incidents of life and adventure in the Rocky Mountains*. Vol. 1, ed. J. Watson Webb. New York: Harper and Brothers. (53-55).

Stirling, Matthew W. 1942. "Origin myth of Acoma and other records." *Bureau of American Ethnology Bulletin* 135. (70).

Stockel, H. Henrietta. 1993. *Survival of the spirit: Chiricahua Apaches in captivity*. Reno: University of Nevada Press.

Stoller, Paul. 1979. "Social interaction and the development of stabilized pidgins." In *Readings in creole studies*, ed. Ian F. Hancock, 69-79. Ghent: E. Story-Scientia.

Stoller, Robert J. 1976. "Two feminized male American Indians." *Archives of Sexual Behavior* 5(6): 529-38.

Stone, Sandy. 1991. "The empire strikes back: A posttranssexual manifesto." In *Body guards: The cultural politics of gender ambiguity*, ed. Julia Epstein and Kristina Straub, 280-304. New York: Routledge.

Strachey, William. 1953. *The historie of travell into Virginia Britania (1612)*. Ed. Louis B. Wright and Virginia Freund. London: Hakluyt Society. (113, 206).

———. 1969. *For the colony in Virginea Britannia lawes divine, morall and martiall, etc.* Ed. David H. Flaherty. Charlottesville: University of Virginia Press.

Swanton, John R. 1922. "Early history of the Creek Indians and their neighbors." *Bureau of American Ethnology Bulletin* 73. (373).

———. 1928a. "Aboriginal culture of the Southeast." *Bureau of American Ethnology Annual Report* 42. (697, 700).

———. 1928b. "Social organization and social usages of the Indians of the Creek Confederacy." *Bureau of American Ethnology Annual Report* 42. (364).

Symonds, John A. [1896] 1956. "A problem in modern ethics: Being an inquiry into the phenomenon of sexual inversion addressed especially to medical psychologists and jurists." In *Homosexuality: A cross cultural approach*, ed. Donald Webster Cory, 3-100. New York: Julian.

Tafoya, Terry. 1989. "Pulling Coyote's tale: Native American sexuality and AIDS." In *Primary prevention of AIDS*, ed. V. Mays, G. Albee, S. Schneider, 280-89. Newbury Park: Sage.

———. 1992. "Native gay and lesbian issues: The two-spirited." In *Positively Gay: New approaches to gay and lesbian life*, ed. Betty Berzon, 253-60. Berkeley: Celestial Arts Publishing.

Talayesva, Don C. 1942. *Sun chief: The autobiography of a Hopi Indian*. Ed. Leo W. Simmons. New Haven: Yale University Press. (xi, 27, 38-39, 40, 103, 108, 117, 153, 186, 294).

Tanner, John. [1830] 1956. *A narrative of the captivity and adventures of John Tanner (U.S. interpreter at the Saut de Ste. Marie) during thirty years residence among the Indians in the interior of North America*. Ed. James Edwin. Reprint. Minneapolis: Ross and Haines. (89-91).

Taylor, Edith S. and William J. Wallace. 1947. "Mohave tattooing and face-painting." *The Masterkey* 21(6): 183-95.

Tedlock, Dennis. 1993. "Torture in the archives: Mayans meet Europeans." *American Anthropologist* 95(1): 139-52.

Teit, James. 1900. "The Thompson Indians of British Columbia." *American Museum of Natural History Memoir* 2(4). (321).

———. 1906. "The Lillooet Indians." *American Museum of Natural History Memoir* 4(5). (267).

———. 1930. "The Salishan tribes of the Western Plateau." *Bureau of American Ethnology Annual Report* 45. (384).

Thatcher, B. B. 1900. *Indian biography, or an historical account of those inividuals who have been distinguished among the North American natives. . . .* Vol. 1. New York: A. L. Fowle.

Thomas, Wesley. 1992. Lecture presented at the Women's Building, 1 December 1992, San Francisco, Calif.

———. 1997. "Navajo cultural constructions of gender and sexuality." In *Two-spirit people: Native American gender identity, sexuality, and spirituality*, ed. Sue-Ellen Jacobs, Wesley Thomas, and Sabine Lang, 156-73. Urbana: University of Illinois Press.

Thompson, David. 1916. *David Thompson's narrative of his explorations in western America*. Ed. J. B. Tyrrell. Toronto: The Champlain Society. (512-13, 520-21).

Thompson, Mark. 1994. *Gay soul: Finding the heart of gay spirit and nature*. San Francisco: Harper.

Tilton, Robert S. 1994. *Pocahontas: The evolution of an American narrative*. Cambridge Studies in American Literature and Culture 83. New York: Cambridge University Press.

Titiev, Mischa. 1944. "Old Oraibi: A study of the Hopi Indians of Third Mesa." *Papers of the Peabody Museum of American Archaeology and Ethnology* 22(1). (205).

———. 1972. *The Hopi Indians of old Oraibi*. Ann Arbor: University of Michigan Press. (214-15, 225).

Tixier, Victor. [1844] 1940. *Tixier's travels on the Osage prairies*. Ed. John F. McDermott. Norman: University of Oklahoma Press. (182, 197, 234).

[Tonti, Henri de]. 1697. *Dernieres decouvertes dans l'Amérique Septentrionale de M. de La Salle: Mises au jour par M. le chevalier Tonti, gouverneur du Fort Saint Louis, aux Islinois*. Paris: J. Guignard.

————. [1698] 1814. "An account of Monsieur de la Salle's last expedition and discoveries in North America." Reprint. *Collections of the New York Historical Society.* Ser. 1, vol. 2, 217-314. (237-38).

Torquemada, Juan de. [1615] 1943. *Monarquia Indiana,* 3rd ed. Vol. 2. Mexico City: Salvador Chavez Hayhoe. Originally published as *I-III Parte de los veynte y un libros rituales y Monarchia Indiana con el origen y guerras de las Indias Occidentales. . . .* Seville: Mathias Clavijo.

Trexler, Richard C. 1995. *Sex and conquest: Gender construction and political order at the time of the European conquest of the Americas.* Cambridge, Mass.: Blackwell Publishers.

Trowbridge, Charles C. 1938. *Meearmeear traditions.* Ed. Vernon Kinietz. Occasional Contributions, Museum of Anthropology, University of Michigan 7. (68).

Truman, Ben C. 1893. *History of the World's Fair, being a complete description of the World's Columbian Exposition from its inception.* N.p.

Trumbach, Randolph. 1994. "London's Sapphists: From three sexes to four genders in the making of modern culture." In *Third sex, third gender: Beyond sexual dimorphism in culture and history,* ed. Gilbert Herdt, 111-36. New York: Zone.

Turner, Victor W. 1969. *The ritual process: Structure and anti-structure.* Chicago: Aldine Publishing Co.

Turney-High, Harry H. 1937. "The Flathead Indians of Montana." *American Anthropological Association Memoir* 48. (85, 156-57).

————. 1941. "Ethnography of the Kutenai." *American Anthropological Association Memoir* 56. (128).

U.S. Board of Indian Commissioners. 1920. *Fifty-first annual report of the Board of Indian Commissioners.* Washington, D.C.: Government Printing Office.

U.S. Census Office. 1900. Twelfth Census of the United States. Indian Population, Fort Yuma Agency, San Diego County, Calif.

U.S. Department of the Interior. 1896. *Report of the Secretary of the Interior.* Vol. 2. 54th Congress, 2d session, doc. no. 5. Washington, D.C.: Government Printing Office.

————. 1898. *Annual reports of the Department of the Interior for the fiscal year ended June 30, 1898: Indian affairs.* Washington, D.C.: Government Printing Office.

Uldall, Hans J. and William Shipley. 1966. *Nisenan texts and dictionary.* University of California Publications in Linguistics 46. Berkeley: University of California Press. (249).

Ulrichs, Karl H. [1864] 1975. "'Vindex': Social-juristische Studien über mannmännliche Geschlechtsliebe." *Forschungen über das Rätsel der mannmännlichen Liebe,* ed. Magnus Hirschfeld. Reprint. New York: Arno.

Underhill, Ruth M. [1936] 1979. *Papago woman.* New York: Holt, Rinehart and Winston. (64, 67-68, 74).

————. [1939] 1969. "Social organization of the Papago Indians." *Columbia University Contributions to Anthropology* 30. (186-87).

Upton, Richard, ed. 1973. *Fort Custer on the Big Horn 1877-1898: Its history and personalities as told and pictured by its contemporaries.* Glendale, Calif.: Arthur H. Clark Co.

van Kirk, Sylvia. 1974. "Thanadelthur." *The Beaver* (spring): 40-45.

Vaughn, J. W. 1956. *With Crook at the Rosebud.* Harrisburg, Penn.: The Stackpole Company.

Vizenor, Gerald. 1991. *The heirs of Columbus.* University Press of New England/Wesleyan University Press.

Voegelin, Erminie W. 1938. "Tubatulabal ethnography." *University of California Anthropological Records* 2(1). (47).

————. 1942. "Culture element distributions 20: Northwest California." *University of California Anthropological Records* 7(2). (134-35, 228).

Voget, Fred W. 1964. "Warfare and the integration of Crow Indian culture." In *Explorations in cultural anthropology,* ed. Ward H. Goodenough, 483-510. New York: McGraw-Hill. (490).

————. 1984. *The Shoshoni-Crow sun dance.* Norman: University of Oklahoma Press.

Volk, Robert W. 1988. "Barter, blankets, and bracelets: The role of the trader in the Navajo textile and silverwork industries, 1868-190." *American Indian Culture and Research Journal* 12(4): 9-63.

Walker, James R. 1980. *Lakota belief and ritual.* Ed. Raymond J. DeMallie and Elaine A. Jahner. Lincoln: University of Nebraska Press. (165-66).

————. 1982. *Lakota society.* Ed. Raymond J. DeMallie. Lincoln: University of Nebraska Press. (127, 147).

Wallace, Edith. 1978. "Sexual status and role differences." In *Handbook of North American Indians.* Vol. 8, ed. Robert F. Heizer, 683-89. Washington, D.C.: Smithsonian Institution.

Waltrip, Bob. 1965. "Elmer Gage: American Indian." *ONE Magazine* 13(3): 6-10.

Warner, Mikel, trans. 1972. *Catholic Church records of the Pacific Northwest: Vancouver and Stellamaris Mission.* Ed. Harriet Duncan Munnick. St. Paul, Ore.: French Prairie Press. (84, Index 79, A-59).

Waterman, T. T. 1910. "The religious practices of the Diegueño Indians." *University of California Publications in American Archaeology and Ethnology* 8(6): 271-358.

Weeks, Jeffrey. 1981. *Sex, politics and society: The regulation of sexuality since 1800.* London: Longman.

Weist, Katherine M. 1980. "Plains Indian women: An assessment." In *Anthropology on the Great Plains,* ed. W. Raymond Wood and Margot Liberty, 255-71. Lincoln: University of Nebraska Press.

Weitzner, Bella. 1979. "Hidatsa Indians." *Anthropological Papers of the American Museum of Natural History* 56(2). (226-29).

Weltfish, Gene. 1965. *The lost universe.* New York: Basic Books. (29).

Westermarck, Edward. [1906] 1931. "Homosexual love." In *The making of modern man,* ed. V. F. Calverton, 529-64. New York: Modern Library. Originally published as *The origin and development of the moral ideas.* (472-73).

Wheat, Joe B. 1976a. "Spanish-American and Navajo weaving, 1600 to now." In *Collected papers in honor of Marjorie Ferguson Lambert,* ed. Albert H. Schroeder, 199-226. Papers of the Archaeological Society of New Mexico 3. Albuquerque: Albuquerque Archaeological Society Press.

———. 1976b. "Weaving." In *Arizona Highways Indian Arts and Crafts,* ed. Clara Lee Tanner, 30-67. Phoenix: Arizona Highways.

Whitam, Frederick L. and Robin M. Mathy. 1986. *Male homosexuality in four societies: Brazil, Guatemala, the Philippines, and the United States.* New York: Praeger. (84).

White, Chris. 1974. "Lower Colorado River area aboriginal warfare and alliance dynamics." In *ANTAP: California Indian political and economic organization,* ed. Lowell J. Bean and Thomas F. King, 113-35. Ramona, Calif.: Ballena Press.

White, Leslie. 1943. "New material from Acoma." *Bureau of American Ethnology Bulletin* 136. (310, 324-25).

White, Raymond C. 1963. "Luiseño social organization." *University of California Publications in American Archaeology and Ethnology* 8(2). (146-47, 186).

Whitehead, Harriet. 1981. "The bow and the burden strap: A new look at institutionalized homosexuality in native North America." In *Sexual meanings: The cultural construction of gender and sexuality,* ed. Sherry B. Ortner and Harriet Whitehead, 80-115. Cambridge: Cambridge University Press.

Whitman, William. [1937] 1969. "The Oto." *Columbia University Contributions to Anthropology* 28. (22, 29, 30, 50).

Wikan, Unni. 1978. "The Omani xanith: A third gender role?" *Man* 14: 473-75.

Will, G. F. and H. J. Spinden. 1906. "The Mandans: A study of their culture, archaeology and language." *Papers of the Peabody Museum of American Archaeology and Ethnology* 3(4). (128, 210).

Williams, H. L. 1880. *The aboriginal races of North America, comprising biographical sketches of eminent individuals, and an historical account of the different tribes. . . ,* 15th ed. New York: John B. Alden. (105, 187-90, 239-40, 244, 248-57).

Williams, Walter L. 1986a. *The spirit and the flesh: Sexual diversity in American Indian culture.* Boston: Beacon Press. (4, 227).

———. 1986b. "Persistance and change in the berdache tradition among contemporary Lakota Indians." In *The many faces of homosexuality,* ed. Evelyn Blackwood, 191-200. New York: Harrington Park Press.

Willoughby, Nona C. 1963. "Division of labor among the Indians of California." *Reports of the University of California Archaeological Survey* 60. (57, 59, 60, 62).

Wissler, Clark. 1912. "Societies and ceremonial associations in the Oglala division of the Teton-Dakota." *Anthropological Papers of the American Museum of Natural History* 11(1). (92-93).

Witherspoon, Gary. 1977. *Language and art in the Navajo universe.* Ann Arbor: University of Michigan Press.

———. 1981. "Self-esteem and self-expression in Navajo weaving." In *Tension and harmony: The Navajo rug. Plateau* 52(4): 28-32.

————. 1994. "Cultural motifs in Navajo weaving." *North American Indian anthropology: Essays on society and culture*, ed. Raymond J. DeMallie and Alfonso Ortiz, 355-76. Norman: University of Oklahoma Press.

Wolf, Eric R. 1982. *Europe and the people without history.* Berkeley: University of California Press.

Wrangel, Ferdinand von. 1839. *Reise des kaiserlich-russischen Flotten-Lieutenants Ferdinand v. Wrangel längs der Nordküste von Siberien und auf dem Eismeere, in den Jahren 1820 bis 1824.* Vol. 1, ed. G. Engelhardt. Berlin: Voss' Buchhandlung.

Wyman, Leland C. 1943. "Review of *Navaho Creation Myth.*" *Journal of American Folklore* 56(220): 147-50

————. 1947. "Review of *Hail Chant and Water Chant.*" *American Anthropologist* 49: 633-37. (634-36).

————. 1983. *Southwest Indian drypainting.* Santa Fe and Albuquerque: School of American Research and University of New Mexico.

Wyman, M. P. 1892. "Report of Crow Agency." *Sixty-first Annual Report of the Commissioner of Indian Affairs.* Washington, D.C.: Government Printing Office.

Yengoyan, Aram A. 1986. "Theory in anthropology: On the demise of the concept of culture." *Comparative Studies in Society and History* 28: 368-74.

Young, Bo. 1997. "Common ground: Separatism, spirituality and politics, a conversation with Clyde Hall." *White Crane Journal* 31: 8-9, 18-19.

Young, Robert W. and William Morgan. 1980. *The Navajo language: A grammar and colloquial dictionary.* Albuquerque: University of New Mexico Press. (525).

Zárate-Salmerón. [1626] 1916. "Journey of Oñate to California by land." In *Spanish exploration in the Southwest, 1542-1706,* ed. Herbert E. Bolton, 268-80. New York: Charles Scribner's Sons.

Zigmond, Maurice. 1977. "The supernatural world of the Kawaiisu." In *Flowers of the wind: Papers on ritual, myth and symbolism in California and the Southwest,* ed. Thomas C. Blackburn, 59-96. Socorro, N.M.: Ballena Press. (74).

————. 1986. "Kawaiisu." In *Handbook of North American Indians.* Vol. 11, ed. Warren L. d'Azevedo, 398-411. Washington, D.C.: Smithsonian Institution. (406).

ACKNOWLEDGMENTS

This book is dedicated to Bradley Rose, who died on June 11, 1996, of HIV disease, and to my mother, Harriette Dooling, who is struggling with Alzheimer's.

Bradley supported my work in countless ways throughout the sixteen years we were together. He read and edited all my writings, translated sources, attended countless lectures (and always found things for me to improve), and joined me on research trips to New Mexico and elsewhere until his illness prevented him. Both of us found inspiration in the lives of third and fourth gender natives; Brad often cited them in his own writings.

I had always felt that without Brad I could never write again. But in the eerie way that life unfolds, the seed of this book was planted on Brad's last day. Our friend Michael Tsosie had just returned from Washington, D.C., where he had been doing research at the Smithsonian Institution. When I described Brad's failing condition, he came by to join the friends gathering at our apartment. He brought a photocopy of the picture of the Quechan fourth gender female published here as fig. 13. It is the first known photograph of a traditional fourth gender female.

In the weeks that followed, Mike and I talked about the picture several times. Then one day he came by with his entire personal collection of ethnographic publications on the Yuman-speaking tribes of the Colorado River region. I doubt I would have taken the initiative to start a new project at that point, and, in any case, I lacked access to a research library. Later that fall, Mike drove me to Los Angeles, where we continued our research at UCLA and the Southwest Museum. Mike's discovery of the photograph had put a question in front of me. In the months that followed, when I wasn't grieving, I found myself writing. The chapter titled "Dreams of Power" became the nucleus of this book.

Mike was not the only friend and colleague whose personal support sustained me and whose professional aid and input made this book possible. I especially thank Susan Landess, Frank Brayton, Stephen O. Murray, Winfield and Solin Coleman, Chris Carlsson and Caitlin Manning, Joey Cain, Randy Burns and GAI, Harry Hay, John Burnside, Mary Cappello, Mark Thompson, Christopher Lewis, Pat Whelehan, and Judith Thorne. For feedback on various parts and versions of this book, I am grateful to David Schneider, Clyde Hall, Angukcuaq, James Abrams, Wesley Thomas, Mike Cowdry, James Brust, Gilbert Herdt, John De Cecco, Paula Gunn Allen, David Halperin, David Greenberg, Martin Duberman, Sandra Hollimon, Martin Ottenheimer, Evelyn Blackwood, the affiliated scholars of Stanford's Institute for Research on Women and Gender, and the students of my NAS 190 seminars at the University of California, Berkeley.

Recently, I came across a Christmas card in my files that my mother had received from a relative-in-law who published an influential journal of religion and mythology. "I'm so glad to hear Will is writing about something other than his berdaches!" she wrote. I don't know what it was I was writing about at the time, unless it was one of the odd jobs I have taken to earn a living. In fact, I have never stopped writing about berdaches in the past fifteen years. And thankfully, my mother never has stopped being proud of me, whatever I was writing about, even now, when she can no longer remember why.

INDEX